Corporate Reputations, Branding and People Management

To Sue and Christine for their help and encouragement throughout this project
– Graeme

To my husband, Christopher, and our children, Alexander and James
– Susan

Corporate Reputations, Branding and People Management:

A Strategic Approach to HR

**Graeme Martin
and
Susan Hetrick**

ELSEVIER

AMSTERDAM • BOSTON • HEIDELBERG • LONDON • NEW YORK • OXFORD
PARIS • SAN DIEGO • SAN FRANCISCO • SINGAPORE • SYDNEY • TOKYO
Butterworth-Heinemann is an imprint of Elsevier

Butterworth-Heinemann is an imprint of Elsevier
Linacre House, Jordan Hill, Oxford OX2 8DP, UK
30 Corporate Drive, Suite 400, Burlington, MA 01803, USA

First edition 2006

British Library Cataloguing in Publication Data
A catalogue record for this book is available from the British Library

Library of Congress Cataloguing in Publication Data Control Number:
2006925279

ISBN–13: 978-0-7506-6950-4
ISBN–10: 0-7506-6950-0

For information on all Butterworth-Heinemann publications
please visit our website at http://books.elsevier.com

Typeset by Charon Tec Ltd, Chennai, India
www.charontec.com
Printed and bound in The Netherlands

06 07 08 09 10   10 9 8 7 6 5 4 3 2 1

Working together to grow
libraries in developing countries

www.elsevier.com | www.bookaid.org | www.sabre.org

ELSEVIER   BOOK AID
              International   Sabre Foundation

Contents

Foreword

In the fast-changing, increasingly global and competitive world of business, the ability of organizations to create and sustain strong corporate brands and reputations is one of the only ways to stay ahead. In most organizations, the main responsibility for reputation management and corporate branding rests with marketing, communications and public relations departments. Yet, as most of us working in the field know only too well, it is people who create reputations for excellence and memorable brands; it is also the actions of people that can destroy these vitally important intangible assets. Moreover, attracting, retaining and engaging talented people in industries such as my own means we are increasingly reliant on high-quality reputations and brands. This is one of the reasons why we, as a leading global financial services company, continue to invest so much time, money and effort into building our corporate reputation, and in sustaining our position as an 'employer of choice'. We know that engaged employees equals business success and profitability.

This book is essential reading for CEOs, marketing and HR practitioners who are serious about making a valued contribution to the success of their organization. This book outlines the future scope and contribution of human resources to business strategy. It is one of the first serious studies of the corporate landscape and is very well researched and practical. I hope you get as much out of this book as I have.

Neil Roden
Group HR Director, RBS

Preface

This book is the first in a series designed to help senior practitioners in human resource management (HRM) develop their knowledge and skills in the strategic issues facing them and their organizations. Like others, we believe the term 'strategic' is often over-hyped; we limit its use in this context to mean 'important'. And, in our view, there are few more important considerations for senior managers than creating and sustaining excellent reputations and brands for their organizations. For example, survey evidence produced by a major international consultancy firm, Hill & Knowlton, in 2006 showed that reputations and brands were among the top items on the agenda of CEOs, including those in China. Why this should be the case has been addressed by John Kay, a leading British economist, who opined:

> The distinction between the role of shareholders and employees was clear when shareholders had bought the plant and employees worked in it. But the principal assets of the modern company are knowledge, brands and reputation, which are in the heads and hands of employees (J. Kay, 2004, *The Truth About Markets: Why Some Nations are Rich but Most Remain Poor*. London: Penguin, p. 58)

So organizations need to capitalize on reputations and brands to be *different* from others to create and sustain sustainable competitive advantage; at the same time, they also need to be seen as *legitimate*, especially in an environment in which they are increasingly distrusted by large sections of the community. Thus, in addition to corporate branding, many businesses are paying greater attention to *corporate social responsibility* (CSR) to achieve long-term sustainability. They are also attempting to develop good *corporate governance* and *leadership* to protect their reputations in the light of major instances of corporate malfeasance such as that exemplified by Enron. Thus, we have chosen to take a broader perspective on corporate reputations and brands, incorporating discussions about corporate social responsibility, corporate governance, leadership and strategy, since these issues are part of the emerging agenda of the Reputation Institute, one of the most influential bodies in this field. They are also issues currently not well served by books written for HR practitioners by HR practitioners and academics.

The central message of this book is that achieving differentiation through reputations and brands and legitimacy through CSR and good governance are driven from the 'inside-out'; how people are led and managed, and the extent to which they identify and engage with their organizations, are major, if not *the* major, drivers of the new corporate agenda. Furthermore, the reverse is also true: corporate reputations and brands, including reputations for CSR, good governance and leadership attract, motivate and retain talented people, which is equally important in a world where such talent is at a premium. So, corporate reputations, brands, CSR and governance are inextricably interlinked with HR and people management, which is the rationale for establishing the Centre for Reputation Management at the University of Glasgow (http://www.gla.ac.uk/crmp).

Though there are some excellent contributions to the links between reputations and brands by marketing and communications consultants and academics, and a few on employer branding, we believe this book is one of the few works that explores the broader corporate agenda through the lenses of people management and HR. Because of our perspective, it is most relevant to senior HR and organizational development practitioners, and also senior managers and leaders. It is also relevant to managers working in the profit and not-for-profit sectors. Though reputations and branding in particular are terms usually associated with large commercial companies, especially multinationals, public sector and voluntary organizations are rapidly coming to realize that these intangible assets play a critical role in realizing their long-term strategic objectives.

Although we have written the book primarily for practitioners, hopefully containing practical advice, it is not a 'how-to-cook' book. We believe that many senior practitioners are best served by, and are looking for, an analytical, critically reflective and multi-disciplinary approach to this emerging corporate agenda. So we have drawn on a wide range of topics – organizational behaviour, marketing, HRM, economics, communications, CSR and leadership studies – to make our case. The book is also grounded in recent research and practice, including a number of originally-researched cases by ourselves and others from the UK, USA, Europe and Asia. Among the issues we have covered are:

- The elements of corporateness and the corporate agenda: corporate reputations, brands, social responsibility, governance, strategy and leadership
- The role of reputations and branding in achieving business and organizational success
- Organizational identities and images, and their relationship to the quality of individual employment relationships and organizational actions
- The role of people management, strategic HR and organizational communications in shaping reputations and brands
- The 'business case' for CSR
- Corporate governance and leadership
- The future of HR and the emerging corporate agenda

We have tried to write in an accessible style, using the first person, and, at times, reflecting on our own experiences and careers to make important points. Previous readers of our work have suggested this helps put some life behind the text. Above all, we have tried to be provocative and to provide an agenda for HR that addresses its own, perennial reputation problems; having spent so long in HR careers, it's time to pay something back.

Graeme Martin and Susan Hetrick

Acknowledgements

The impetus for this work began in 2003 following research conducted for the CIPD on the links between branding and HR. When we first met, we debated the role of the HR function in creating and sustaining corporate reputations and brands, a topic that was almost entirely approached from a marketing and communications viewpoint. From our own perspectives as an academic and as a practitioner, we began our journey to explore how people strategies are, and will continue to be, among the most important assets that differentiate success from failure in organizations in all sectors of advanced economies.

Any book is the outcome of the efforts of a number of people: from developing our ideas and challenging our assumptions through to providing organizational insights and case material. Consequently, we would like to thank the authors whose work has informed our ideas and the practitioners who have kindly donated their time to speak to us. In this context, we are especially grateful to those people who have endorsed this book, others who have provided some of the intellectual inspiration and some of the practitioners who have assisted with the research. These include, in alphabetical order: Alison Allan, Greig Aitken, Simon Barrow, Duncan Brown, Sandra Burke, Chris Brewster, Karen Carlton, Anna Commachio, Alma Caldwell, Wayne Cascio, Thomas Clarke, Leslie de Chernatony, Grahame Dowling, Helen Francis, Charles Fombrun, Annette Frem, Ian Gray, Paul Goldsmith, Geraldine Hetherington, Norma Hogg, Irene Johnstone, Liz Kelly, Robin Kramar, Linda McDowall, Jim McGoldrick, Colin McLatchie, Johanne Malin, Colin Moreland, Richard Mosley, Alan Murdoch, Neil Roden, Lynn Rutter, Anne Sloan, Martyn Sloman, Sue Smith,

Paul Sparrow, Mary Spillane, Gordon Teasdale, Susan Thom, Anthony Thomson and Stephen Young. Particular thanks must go to our research assistants and colleagues – Ros Doig, Synove Granly, Martin Reddington and Christine Smith – who have been incredibly valuable in helping us put together material for the book and who have helped with some critical reading of the text. In addition, we would like to thank the companies and managers in the UK, Poland and US, who supported Susan's doctoral research and informed our thinking on global companies, as well as the large number of organizations and blue-chip companies that we have worked with over the past twenty years.

You will also see numerous references to our close colleagues, associates of the Centre for Reputation Management through People at the University of Glasgow's School of Business and Management, Phil Beaumont, Judy Pate and Hong Zhang. We owe these friends an enormous debt for their work over the years and for sharing the burden of writing associated material. We also wish to thank Edinburgh Business School at Heriot Watt University for giving us permission to use material written for their distance learning masters degree programme, especially Alex Scott, Alex Roberts and Charles Ritchie for their help.

Without the excellent team at Butterworth-Heinemann – Maggie Smith, Claire Hutchins, Olivia Warburton, Melissa Read and Elaine Leek – this work would not have been possible. They have been a great team to work with and could not have done more to make the process smooth and effective.

Finally, we both have young families and would like to thank them and our respective spouses for their support.

The authors and publishers would like to thank the following for their permission to reprint material:

Helen Handfield-Jones, *Elements of a talent management approach.* Exhibit from website, www.handfieldjones.com/diagnose/index.html (accessed Feb 2005).

Kaplan, R. and Norton, D. (2001) *The strategy-focused organization: how balanced scorecard companies thrive in the new business environment.* MA: Harvard Business School Publishing. Exhibit 2.1, The employee-customer-service–profit chain at Sears, reprinted with permission.

Harris, F. and de Chernatony, L. (2001) Figure 2, *European Marketing Journal,* **35** (3/4), reprinted with permission of Emerald Publishing.

Davies, G. with Chun, R., Da Silva, R.V. and Roper, S. (2003) *Corporate reputation and competitiveness.* London: Routledge, Exhibit p. 62.

Fombrun, C. J. and Van Riel, C. B. M. (2003) *Fame and fortune: how successful companies build winning reputations,* Upper Saddle River, NJ: Financial Times/Prentice Hall. Exhibit, p. 100; 'A month after Katrina', with kind permission of Knowledge@Wharton, available online at http://knowledge.wharton.upenn.edu.

Bek, D., Jones, I. W. and Pollitt, M. G. (2005) How do multinationals build social capital? Diageo's corporate citizenship programme. *Working paper No. 302, ESRC Centre for Business Research,* March 2005. University of Cambridge, material adapted by permission of authors.

Miles, S. J. and Mangold, W. G. (2005) Positioning Southwest Airlines through employee branding. *Business Horizons,* **49**, Exhibit p. 540, reprinted with permission from Elsevier.

Barrow, S. and Mosely, R. (2005) *The Employer Brand®: bringing the best of brand management to people at work.* London: Wiley. Exhibit, p. 111, reprinted with permission from John Wiley Publishing.

Every effort has been made to contact owners of copyright material; however the authors would like to hear from any copyright owners of material produced in this book whose copyright has been unwittingly infringed.

CHAPTER 1

The importance of the corporate agenda and its links with human resource management

Introduction

In a recent book on branding and reputation management, John Balmer and Stephen Geyser (2003) perceptively argued that the drive towards 'corporateness' was one of the major trends among organizations in developed and emerging economies. This argument reflects the twin problems facing the architects of organizational design – achieving a balance between getting people to cooperate with one another (the corporate agenda) and getting them to display initiative (encouragement of individuality and differences) (Roberts, 2004). Exploring this trend towards corporateness, which we believe to be only partly supported by evidence from Europe, North America and Asia, is the starting point for our book. Let's begin our examination with a small sample of this evidence from two cases of corporate America. We have chosen these two since there can be few better justifications for a book on management than the importance of its subject matter to the fate of the world's most powerful nation and to one of its major corporations. Take a few minutes to read the illustration in Box 1.1, written just after the end of the war with Iraq in 2004.

Box 1.1   America's Image Abroad: Reputation Management, Branding and People Management

According to an *Economist* article published just after the end of the Iraq war, Keith Reinhard, the chairman of American consultants DDB Worldwide, was recently set the task of selling American business and American brands to the rest of the world following the bad post-Iraq war international press. His 2004 message to Yale University business students was that he loved American brands, '... but they are losing friends around the world and it is vital to the interests of America to change this'. He argued that the reputation of America abroad was at an all-time low and this perception, 'however misguided', was damaging the economy.

To tackle the problem, Reinhard, helped by some senior executives in America's advertising industry and university academics, set up a pressure group to improve the reputation of the USA overseas. The idea was not new, since President Bush had speculated on the reasons why 'everyone hates America' after September 11th, 2001. But Reinhard felt the need to use consumer research to tell American business what most people outside the USA seemed to understand about America's declining image.

His worries have been subsequently reinforced by an extensive DBB study covering 17 countries, which provided the feedback that 'America, and American business people, were viewed as arrogant and indifferent toward others' cultures; exploitative, in that they extracted more than it provided; corrupting, in how they valued materialism above all else; and willing to sacrifice almost anything in an effort to generate profits'. Further evidence came in the shape of a survey of global brands by Roper ASW, another consulting firm, which showed a marked decline in support for, and trust in, American brands.

Source: *Economist*, 2004

This case illustrates how important 'corporateness' is for America's continued competitive success and shows how national and organizational reputations and brands are interlinked. It also tells us something about the extent to which America's image abroad and that of its major corporations depend on intangible assets such as brands and reputations (Hagel and Seely Brown, 2005). Because of this increasing dependence, these corporate-level concepts have become major areas of strategic interest among the boardrooms of companies in sectors as diverse as financial services, information and communication technology (ICT), retailing, food and beverages, hospitality and tourism, healthcare, local and national government and charities.

Note also the implication in the case that the reputation and brands of 'USA inc.' and those of its major corporations are closely aligned with the poorly perceived actions, values and attitudes of American managers and employees. To illustrate this relationship, let's drill down a little from the perceptions of the USA as meta-brand to an example of how these perceptions may be formed at a micro level. This second illustration, in Box 1.2, is based on our personal research into a particular US-based company – in fact, one of its most cherished – and we shall return to it later in the book for a few other lessons.

Box 1.2   AT&T's Re-branding of the NCR Corporation

AT&T, a major US telecommunications and technology company, acquired another American giant, the NCR Corporation, in 1991 following a hostile takeover bid. Initially, the headquarters management of AT&T adopted a 'financial control' approach to NCR and did not interfere in its product-market strategy; for the first two years it allowed its subsidiary companies and plants in more than 40 countries to operate as semi-independent units. This hands-off approach particularly applied to its most profitable and high profile subsidiary based in Scotland, at the time, the largest design, development and manufacturing facility of automatic teller machines (ATMs) in the world. The Scottish company was the 'jewel in the crown of NCR' and had featured heavily in the international business press as a model of success. Its CEO was also revered by people inside and outside of the UK-based company as a model leader. The rationale for allowing the Scottish operation substantial autonomy was two-fold. First, its product range and expertise fell outside top management's main interests, which were in acquiring a computer technology company. Second, it was a major contributor to NCR's profits, highly disproportionate to its size and investment requirements.

However, after a period of two years of little or no strategic intervention, AT&T's corporate management team decided to transform its NCR acquisition *en masse* by adopting a global branding strategy. The name of NCR, a company with a 100 year history, was destined to be expunged from history and replaced by the more corporate-sounding name of AT&T Global Information Solutions (AT&T (GIS)) and headquarter management decided to take a more interventionist approach to all aspects of the business, including its previous technology-based, 'macho' culture. This radical change was justified by headquarters because large financial losses were being incurred by virtually every business unit in NCR, that is, apart from the Scottish subsidiary.

AT&T's president brought in Jerre Stead, a new US-based CEO for AT&T (GIS), because of his high profile track record in turning around an ailing electrical contracting company and another AT&T acquisition. Strongly influenced by a US academic-consultant 'guru', the new CEO embarked on a near-messianic attempt to re-brand AT&T (GIS) by using corporate and organizational identity management techniques, constructing a new vision statement and introducing a culture change programme. This re-branding process was also marked by: (1) disposing of many of the old NCR management team in America; (2) developing a much more strategic and 'hands-on' approach to strategy and tactics, in contrast to the sole concern with financial control by the previous NCR management team in Dayton, Ohio; and (3) basing the cultural/identity change programme on putting employees and customers at the heart of the new corporation's policies. This programme involved three central elements. The first was christened the 'Common Bond', which included a best-practice, ethical mission statement, new values framework and set of working principles designed to 'empower employees and customers'. The ethical and empowering features of this programme are worth emphasizing at this stage, because it has been argued that the 'mutuality model' of HRM, based on treating people with respect, was more likely to lead employees to view the effort positively and to accept company actions that might have negative consequences for a minority of employees. Second, the programme involved flattening existing organizational structures and attempting to empower the local managers and workforce by, among other techniques, re-labelling managers and supervisors as 'coaches' and workers as 'associates'. Third, Stead took a personal lead in the programme by attempting to drive the changes through in a matter of nine months, including many personal appearances in the UK and an enormous investment in corporate communications.

We tracked the effects of the programme on employee attitudes, values and acceptance of the new identity over a four-year period to allow changes to bed down. However, Stead left the company after only 18 months following the sale of NCR by AT&T, which more or less signified a failed acquisition and the end of the programme. It should come as little surprise to readers that the attempted identity and culture change failed miserably during the 18-month period of Stead's stewardship. The explanations we unearthed were quite complicated but centred on:

■ The programme being seen by local management and employees in the Scottish subsidiary as an American-originated and orientated programme, and a one-size-fits-all solution. It was viewed as the personal mission of two US nationals based at headquarters (Stead and his academic guru). Stead was also seen to lack a track record in managing international companies, which showed in the extremely US-biased, evangelical language and content of the programme.

■ This sense of US parentage was markedly enhanced by an absence of prior consultation and discussion with local management in the Scottish subsidiary, apart from some HRM staff who stood to gain from the process. Quite simply, the views of the prominent and well-respected local CEO and many of his staff had not been sought on the appropriateness of re-branding a company that was an acknowledged world leader in its field.

Source: Based on Martin, Beaumont and Pate, 2003

This second case not only illustrates the desire by firms such as AT&T for a strong sense of 'corporateness' as a means of competitive advantage, but also details how reputations and brands are made or broken by the values, attitudes and behaviour of people, most notably leaders and board members, who shape the cultures and identities of their firms. Perhaps just as important from our perspective, it also implies great potential for more effective human resource management (HRM) to contribute to the corporate agenda by designing and executing HR strategies that *support* and *drive* corporate strategy rather than those that hinder or follow it.

This book, then, addresses these issues from an HRM perspective, uniquely as far as we are aware, because a strong case can be made that brands and reputations are driven from the inside – sometimes well but often poorly. Because of this 'inside-out' thesis, it follows that HR specialists have a great deal to contribute if they can grasp the corporate agenda, organizational needs for corporateness and begin to understand and use the language and insights of branding, marketing, communications, public relations and corporate social responsibility (CSR) specialists. Such a grasp has become progressively more important because of the so-called 'war for talent', which will become even more intense given the changing demographics of the major world economies of Europe, Asia and even the USA (Pfeffer, 2005), the changing basis of competition towards the knowledge-based and creative industries (Florida, 2005) and the calls for more socially responsible, sustainable and well-governed organizations (Clarke, 2004; Jackson, 2004).

For example, IBM is warning firms of the persistent talent shortages brought about by the baby-boom generation reaching retirement age, with their head of human capital management cautioning that the ageing population will be one of the major issues facing organizations in the 21st century. Most European and Asian governments are facing quite rapidly ageing populations, but even the USA, which benefits from high levels of talented immigration, is estimated to be short of 17 million people of working age by 2020. Another example comes from a recent set of consulting surveys on the importance of corporate reputations and corporate branding not only to senior executives in America and Europe but also to Asian executives, including Chinese CEOs (Hill and Knowlton, 2004). One of these surveys conducted in 2004, in conjunction with *The Economist*'s panel of more than nine hundred senior executives worldwide, showed that 93% of these respondents believed customers considered corporate reputation to be either important or extremely important while 31% of them also believed that corporate reputation was one of the top three factors that customers consider in deciding to purchase from a company. Seventy-nine per cent of these senior executives also believed corporate reputations were one of the top three factors that influenced investors in investment decisions. Recruiting and retaining talent was seen as the most important benefit of building and maintaining a strong corporate reputation, with 43 per cent seeing it as one of the top three factors in attracting people to join (second only to compensation and career growth). The survey of 120 senior leaders of major Chinese companies showed that corporate reputation and brand building were the most important objectives for their organizations. Three-quarters of respondents said that brand building was the most important business outcome of their companies' reputations. Nearly all of these executives saw these brands as very important for developing strategic partnerships and for recruiting and retaining talented people.

Before going any further, however, we need to define our terms a little more accurately and consider the reasons why corporateness has become part of the strategic agenda for organizations (and, increasingly, cities, regions and nations). The box below gives a working definition.

Key definition: Corporateness

We use the term 'corporateness' as an umbrella term for the various powerful and revealing corporate-level concepts, including reputation, identity, image, brand, vision, strategy, communications, culture, social responsibility and governance that have come to form a new way of thinking about organizations. Corporateness implies the desire for many, especially large and complex, organizations to develop a unified approach to business and present a distinctive corporate identity in key areas such as branding, reputation, cost control and, increasingly, legitimacy to all stakeholders. This does not imply that such organizations are uninterested in encouraging diversity or acknowledging, and often promoting, the existence of legitimate sub-cultures, multiple identities and employee segments, but that they need to balance the classic trade-off, as economists put it, between the requirements for people to *cooperate* to fulfil common goals and to show individual *initiative* in achieving sub-unit goals (Roberts, 2004). Sometimes, organizational scholars refer to this trade-off as the integration-differentiation problem.

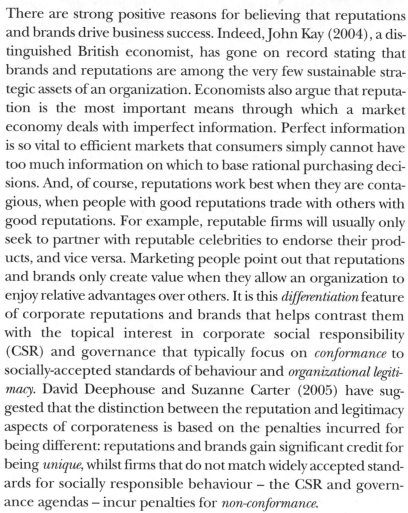

Corporate reputations, brands and business success

There are strong positive reasons for believing that reputations and brands drive business success. Indeed, John Kay (2004), a distinguished British economist, has gone on record stating that brands and reputations are among the very few sustainable strategic assets of an organization. Economists also argue that reputation is the most important means through which a market economy deals with imperfect information. Perfect information is so vital to efficient markets that consumers simply cannot have too much information on which to base rational purchasing decisions. And, of course, reputations work best when they are contagious, when people with good reputations trade with others with good reputations. For example, reputable firms will usually only seek to partner with reputable celebrities to endorse their products, and vice versa. Marketing people point out that reputations and brands only create value when they allow an organization to enjoy relative advantages over others. It is this *differentiation* feature of corporate reputations and brands that helps contrast them with the topical interest in corporate social responsibility (CSR) and governance that typically focus on *conformance* to socially-accepted standards of behaviour and *organizational legitimacy*. David Deephouse and Suzanne Carter (2005) have suggested that the distinction between the reputation and legitimacy aspects of corporateness is based on the penalties incurred for being different: reputations and brands gain significant credit for being *unique*, whilst firms that do not match widely accepted standards for socially responsible behaviour – the CSR and governance agendas – incur penalties for *non-conformance*.

Let's begin, however, by looking at the legitimacy problems of organizations since, as we write, CSR and requirements to improve corporate governance are two of the reasons driving much of the current interest in corporateness. Recent corporate scandals in almost every country in the world have demonstrated the risk associated with irresponsible behaviour and poor governance to damaged reputations, brands and, in some cases, the demise of companies. These include:

> ■ *The decline in general levels of trust and consumer confidence* following the highly publicized cases of *questionable*

(and, sometimes criminal) corporate governance and *unethical behaviour*. Well-known examples include the US cases of Enron, Andersen Consulting and WorldCom financial scandals during the early part of this decade, and the long-running case of Philip Morris (now Altria), the tobacco and food conglomerate, which has fought a constant battle over the social legitimacy of its products. In the UK, Shell and the Rover group have suffered public condemnation for dubious practices of their senior managers, whilst in Italy and Germany, companies such as Parmalat and Mercedes have shown that family-based and joint management–employee governance structures are not immune from criticism. Even organizations such as the European Union and the United Nations have been charged with corruption and ethical malpractice.

■ *Problems associated with inferior ideas and dangerous lines of business, products and services.* Matt Haig's (2003) book on the 100 biggest branding mistakes is a catalogue of failures that fall under this heading, including the well-known cases of the Ford Edsel, Sony Betamax and New Coke. Other examples include: Intel's problems with its Pentium processor that could not handle some simple mathematical calculations; the Ford/Bridgestone fiasco, during which Ford sued the Japanese company Bridgestone for providing faulty tyres that caused their Explorer 4 × 4 to be involved in a number of fatal accidents; the UK high street jeweller Ratners, whose products were so cheap that the chairman, with a disarming but fatal honesty, admitted that many of his products were 'total crap' and even he wouldn't buy them; Sunny Delight's high-sugar orange juice, which was marketed to children as a healthy way to begin a day but was associated with dental decay and obesity; and the continuing problems of poor reputation faced by motor vehicle servicing companies in the UK over the past 30 years, reported by the consumer magazine *Which?* In October (2004).

■ *The more fundamental concerns of the critics of big business who point to the apparent encroachment of corporate interests and economic globalization on nearly every aspect of social and political life, and the declining influence of governments to represent the interests of ordinary people.* A powerful example of this line of criticism is Joel Bakan's (2004) book and film *The Corporation*, which argued that corporations are rapidly becoming more powerful than many governments but are mandated by statute to a single-minded pursuit of shareholder value; only when a convincing business case has been made, do they consider exercising social responsibility and addressing stakeholder interests. Another example of a best-seller dealing with these is Naomi Klein's (1999) *No Logo*, which claimed that the power of global brands was at the heart of major injustices in the world and thus became something of a bible for the anti-globalization movement.

However, there are also more positive reasons why companies are interested in their corporate brands, identities and reputations, all of which are associated, in one way or another, with improvements in long-term financial performance and returns to other stakeholders in an organization.

First, corporate brands are increasingly being treated as significant intangible assets, sometimes worth up to twice the book value of their tangible assets (Hatch and Schultz, 2001; Fombrun and Van Riel, 2003). This is especially the case for so-called celebrity firms that take bold or unusual actions and display distinctive identities (Rindova *et al.*, 2006). For instance, the world's best-known brand, Coca-Cola, was estimated to be worth \$67bn in 2004 (see Table 1.1), whilst the newer brand images of companies like Nokia, Sony, Virgin, Tesco and the UK-based budget airline EasyJet, have allowed them to leverage their super-brands by offering new products and services to new markets (Haig, 2004). The valuation of such intangible assets is slowly being recognized by the accounting bodies of many developed countries and will become an even bigger factor in the market for corporate control in these countries. Second, there is emerging empirical proof of a strong and positive link between corporate reputations and financial performance (Roberts and Dowling, 2002; Deephouse and Carter, 2005). The basis for both of these financial outcomes – improved book market values and long-run profitability – arises from the ability of companies to *differentiate* themselves consistently from competitors to enjoy the benefits of *customer captivity,* since intangible assets are difficult to copy and take years to perfect (Fombrun and Van Riel, 2003; Greenwald and Kahn, 2005).

Table 1.1
Top ten brands by value, 2004

Brand	Estimated value ($bn)
Coco-Cola	67.39
Microsoft	61.37
IBM	53.79
GE	44.11
Intel	33.50
Disney	27.11
McDonald's	25.00
Nokia	24.04
Toyota	22.67
Marlborough	22.13

Source: Business Week Online. http://www.businessweek.com/magazine/content/04_31/b3894096.htm. (accessed 8 December 2004)

As noted earlier, both cases illustrate the role of *employees and managers* in creating and maintaining these valuable assets, largely through their *unscripted and discretionary* actions, attitudes and behaviours, which lead customers, investors and other key stakeholders to infer favourable or unfavourable impressions of the company (Boxall and Purcell, 2003; Sjovall and Talk, 2004). The key point here is that it is not only the formal communication of corporate identity and image which is important. It is also the informal impressions created by managers and employees in the normal day-to-day conduct of their work. These impressions, in turn, lead stakeholders to attribute to the company important positive or negative qualities, such as its reputation. So, many organizations have come to recognize that one of their few unique and inimitable assets is their *human resources* in creating *reputational capital,* since other forms of capital, including their products and services, and many of their internal management processes, including financial engineering, supply chain management and purchasing strategies, are all tangible and, therefore, open to imitation by any firm wishing to dig deep enough into their operations (Joyce *et al.*, 2003; Jackson, 2004).

Key definition: Reputational capital

Reputational capital is often defined as the difference between the book valuation of an organization and its market valuation. It is built on the trust and confidence of stakeholders in an organization that it will act in their best interests, and for a reputation to be effective, in each interaction between the organization and its key stakeholders (customers, employees, suppliers, etc.), 'the returns from maintaining an unsullied reputation must exceed the gains from violating trust and reneging on promises' (Roberts, 2004, p. 161). From an economist's perspective, it is the timing of these returns that determines the value of these returns. Since these are largely in the future, the value of a good reputation to a company depends on the number of times and the range of situations in which it can be used to generate such value (Dowling, 2001, p. 23).

For example, marketing managers are likely to place high value on a corporate reputation if it could influence consumers during the search phase of their purchase and during the postpurchase phase when they can use the brand or company reputation of its product or services to ensure repeat buys. HR managers are also likely to place high value on a corporate reputation if it helps them attract talented people to apply for posts, to accept offers and to remain with the organization during bad as well as good times. In both of these situations, a reputation for ethical trading and socially responsible behaviour has been used successfully – the Body Shop being the most notable example. Indeed a strong business case has been made for CSR by the American academic Kevin Jackson (2004), who has argued that a 'reputation for integrity and fair play is the most overlooked intangible asset that a business has'.

As is often the case with intangible assets, however, measuring the implicit contracts between organizations and their stakeholders, recognizing when they are breached and punishing transgressors, are difficult issues. It is these characteristics of reputations that place a limit on their value to organizations. Opportunistic or criminal behaviour often only becomes evident long after the acts took place.

The business literature is replete with anecdotal evidence of how customer service and good human resource management makes a significant difference to consumer purchasing decisions. Companies throughout the world have sought to link good human resource management to consumer purchasing decisions. Well-known examples, which we shall use as illustrations in this book, include: Hewlett Packard, Yahoo!, Sears, and Southwest Airlines in the USA; Agilent Technologies, British Airways, Royal Bank of Scotland, HSBC, Scottish & Newcastle Breweries and Tesco based in the UK; and Evian, Orange, Mars, BenQ and Acer in continental Europe and the Asia–Pacific region. More rigorously researched justifications for this proposition come from our own case research, work and consulting experience, and at least four sources of literature we will examine further in this book:

- Mary Jo Hatch and Majden Schultz's (2001) work on more than a hundred leading companies in the USA and Europe found that organizations wishing to create a strong corporate brand had to align three essential, interdependent and largely intangible elements – the organization's vision, image and culture.
- Charles Fombrun and Cees Van Riel's (2003) work on corporate reputation management since the early 1990s, which has demonstrated a close link between the financial fortunes of companies worldwide and their reputations. They have found that bottom line returns, operating performance cash flows and growth in market values are closely tied to their reputation quotient (RQ), a measure that includes important people and culture management variables.
- Grahame Dowling, along with his colleague P. W. Roberts, who have shown that companies with an

above-average Fortune reputation score are more able to sustain or attain an above-average return on assets.

■ Gary Davies and his colleagues at Manchester Business School in the UK, who have been working hard, especially in the retail industry, to develop a link between organizational identity and external image, have shown how an alignment between the two can lead to superior performance.

So, in this opening chapter, we will look at the relationship between corporateness and strategic human resource management, since this is one of the most important areas in which the effective management of people has been proved to impact directly on performance. It is also, as we have argued, one of the areas in which the HR profession can make a profound and distinctive contribution to all types of organizations and in all sectors of the economy.

Definitions, a model and a storyline

First, however, we need to be a little more specific about the ideas underlying corporateness and how they relate to each other because there is a great deal of confusion among practitioners and academics about the meaning of concepts such as image, branding, reputation and identity. This is a practical problem, because if you cannot define something you are unlikely to be able to measure it or manage it effectively, a constant theme of this book. Second, being a little more clear about definitions helps us develop a model that links HRM to the leading corporate-level indicators that focus on differentiating organizations – corporate reputations and corporate branding – and, thereafter, to outcomes such as financial performance and CSR (see Figure 1.1).

The storyline for our model can be summed up in relatively simple terms:

■ Corporations in all sectors of the economy have a need to differentiate themselves to achieve long-run success,

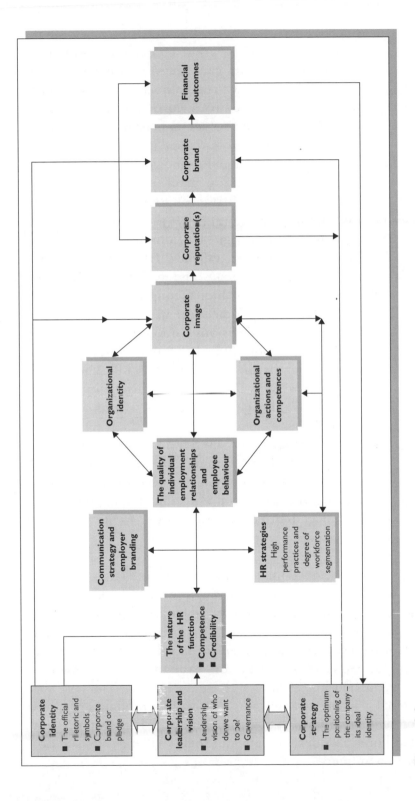

Figure 1.1
Modelling the relationship between people management, reputations, brands and performance.

which is often measured in financial outcome or in the public sector, by public good. One of the most important ways in which they can achieve this aim is to create and maintain positive reputations for being unique, which helps build a strong corporate brand, and by conforming to stakeholder expectations for socially responsible behaviour and good governance.

- ■ Corporate vision, leadership and good governance, corporate strategy and the design of an appropriate corporate identity are the first-level, strategic decisions that drive this process.

- ■ These first-level strategic decisions have to be executed through second-level, effective HR and communications strategies to create and maintain high quality employment relationships among individuals, and to have them identify and engage with the overall corporate direction and decisions flowing from them.

- ■ In turn, these individuals help create a unique organizational identity and, in conjunction with leaders, take actions collectively that reinforce this identity to project a positive image to customers, clients and other stakeholders.

- ■ How this image is perceived by relevant outsiders (and by employees) will determine how successful the whole process has been, but there is good evidence to believe that alignment between HR strategies, identity, action and image is critical to strong reputations and corporate brands.

We have developed this storyline into a model to organize the rest of the book in Figure 1.1, though you should be aware that the relationships among these variables are two-way and circular. So, just as good HR is likely to enhance reputations and performance, high levels of performance are likely to attract good human resources in the increasingly global competition for talent (Florida, 2005).

Finally, in this chapter, we shall begin a preliminary discussion of the significance of corporateness for the HR profession; what potential does it create and what challenges does it pose for practitioners?

Defining corporateness: corporate branding, identity and corporate reputation

As we noted at the beginning of this chapter, Balmer and Greyser (2003) have argued that the interest in corporateness has never been higher, providing a new and powerful lens to show corporations how they can improve their overall perform-ance. The promised benefits derived from strong corporate brands, images and reputations are now being taken seriously by businesses on a global scale. Witness the various rankings of companies in the business press, which we have already referred to, and the attention paid to these rankings by major organiza-tions. Yet, corporateness also creates a great deal of confusion because a variety of corporate-level concepts compete for prom-inence. These include corporate identity, image, branding, repu-tation and communications. Rather unhelpfully, these concepts are sometimes used as synonyms for one another and create con-fusion among the people who have to work with them.

To help shed light on these problems, Balmer and Geyser set out six questions that explain corporateness. These questions relate to six distinctive corporate-level concepts (see Table 1.2).

Table 1.2

What 'corporateness' means: six questions and related concepts.

Key question	Key concept
What are the corporation's distinctive attributes?	Corporate identity
To whom and what do/should we communicate?	Corporate communications
What is our corporate promise or pledge?	Corporate branding
What are organizational members' affinities, or 'who are we'	Organizational identity
How are we perceived as time goes on?	Corporate reputation
How are we perceived right now?	Corporate image

Source: Adapted from Balmer and Geyser, 2003, p. 4

They have also pointed out that each of these concepts has been popular with practitioners and academics at different periods during the past 40–50 years, probably reflecting the contemporary problems that organizations faced and the various disciplinary interests and ambitions of those contributing to the debate. For example, at the time of writing this book, corporate branding is a pre-eminent concept, perhaps because marketing specialists are asserting their claims to ownership of this field of study and practice, no doubt since it serves their professional identities and interests to do so. However, from the perspective of HR, and to repeat our core message, what is common to all of these concepts is the crucial role of people management in shaping, making or 'breaking' them. As a number of senior HR academics have commented in a recent, wide-ranging review of the links between HR strategy and organizational performance, it is not the fact of the existence of sound HR policies that is important, but how employees actually experience the intent and implementation of these policies by senior leaders and their managers (see Special Issue of the *Human Resource Management Journal* on HRM and performance, 2005).

Let's take a brief look at some of these ideas to help us sketch out our model in Figure 1.1 that shows how they stand in relation to each other, and how HR strategies might be used to influence them. We will spend a little more time on each of them later in the book but it will help you when we begin to get into more detail in later chapters to refer back to the overall picture in Figure 1.1.

Corporate branding

Branding product and services has played a significant part in the marketing strategy of firms for many years, with a number of products and services having worldwide recognition and helping create market values well in excess of book values (see Table 1.1). We have already highlighted the example of Coca-Cola. Another good example from the service sector is the MBA, which is the single most recognizable global brand in educational services. The classic case of branding lines of products, however, is associated with Procter & Gamble, the American multinational that is attributed with 'inventing' the branded strategy for its household cleaning, personal hygiene, baby and pet care goods (see http://www.pgprof.com/). Although some of its brands are global, such as Crest toothpaste, Sure deodorant and Old Spice aftershave, others are specific to particular countries. This strategy is sometimes referred to as a 'house of brands' (Aaker, 2004).

Nevertheless, it is the *branding of companies* that has become increasingly valuable, especially in industries such as financial services and consumer goods and services (Schulz and de Chernatony, 2002; Alessandri and Alessandri, 2004). Marketing jargon for company or corporate branding is *monolithic branding* since it reduces the needs of firms to promote individual lines of business or products/services to capture customers (Berthon Hulbert and Pitt, 1999; Harris and de Chernatony, 2001). Such developments are not new: some strong corporate brands have retained their place in the top 100 global brands for 50 years or more, including Coca-Cola itself, Hewlett-Packard, Gillette, Volkswagen and Kellogg's. In the case of the MBA, it is Harvard that is mostly associated with this brand, although it was not the first business school to develop such a course. So, to some extent at least, the fact of the continued existence of these organizations reflects the power and functions of corporate brands to *look outwards* by bestowing the following advantages on their companies:

- building long-term trust by increasing customer loyalty and convincing consumers of the benefits of their products and services
- reducing customers' search costs for perceived quality products and services and also providing them with certain psychological rewards
- ensuring repeat purchases, assist in the development of new product launches, facilitating market segmentation by communicating directly to the intended customers of the product or service, and facilitating premium pricing.

Corporate branding, however, is also recognized for a further, important reason, and that is its ability to *look inwards* to engage the 'hearts and minds' of employees. Marketers increasingly acknowledge that corporate branding *depends* on the hearts and minds of employees, since, as we have already seen, much of the value of corporate brands is delivered through people, having employees identify with the brand and align their efforts behind the brand. As one leading academic in this field has argued: 'One of the challenges of brand management is ensuring that staff have values that concur with those of the firm's brands' (De Chernatony, 2001, p. 5). A well-known example of this relationship is the service–profit chain in retailing, which is based on the propositions that (a) a 'compelling place to invest in' will derive from a 'compelling shopping experience', and (b) a compelling shopping experience will, in turn, be driven by employees' experience of a 'compelling place to work' (Kaplan and Norton, 2001). We shall return to this idea in the next chapter.

As a result, corporations have begun to use the language and tactics of internal branding to create employer brands, a practice which is quite widespread in the USA, Europe and Asia (Barrow and Mosley, 2005). One good example is the financial services company HSBC. This is a bank with a long history and until recently had grown quite slowly and mainly organically. In recent times, however, it has grown through acquisitions, some of them large, including companies in Brazil and Mexico. Part of the secret of its success has been its ability to transfer the brand equity of these acquired firms into the corporate brand equity, so that customers and employees identify with the corporation rather than the local banks they used to be served or employed by. Again, we will return to this idea of employer branding later in this book, with cases of Yahoo!, Southwest Airlines and others. At this point, however, we wish to flag a note of caution regarding the importance and desirability of corporate branding; not every organization needs it nor does a corporate brand always deliver the benefits promised, as our case of AT&T and NCR illustrated.

Corporate reputation and corporate image

Organizations have always had a concern for their image and, in the 1950s, academics began to examine the idea of image in terms of personality theory in the retailing sector. This concern led a number of commercial research organizations to conduct image studies, such as Marketing and Opinion Research International (MORI) in the UK and the Opinion Research Center (ORC) in the USA. The concept of image and image research, however, has been bedevilled by a number of problems because the concept has been used to refer to quite different aspects of an organization. These include the *transmitted* image (the visual image or desired image, transmitted by the corporate designers), the *received* image (how stakeholders perceive the brand, corporate reputation, or the organizational symbols), and the *construed* image (how, for example, employees believe customers see the organization). As a consequence, image is a concept that is difficult to pin down and, according to Balmer and Geyser (2003), has ceded ground to corporate reputation as a more useful concept. In a landmark paper, however, Dave Whetten and Alison Mackey (2002) have attempted to clear up the terminological confusion and have rescued image as a key concept in explaining corporate reputation. We will draw on this concept in Chapter 3.

The study of reputation has grown rapidly since the 1990s, bringing together scholars and practitioners from marketing and branding, organizational studies, communications and strategic management (Dowling, 2001; Hatch and Schultz, 2001; Davies *et al.*, 2003; Fombrun and Van Riel, 2003), and, more recently, our own work in HRM (Martin and Beaumont, 2003; Martin *et al.*, 2005). Whetten and Mackey (2002) see the identity-image-reputation process as a fundamental component of an organization's 'self-management project'. To make their point, they draw on a useful analogy and distinction between an organization's autobiography (self-authored narratives about identity that influence the projected image) and its biography ('official' and 'unofficial' assessments of the organization by outsiders – its reputation).

This biographical metaphor then helps stake out a claim for the notion of reputation to feature prominently in the corporate agenda. There are other justifications, however, which are equally important. Though corporate branding and reputation have common origins in their concern with the external image of an organization, proponents of corporate reputation claim it to be a more distinctive 'root' and intuitive concept than branding. This can be attributed to the notion of reputations taking into account the past as well as present and future impressions of a company's image and incorporating a wider range of measures and wider range of stakeholders in defining a reputation. It is also arguable the term reputation is more widely acceptable to people, especially in the public and voluntary sectors of economies, particularly as it has become to be progressively associated with companies' efforts at socially responsible and sustainable behaviour. Ask any person in the street if they understand what reputation means and they will be able to give you an answer; the same is unlikely to be said about a brand. One important attempt to spell out the relationship between corporate reputation and corporate branding is by Grahame Dowling (2001, 2004). He has argued that corporate reputations are lead indicators of brands; without a positive reputation it would be impossible to create a powerful corporate 'super-brand' or celebrity brand (Rindova *et al.*, 2006) (see Box 1.3). The brand pledge or covenant, created by the designers of corporate identity, has to be positively evaluated by key stakeholder groups, including customers, employees and, increasingly, financial analysts, the press, non-government organizations (NGOs), the general public and, of ever greater importance, the media, which help create celebrity status; it is on the basis of these evaluations that corporate brand reputations and brand equity are built. As a result, corporate reputation is slowly beginning to compete with branding and identity as the superior organizational lens.

Box 1.3   Google and Apple as Celebrity Brands

According to Rindova *et al.* (2006), a celebrity firm is developed from the media's search for organizations that serve as dramatic examples of important changes in society by taking bold or unusual actions and attempt to create distinctive identities (see next section in this chapter). These firms are natural targets for 'dramatized realities' created by the business press.

A good example is Google, one of the most widely discussed success stories in the business press, and an organization like Apple whose products define the industry standard. Just as the iPod is synonymous with digital music players, Google is with search engines. We now talk about 'doing a Google'.

Most of the business press coverage is on the founders, two young Stanford graduates, Larry Page and Sergey Brin. For example, an *Economist* article of January 2006 portrays Page as the 'visionary geek-in-chief', pronouncing at software conferences on the range of new products that will help Google achieve its ambition to 'organize all the world's information'. The storyline portrays the firm's celebrity through Page's missionary fanaticism, claiming that visitors feel they are in the company of religious zealots rather than employees (in much the same way that Apple was portrayed in the 1980s under the guidance of Steve Jobs). They also hint that Google may have an even grander design, to produce artificial intelligence that surpasses human capacity in written conversations – a 'god from a machine'.

In the context of celebrity brands and people management, two questions are worth reflecting on:

- Could this dramatization rebound on Google in the future?
- Will Apple's iPod celebrity conflict with its earlier image as a counter-culture? Apple wants to use the iPod success to sell more computers, which have always been seen as the niche product produced by niche people.

Much of this interest in reputations can be attributed to the work of the Reputation Institute, a worldwide network of companies, consultants and academics (www.reputationinstitute.com), which has been a forum for discussion of these concepts and the development of measures of the components of reputation since the mid-1990s. Charles Fombrun, the originator of the Institute, began his academic work in the field by examining the extraordinary impact of *Business Week* reputation rankings of US business schools on their ability to compete in the marketplace for students, donations and faculty, and the factors that underlay these rankings. Since then, we have witnessed an explosion of similar rankings in the business world, including rankings of companies' overall reputations (*Fortune* magazine, *Asia Business* and *The Financial Times*), best-managed companies (*Management Today*), rankings of good companies to work for (*The Sunday Times*) and, more recently, CSR (the Dow Jones Sustainability Index – see Chapter 9), which have lent the idea of reputation great credibility with the general public and other stakeholders. We examine this issue in more detail in Chapter 2.

Identity

The interest of reputation management in organizational identity has its origins in earlier work by academics on individual identity. Interest focused on how individuals came to take on the identity of the groups and organizations with which they interacted (the process of identification). Since then, this notion of identity has metamorphosed into the idea of an organization having an identity in its own right (an organizational identity), either as a kind of collective supra-personality or, borrowing from the legal concept of the firm, as a 'social actor' capable of being held accountable and 'finding one's own place in society' (Whetten and Mackey, 2002).

In a classic interpretation of organizational identity, Albert and Whetten (1985) outlined three of its central principles:

- It should capture the essence or 'claimed central character' of the organization
- It should set out its claimed distinctiveness
- It should show continuity over time.

These principles are the usual starting point for more recent discussions of the topic. Two of the most interesting concern its continuity and central character. First, some writers claim that fluidity and flexibility constitutes a requirement for organization identities to cope with rapid environmental changes in the modern world (Goiia *et al.*, 2000). Arguably, then, this third principle should capture the idea of flexibility as well as endurance; what Goiia *et al.* refer to as a 'mutable identity', capable of helping an organization change over time. One good example these researchers draw on is how IBM managed to change its view of itself and its projected image as a single-minded mainframe company in the 1980s in response to market changes so that it could compete with small PC companies. Since then it has undergone another identity change to a solutions-based company, but all the time retained elements of its original character.

Second, other writers point to the existence of multiple identities in organizations. This idea runs counter to the idea of a monolithic corporateness but is probably a more realistic picture of, and for, many organizations. For example, just as an individual can be a mother, doctor, athlete and daughter at the same time, a hospital can be seen by its members as a business, a caring organization and a professional organization. Thus, how you see an organization at any point in time depends on where you are viewing it from – from the perspective of a politician or financier looking for value for money, as a patient looking for high levels of care, as a doctor looking for a place to practise a craft and develop a reputation, or as a business journalist looking for a dramatic story (as in the case of Box 1.3). We examine these issues more closely in Chapter 3 but they do suggest that attempts by corporate communication departments (in conjunction with a willing business press), to create corporate identities which are unrecognizable to employees, are counterproductive in the long run; often they generate unofficial, opposed identities and resentment towards heroic leadership.

Organization actions, governance and leadership

Just as organizations can be said to have identities in their own right they are often attributed with the ability to act. Whereas organizational identity deals with the 'Who are we?' question and how such conceptions influence the corporation's autobiography, its image cannot be sustained without supportive organizational actions. Though the idea of organizations acting (or making decisions, having an identity, learning, etc.) can be considered as an anthropomorphism (attributing human forms or qualities to entities that are not human), the idea is a useful one in so far as it draws attention to the question: which people are most influential in shaping organizational direction and actions?

The usual answer, of course, is the board of directors, leaders and senior managers. Good governance and leaders help bind an organization together as it changes. They help organizations to differentiate themselves from others and meet social legitimacy goals. Leaders' actions symbolize the organizational identity. Finally, they also meet the needs of individuals and the organization by taking on its collective work. One only needs to look at cases of bad governance and leadership to see its impact on organizations, and indeed, nation-states; witness the cases of malpractice and unethical behaviour referred to earlier in the well-documented cases of Enron and others (Clarke, 2004; Kellerman, 2004). Particularly important to our framework, it is through their actions or inactions that employees come to understand and experience the 'true' identity of an organization rather than that which is portrayed in mission statements and public pronouncements (see Box 1.3). Governance and its problems are embedded in the identity of organizations, or more probably, their multiple identities.

In an enlightening participant observation study of a US voluntary organization, Golden-Biddle and Rao (1997) have shown how its directors' behaviours were embedded in the multiple identities of the organization *and* helped create and sustain them. These directors experienced not only role conflict resulting from competing expectations from their legal and fiduciary obligations but 'conflicts of commitment' as they struggled to reconcile incompatible expectations ensuing from their desire to uphold two primary identities – 'volunteer governance', in which the direction of the organization was invested in volunteers rather than professional managers, and to act as a 'family of friends', which implied strong feelings of friendship among directors and conflict avoidance at all costs. When faced with a challenge to its ways of operating by a senior volunteer board member who broke the rules of conflict avoidance, the organization's identities were severely tested, but were effectively repaired by breaching the contradictions between them through an acceptable compromise. As this case demonstrates, governance and leadership action are embedded in the multiple organizational identities that helped create the problems of dual commitment but also helped them work out a compromise solution that reinforced these identities. It also hints at how more recent and well-documented problems of governance may have arisen and been dealt with, in many cases unsatisfactorily, at least from the perspective of the media and general public.

Leadership *styles* are also important in translating organizational identity into an image. We often refer to senior leaders' (in)abilities to 'walk the talk' by acting out the mission and values statements, and to the gaps between 'rhetoric and reality' in which the leadership style is totally inconsistent with the usual mantra of 'people are our most important asset'. From an employee perspective, there are few more important breeding grounds for cynicism than the failure of senior leaders to match organizational identity and image with action, as we have discovered in a number of studies of organizational change (Pate *et al.*, 2000). The reverse is also true, however: employees are known to invest their leaders with almost mythical qualities to inspire them to achieve radical organizational transformations (Martin and Riddell, 1996), though the higher the pedestal the further the potential for a fall from grace. The major debate in leadership most obviously related to this issue is the ubiquitous division in nearly all studies on management between task-oriented behaviours and person-oriented behaviours; like most solutions in management, the idea of a compromise or 'optimization' between them is the most favoured way forward. Without attention to both performance and people, it is unlikely the employees will identify with the organization and act in ways that will enhance its image.

The individual employment relationship, individual behaviours and their links with organizational identity

We contend there are processes at work in which individuals may, *under certain circumstances*, come to incorporate elements of their organization's identity into their self-perceptions. These processes draw on social identity and self-categorization theories. One of our core messages for practitioners is as follows: changing employees' identities is a more difficult and uncertain task than most of basic culture management and communications-driven, customer relationship texts would have readers believe, notwithstanding the ethical problems and potential backlash from so-called 'brandwashing'. Organizational identity (the 'Who are we?' question) and the relationships between leadership and followers will depend on the ability of key managers to understand and manage the psychological contracts that exist in the organization, that is, the perceptions held by individuals concerning organizational 'promises' and the relative values they place on these promises or expectations (Conway and Briner, 2005). It will also depend on other key individual–organizational linkages that contribute to the quality of individual employment relations (see Chapter 4). These include: *individual identification* (the 'Who am I?' question), *internalization* ('What do I believe in?'), *psychological ownership* ('Do I feel that the organization is mine?') and *commitment* ('Will I stay?') (Pierce *et al.*, 2001; Sparrow and Cooper, 2003). Such a list is often confusing for practitioners and is probably why the idea of *employee engagement* has become so popular in recent years, since it promises to tap into or overlay all of the others as a form of temperature check for HR managers. However, like any idea or tools claiming to do everything, it may end up doing nothing particularly well; this, we believe, is the problem facing many of the consultancy-based engagement approaches. Nevertheless, engagement does bring something extra that organizational psychologists have sometimes failed to consider, including, most importantly, measures of attitudes relevant to business-related behaviours. These attitudinal dimensions of business-related behaviours usually refer to a belief in the organization and its mission; a desire to work to make things better, an understanding of the business context and the strategic drivers of the organization; respect for colleagues and willingness to help them, willingness to go beyond contract, and keeping up to date with developments in their field (Robinson *et al.*, 2004).

Recent academic research on engagement, and there has been very little of that, has shown it to be positively related to customer satisfaction (Harter *et al.*, 2002), a lead indicator of financial performance in tests of the service–profit chain in the retailing and banking industries (Gelade and Young, 2005). Though more work needs to be done on defining engagement and its correlates, it shows promise as a concept.

Finally, it almost goes without saying, critical behaviours for reputations and brands also depend on the outcomes of knowledge, skills and abilities – the human capital pool. Investment in knowledge stocks and knowledge flows is one of the key messages of strategic human resource management (Dunsford *et al.*, 2001).

HR strategies and the quality of individual employment relations

The central premise of this book is that HR can contribute significantly to corporate reputations and branding by influencing the lived experience of employees, the quality of their individual employment relationships, and through these, organizational identity, governance and leadership. The connections between HR drivers and these variables, however, are not clear-cut: how HR fast-forwards into individual employment relations and interpenetrates with corporate strategy is a complex process; it is not just a question of aligning HR with the business strategy and pulling the right levers to generate positive psychological contracts, engaged and competent employees.

Some HR researchers and many practitioners advocate a 'one-best-way' set of practices masquerading under a range of guises – high involvement HR, high commitment HR or high performance work systems. The basic but compelling message (not always intended but often read as such) is: search for best practices among 'best-in-class' firms on a range of HR variables, benchmark yourself against these firms and implement those practices that fit your needs. Yet, the very idea of best practices has been roundly criticized, most importantly, on the grounds that context is all important, whether it be the strategic, industry or national context (Leseure *et al.*, 2004). This has resulted in another school of thought in strategic HRM, focusing on the 'fit' between 'bundles of practices' and organizational contexts. Best fit approaches have tended to dominate the academic, rather than practitioner, literature on HRM, reflecting the portfolio planning/life cycle approaches in marketing during the 1970s and the competitive positioning work of strategy writers such as Michael Porter during the 1980s (see Chapter 5).

However, best fit is not only concerned with this external fit between HR systems and strategy, but also with internal fit. This latter concept comes in two varieties. The first is the degree of coherence among HR policies and practices themselves, required to create powerful combinations but avoid deadly cocktails. The second type of internal fit focuses on creating synergies between HR policies and practices themselves and between HR systems and other organizational systems. One of the most insightful of these is the 'architectural' approach which we shall discuss in Chapters 5 and 6. The basic argument of this approach is the need to segment the labour force in much the same way that we segment customers. Also it suggests that, while talented people matter, more importantly, it is managing talent that matters: the value and uniqueness of human capital to organizations differ, and these different groups should be treated differently – the so-called talent management approach.

Modelling the relationship between people management and corporateness

We are now almost in a better position to explain our model in basic terms (see Figure 1.1). First, corporate brands depend on corporate reputation(s), which is set out in more detail in Chapter 2. Corporate brands result from the levels of confidence that people place in the ability of an organization to deliver high levels of what they value about its corporate image and the support they give to its products and/or services. Reputations represent the degree of alignment between the beliefs and feelings held by a group about an organization's overall projected image and its values (Whetten and Mackey, 2002).

Second, the drivers of corporate image lie in the interactions between organizational identity and individual identification with their organizations, together with organizational governance and effective leadership. These interactions are the subject of Chapter 3. Third, these interactions depend on the quality of individual's employment experiences, including their perceptions of psychological contracts, their levels of engagement and their skills, which is the subject of Chapter 4. Fourth, how employees experience their employment relationships depends on the sophistication of human resource and communication strategies, which we explore in our four-part discussion of strategic human resource management in Chapters 5, 6, 7 and 8. It is these people management variables that represent the operational but core element of our model and form our particular contribution to the emerging literature and practice in the field of reputation management and branding. We will set out exactly what challenges they bring for the HR function in the last chapter of the book. In the penultimate chapter, however, we discuss how strategic human resource management and the HR function are related to three, leading corporate-level indicators: corporate strategy, senior leaders' vision and governance, and corporate identity, increasingly through a CSR agenda, to influence reputations and brands.

So our model, which we shall use to organize the rest of this book, is based on explaining the related concepts of corporate branding and corporate reputation and their links with people management. In turn, these work through organizational identity, actions and the processes of psychological contracting and identification.

The core propositions of the model, which are a slightly more formal re-statement of our storyline for the book, are threefold:

- Corporate reputation and evaluations of corporate brand strength are ultimately dependent on effective people management strategies and behaviour, including HR strategies, formal and informal organizational communications, policies designed to connect and engage employees with the organizational aims and the kinds of behaviours they engender. This contention is the central one of the book.
- The competence and credibility of the HR function, working in tandem with other functions such as marketing, are key variables in translating important corporate-level antecedents, including senior leaders' corporate vision of leadership, corporate strategy and the expressed desire of leaders to have a corporate identity, into effective people management strategies.
- Finally, these people management strategies work through the interrelationships between organizational identity, governance and leadership styles, competent

employees and supportive behaviours to influence the links between corporate image, corporate reputation(s) and the corporate brand.

The significance of corporateness for HR professionals

If human resources are at the heart of corporateness in any organization, what role does this imply for human resource professionals? This question leads us to our third main contention, that corporateness presents a significant challenge and opportunity for senior HR professionals. These challenges are especially relevant for practitioners working in complex and often fragmented organizations, those in internationally differentiated organizations, those in highly customer-focused or knowledge-based organizations, and those that seek to develop reputations and brands for CSR. More and more, HR specialists are witnessing calls for the HR function to play a strategic role as business partners, strategic partners and leaders (CIPD, 2004; Ulrich and Brockbank, 2005). Though this concept has not been particularly well articulated, we see it as working directly with the senior management team and other functions to play a leading role in interpreting changing external environments for organizations and creating added value by managing talent, helping create strong individual–organizational linkages, shaping organizational cultures and contributing to the change management process. So, in such contexts, HR will require a more expert understanding of these corporate-level concepts, organizational identity and identification, and their potential in building and sustaining corporateness. By doing so, they will become better equipped to become not only business partners but also 'corporate partners' or corporate HR leaders, an idea to which we will return to the final chapter on creating a fit-for-purpose HR function.

What has been a surprise to us in doing the research for this book, and for our previous work in this field, is that the human resource literature is almost silent on the relationship between corporate-level concepts and people management. This silence, however, is becoming much less deafening. For example, recent evidence drawn from research into the strategic issues facing international firms, showed that employer branding, one of the key ideas associated with corporate branding, was one of the most important of these issues for international HR managers (Sparrow *et al.*, 2004). In addition, an unpublished panel survey undertaken by *The Economist* in 2003 showed high levels of awareness among US, Europe and Asia international firms of the importance of the branding-people management link (Martin *et al.*, 2005). These trends are supported by our own research,[1] and by the extensive interest shown recently by practitioners at numerous conferences on employer branding and the like.

This lack of previous interest in issues such as reputation, branding and identity management from the HR community – practitioners, HR consultants and academics – contrasts markedly with marketing and communications specialists, both of whom have produced a substantial literature on the connections between brand advantage, customer service and people management strategies (de Chernatony, 2001), corporate reputation and people management (Davies *et al.*, 2003) and communications, branding, corporate reputation and people management (Van Riel, 2003). The central message of much of this work, like our own, is that external image and reputations are intimately linked to employee values, attitudes and behaviours, especially in customer-facing industries, knowledge-based and creative organizations, and those seeking to promote CSR. In the field of branding, for example, two leading UK marketing experts argue that employees exert a powerful influence on linking the external and internal interface (Harris and de Chernatony, 2001), and that employees are at the heart of delivering the 'promises' of the brand. That same message has also been delivered by two marketing professionals who have recently moved into HR consulting (Barrow and Mosley, 2005).

Yet, despite all of this interest shown by marketing and branding specialists, we do not have a sophisticated enough

[1]We have been examining the relationship between HR, branding and corporate reputation since 2003 as researchers, consultants and practitioners(see Martin and Beaumont, 2003; Martin *et al.*, 2005; Hetrick and Martin, forthcoming. This work has led to the establishment of a Centre for Reputation Management through People at the University of Glasgow's School of Business and Management, http://www.gla.ac.uk/crmp).

understanding of the linkages between HR and marketing in the brand management and reputation building processes (see also Sparrow *et al.*, 2004). Naturally enough, given their backgrounds, education and interests, marketers have been good at using the language of branding and communications to shed new light on people management, and have produced practical tools for assisting HR professionals to apply the language of branding to people management problems. However, they have said little about the complex nature of employee identification with brands and organizations, other than at a general level and usually in highly prescriptive manner. As befits business disciplines that are essentially normative, marketing and communications sometimes fail to deal with the realities or causes of much of organizational life, such as cynical or apathetic employee attitudes to customer service, unethical products and practices, disenchanted managers and the competing professional identities of many knowledge workers that have little connection with advancing ideas of corporateness.

So, for HR professionals, the rising star of corporateness marks a watershed and a real opportunity to become corporate, as well as business, partners. However, it also brings significant challenges for the role of the HR function, as well as the capability of HR professionals to 'round themselves out', lead and deliver people strategies that support corporate reputations and brand, CSR and good governance.

References

Aaker, D. A. (2004) Leveraging the corporate brand, *California Management Review*, **46** (3), 6–18.

Albert, S. and Whetten, D. (1985) Organizational identity, in L. L. Cummings and B. M. Staw (eds), *Research in organizational behaviour* 7. Greenwich, CT: JAI Press, pp. 263–295.

Alessandri, S. W. and Allessandri, T. (2004) Promoting and protecting corporate identity: the importance of organizational and industrial context, *Corporate Reputation Review*, **7**, 252–268.

Bakan, J. (2004) *The corporation: the pathological pursuit of profit.* New York: Free Press.

Balmer, J. T. and Greyser, S. A. (2003) *Revealing the corporation: perspectives on identity, image, reputation, corporate branding and corporate-level marketing.* London: Routledge.

Barrow, S. and Mosley, R. (2005) *The Employer Brand®: bringing the best of brand management to people at work.* London: Wiley.

Berthon, P., Hulbert, J. M. and Pitt, L. F. (1999) Brand management prognostications, *Sloan Management Review*, **40** (Winter), 53–65.

Boxall, P. and Purcell, J. (2003) *Strategy and human resource management.* London: Palgrave Macmillan.

CIPD (2004) *Business partnering: a new direction for HR.* Wimbledon: CIPD.

Clarke, T. (ed.) (2004) *Theories of corporate governance: the philosophical foundations of corporate governance.* London: Routledge.

Conway, N. and Briner, R. B. (2005) *Understanding psychological contracts at work: a critical evaluation of theory and research.* Oxford: Oxford University Press.

Davies, G. with Chun, R., Da Silva, R. V. and Roper, S. (2003) *Corporate reputation and competitiveness.* London: Routledge.

Davies, G., Chun, R., Da Silva, R. V. and Roper, S. (2004) A corporate character scale to assess employee and customer views of organization reputation, *Corporate Reputation Review*, **7**, 125–146.

de Chernatony, L. (2001) *From brand vision to brand evaluation.* Oxford: Butterworth–Heinemann.

Deephouse, D. L. and Carter, S. M. (2005) An examination of differences between organizational legitimacy and reputation, *Journal of Management Studies*, **42**, 329–360.

Dowling, G. R. (2001) *Creating corporate reputations: identity, image and performance.* New York: Oxford University Press.

Dowling, G. R. (2004) Corporate reputations: should you compete on yours? *California Management Review*, **46** (3), 19–36.

Dunsford, B. B., Snell, S. A. and Wright, P. M. (2001) Human resources and the resource based view of the firm. *CAHRS Working Paper 01-03*, School of Industrial and Labor Relations, Ithaca, NY: Cornell University Press.

The Economist (2004) Selling the flag, *The Economist*, 26 February.

The Economist (2006) St Lawrence of Google, *The Economist*, 14 January.

Florida, R. (2005) *The flight of the creative class.* New York: Harper-Collins.

Fombrun, C. J. and Van Riel, C. B. M. (2003) *Fame and fortune: how successful companies build winning reputations.* Upper Saddle River, NJ: Financial Times/Prentice Hall.

Gelade, G. A. and Young, S. (2005) Test of a service profit chain model in the retail banking sector, *Journal of Occupational and Organizational Psychology*, **78**, 1–22.

Goiia, D. A., Shultz, M. and Corley, K. G. (2000) Organizational identity, image and adaptive instability, *Academy of Management Review*, **25** (1), 63–81.

Golden-Biddle, K. and Rao, H. (1997) Breaches in the boardroom: identity and conflicts of commitment in a nonprofit organization, *Organizational Science*, **8**, 593–611.

Greenwald, B. and Kahn, J. (2005) *Competition demystified.* New York: Portfolio/Penguin.

Hagel IIIrd, J. and Seely Brown, J. (2005) *The only sustainable edge: why business strategy depends on productive friction and dynamic specialization.* Boston, MA: Harvard Business School Press.

Haig, M. (2003) *Brand failures: the truth about the 100 biggest branding mistakes of all time.* London: Kogan-Page.

Haig, M. (2004) *Brand royalty: how the world's top 100 brands thrive and survive.* London: Kogan-Page.

Harris, F. and de Chernatony, L. (2001) Corporate branding and corporate brand performance, *European Marketing Journal*, **35** (3/4), 441–456.

Harter, J. M., Schmidt, F. and Hayes, T. L. (2002) Business unit level relationships between employee satisfaction/engagement and business outcomes: a meta-analysis, *Journal of Applied Psychology*, **87**, 268–279.

Hatch, M. J. and Schultz, M. (2001) Are the strategic starts aligned for your corporate brand?, *Harvard Business Review*, Jan–Feb, pp. 129–134.

Hill and Knowlton (2004) Global corporate reputation watch survey. http://www.hillandknowlton.com/crw/ (28 February 2006).

Human Resource Management Journal (2005) Special issue: The link between HRM and performance, *Human Resource Management Journal*, **15** (4).

Jackson, K. T. (2004) *Building reputation capital: strategies for integrity and fair play that improve the bottom line.* Oxford: Oxford University Press.

Joyce, W., Nohria, N. and Robertson, B. (2003) *What really works: the 4+2 formula for sustained business success.* Boston, MA: Harvard Business School Press.

Kaplan, R. and Norton, D. (2001) *The strategy-focused organization.* Boston, MA: Harvard Business School Press.

Kay, J. (2004) *The truth about markets: why some nations are rich but most remain poor.* London: Penguin Books.

Kellerman, B. (2004) *Bad leadership: what it is, how it happens and why it matters.* Boston, MA: Harvard Business School Press.

Klein, N. (2000) *No logo: no space, no choice, no jobs.* New York: Picador.

Leseure, M. J., Bauer, J., Birdi, K., Neely, A. and Denyer, D. (2004) Adoption of promising practices: a systematic review of the evidence, *International Journal of Management Reviews*, **5/6**, 169–190.

Martin, G. (2006) *Managing people and organizations in changing contexts.* Oxford: Butterworth–Heinemann.

Martin, G. and Hetrick, S. (forthcoming) Corporate reputation, branding and people management: the case of Finco.

Martin, G. and Riddell, T. (1996) 'The wee outfit that decked IBM': manufacturing : strategic change in the 'Cash', *Strategic Change,* **5** (1), 3–25.

Martin, G. and Beaumont, P. B. (2003) *Branding and people management: what's in a name?* Wimbledon: CIPD.

Martin, G., Beaumont, P. B. and Pate, J. M. (2003) A process model of strategic change and some case study evidence, in W. Cooke (ed.), *Multinational companies and transnational workplace issues.* Westport, CT: Quorum Press.

Martin, G., Beaumont, P. B., Doig, R. M. and Pate, J. M. (2005) Branding: a new discourse for HR?, *European Management Journal,* **23** (1), 76–88.

Pate, J., Martin, G. and Staines, H. (2000) The new psychological contract, cynicism and organizational change: a theoretical framework and case study evidence, *Journal of Strategic Change,* **9** (1), 481–493.

Pfeffer, J. (2005) *Creating a performance culture.* Presentation at University of Strathclyde, 23 September.

Pierce, J. L., Kostova, T. and Dirks, K. T. (2001) Towards a theory of psychological ownership in organizations, *Academy of Management Review,* **26**, 298–310.

Rindova, V. P., Pollock, T. G. and Hayward, M. L. A. (2006) Celebrity firms: the social construction of market popularity, *Academy of Management Review,* 31: 50–71.

Roberts, J. (2004) *The modern firm: organizational design for performance and growth.* New York: Oxford University Press.

Roberts, P. W. and Dowling, G. R. (2002) Corporate reputation and sustained superior financial performance. *Strategic Management Journal,* **23**, 1077–1093.

Robinson, D., Perryman, S. and Hayday, S. (2004) *The drivers of employee engagement.* Institute of Employment Studies, Report No. 404. Brighton: IES.

Schultz, M. and de Chernatony, L. (2002) Introduction: The challenges of corporate branding, *Corporate Reputation Review,* **5** (2/3), 105–112.

Sjovall, A. M. and Talk, Andrew C. (2004) From actions to impressions: cognitive attribution theory and the formation of corporate reputation, *Corporate Reputation Review,* **13**, 269–281.

Sparrow, P. R. and Cooper, C. L. (2003) *The new employment relationship.* Oxford: Butterworth–Heinemann.

Sparrow, P. R., Brewster, C. and Harris, H. (2004) *Globalizing human resource management.* London: Routledge.

Ulrich, D. and Brockbank, W. (2005) *The HR value proposition.* Boston, MA: Harvard Business School Press.

Van Riel, C. B. (2003) The management of corporate communications, in J. M. T. Balmer and S. A. Geyser (eds), *Revealing the corporation: perspectives on identity, image, reputation, corporate branding and corporate-level marketing.* London: Routledge.

Whetten, D. and Mackey, A. (2002) A social actor conception of organizational identity and its implications for the study of organizational reputations, *Business and Society*, **41**, 393–414.

CHAPTER 2

Managing corporate brands and reputations

Making the connections between strategy, corporateness and HRM

In the opening chapter we introduced two of the most important corporate-level concepts in our model – branding and reputation management – and showed how these are important to the key strategic interests of organizations and nations in market economies. Reputations and brands provide essential information to consumers and other stakeholders in an imperfect world. Our second message was that brands and reputations, though validated on the outside by consumers and other external stakeholders, are usually driven from the inside by the quality and actions of employees. In this chapter we wish to develop this last message by shedding some light on the meaning of brands, branding and reputations, especially for non-specialists in these fields, and discuss how they may be related to each other.

However, since all ideas in business and management are something of a contested terrain, there are different schools of thought on branding and reputation management, so we also discuss and evaluate some of these. This is of great practical importance because of confusion over what is meant by branding and reputations. Thus *we* need to be clear about what *we* mean, how these ideas might be related to each other and what their specific connections are with people and HRM. To do this, it is first necessary to trace their intellectual justifications and links to the literature and practice of strategic management, which deals with the highest level and most long-term decisions of organizations.

Corporateness and strategic management

Strategic management as a body of knowledge and practice has been dominated by an 'outside-in' perspective, often simplified for students and practitioners into the ubiquitous SWOT framework. This portrays strategy as a three-stage process of examining the *opportunities and threats* in external environments of organizations, considering the *strengths and weaknesses* of internal resources, and bringing both into alignment. The usual emphasis and core message of this framework, however, is that it is the *external opportunities and threats that drive strategy* with internal resources needing to be brought into line with these environmental pressures. The major figure in this outside-in approach to strategic management is Michael Porter (1985, 1996), whose views on strategic success are characterized as being driven by fit with the external environment. Porter's original focus was on the attractiveness of industries as the driver of strategy and the forces that shape attractiveness of industries to firms – *buyer and supplier power, the threat of substitute products/services and new entrants into the market, and the intensity of competitive rivalry*. Based on this external analysis, the main strategic choice for firms was how to position themselves competitively, either through *differentiation* in the minds of customers, *cost leadership* throughout the value chain or *focus*, niche marketing strategies. Accordingly, people and HRM were treated as downstream or derived decisions that followed strategic marketing, planning and branding, and were rarely considered to be of significant strategic importance.

It should come as no great surprise that marketing and branding specialists have drawn intellectual inspiration from such a model, and how they may have contributed to its dominance by elevating the 'cult' of the customer (Du Gay, 1996) and, indeed, product branding to an all-time high during the 1980s and 1990s. We use the term cult here because there was some ideological as well as rational reasoning used to justify outside-in perspectives. Ideology can be thought of as the use of ideas to promote certain interests, often beyond what might be justified by the evidence or interests of society in general. And there is little doubt that the interests of marketing and branding specialists, especially the major marketing consultants, were served by promoting customers at the expense of other stakeholders in organizations.

However, when developed economies began to move away from competing on the basis of tangible products and manufactured goods to intangible services and, increasingly, knowledge assets, strategic management began to look for alternative explanations of success. Perhaps the best known of these 'new strategic management' approaches is the resource-based view (RBV) of the firm (Barney, 1991, 2002; Grant, 1991). This 'inside-out' strategic perspective has become a counterpoint to the outside-in caricature of Porter's perspective and speaks to the differentiation/ initiative agenda proposed by unique organizational identities in the opening chapter. Though this picture is a little unfair, since Porter has acknowledged the importance of internal resources in driving strategy (Argyres and McGahan, 2002), his debates with Jay Barney are worth reviewing. In contrast to Porter's focus on the attractiveness of industries, Barney's resource-based view on strategy and, by implication, on HRM, sees the fundamental and, indeed, only sustainable route to competitive advantage as arising from how you put together unique and enviable combinations of internal, usually intangible, resources, the principal justification being that everything else is open to inspection and copying. The most important of these are often seen to be information and people, and their relationships to other key processes and intangible assets, such as knowledge creation and dissemination, brands and the creation and maintenance of reputations (Boxall and Purcell, 2003; Martin *et al.*, 2005). Since these intangibles are, in many respects, the products of specific organizational cultures, defined by the guiding assumptions and values, attitudes, norms of behaviour and key artefacts such as structures, systems and processes, this has led some writers to believe it is how such cultures are managed and how people are selected, developed, rewarded and organized that differentiates firms, especially in the modern knowledge-based industries and growing service sectors of Europe and North America (Pfeffer, 1998, 2005).

So, the RBV has provided a major intellectual and empirical justification for the importance of HRM and its links to key strategic decisions on issues such as branding and reputations, and we will return to it in later chapters in this book. Just as the interests of marketing people have been served by the outside-in approach, we have to be a little wary of any perspective that offers a one-best-way analysis and solution. This is especially so for one that promotes another sectional interest – human resources – at the expense of other key aspects of business (Porter, 1996; Argyres and McGahan, 2002). For example, as Porter (1996) has argued, internal resources – people, brands, reputations or knowledge – are of no intrinsic competitive value; it is how they are used and in what contexts they are used that create value for organizations and economies. The RBV has also been criticized for at least two other reasons (Lado *et al.*, 2006), who state that:

- Resources are intangible (such as organizational knowledge and reputations), so they cannot be open to measurement, making proof of the idea a near impossibility.
- An organization's truly valuable (human) resources are difficult to imitate because they are opaque, so how can employees and managers understand and build on them to create sustainable advantages?

These criticisms have important practical implications for reputation management and branding because they have been traditionally seen as part of 'soft' management, not the numbers game that most managers understand. Nevertheless, the RBV has managed to rebalance the debate, based on the rationale that you don't move a seesaw by sitting in the middle. As these two camps are beginning to recognize, however, the answer to this fundamental question on the sources of competitive advantage question probably lies somewhere in the middle, with both perspectives having something to offer (Boxall and Purcell, 2003). We shall examine these perspectives in Chapters 6 and 9.

Core competences and the service–profit chain

Sitting alongside the RBV is another stream of influential strategic management literature that has been used to explain effective and sustainable strategic advantage. This is based on the notion of *core internal competences* (Hamel and Prahalad, 1994; Hamel, 1998) and the complementary idea of the '*balanced scorecard*' (Kaplan and Norton, 1996, 2001). The balanced scorecard is particularly relevant to the relations between HR and branding since it makes explicit the practical links to balancing the needs and measurement of different stakeholders in an organization – satisfying customers and financial objectives with the effective management and measurement of internal business processes, including people, and individual and organizational learning and growth. Kaplan and Norton (2001) have also developed a strategy map or 'theory of the business', which is, in effect, a cause-and-effect model designed to help managers understand the relationships between critical performance drivers and their associated outcomes. A popular and important derivation of this theory of the business is an approach linking the marketing of services, customer relationship management and customer satisfaction to internal markets and human resource management – the *service–profit chain*, first identified by the Sears corporation in the USA (Heskett *et al.*, 1997; Kirn *et al.*, 1999) (see Figure 2.1).

The service–profit chain has been widely used in service industries such as retailing, the hospitality industry, airlines and financial services to explain the links between employee attitudes, customer satisfaction and superior business performance. For example, drawing on the service–profit chain, Hemmington and Watson (2003) have argued that the service encounter provides the best and probably only unique opportunity to differentiate service to individual customers, thereby creating higher levels of customer satisfaction and repeat business in the hospitality industry. The reality of the delivery of employee-centred actions was more important than the marketing communications literature of hotels; through promising high levels of customer service, often through vague and clichéd statements, they failed to differentiate between hotels and had the negative potential to over-promise what could not be delivered.

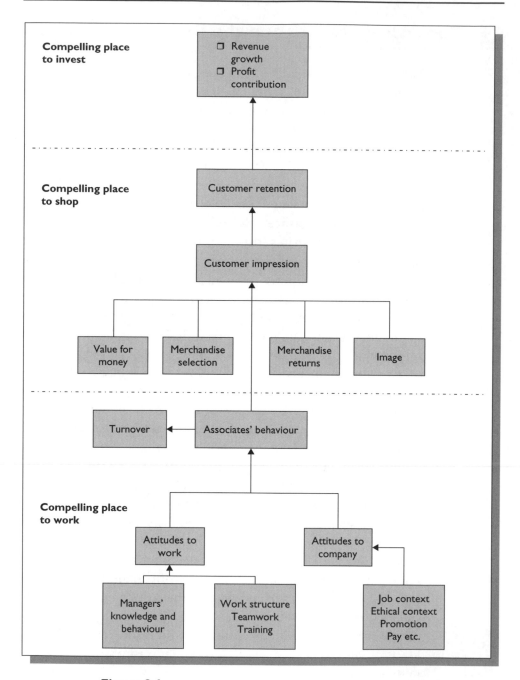

Figure 2.1
The employee–customer–profit chain at Sears (adapted from Kaplan and Norton, 2001).

Further support for the central nature of the service encounter came from a Gallup poll in the USA of six major sectors on the factors influencing brand performance; it found that, for all sectors, the single most important factor in building brand loyalty was employee behaviour (McEwen and Buckingham, 2001). In the case of the airline industry, interaction with employees was three times more powerful than any other factor, including product performance. On the negative side, poor employee performance was also important in customer dissatisfaction, particularly when there were no other features to differentiate among products or services. Nevertheless, the direct evidence in support of this service–profit chain is not all that convincing. Read the summary of a banking study in Box 2.1.

Box 2.1   The service–profit chain in the UK retail banking industry

Garry Gelade and Stephen Young, two psychologists working for major international consultants, have access to enormous data sets in the British retail banking sector that allowed them to conduct a rigorous study of the service–profit chain in four banks. Data were collected on the attitudes of 37 000 employees to the jobs and organizations; they also had access to customer satisfaction surveys and sales performance at bank branch level.

These data allowed them to test the simple proposition of the service–profit chain that 'satisfied and motivated employees produce satisfied customers, and satisfied customers tend to purchase more, increasing the revenues and profits of the organization' (Gelade and Young, 2005, p. 2). The key link here is customer satisfaction being the mediating variable between employee attitudes and organizational performance (see Figure 2.1). The model Gelade and Young used involved a causal relationship linking positive employee perceptions of team working, job enablers and job support to organizational climate and commitment. These people management variables were thought to be the lead indicators of sales achievement, though mediated by customer satisfaction.

Their data provided high levels of support for positive correlations of employee attitudes and climate evaluations with customer satisfaction and sales performance at the business unit level of analysis, i.e. the banks. From these data, they concluded that, in theory at least, an improvement in one standard deviation from the mean of scores in employee commit-ment would lead to an average 6% increase in bank sales. So if banks worked very hard to achieve such improvements in attitudes by raising average levels of commitment to at least the level of the most committed top third of employees, they would reap significant benefits.

However, their data provided little support for the mediation effects of customer satisfaction and, thus, the role it plays in the theory of the service–profit chain. Though this should not be interpreted as meaning customer satisfaction is irrelevant to the links between employee atti-tudes and sales performance, other branding research also questions the idea that customer satisfaction is closely associated with customers buy-ing more or remaining loyal to the firm (Miller and Muir, 2004).

Source: Based on Gelade and Young, 2005

As you can see from this discussion on the RBV and related ideas such as the service–profit chain, brands and reputations are dynamically linked to HRM. However, we need to be a little clearer about what brands, branding and reputations mean and how they are linked. We shall now discuss this question in a little more detail.

Developments in branding and definitions

Proponents of branding view brands as the central organizing principle for good management of a business and the most important intangible asset that an organization can possess. By and large, most big organizations with well-known brands, whether in the for-profit or not-for-profit sectors, offer com-modity products or services that can be relatively easily substi-tuted by others. One only need examine the competitive offerings of high profile brands such as Coca-Cola, Heinz, HSBC, Wal-Mart, McDonald's, Nokia, Ford or even Cancer Research, and premium brands such as BMW and Moet-Chandon to see this. What they do share, however, are three attributes that distinguish them from their rivals: an attempt to create a *compelling idea*, supporting core *values* and a role in the organization that places *brand* positioning, purpose and values at *the heart of all key decisions* (Brymer, 2003; Sherry, 2005). Many branding specialists share these ideas but offer additional attributes as their own contributions to the meaning and value of branding (see Box 2.2). They would also have little difficulty in subscribing to a definition of brands that suggests more than a name or symbol used to sell products and services, the usual impression held by non-specialists. We offer our own variation of a well-known definition by Kristin Zhivage as a working one for this book. This incorporates the people management dimension with the external view of marketers.

> A brand is a promise made and kept in every strategic, marketing and human resource activity, every action, every corporate decision and every customer and employee interaction intended to deliver strategic value to an organization.

Box 2.2   Brands and business success

Jon Miller and David Muir (2004) are consultants who argue cogently that brands and branding are, or should be, at the heart of business and treated as a key approach to creating shareholder value. They have identified five themes that are fundamental to understanding brands:

- Brands enhance the value of a product or service beyond its functional value, so enabling organizations to gain by selling more and/or charging higher prices. By generating better cash flows, they help create shareholder value.
- Brands are the source of alignment between an organization and its stakeholders, providing the basis for continuity and trust. Trust and loyalty, not just satisfied customers, are what generate revenues and long-term sales performances.
- Brands are the outcomes of behaviour – every action taken by members of an organization has the potential to influence a brand reputation, for good or bad. Brand promises create expectations that are judged by the behaviour of organizational decisions and actions; promises have to be matched by delivery in every action, decision and customer interaction.

■ Brands only exist in the minds of people – they are perceptions held by consumers and are therefore public objects, not only assets of the organization. It is in this sense that people can be said to 'own' brands.

■ Brands can provide organizations with purpose and direction, helping align stakeholders behind the brand. In this sense, branding should be part of the vision and mission of the organization.

Box 2.3   Evian: an exceptional case that proves the rule?

We have made the claims that brands and reputations are usually driven from the inside and that many brands are built on commodity products which are easily substituted. Evian demonstrates how powerful marketing and branding can be in creating a brand from a commodity like water; however HR and people management seem to have no part to play in this success. But is this case unique and the exception that proves the rule that 'it all stems from people'?

Evian water began life as a medicinal product in the 19th century sourced in Evian-les-Bains on the shores of Lake Geneva, overlooked by the Alps. Matt Haig (2004) points out that the success of this product, sold in 120 countries and brand leader in the increasingly popular mineral water market, is remarkable, because it costs many times more than ordinary and free tap water, which is sometimes more pure than bottled water, and tastes little or no different. So what is behind its success? Clearly not price and product quality. According to Haig, it is the purity of its branding that has driven Evian into its leading position.

Evian is marketed as a pure water, filtered many times, 'untouched by man', in an idyllic Alpine setting. It is also pure in the sense that there have been no attempts to extend the brand into other water products, such as fruit-flavours or sparkling water. In these senses, its success seems to be driven by marketing and image-making, which benefits from its chilly Alpine associations and from health and lifestyle advice that tells us to drink more water.

The value of brands

As noted in Chapter 1, the economic and social value of brands to organizations is increasing significantly. Studies by academics and consultants have shown that the contribution of brands to the top-branded companies can contribute between 20 and 70%

to the market capitalization of the parent companies, and that companies with strong brands consistently outperform those with weaker brands (Lindeman, 2003). The key message here is that brands matter a great deal in the valuation of companies and in helping those companies outperform their competitors. As a result, the valuation of brands on the balance sheet is becoming much more widely accepted in most advanced countries. National accounting standards are changing to follow the early lead of the UK, Australia, New Zealand and France in allowing brand values to appear on balance sheets, with the expectation that most countries will follow American Generally Accepted Accounting Principles (GAAP) in capitalizing 'goodwill' on company balance sheets and depreciating it according to its useful life, normally a much longer period than technology or other capital investments.

These changes in capitalization have led some companies that once owned factories and other forms of physical, but depreciating, assets to divest themselves of these tangible assets and invest more heavily in intangibles such as brands that have a much longer useful life. Thus we are witnessing the development of companies that are little more than a collection of brands; 'manufacturers without factories' reliant on outsourcing production and services to developing economies such as India and China. Nike is a good example of this approach to doing business. However, as we can see in Box 2.4, these developing countries also recognize the importance of brands to the future of their economies and their major organizations.

Box 2.4   The re-branding of Taiwan

The Economist (2005a, 2005b) reported on the critical importance of branding strategy to Taiwan, which, according to the World Economic Forum in 2005, is the world's 5th most competitive economy. In 2000, Taiwan made three-quarters of the world's notebook computers. It also makes two-thirds of LCD monitors and four-fifths of PDAs. Now, apart from some high quality products, manufacturing is moving to China, in line with global trends in developed economies to shift manufacturing offshore.

A few years ago no one would have heard of Taiwanese brands such as BenQ; now the Taiwan government sees branding of its companies as the only way to compete. Previously, many of its companies made a living, just like BenQ, by making IT products for other companies that sell them under their own brands. This process is known as original design manufacturing (ODM) or original equipment manufacturing (OEM), depending on the amount of design and development content. Taiwanese companies, however, are facing increased competition from China, which is developing ODM business too. At the same time, the number of big IT brands is consolidating, thus reducing the number of potential customers for ODM manufacturers.

Since IT manufacturing accounts for 15% of the island's output, Taiwan's government has long seen its mission to be to help guide these companies in new directions. In 2003, it created a development plan known as 'Challenge 2008', which set out a vision for Taiwanese companies being based on building world-class brands and concentrating on cutting-edge technologies. 'It called for an increase in total R&D spending from just over 2% of GDP to 3% within six years' (*Economist*, 2005b). This would bring Taiwan up to the current level of the United States and Japan. The government would do its bit by providing low interest loans and launching new transport infrastructure projects.

BenQ was among the first of Taiwan's big ODM firms to rise to this challenge of brand-building, when it was spun off from its parent, Acer, BenQ in 2001. Since then its branded business has increased from 25% to 35–40%. In 2005, it announced its intentions to buy an established brand – the mobile hand-set business of Siemens. Similarly, Acer was by 2005 the fifth-biggest producer in the world of personal computers and is one of the top sellers of notebook computers in Europe. Taiwan is also developing the flat-screen markets and those of computer games.

One of the articles concludes by reflecting on the need for China to adopt a similar strategy, noting how some Chinese companies are spending heavily on building brands. This process is already evident following the purchase by Chinese companies of famous brand names, such as IBM's computing division and Rover cars in the UK.

Corporate social responsibility (CSR)

The social value of brands is less clear but no less important. We have touched on the arguments that the global brands are a threat to governments and to ordinary people, again with Nike and Gap being a good example during the 1990s, when they were accused of exploiting workers in 'sweatshops' in Indonesia, Thailand and other parts of South-East Asia. A report from the San Francisco Global Exchange revealed that Nike workers in Indonesia were being paid 80 US cents a day, and asked the company to double this rate, the cost of which would have been around $20 million, the amount that Michael Jordan was being paid annually to endorse the brand (Haig, 2004). The consequences of this negative publicity placed pressure on Nike and similar companies to champion the cause of exploitative working conditions and human rights abuses in these countries (Hilton, 2003) by raising wages and proposing codes of practice for working overseas. It is due to cases such as this one that companies have begun to take a genuine interest in CSR to minimize the risk to their brands associated with their social and environmental performance.

CSR, discussed more extensively in Chapter 9, is sometimes seen as a cynical attempt by business to escape their responsibilities or as the latest in a long list of management fads; but it has at least two important justifications. The first is the commercial incentive to enhance brand reputations by being seen as a trustworthy business, good employer, good place to work and good neighbour in the community. As we shall see, becoming an employer of choice and securing a high rating in the various benchmarking exercises that rate companies on these issues has a major impact on their ability to attract and retain top talent. The second is the more defensive reason, which is to enforce companies that 'breach the rules' to adapt their practices to meet ever-changing societal expectations. McDonald's introduction of healthy meals to its menu is a good example of company responding to criticisms and legal challenge over its impact on rising obesity levels in the USA and UK. During 2002 it experienced its first drop in profits as consumers reacted to almost epidemic levels of obesity, associated in part with the high-fat fast foods McDonald's and other fast food chains offered (*Economist*, 2005c). These chains began to compete on price, which was a sign that their brands were beginning to lose relevance to consumers. McDonald's and other fast food companies responded by introducing new, healthier food lines, though whether this strategy will convince consumers that the companies have their interests at heart is another thing. Another example is British American Tobacco (BAT), which published its CSR policy in 2005 as a response to the public concern about its products (Arkin, 2005). Its senior managers argue that the health risks associated with smoking make it all the more imperative to act responsibly.

In addition to the CSR arguments, social value is also associated with extra investment needed by branded companies to improve products and services continuously and to keep them relevant. Again, research into this aspect of branding showed that less-branded companies launched fewer products and spent less on R&D than their more heavily branded counterparts. Indeed, economists who have looked into the effects of advertising support this line of reasoning (Kay, 2004). Modern advertising contains very little information about the nature of products and services on offer, especially commodity products and services. What they do contain is information that the company is able and willing to invest in the product/service and in developing a relationship with consumers. And because most marketing people understand this 'theory', advertisers are drawn into ever more costly (some would say wasteful) advertising campaigns.

Brand equity

As the above theory of advertising implies, understanding strong brands requires a measure of relative value. For example, when comparing the brands of British Airways with Singapore Airlines or Virgin, or Dell with Acer and IBM, on what basis can we say that one is stronger than the other? The usual measurement is brand equity, which identifies the potential of a brand to add value:

> a set of assets (and liabilities) linked to a brand's name and symbol that adds to ... the value provided by a product or service to a firm and/or that firm's customers. (Aker, 2004)

Brand equity comprises four components, set out below in Table 2.1. We shall develop these ideas in Chapter 8, which deals with employer branding in more detail.

Table 2.1

Brand equity.

	Components	What is it?	Creates value by:
Brand equity	Loyalty	An emotional link between the brand and customers that cause them to repeat purchases	Reduced costs of gaining new customers Loyalty creates brand 'ambassadors' Gives breathing space when changes are made
	Awareness	Consumers' familiarity with brand	People prefer the familiar over the unknown Enables people to compose a quick mental shortlist of potential purchases
	Perceived quality	Assessment of expected quality that a brand will deliver	People more likely to pay for what they believe to be high quality Associated organizations, e.g. retailers, more likely to 'rent' brand by stocking, networking, etc. Launch-pad for brand extensions
	Associations	The images and ideas connected with the brand – what it means to customers	Creates interest and relevance to customers Helps differentiate from competitors Sends signals to customers' significant others – says something about purchaser to others

Source: Based on Miller and Muir, 2004, p. 210

Linking brands and branding to HRM

Branding research and the importance of people

From this discussion of brands, it should now be apparent that there is a trend in the marketing literature towards recognition of effective people management in the branding process. In addition to the practitioner works we have cited, academics in the branding field have been sending out relatively similar messages for a number of years (Berthon *et al.*, 1999; Harris and de Chernatony, 2001; Ewing *et al.*, 2002; Buckley, 2005).

Are branding specialists on the ground taking this message to heart? The answer, it seems, is a qualified 'yes'. De Chernatony (2001a, 2001b) has explored the differing interpretations held by brand managers about branding, some of which have immediate relevance for HR and people management. These interpretations with some examples include:

- brands as visual logos and signifiers, which create differentiation in the minds of customers, e.g. the Nike swoosh logo, Adidas's three stripes
- brands as legally enforceable statements of ownership, e.g. among the ancient or prestige universities such as Cambridge, Oxford and Harvard
- brands as a form of shorthand for consumers, e.g. Hoover or McDonald's, which:
  - ◻ assist the information processing limitations of individuals and help them to make attributions about products and services
  - ◻ reduce the risk for customers in imperfect markets
- brands as positioning by helping associate brands with particular benefits for customers, e.g. the Virgin brand and Virgin Blue in Australia, Rolex
- brands as personality, in which brands are infused with emotional values beyond their functional benefits, e.g. Coke helping the world to come together, Calvin Klein underwear
- brands as a relationship builder, which is an extension of the idea of brands as embodying a personality into the notion of customers having a relationship with the brand, e.g. Disney, British Airways
- brands as clusters of values, which help organizations extend into new markets with related values, e.g. Virgin and its moves into the soft drinks market, Sony and its moves into entertainment

- brands as added value beyond the basic product or service offering, for which customers value and are usually willing to pay a premium price, e.g. Kellogg's, Colgate, Unilever's soap powders
- brands as visions, which are mainly used to galvanize stakeholders into actions designed to attain some future desired state, e.g. Sony's pioneer brand offering innovation, British Airways and the 'world's favourite airline' culture change programme, Audi's 'Vorsprung Durch Technik' (advance with technology) strapline, political parties such as the re-branding of 'New Labour' in the UK during the 1990s
- brands as identity that set out an ethos with which organizational stakeholders can readily associate, e.g. the Body Shop, Apple, Ben & Jerry, Hewlett-Packard, Cancer Research
- brands as image, which focuses on what customers perceive to be real, e.g. Barbie, Harry Potter, Evian and BMW
- branding companies, which reduce the needs to promote individual lines of business or products, and are increasingly seen as a way of engaging new and existing employees in the corporate brand, the key focus of this book.

You should be able to see from these diverse interpretations that the brand managers in this study viewed branding not only as playing a key external role in adapting their organizations to market circumstances, but also in aligning people behind the brand. In Figure 2.2 we have adapted de Chernatony's (2001a, 2001b) ideas to construct a representation of the internal and external views on branding.

Of the 12 roles of branding identified above, at least three are strongly internally focused and have major implications for people management and HR professionals. It should also be noted that there is a 'clear line of sight' between people management, the employee-focused definitions of branding and the externally focused definitions. So, for example, in one of the cases we researched for this book, Agilent Technologies (an off-shoot of Hewlett-Packard), senior HR managers were

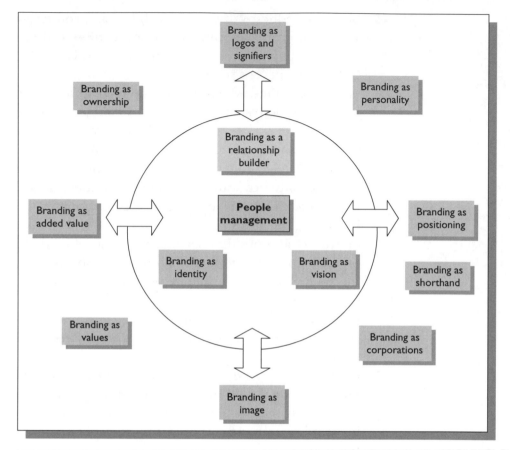

Figure 2.2
Interpretations of branding and the links with HR (based on
de Chernatony, 2001; Martin and Beaumont, 2003).

unable to make a distinction between the notion of branding
as identity and branding as a cluster of values, seeing instead a
strong interpenetration between the two concepts. Given Hewlett-
Packard's long history as an employee-oriented brand, this
should not be surprising. Similarly, one might expect the same
degree of interpenetration between brands as visions and corporate branding, as we shall argue later in this text.

This marketing and branding literature, however, is to be
treated with a little caution as we have already noted in our
point about its ideological basis. There is little doubt that it is
stronger on prescription and on how things should be than on
description of how things are. For example, to argue that brands

should be at the heart of all key decisions in an organization is inconsistent with how many successful organizations operate in practice. Moreover, as we have seen, consumers are increasingly wary of the negative connotations of brands and the 'spin' associated with brand managers, public relations and communications departments. Most branding and marketing literature is underpinned by a unitary, communications perspective which is based on an assumption that organizations are essentially conflict-free and made up of homogeneous cultures. If they are not, the argument goes, they should be made so through effective communications. From this perspective, conflict, politics and sub-cultures are seen as unnatural, malfunctions of naturally ordered systems, to be treated by having consumers, employees and other stakeholders understand the truth of where their true interests lie. As a result, this branding literature, just like the dramatized accounts of celebrity firms we discussed in the opening chapter, tends to restrict the role of HR to communicating brand values downwards, rather than as being the source of such values and the driver of key aspects of strategy. As many of us schooled in the university of life will be aware, however, communications will only get us so far; not everyone has the same interests, nor are organizations necessarily better off without a legitimate expression of conflict over competing interests, since it is usually only through conflict and speaking up to power that often-needed change results. Indeed, it is incumbent on good followers to express legitimate concerns. We will deal with this aspect of leadership and governance in Chapter 9.

Harris and de Chernatony's (2001) model, though strong in some respects, illustrates these criticisms quite well. The starting point for these authors is the need for employees to become 'brand ambassadors' in their role as the key interface between the internal and external environment of the organization and in having a potentially powerful influence on customers' perceptions of the brand offering and the corporation. Nevertheless, we should not 'throw the baby out with the bathwater'. They make a useful attempt at bringing together a number of the previously discussed different interpretations of brands to explain the concept of brand identity, defined by them as 'an organization's ethos, aims and values that create a sense of individuality which differentiates a brand' (p. 442). From Figure 2.3 we can

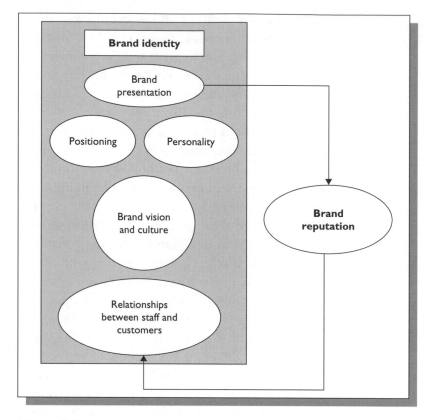

Figure 2.3
The relationships between brand identity and brand reputation (based on Harris and de Chernatony, 2001, p. 443).

see that brand identity comprises the connections between its core vision and culture, the company's positioning in the marketplace, the emotional or personality characteristics of potential customers with which it wishes to associate, its presentation styles and, finally, the consistency between employee relationships and customers.

They further argue that a brand's identity is not always the same as its reputation, which they define as 'a collective reputation of a brand's past actions and results' (p. 445) that describes its ability to deliver value to key stakeholders. These authors regard brand reputation as more important in establishing and measuring brand performance, precisely because reputation takes into account the *past* as well as the *present* and it also encompasses *all organizational stakeholders*.

Thus, it is this key development in branding, which moves us away from a focus on products to corporate level branding, that has caused organizations to think more inclusively about how front line customer service staff, designers and developers, knowledge workers and a whole range of other employees can influence brand reputation. Moreover, as these writers suggest, corporate branding requires consistency and uniformity in delivering the brand identity by all members of the brand management team and all stakeholders, including customers and employees. Let's have a look at an example from the technology sector.

Box 2.5   Building a brand at Yahoo!

Yahoo!, one of the best-known Internet companies, underwent a major re-branding exercise in 2004 to position itself for 'its bigger future'. Like Google, Amazon and eBay, Yahoo! is coming of age and is past the start-up phase but does not want to lose the energy and values of those early years.

Yahoo! is an interesting contrast to Google. Again founded by two Stanford graduates, but they are much lower key. From an HR perspective it is interesting that the author of the article that is the source of this case is Senior Vice President for HR at Yahoo!, and claims that the internal branding process was the starting point defining a mission and values statement, which began with simultaneous internal research conducted on the founders, executives and employees and external research on customers.

Since the company saw itself as a young, rather irreverent organization, it did not want to begin with a list of values that every other organization would aim for, so the question they addressed was: 'What sucks and aren't you glad you won't find these at Yahoo!?'. Following research conducted jointly with marketers and HR staff, they developed a series of workshops to explore brand characteristics, competencies, values and territories. In addition extensive market research on what customers thought about the brand helped identify core, internal competences and defining experiences for customers.

Libby Sartain argues that this simultaneous inside-out and outside-in approach helped define the target customer as a heavy user of the Internet with a YI gene, who was interested in efficiency, engagement and expansion. The Yahoo! brand, signified by the 'Life Engine' had to address the needs of that customer. However, it also had to address the needs of

employees (Yahoos), who made the Life Engine come to life, first by identifying what attracted them to work for the company, and the kinds of
development and experiences that would bring out their potential and
retain them.

Yahoo! is addressing the internal branding position and applying it to
every dimension of the employee experience to find and keep 'Yahoos
with the Y! gene', through a mixture of internal marketing techniques and
career development tools. One example is its 'My Life: My Benefits' programme that attempts to match company rewards, benefits and experiences to different stages in the career life cycle of Yahoos.

Source: Adapted from Sartain, 2005, pp. 89–93

Stage models, branding and HRM

One useful way of thinking about the links between corporate
branding and HRM is to see the relationship as a series of stages
through which organizations may pass en route to full-blown
corporateness. Figure 2.4 maps out two of the key dimensions
we have discussed in this chapter. The first is the extent to which
organizations differ in attaching importance to corporate branding in their general business strategy, drawn from a study by
Interbrand (2002) on the global financial services industry. The
second dimension is the extent to which organizations perceive
HRM to be a key variable in delivering their corporate branding
strategy, if indeed they have one.

Stage 1 corresponds to a limited role for branding in corporate strategy, in which brands are restricted to symbols for particular products, services or individual businesses, and in which
HR plays little or no role in supporting the brand. There is no
attempt to connect individual brands to employees' motivations, values or behaviours. Such a stage is likely to describe the
position of many smaller or newer companies, especially in the
non-service sectors, which fail to see how brands can embody
values that relate to employees (or customers for that matter).

Stage 2 applies to organizations that may have a master brand
as a corporate logo but place more emphasis on building a vision
and value proposition for existing or new product or service

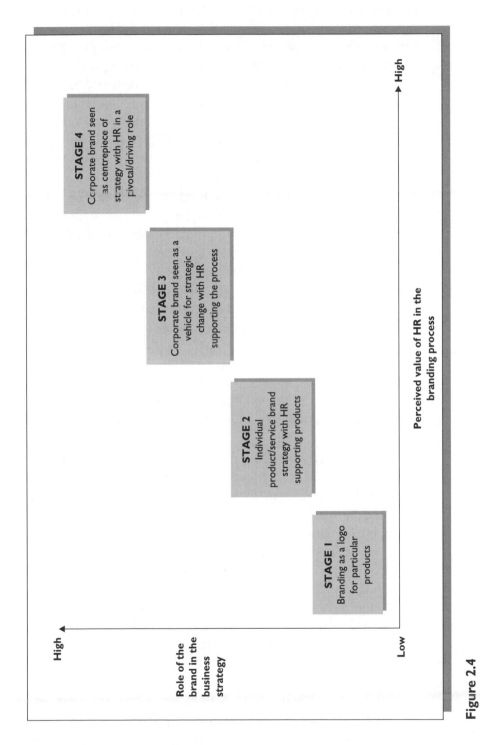

High

**Role of the
brand in the
business
strategy**

STAGE 4
Corporate brand seen
as centrepiece of
strategy with HR in a
pivotal/driving role

STAGE 3
Corporate brand seen as a
vehicle for strategic
change with HR
supporting the process

STAGE 2
Individual
product/service brand
strategy with HR
supporting products

STAGE I
Branding as a logo
for particular
products

Low

High

**Perceived value of HR in the
branding process**

Figure 2.4
Stages on the road to corporateness (based on Interbrand, 2002; Martin and Beaumont, 2003).

brands. This may be because of the strength of existing brand reputations that the company may have acquired or because they wish to launch a new line of business distinct from the values of the master brand. This stage is associated with companies being a 'house of brands' and the role of HR in this context is to provide support for the individual brands and the connection with employees' values is to identify with these individual brands. A good example here was the early approach of RBS, the Royal Bank of Scotland Group, which has grown rapidly to become one of the world's major banks by acquiring major UK brands such as Natwest and Coutts, and Citizens Bank in the USA. RBS made a conscious decision to allow these brands to function as normal rather than re-brand them with the RBS logo. Similarly, established brands in financial services and the airline industry established separate brands to deal with new ventures in internet banking and low cost air travel, such as Cahoot and Egg, the Internet arms of the ANG and the Prudential, respectively, and British Airways now-aborted attempt to launch Go!, their low cost subsidiary. Yet another example is the little known, but extremely profitable, Kentucky-based, Yum! Brands. This company owns the much better-known Kentucky Fried Chicken, Pizza Hut and Taco Bell. These three brands account for 4% of all restaurant sales in America, second only to McDonald's, which accounted for 6.5% in 2005 (*Economist*, 2005c). The potentially negative effects, however, of such strategies, which are strong on product or service differentiation but weak on integration with the corporate values and cost sharing in areas such as HR, IT and property, have led some companies to move to the third stage of development.

Stage three attempts to capitalize on the vision and values of a strong corporate brand for significant organizational change, for example, in bringing together previously disparate business operations, such as the Swiss-Swedish multinational ABB in the late 1980s and early 1990s (Belanger *et al.*, 1999), or in improving service offerings, such as HSBC, which acquired banks in the UK, France and the USA (Haig, 2004). The role of HR in providing support for this process of corporate branding lies in designing programmes for change and the role of the corporate brand is to provide a compelling employment brand proposition for staff as well as providing an identity for customers (Barrow and Mosley, 2005). Whilst the payoff for such a strategy can be significant in having employees 'live the brand' and in building strong relationships with customers, such changes are difficult to implement universally and usually require many years to become fully embedded, as we have already seen from our example of AT&T and NCR in Chapter 1.

Stage four is when the corporate brand becomes the focal point of corporate strategy, with HR playing a pivotal role in driving the corporate branding process and employees identifying closely with the corporate brand values and acting as brand ambassadors. The role of individual product or service brands and employee identification with them is secondary, with recruitment and deployment of employees frequently used to underpin the corporate branding strategy. It is at this stage that employer of choice and employer branding policies are most likely to be found, with employees being recruited, developed and rewarded for identification with the corporate brand as much as, or more than, for a specific job. The payoff to the organization, in addition to having employees identify with existing business, is believed to be that employees will be more flexible and innovative in delivering future business or service improvements, good examples being Hewlett-Packard, Ben & Jerry, BP, Orange, Virgin, Sony, Google, the Body Shop and even Heinz, which is well known for its employee orientation (Haig, 2004). In the case of some companies, heavy investments in corporate branding and HRM will help them through the difficult circumstances by engaging employees and retaining their loyalty. We shall refer to one such case, that of Agilent Technologies, at various points throughout the book.

A cautionary note needs to be added at this point. Stage theories usually connote a sense of progress, inevitability and best practice. We do not wish to imply any such linear thinking or assumptions since our belief is that context and timeframes play an important part in shaping the strategic positions of organizations. The case of the RBS, with its early decision to retain separate brands in the UK and the USA following recent merger activity, illustrates this point well. So, at best, stage theories highlight no more than promising practices and ours is no different, indeed, the question of benchmarking against best practice is arguably flawed because there is little sustainable differentiation to be gained from following the pack.

Nevertheless, it is also interesting to note that RBS, like HSBC before it, is moving slowly to becoming a 'branded house', by endorsing its major businesses with the RBS logo and investing heavily in the RBS (rather than Royal Bank of Scotland) brand at major international sporting events and other forms of promotion, perhaps with a view to establishing a more corporate feel to its image (see also Chapter 7).

Corporate reputations

As we noted in Chapter 1, the concepts of branding and corporate reputations have a common origin in their focus on the image of organizations. Furthermore, as we have already noted in this chapter, branding specialists sometimes use the term reputation to refer to key attributes of brands. Nonetheless, one of our central key contentions in this book is that the idea of a reputation is a more distinctive, root concept, less redolent of communications 'spin' than branding, is plural in its outlook and addresses a wider range of stakeholders and agendas. These include CSR, diversity and governance, which are important topics in this book. Thus, for our purposes, reputation is a broader, more inclusive and more useful focal concept than branding, and has a distinctive meaning which we will discuss later.

Like branding, corporate reputations have become the subject of a number of influential press ratings, including *Fortune Magazine, Asia Business* and *The Financial Times*, which have lent it credibility with the general public and other stakeholders. As we also indicated in Chapter 1, positive reputations can lead to significant financial advantages. However, reputations have also become notable because of their ability to help defend an organization when it encounters adverse publicity. For example, Johnson & Johnson was able to survive the catastrophic, malicious tampering with Tylenol, one of its core products, by recovering well from a small decline in its market value because of the company's past reputation for good business principles and socially responsible behaviour – its reputational capital (Haig, 2004). Other companies, when facing similar disasters, have suffered more severe and sustained declines in market value because they did not have the depth of reputational capital to sustain them through their crises (Fombrun and Van Reil, 2003). As we write, Merck, the US pharmaceutical company, is in the middle of a crisis. It had £27 billion wiped off its share value following the successful legal action taken against it for its now infamous marketing of Vioxx, the anti-inflammatory drug that was associated with heart problems (*Economist*, 2005b). Corporate reputation is also important in the wake of the corporate governance and financial irregularities of Enron, WorldCom and Andersen Consulting in the USA, Parmalat in Italy, Shell in the UK and Mannesmann and Volkswagen in Germany because it acts as a form of ethical control by creating a culture of ethical values and standards of behaviour that help guide employees in their dealings with customers, clients and governments and answer the question: Would my actions be in line with the organization's reputation? Clearly in the case of the most recent of these scandals, the answer would be negative.

Approaches to reputation management

So, what do we understand by corporate or organizational reputation(s)? Like identity, image and brands, this whole area is confused by different people using the term in slightly different ways. For example, some writers and practitioners treat reputation and image as the same thing, others suggest that they are different but closely related, while yet others treat reputations as a combination of image and identity. Following Whetten and Mackey (2002), we have already made an initial attempt to define reputation in Chapter 1 as an organization's biography, the official and unofficial assessments of the organization by significant outsiders. This is distinguished from its autobiographical image, its own account of how it wants to be regarded. In slightly more formal terms, reputation can be defined as the mirror of image: 'the feedback from others concerning the credibility of an organization's self-definition' (p. 400).

There are some important implications of this definition. First, outsiders only have partial information on which to base their assessments and, thus, what they come to expect of an organization. Second, they are likely to make assessments on the basis of what they value and expect to find in the projected image. As we shall see, however, there is some disagreement over whether an organization enjoys a reputation singular or reputations plural. Let's look at four slightly different interpretations, each of which has a contribution to make to the reputation management field.

Strategic stars

In Chapter 1 we noted the work of two leading writers, Mary Jo Hatch and Majken Schultz (2002), who have significantly influenced practitioners. They see reputations resulting from the interaction between the objective and subjective evaluations of existing and potential stakeholders. These evaluations comprise three interrelated dimensions:

- **informal** interactions among stakeholders, for example through sales meetings, employee storytelling or accounts from satisfied or dissatisfied customers; these incidents strongly influence an organization's reputation or external image but are largely uncontrollable
- **the business press**, such as the rankings of the best places to work and industry press ratings of organizations
- **potential stakeholders**, such as possible recruits, shareholders and other funders, government organizations and the community at large.

Hatch and Schultz (2001) have developed from earlier, more academic, work a practitioner-orientated tripartite framework based on corporate image, corporate vision and organizational culture. By image they mean the outside world's or stakeholder impression of the company, including customers, shareholders, the media and general public. Vision refers to what senior managers aspire to for the company and culture refers to the organization's key values, behaviours and attitudes (p. 130). Hatch and Schultz have argued that, to build an effective corporate reputation, organizations must ensure that these three elements of an organization, the *three strategic stars*, need to be aligned. According to these authors, misalignments occur when there are significant gaps in the following areas:

- The **vision–culture** gap results from senior managers moving the company in a direction that employees either do not understand or do not support. Sometimes this is a consequence of the pace of change, in which the vision is too stretching, whereas at other times it results from visions that sit uneasily with ethical or traditional values, such as the attempted re-branding of the UK Post Office to Consignia or British Airway's attempt to re-brand itself as 'the *world's* favourite airline' by dropping the union jack from its tailfins and adopting diverse motifs from different countries to reflect its new global image. Both of these attempts failed badly because they did not fit the established culture and traditions of the organization, nor did they command the respect of existing employees (Miller and Muir, 2004). Another illustration of this gap one of us researched with a close Chinese colleague is drawn from joint ventures between European and Chinese companies. These Sino-foreign joint ventures all had problems merging the Chinese ways of doing HR, embedded in the 'Iron Rice-Bowl' culture and previously limited discretion over hiring, firing and setting wages, with inwardly investing companies' more market-oriented visions and practices (Zhang and Martin, 2003).

- The **image–culture** gap usually results from organizations not putting into practice their brand values and leads to confusion among customers about the company's outside image. This gap is usually most apparent when employees' views of the company are quite different from those held by customers. One example cited in a *Harvard Business Review* article by Peter Cappelli was of United Parcel Services (UPS). It discovered a major problem in retaining truck drivers with an in-depth knowledge of local routes. UPS had assigned these drivers tedious and difficult work of loading vans at the beginning of their routes, which conflicted with the image that drivers had of themselves as guardians of a proud heritage of delivery. Re-assigning this boring work to warehouse staff reduced driver turnover and increased the alignment between cultural values and the image of the company.

- The **image–vision** gap occurs when there is a mismatch between the external image of the organization and senior management's aspirations for it. Again the British Airways example to globalize its image by removing the Union Jack from its tailfins provides a dramatic illustration of how customers, in this case embodied by the criticisms of Margaret Thatcher and other key customers, can cause a company to re-think its reputation. This image–vision gap can also occur at national level. For example, Australia has taken a long time to shake off its image to the rest of the world as the 'land of the long weekend', good for holidays but not good for the kinds of investment needed for it to compete on a global scale in the new, knowledge-based economy. The fact that it has done so, and was by 2005 one of the world's most competitive economies speaks volumes for the vision of recent Australian governments and those of its major companies (World Economic Forum, 2005).

Hatch and Schultz have developed a framework (or 'toolkit') that comprises a set of three areas for diagnosis to assess the extent of misalignment between these three strategic stars:

1 Who are the stakeholders – what do they want – is the company communicating with them effectively?
2 Does the company live the values it promotes – is the vision a compelling one for all sub-cultures?
3 What images do stakeholders associate with the company – in what ways do employees and stakeholders interact – what is the potential for problems in these interactions?

These questions do not break new ground in assessing culture, but they do point to the complex relationships between the external and internal aspects of managing effective corporate branding, placing equal weight on these dimensions.

Corporate character

Another influential approach to reputation management has been developed by Gary Davies and his colleagues in the UK (Davies *et al.*, 2003), who see organizational reputations as the alignment of identity and external image. They have developed a unified and objective way of measuring the gaps between external image and internal identity. Their argument is that reputation is 'the collective term referring to all stakeholders' views of corporate reputation' (p. 62), including internal (organizational) identity and external image, which they define as the views of the company held by external stakeholders, especially customers. Their framework is set out in Figure 2.5, and highlights the potential for gaps between desired image, actual image and internal identity.

It is the way in which these gaps are measured, however, that is of most interest because they use a single concept and set of measures to gauge differences, which is very unusual in this type of research. To gain a 'clear line of sight' between internal and external perceptions of the organizations they make use of the

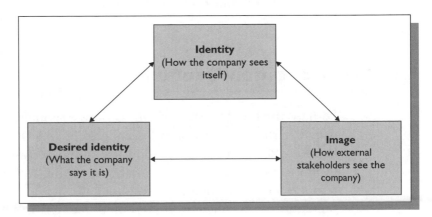

Figure 2.5
Gaps in reputation (based on Davies *et al.*, 2003, p. 62).

notion of stakeholder perceptions of the **organization's personality**, a construct borrowed from the psychology literature to describe generic organizational personality types. Organizational personality is defined by eight dimensions: *agreeableness, trustworthiness, enterprise, chicness, competence, masculinity, ruthlessness* and *informality*. Questions have been derived to assess these personality dimensions, and internal and external stakeholders are provided with the same questions. By doing so, the extent of the gaps can be measured and used to realign the three components of reputation. This work has been extensively used in research and consulting, and is useful in helping us understand the various views of the organization held by different stakeholders using the same set of measures.

More recently, Davies and his colleagues have dropped the term 'personality', and replaced it with 'character', a wise decision given the problems of conflating organizational attributes with those of individuals. The idea of an organization having a character is more widely accepted perhaps because it is more vague, is a synonym for reputation and, unlike personality, has a lineage in organizational studies. For example, Rob Goffee and Gareth Jones (2003) have developed a sophisticated analysis of corporate cultures based on the notion of character. We shall discuss these ideas in a little more detail in the next chapter on Image and Identity, which Davies and his colleagues, along with most writers in the reputation management field, see as a key element in linking the internal and external dimensions of organizations.

The Reputation Quotient

Perhaps the best-known work on corporate reputation, however, is by Charles Fombrun and his colleagues (e.g. Fombrun and Van Riel, 2003) at the Reputation Institute (see www.reputation-institute.com), based in New York but involving academics, practitioners and consultants throughout the world. They define reputation as 'a collective representation of a firm's past actions and results which describe its ability to deliver valued outcomes to multiple stakeholders. It gauges a firm's relative standing with employees and externally with stakeholders, in both its competitive and institutional environments' (Fombrun, 1996). This collective representation creates favourable accumulated impressions which, as Fombrun and Rindova (2000) propose, 'crystallize into the intangible asset of a corporate reputation'. Their definition of corporate reputation has five characteristics:

- Corporate reputation is rooted in the past, as well as the present.
- It is of equal concern to internal and external stakeholders.
- It is based on past actions and achievements.
- It is best assessed by examining the benefits accruing to individual stakeholder groups.
- It can be used to position the organization against competitors and benchmark against the best ones; it can also be used to relate the organization to its external environment.

To measure corporate reputation, they have developed a widely used 'global' index called the **reputation quotient**. This aggregate measure scores organizations on emotional appeal, products and services, workplace environment, social responsibility, financial performance, and vision and leadership through extensive questioning of stakeholders' views. These views can be drawn from stakeholders of companies in an industry and across industries and countries. It is interesting to note that even among countries as close in culture and institutional background as Norway, Denmark and Sweden, the relative weighting of these factors varies significantly (Aperia *et al.*, 2004). It is also noteworthy that the most important factor in the minds of the general public concerning CSR is the perceived treatment of employees. This factor, when combined with perceptions of the workplace environment, tends to rank highly in influencing evaluations of corporate reputations (see Chapter 9).

Fombrun and Van Riel (2003) have tackled the people management contribution to corporate reputation building by developing an **employee-expressiveness quotient** (EQ). This, in turn, is linked to strong identification with companies and to supportive employee behaviours (see Figure 2.6). They contend that companies have to express themselves effectively to

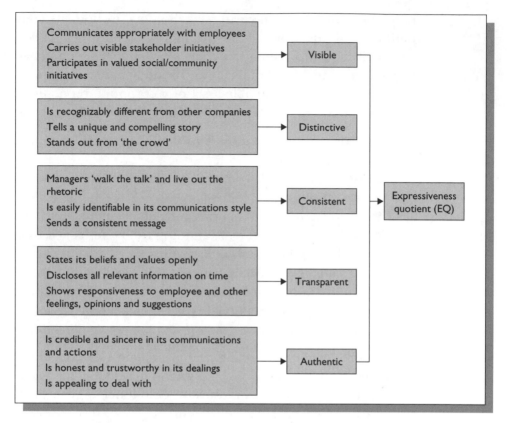

Figure 2.6
The expressiveness quotient (adapted from Fombrun and Van Riel, 2003, p. 96).

employees to build emotional appeal, which comprises good feelings about the company, admiration, respect and trust in the company. Expression, in this context, refers to the corporate communications process in which companies are willing to 'put themselves out there, to convey who they are and what they stand for' (Fombrun and Van Riel, 2003, p. 95). Figure 2.7 shows the drivers of expression for employees and their relationship to the EQ. Their central proposition is the greater the EQ, the greater the emotional appeal of the company to its workforce.

The EQ is close in tone and language to the notion of employer branding, which we shall discuss in Chapter 8. Both ideas share an interest in telling credible, unique and compelling stories to employees concerning why they should identify with the

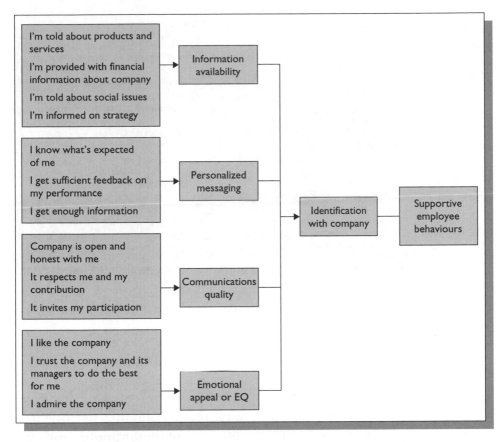

Figure 2.7
Measuring identification with the company and the links with employee
behaviours (based on Fombrun and Van Riel, 2003, p. 100).

company. Fombrun and Van Riel also propose a two-way relationship between identification with the company and expressiveness: the greater the level of identification, the greater the
expressiveness and resulting reputation. High levels of identification are likely to lead to employees engaging in supportive
behaviours, such as managers 'walking the talk', senior executives
constantly communicating results and front-line, customer-
facing staff communicating honestly with customers, behaviour
which, in turn, will enhance the corporate reputation over time.
Conversely, they argue, the higher the reputation of the company, the more likely employees will identify with the company
and its mission, act as its 'ambassadors' to potential recruits, to
other less-committed employees and, of course, to customers.

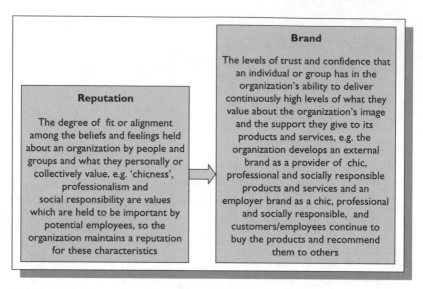

Figure 2.8
The relationship between reputations and brands (based on Dowling, 2001).

We will discuss this link between identification in Chapters 3 and 4, when we look more closely at engagement.

Their cause-and-effect model is set out more formally in Figure 2.8, which shows how reputation building, personalized communications, the quality of communications and the EQ (or emotional appeal) are linked through increased levels of organizational identification with behaviours that are supportive of corporate reputation. The model also highlights the questions used to assess the levels of organizational identification.

Plural reputations are lead indicators of brands

Though Fombrun and his colleagues have certainly advanced our understanding of corporate reputation, there are two criticisms we can make. The first is that it is not quite clear enough in setting out the relationship between reputation and branding, which are sometimes treated synonymously. Grahame Dowling's (2001) work is particularly helpful in this regard by making clear links between reputations and what he calls 'super-brands'. In line with our earlier discussion on the importance of corporate brands, he sees the valued outcomes of reputations as follows:

- **building trust** among customers, employees and other stakeholders that the organization will act in their best interests or that of the community
- **building confidence** among customers, employees and other stakeholder that the organization will continue to value their contributions and their trust
- **lending support** to the organization by continuing to use its products and services and to recommend others to use them.

It is from high levels of such confidence, trust and support for organizational reputations (for valued characteristics such as superior performance, fairness, honesty, social responsibility and professionalism) that super-brands result.

The second criticism is of the unitary approach of Fombrun and his colleagues, which culminates in the global measure of reputation. Again, Dowling's work is helpful in this regard in pointing out the plural nature of reputations. His argument, like some of the writers on organizational culture and identity, is that we cannot sensibly talk about a corporate reputation in a unitary sense because reputations will be judged differently according to who is doing the judging, when and why they are judging, and the criteria they use to judge. Reputations, he argues, arise from the degree of fit or alignment between two key elements:

- the beliefs and feelings of different groups of stakeholders about an organization (which he defines as image but we see as part of reputations)
- their individual or collective values (personal values) (see Figure 2.1).

Since, as he contends, brands flow from the levels of trust, confidence and support that stakeholders have in the ability of the organization to deliver what they value about the organization's image/reputation, by definition perceptions of brands will also be different, e.g. among different customer segments, different groups of employees, potential employees, etc.

Dowling is not alone in emphasizing the plural nature of reputations. For example, Hatch and Schultz (2001) point to the interaction between the objective and subjective evaluations of four distinct groups as the source of reputational pluralism. These groups are:

- **Functional groups** – for example, through informal interactions at sales meetings, employee storytelling or accounts from satisfied or dissatisfied service providers. These incidents strongly influence an organization's reputation but are largely uncontrollable.
- **Different customer segments** – for example, young, old, educated, urban, suburban, class, etc.
- **The business press and special interest groups** – such as the rankings of the best places to work and industry press ratings of organizations, as outlined above.
- **Normative and potential stakeholders** – such as possible recruits, shareholders and other funders, trade associations, government regulatory agencies, professional organizations and the community at large.

So it follows that no organization in reality has a single reputation since different stakeholders are likely to value different images of an organization. Indeed, what you see is likely to depend on where you stand; if you place high value on professionalism, you are likely to look for that element in an organization's projected image, say from a business school that is research-led with well-known teachers. On the other hand, if you place a high value on friendliness or leading-edge enterprise, you would probably look for a different kind of school. As a result, the 'designers' of corporate reputations need to be clear about who they are aiming to influence and the best methods of influencing different groups of stakeholder.

However, at a practical level, the debate between the singular and global view of reputations and brands may be a false one, since Fombrun has always acknowledged the problems of an aggregated notion of corporate reputation. He points, instead, to its practical value in helping organizations identify their relative standing, understand the factors that have contributed to it and highlight the kinds of actions that might be needed to improve it. In effect, he has gone for simplicity and practicality in moving the conversation along on reputations rather than overcomplicating the story before readers begin to understand it. At the time of writing Fombrun and Van Riel are working on a development of the RQ to address the problems of using aggregate measures with different stakeholders and to address one of the key problems of understanding, what they acknowledge to be a key driver of reputations – human resource management and employee communications (Fombrun, 2005).

Conclusions

In this chapter we have examined, in more depth, the notions of branding and reputations, showing how these are distinctive but related ideas. Whilst branding is the better-known concept, especially among practitioners in the for-profit sector, our argument is that we have to work with both notions. In our model, we have described reputations, which are best thought of as plural, as lead indicators of corporate brands. Brands flow from good or poor reputations held by different groups of people about the organization's image. These evaluations are quite specific to the particular values of different groups, so are more usually associated with a wider range of stakeholder and agendas, including good governance, CSR, diversity and human resource management. Reputation is also a more intuitive idea, takes longer to build and is a more acceptable term to organizations in the not-for-profit sector. Moreover, there is an increasing volume of material on reputation management, which is very well researched and is shown to have strong links to performance. At the heart of the reputation management approach is the link between external image and internal identity, to which we now turn in Chapter 3.

References

Aker, D. A. (2004) *Brand portfolio strategy: creating relevance, differentiation, energy, leverage and clarity.* New York: Free Press.

Apéria, T., Brønn, P. S. and Schultz, M. (2004) A reputation analysis of the most visible companies in the Scandinavian countries, *Corporate Reputation Review,* **7**, 218–230.

Argyres, N. and McGahan, A. M. (2002) An interview with Michael Porter, *Academy of Management Executive,* **16** (2), 43–45.

Arkin, A. (2005) Is it possible for a tobacco company to act responsibly?, *People Management*, 1 September, pp. 28–31.

Barney, J. (1991) Firm resources and sustained competitive advantage, *Journal of Management*, **17** (1), 99–120.

Barney, J. (2002) Strategic management: from informed conversation to academic discipline, *Academy of Management Executive*, **16** (2), 53–58.

Barrow, S. and Mosley, R. (2005) *The Employer Brand®: bringing the best of brand management to people at work*. London: Wiley.

Belanger, J., Berggren, C., Bjorkman, T. and Kohler, C. (eds) (1999) *Being local worldwide: ABB and the challenge of global management*. Ithaca, NY: Cornell University Press.

Berthon, P., Hulbert, J. M. and Pitt, L. F. (1999) Brand management prognostications, *Sloan Management Review*, **40** (Winter), pp. 53–65.

Boxall, P. and Purcell, J. (2003) *Strategy and human resource management*. Basingstoke: Palgrave Macmillan.

Brymer, C. (2003) What makes brands great?, in R. Clifton and J. Simmons (eds), *Brands and Branding*. Princeton, NJ: Bloomberg Press, pp. 65–76.

Buckley, E. (2005) Internal branding, in A. M. Tybout and T. Calkins (eds), *Kellogg on branding: the marketing faculty of the Kellogg School of Management*. Hoboken, NJ: John Wiley, pp. 320–327.

Davies, G. with Chun, R., Da Silva, R. V. and Roper, S. (2003) *Corporate reputation and competitiveness*. London: Routledge.

de Chernatony, L. (2001a) *From brand vision to brand evaluation*. Oxford: Butterworth–Heinemann.

de Chernatony, L. (2001b) The diverse interpretations of brands, *The Marketing Review*, **1**, 283–301.

Dowling, G. R. (2001) *Creating corporate reputations: identity, image and performance*. New York: Oxford University Press.

Du Gay, P. (1996) *Consumption and identity at work*. London: Sage.

Economist (2005a) Moving on: manufacturing is out; knowledge-based industries are in, *Economist*, 13 January.

Economist (2005b) Face value: the man with two daggers, *Economist*, 27 August, p. 60.

Economist (2005c) Fast food's yummy secrets, Special Report, Yum! Brands, *Economist*, 27 August, pp. 61–62.

Ewing, M. T., Pitt, L. F., de Bussy, N. M. and Berthon, P. (2002) Employment branding in the knowledge economy, *International Journal of Advertising*, **21** (1), 3–23.

Fombrun, C. J. (1996) *Corporate reputation: realizing value from the corporate image*. Boston, MA: Harvard Business School Press.

Fombrun, C. J. (2005) Keynote address to the annual conference of the Reputation Institute, Madrid, 23 June.

Fombrun, C. J. and Rindova, V. P. (2000) The road to transparency: reputation management at Royal Dutch/Shell, in Majken Schulz, Mary Jo Hatch and Mogens Holten Larsen (eds), *The expressive organization: linking identity, reputation, and the corporate brand*. Oxford: Oxford University Press.

Fombrun, C. J. and Van Riel, C. B. M. (2003) *Fame and fortune: how successful companies build winning reputations*. Upper Saddle River, NJ: Financial Times/Prentice Hall.

Gelade, G. and Young, S. (2005) Test of a service profit chain model in the retail banking sector, *Journal of Occupational and Organizational Psychology*, **78**, 1–22.

Goffee, R. E. and Jones, G. (2003) *Character of a corporation*. London: Profile Books.

Grant, R. (1991) The resource-based view of competitive advantage: implications for strategy formulation, *California Management Review*, **33** (2), 114–135.

Haig, M. (2004) *Brand Royalty: how the world's top 100 brands thrive and survive*. London: Kogan-Page.

Hamel, G. (1998) *Leading the revolution*. Boston, MA: Harvard University School Press.

Hamel, G. and Prahalad, C. K. (1994) *Competing for the future*. Boston, MA: Harvard Business School Press.

Harris, F. and de Chernatony, L. (2001) Corporate branding and corporate brand performance, *European Marketing Journal*, **35** (3/4), 441–456.

Hatch, M. J. and Schultz, M. (2001) Are the strategic starts aligned for your corporate brand?, *Harvard Business Review*, Jan–Feb, pp. 129–134.

Hemmington, N. and Watson, S. (2003) Managing customer expectations – the marketing communications *vs* service delivery conundrum, *International Journal of Customer Relationship Management*, **5** (3), 271–283.

Heskett, J. L., Earl, W. and Schlesinger, L. (1997) *The service profit chain*. New York: Free Press.

Hilton, S. (2003) The social value of brands, in R. Clifton and J. Simmons (eds), *Brands and branding*. Princeton, NJ: Bloomberg Press, pp. 47–64.

Interbrand (2002) Bank on the brand, *Business Papers*, No. 1.

Kaplan, R. and Norton, D. (1996) *The balanced scorecard: translating strategy into action*. Boston, MA: Harvard Business School Press.

Kaplan, R. and Norton, D. (2001) *The strategy-focused organization.* Boston, MA: Harvard Business School Press.

Kay, J. (2004) *The truth about markets: why some nations are rich but most remain poor.* London: Penguin Books.

Kirn, S. P., Rucci, A. J., Huselid, M. and Becker, B. (1999) Strategic human resource management at Sears, *Human Resource Management,* **38** (4), 329–335.

Lado, A. A., Boyd, N. C., Wright, P. and Kroll, M. (2006) Paradox and theorizing within the resource-based view, *Academy of Management Review,* **31**, 115–131.

Lindeman, J. (2003) The financial value of brands, in R. Clifton and J. Simmons (eds), *Brands and branding.* Princeton, NJ: Bloomberg Press, pp. 27–47.

McEwen, B. and Buckingham, G. (2001) Make a marque, *People Management,* 17 May, pp. 40–44.

Martin, G. and Beaumont, P. B. (2003) *Branding and people management: what's in a name?* Wimbledon: Chartered Institute of Personnel and Development.

Martin, G., Beaumont, P. B., Doig, R. M. and Pate, J. M. (2005) Branding: a new discourse for HR?, *European Management Journal,* **23** (1), 76–88.

Miller, J. and Muir, D. (2004) *The business of brands.* Chichester: Wiley.

Pfeffer, J. (1998) *The human equation: building profits by putting people first.* Boston, MA: Harvard Business School Press.

Pfeffer, J. (2005) Creating a performance culture. Presentation at University of Strathclyde, 23 September.

Porter, M. E. (1985) *Competitive advantage: creating and sustaining superior performance.* New York: Free Press.

Porter, M. P. (1996) What is strategy?, *Harvard Business Review,* Nov–Dec, pp. 61–71.

Sartain, L. (2005) Branding from the inside out at Yahoo!: HR's role as a brand builder, *Human Resource Management,* **44** (1), 89–93.

Sherry Jr, J. F. (2005) Brand meaning, in A. M. Tybout and T. Calkins (eds), *Kellogg on branding: the marketing faculty of the Kellogg School of Management.* Hoboken, NJ: John Wiley, pp. 40–72.

Whetten, D. and Mackey, A. (2002) A social actor conception of organizational identity and its implications for the study of organizational reputations, *Business and Society,* **41**, 393–414.

World Economic Forum (2005) *The global competitiveness report, 2005–2006.* London: Palgrave Macmillan.

Zhang, H. and Martin, G. (2003) *Human resource management practices in Sino-foreign joint ventures.* Nanhchang: Jiangxi Science and Technology Press.

CHAPTER 3

Organizational identity, action and image: the linchpin

We now turn to an examination of the core relationship between what Ed Schein (1985) described as the external adaptation/ internal integration problem. This relationship is at the heart of our model linking HR, reputations and corporate branding; it also presents organizations seeking to create new identities and images with enormous challenges. Consider an advertisement placed by GE, one of the world's largest companies, in *The Economist* during September 2005. In this advertisement, they portrayed an image of the company as an ecologically friendly and innovative organization, summed up in the strapline, 'eco-magination at work', and pointed out how they could produce quieter and more energy-efficient aircraft engines, energy-efficient wind turbines, advanced water desalination, advanced plastics for cars, which reduce the needs for paint, and energy-efficient light bulbs (see Chapter 9 for a further discussion of this case).

Recapping on our basic storyline in Chapter 1, there are four key processes at work that have to be addressed in meeting such challenges, which the GE example illustrates well (see Figure 3.1). First, organizational image is what senior people in the company want different groups of stakeholders to believe and feel about it in terms of its most enduring and distinctive features, e.g. a traditional engineering conglomerate wishes to project a socially responsible and technically professional image. Second, whether GE can secure a reputation for ecomagination will depend on what different people and groups expect from, perceive and value about its image, e.g. do they expect to see this image, do they value these characteristics of professionalism and eco-friendliness, and do they see GE acting out their image? Third, this image and reputation, in turn, will depend on GE's organizational identity ('Who are we?') and its collective actions, including its governance and senior leadership behaviours, e.g. leaders collectively identify with the agenda, understand their relevance to the business context and act with high regard for professionalism and eco-friendliness in their decisions and dealings with stakeholders. Fourth, the quality of individual employment relationships and employee behaviour in GE will shape the projected image, the organizational identity and organizational actions. In turn, these factors feed back into the quality of individual employment relationships through a process of identification.

In this chapter, we will explore these ideas in more depth, focusing on the organizational identity, actions and image relationship, though we cannot discuss these in isolation from how they shape individual employment relationships, an issue covered in depth in Chapter 4.

The core relationship

As we have become all too aware in writing this book, there is a great deal of confusion among practitioners and academics over terms such as identity, image, reputation and culture. So, it is extremely important for readers that we attempt to clear up the confusion and make our position clear on these issues for sound practical reasons. If you cannot define your concepts and show how they are related, you are unlikely to be able to measure them, explain how one may cause the other (account for them) or justify them (why they matter). As a result, you will never be able to manage them in the proper sense of that term.

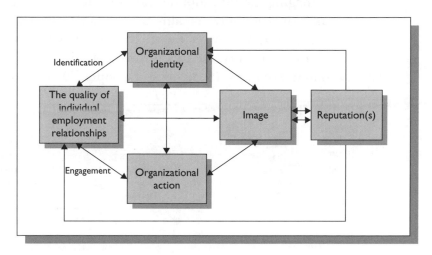

Figure 3.1
Linking reputation, image, actions and Identity.

Dave Whetten and Alison Mackey (2002) illustrate this problem well when discussing the field of reputation management (see Figure 3.2). They point out that most models of reputation management that build on the notion of identity fail to make a distinction between identity as a *cause* and identification as an *effect*. As we shall see, identity has come to be seen as a property of the organization as a whole, and not just the sum of its parts (e.g. individual attributes, opinions and personalities). Thus organizations have to create and manage these identities (cause) to influence their reputation(s) (effect). However, the management of reputations is also justified because it helps create greater identification among individuals (the justification), e.g. customers with the brand, employees who internalize the values of the product or service and investors with the mission of the organization. The most important practical point here is that measuring and managing organizational identity is not the same as measuring and managing individual identification and the quality of individual employment relationships; though these may be closely related ideas, again as we shall see later in this chapter. As HRM specialists or boards of directors, we probably have a greater chance of managing at the organizational identity level because we have more control over its key elements and drivers (e.g. its distinctiveness from other organizations) than managing identification at the individual level. This is because individual identity remains the property of individuals and is driven by how they see themselves, not how they see the organization. Individual identity is thus more diffuse and difficult for others to control (Sparrow and Cooper, 2003).

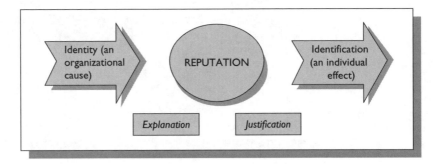

Figure 3.2
Identity as a cause and identification as a justification (based on Whetten and Mackey, 2002, p. 407).

Two examples serve to illustrate why this might be the case. The first arises from some research we have conducted on the impact of information and communications technologies (ICT) and HR. Many organizations use web-based HR portals to create a corporate feel (organizational identity) in their organizations. Not only are such portals seen to lead to a more corporate identity, but, once in place, are used to justify further investment in e-HR to promote employee self-service for HR services and have line managers take on more responsibility for people management. However, there is evidence that some employees and line managers perceive this process as little more than cost-cutting; even worse, it causes them to re-evaluate their traditional relationship with HR as a de-personalized one, in turning reducing their individual identification with the organization. So although the understanding of who we are may be advanced, the levels of identification may decline because the interests and perceptions of some individuals are not seen to coincide with the organizational aims of self-service.

The second example is from research conducted by our close colleagues Judy Pate and Phil Beaumont into a public sector organization responsible for environmental protection. In this organization there are many professional scientists with high levels of qualifications and external interests/affiliations. Some of these professionals agree with the overall values of the organization and understand 'who we are'; however, some individuals identify more closely with their professional careers and in their answer to the question 'Who am I?' is more wrapped up with their personal identity as a scientist. Many years ago, the sociologist Alvin Gouldner (1954), described this conflict in terms of the relative strength of different kinds of loyalty to firms – the 'cosmopolitan' expert, whose power and interests are linked to their technical expertise and the 'local', true bureaucrats, whose power and interests are linked more closely with the traditional administrative bureaucracy and agenda of organizations. The critical point of this analysis is that, in modern organizations, experts are always subordinate to the bureaucracy and bureaucrats, and are likely to experience tensions in being subordinated. As a result, they perceive their interests are often best served by enhancing their technical expertise, sometimes at the expense of the corporate agenda; in turn, this self-centred or self-interested behaviour is often reinforced by the approach of organizations in tearing up the old, relational, employment deal and replacing it with a new, more transactional deal (see Chapter 4 on psychological contracts).

This work by Gouldner foreshadowed the current concern with knowledge workers and their attachments to organizations; it is also relevant to the often-experienced role conflict arising from the competing pressures of HR to become strategic partners by their organizations and their, some would say, natural inclinations to act as employees' champions. Arguably, the HR business partner model, so favoured by many companies, is a compromise between these two claims for identification, a concept we examine in the final chapter of this book.

Let's look at a case we researched for this book to illustrate some of the practical problems involved in the image-identity relationship and the problems of managing across the individual–organizational levels.

Box 3.1   Image and identity problems at Scottish Enterprise (adapted from Martin et *al.*, 2005)

Scottish Enterprise (SE) is the major national economic development agency for Scotland, the senior managers of which report directly to the Scottish Executive (the civil service) and, through them, the Scottish Parliament on issues such as economic growth, industry development. In 2004, SE employed 2500 people with a budget of £500 million per annum. According to its website (http://www.scottish-enterprise.com/sedotcom_ home/about_se.htm?siblingtoggle = 1; 28 February 2006), its key priorities are to provide a range of high quality services to:

■ help new businesses get under way
■ support and develop existing businesses
■ help people gain the knowledge and skills they will need for tomorrow's jobs
■ help Scottish businesses develop a strong presence in the global economy – building on Scotland's reputation as a great place to live, work and do business.

SE developed from 14 relatively autonomous local enterprise councils (LECs) that had served the regions of Scotland during the 1980s and early 1990s. Whilst having a common charter, each of these LECs had its own ways of doing business, its own cultures and internal identities and own external images. As such, there was a great deal of confusion in the business community and among the general public about the role of the LECs. For example, it was possible for individual businesses to seek assistance from two LECs and be made quite different offers of service and grants. In addition, the majority, though not all, of the LECs interpreted their role effectively to exclude service to the large organizations in their respective communities, instead preferring to see themselves as the champions of the small and medium-sized enterprise (SME) sector. As a direct result, the LECs suffered in terms of corporate reputation among the key 150 companies in Scotland, a condition which was reflected and reinforced by damaging attacks by certain sectors of the business press that saw no useful role for public sector organizations in essentially private business.

To make matters even more complicated the Scottish Executive decided to have SE incorporate 'Careers Scotland', a previously autonomous branch of the Scottish Executive employing 1100 staff. The careers service and many of the people who worked for it embraced an agenda of social inclusion by championing the less successful people in society. This social inclusion agenda and culture of the careers service have not always sat easily with the more market-oriented, business-driven image that SE sought to create.

In 2000, a new Chief Executive, Robert Crawford, put into place a major exercise of corporate change to address these damaging image problems and the incorporation of Careers Scotland. This new, larger version of SE was intended to provide a single shared service for economic development for Scotland,[1] and for vocational training, career development and international business development. As part of this change programme, SE sought to reorganize internally to bring the LECs under more close control but, at the same time, allow them substantial autonomy in carrying out their regional economic development and training roles. Such reorganization was also to be accompanied by a decision to make substantial reductions in staff numbers and to introduce efficiency savings in the operating budget of £50 million. The senior directors of SE took the initial line that this strategy would need to be accompanied by a strong corporate brand image and to have the LECs support that corporate image in every aspect of their operations. To test their thinking, they set up a 'Values and Brand' team comprising two marketing staff, two HR staff and five operational staff, each with different backgrounds. Diversity of backgrounds of team members was seen to be essential in configuring the team to reflect the make-up of the SE network. The task they were given was to research the need for a corporate brand image and to develop a brand strategy, for the period 2002–05, if they sensed that external image and internal identity were a problem. They were also asked to work and liaise with an HR-led group which was researching into the need for culture change in the organization.

Early research commissioned by the team in 2000 showed the extent of the problem faced by Scottish Enterprise in presenting a coherent image. A total of 272 logos and 160 websites were being used throughout the network of LECs. This lack of corporate coherence was reflected in more subjective assessments of the multiplicity of sub-cultures, different identities of professional groupings and employment practices used throughout the network. The people-management dimension of the problem was made especially difficult given the simultaneous decision by SE to reduce staff numbers from 2000 to 1500 to make efficiency savings of £50 million.

[1] Except the Scottish Highlands and Islands, which was thought to be unique enough to require its own economic development agency.

Following the research phase, which had confirmed the initial expectation that a unified corporate image and values framework would need to be created for the transformed SE, the team began to realize that they did not have the expertise to develop the strategy on their own. Consequently, they sought advice from a leading academic in the field and from a leading consulting organization to help them develop the brand strategy. By January 2002, the team, in conjunction with the consultants, had developed a coherent brand strategy and implementation plan, comprising the following elements:

- brand concept and values
- brand personality tone and style
- brand strategy objectives and targets, 2002–05
- brand architecture and guidelines for the promotion of products and services (including a comprehensive Visual Identities Audit, the development of an online Intranet Brand Guidance Tool and the creation of SE's first comprehensive Visual Style Guide)
- brand monitoring and evaluation framework
- 'Living the Values' staff programme
- internal communications plan
- external communication priorities guidance.

Since January 2002, there has been a major effort to implement this strategy, with cascaded workshops designed to communicate the brand values as part of the 'Living the Values' staff programme and major exercises in consultation with external stakeholders and employees throughout the network on the external and internal brand image and identity. One of the key features of the SE programme has been the systematic implementation of the brand monitoring and evaluation framework, culminating in an annual brand strength report. This report tracks progress against objectives through quantitative and qualitative research on the external and internal aspects of the SE brand. The report has been used as a starting point for an annual 'conversation' with the SE board and throughout the network more generally on how to develop the external corporate image and internal organizational identity. In 2003, the following results, which give some indication of the progress that has been made within SE, were reported:

- Internal measures from the annual staff survey showed that the composite 'score' on questions relating to employee understanding of the SE vision, purpose and objectives had increased substantially by 16%. Currently, 84% express agreement or strong agreement with statements referring to understanding of the vision.

■ Business customer satisfaction ratings were increased by 3–83%.

■ The 272 logos previously in use had been reduced to nine throughout the network.

■ The 160 websites were reduced to three channel sites, all supported through one SE server.

■ An annual marketing budget saving of £6.42 million (32%) was made in 2002/03 and the marketing department was on target to save £5.1 million in 2003/04.

From an HR perspective, the annual staff surveys from 2002 and 2003 provided additional data that showed the extent to which the corporate internal identity had been developed.

Percentage of staff agreeing or strongly agreeing with statements related to the new values framework between 2002–2003.

Statement	2002	2003
I am aware of the SE values	70	90
I fully understand what the SE values mean to my work	61	74
I am fully committed to the SE values	61	71
I 'live' the values when performing my work	42	59

This case shows the problems experienced by one public sector organization, created by the merger of semi-autonomous regional units and the forced incorporation of another organization that did not fit easily with SE's original mission. Drawing on the ideas of Schein discussed earlier, it exhibited the problems of internal integration (the identity problem) and external adaptation (the image problem), especially with a Scottish business community that was confused over its mission and sometimes hostile to the idea of a public sector organization intervening in private sector business. The case also shows how HR and marketing, by working together, can create impressive results by producing improvements in organizational identity and image. However, you may wish to speculate, for a moment on the reasons why people in the two surveys were much less inclined to report that they 'lived' the SE values when performing their work than being fully committed to them. Our discussion of the organizational identity–individual identification relationship, and cosmopolitans and locals, may help you think about this issue.

Let's look a little closer at some further material that might help us analyse SE's problems in more depth by examining some of the ideas that help clear up some of the conceptual confusion in this field and some of the practical approaches that result from such work.

Organizational identity and image

As we noted in Chapter 1, organizational identity has its origins in earlier work by academics on individual identity and the identification process: how individuals come to take on the identity of groups and organizations. We will examine this issue of individual identification later in this chapter and the next one, which deals more specifically with individual–organizational linkages. To recap, we also suggested that much of the recent work on identity has focused on *organizational* identity, a relatively new idea. This has been conceived of in two, rather different, ways – a stronger and weaker version – both of which have different practical implications. The weaker version of organizational identity is to see it as little more than a summation of the shared beliefs of those individuals who make up the organization – a kind of collective personality. We shall discuss an example of this approach later in this chapter when looking at the notion of Corporate Character approach of Gary Davies and his colleagues. The other, stronger version is to see an organization as a 'social actor' in its own right, independent of the particular individuals comprising it, capable of, and authorized to, take actions, entering into contracts and projecting an image to the outside world in its own right (Whetten and Mackey, 2002). Often a sports metaphor is used to explain this social actor perspective, as when senior managers invoke the idea of a team being bigger than any of its players and outliving their narrow career interests.

The basic premise of this latter view is one of self-reference, which is sometimes equated with the idea of organizational agency – that an organization can develop a self-concept or self-definition independent of how outsiders see it. Such a notion meets the needs of other stakeholders, including government, to hold it to account in its own right, in much the same way individuals are held to account for their beliefs and actions. A further, key implication of self-reference is that an organizational identity, which is evident in the resource-based view (RBV) of strategy discussed in Chapters 2 and 9, is one of the most important ways that organizations can promote a strategy of differentiation (or focus, if operating in a more narrow product-market segment). For, as we noted, collective identity, like individual identities, is a claim for difference as well as similarity with others. Just as we define ourselves as individuals to be different from groups we don't want to belong to and to be similar to groups we want to receive affirmation from, organizations need to differentiate themselves through their own agency *and* conform to expectations set by stakeholders such as government, the state and industry bodies. It is this view that most closely informs our own ideas, but let's look at a number of other important contributions to this organizational identity-image relationship. These contributions embody some of the ideas just expressed but also offer variations on the theme and provide other insights for HR practitioners.

Culture, image and identity

For those readers with an understanding of the literature on organizational change and development, you might be asking the question: what is the difference between identity and culture? And you would be right to do so. For example, recapping on the three principles of organizational identity by Albert and Whetten (1985) in Chapter 1: that (a) it should capture its essence or 'claimed central character' of the organization; (b) it should set out its claimed distinctiveness; and (c) it should show continuity over time – it is clear that they could equally apply to culture. This is not helpful in distinguishing between them and in clearing up the conceptual confusion that bedevils this field, especially for practitioners trying to make sense of the multiple voices competing for airspace. One way of doing so is to see organizational identity as the link between culture and image, the approach taken by Hatch and Schultz (2002). Their reasoning is quite complicated and subtle, but basically suggests a two-way, recursive relationship between the three core ideas of culture, organizational identity and organizational image (see Figure 3.3 for a simplified version of their model).

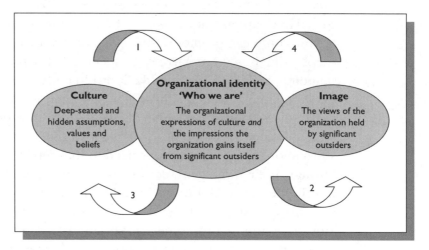

Figure 3.3
The relationship between culture, identity and image (based on Hatch and Schultz, 2002, p. 995).

The first relationship (1) is between culture and identity. Cultures can be thought of as the deeper, often hidden, values, beliefs and assumptions that shape how organizations define themselves collectively (Schein, 1985). Over time, through self-conscious, collective reflection on culture, an organizational identity emerges. This is a more surface-level, collective sense of 'who we are'. The key point about this relationship is that identity does not have to depend on people outside of the organization for confirmation; instead it is largely internally driven. The organizational identity that emerges helps create (2) the second relationship, an impression on significant others, e.g. potential and existing customers, potential employees, investors, the media and the general public. The processes, however, are not just one-way: identities reflect back on cultures (3) as the collective organizational behaviour of employees helps sustain and confirm the cultural values, beliefs and assumptions of the organization over a period of time.

As an example of relationships (1) and (2), Hewlett-Packard (HP), which began life as an electronic test and measurement instrumentation manufacturer in 1939, is well known for having an organizational identity that is expressly defined by a 1961 internal memo from Dave Packard. This memo stated that the mission of the HP was 'to design, develop and manufacture the finest products for the advancement of science and the welfare of humanity'. It has also become known worldwide for an open, caring and sharing style of HRM that places employees at the centre of its operation and as one of the best places to work in international league tables of such issues. It is generally held that this identity was the product of the values and assumptions of the founders, and of the success generated by following its founding culture and principles. When HP moved into the computing business, for which it is now known, this identity remained core to its operations. In 2001, HP sold off its original test and measurement division to create Agilent Technologies, a completely separate company. Unsurprisingly, however, Agilent had all of the hallmarks of HP's founding culture, expressed in its organizational identity, operations, policies and practices, such as HR, ethical business policies, diversity management and so on. During research for this book, managers at Agilent have told us that you cannot understand the 'who we are' without understanding the cultural origins and values of HP in its early days, deeply engrained in how HP does its business.

The final relationship (4) shows how identities may also be externally generated. Identities – 'who we are' – are not only formed culturally by reference to internal values and beliefs, but are also formed by feedback from significant others of the projected image. Quite literally, significant others act as a mirror for the organization to help form its sense of who it is and what it looks like. For example, certain sections of the media that feed off the need for celebrity sometimes play an important role in creating heroic 'leaders' in organizations and heroic or 'celebrity organizations' (Rindova *et al.*, 2006), often at odds with how an organization sees itself or would like to see itself. Arguably, our current concern with the 'cult of leadership' and the increasingly high salaries being paid to CEOs, reflect media and investor needs to hold individuals, rather than teams of leaders, to account and the need to make news (Kellerman, 2004). We return to this issue in a discussion of Hurricane Katrina later in this chapter.

Another illustration of this relationship has been the creation of the Beckham brand. David Beckham, who is one of the world's most famous footballers and has become an icon among teenagers in Asia and Europe, is behind one of the best-known personal brands. It is often suggested, however, he owes his image to his ability to appeal to many different groups, all of whom can project on him what they will – footballer, star symbol, family man, new man and even saviour of English national identity through football. In other words, he is, according to some observers, a media and consumer creation with a celebrity status extending far beyond his abilities as a footballer. (The same argument can be applied to the 'celebrities' of reality TV shows whose reputations have grown because of a complicit relationship with the media in creating them and the market for 'non-celebrities'.) It is argued that Manchester United, the club with which he grew up and who helped him build his image, were happy to transfer him to Real Madrid because the Beckham image had become 'bigger than the club' and detracted from the team that had shaped his football (and, in part, commercial) success. For example, his manager, Sir Alex Ferguson, accused him of playing (long, showy) 'Hollywood' passes that were intended to enhance his own image, often to the detriment of his team members and the club (because they cut out his midfield colleagues and had little regard for the ability of the receiver to deal with the long ball). This is only one of many illustrations that show the dark side of talent management, a topic we explore in Chapter 6, often revealing tensions between individuals whose image is created by significant outsiders and the collective identity of the internal teams they work with. Good examples here are the 'stars' of the knowledge-intensive industries such as financial investment, consulting, medicine and academia, whose external reputations are effectively 'rented' by the organizations that employ them. As we have noted in our discussion of cosmopolitans and locals, tensions often arise between such talented individuals and the groups they work with (and which often help create their 'stardom') (Groysberg *et al.*, 2004).

Multiple identities and the 'AC³ID test'

Another helpful way of thinking about the identity-image relationship has been developed by John Balmer and Stephen Geyser (2003). They seek to apply the concepts of identity to the whole field of corporate-level studies, which they argue can cohere around the management of these *multiple identities* of a corporation (though this is a different usage of multiple identities to our own). As a result, they have proposed a multi-disciplinary approach – now called the AC³ID framework – to the management of image and identity. According to them, identity has five meanings which incorporate not only the previously discussed organizational identity and image but also other corporate-level concepts such as corporate identity, strategic vision and corporate strategy (see Figure 3.4).

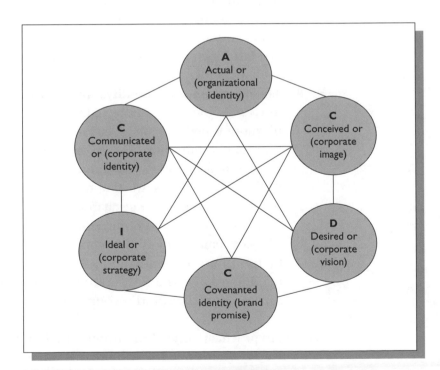

Figure 3.4
The AC³ID framework (adapted from Balmer and Geyser, 2003, p. 17; Balmer and Stuart, 2005).

■ The **actual identity** is defined as the current attributes of the corporation, including the management values, leadership styles, organizational structure, business activities and markets, and the range of products and services.

■ The **conceived identity** refers to the past, present and future perceptions of internal and external stakeholders, close to Hatch and Schultz's image and identity relationship, and to reputation.

■ The **ideal identity**, which is the optimum positioning of the corporation in its given markets at a point in time, based on an analysis of external environmental–internal resources fit. This identity is associated with the work of strategic planners and is close to the notion of corporate strategy and strategic positioning.

■ The **desired identity** is synonymous with the vision of the organization held by its leadership. It is not the same thing as ideal identity, which is mostly the result of serious analysis. The desired identity is very often a personal and egotistical statement made by senior leaders, but which is no less important in its consequences than ideal identities.

■ The **communicated identity** is the 'official' identity put into the public domain through the corporate communications function – the official rhetoric of the organization that communicates what the organization wishes to be. It is also, however, communicated by less controllable media, such as 'word of mouth' and the financial press, which requires a great deal of management time spent on internal communications and public relations.

■ The **covenanted identity**, which is the 'promise' made by the brand to persuade us to place our trust and confidence in it and to continue to support it through repeat 'purchases' and recommendations.

The main practical value of this framework is the proposition that all five identities need to be broadly aligned over time. Balmer and Geyser maintain that if any two of these are out of alignment at a particular point, this will be manifested as a 'moment of truth' from which a corporation's reputation is in danger of suffering serious damage. So, for example, the dangers of communicated identity (or corporate identity) running ahead of the actual identity (or organizational identity) can, as we discuss in later chapters, lead to persistent cynicism among employees and also lead to distrust among customers if this cynicism is communicated by disaffected employees. Another example is redundancies or retrenchments that lead to mass disaffection among employees (negative organizational identity) who are simultaneously being exhorted to 'live the brand' image that 'puts people first' (the conceived identity). So, Jeff Pfetter (2005) has argued that as 'employees are increasingly disengaged and distrustful of their employers, organizations have moved to become less like communities and adopt more arm's-length and distant relationships with their people. Organizations that are more communal have arrangements for helping employees in need ... are better at resolving work–family issues, and foster long-term employment relations' (p. 1).

The Balmer and Geyser model has been applied to the analysis of British Airways progress over the past few decades (see Box 3.2).

Box 3.2   The changing identities of British Airways (BA)

BA can be traced to 1924 when four small airlines merged to form Imperial Airways, encouraged by the British government. It operated as a virtual monopoly until 1935, when British Airways was established to further the UK's aviation interests in South America and Europe. The brand name temporarily disappeared but was re-established in 1974 following the merger of British Overseas Airways Corporation (BOAC) and British European Airways (BEA). Balmer and Stuart trace six periods during which there has been a mismatch in BA's changing identities.

■ **'Appalling' identity (1974–1980).** Following the merger of BOAC and BEA, there were tensions between the two groups of staff, with the former seeing themselves as superior to the latter. This manifested itself in poor service which was exacerbated by the attitudes of BA pilots, many of whom had joined from the Royal Air Force and saw passengers as cargo to be transported, and as a near-unnecessary evil. This became a major problem for customers since the airline held a virtual monopoly of many routes in and out of Heathrow. BA came to stand for 'Bloody Awful'.

■ **'Adjusting identity' (1981–1983).** Margaret Thatcher gave Sir John King the chairmanship to turn it around from a loss-making nationalized carrier to a profitable private sector organization. Inheriting a huge overdraft, King and his new board embarked on a series of initiatives to improve employee morale and self-image, which was seen to be a major problem. This included an expensive advertisement, called the Manhattan ad, that was designed to change the identity and self-respect of employees as much as convince customers that the airline was changing.

■ **'Appealing identity' (1984–1987).** King and his new CEO, Sir Colin Marshall, who had a service industry background, were experienced communicators, who recognized the need to change the image and self-image of the company to improve customer service. This began with a major culture change programme called 'Putting People First', in which Marshall led from the front. It was also a period during which BA introduced a new livery that emphasized its 'Britishness', incorporating the Union Jack flag and a coat of arms. There is evidence, however, that this culture change programme had only a limited impact, especially among lower levels of employees.

■ **'Adoring identity' (1988–1995).** BA adopted the claim that it was 'the world's favourite airline', which was supported by customer satisfaction surveys. King and Marshall were insistent that this brand promise was supported by employee behaviour and HR became a major player in delivering the brand warrant.

■ **'Ailing identity' (1996–2000).** Robert Ayling became CEO in 1996 in its lead up to privatization in 1997. Ayling and his team determined that BA had to change its image from being Britain's national flag carrier to an international business, since more than 60% of its customers were non-UK citizens. It was during this period that BA changed its communicated identity by, among other design efforts, introducing a series of international images on the tailfins. This soon became seen a major mistake when Margaret Thatcher described them as 'appalling'. Employees resented the changes, especially since they cost £60 million, and Richard Branson of Virgin exploited the criticism of many US customers that they wanted BA to look more British, by changing the livery of Virgin airlines to carry the Union Jack. The ethnic tailfins were replaced after two years and

Ayling accepted the position of BA as a British-based global airline. The period was financially disastrous with £4.2 billion being wiped off BA's balance sheet. Needless to say, Ayling stepped down in 2000, following his failed attempt to change the image of BA through graphic design.

■ **'Affirming identity' (2000–2005).** A new CEO, Rod Eddington, was appointed, whose job has been to deal with the problems posed by low cost air carriers on short-haul journeys. The British airline industry has become one of the most competitive in the world, with a large number of 'no-frills' airlines offering extremely cheap fares all over the UK and Europe. BA has attempted to affirm its traditional identity by affirming its 'Britishness' and by re-positioning itself ever more as a carrier that deals with premium service and business class passengers. It has done so quite successfully, posting huge profits in 2005, but has run into employee relations problems with its full-time staff and contractors causing it to lose reputation for customer service.

Balmer and Stuart analyse each of these periods in terms of either a mismatch between the multiple identities or of bringing them into alignment. For example, the first period, the appalling identity, was seen as a misalignment between actual and ideal identities, while the adjusting identity period was seen as bringing the covenanted identity and actual identity into alignment. You may wish to reflect on how they analyse the other periods.

Source: Adapted from Balmer and Stuart, 2005

Corporate character, image and identity

As we discussed in Chapter 2, the reputation management approach developed by Gary Davies and his colleagues in the UK (Davies *et al.*, 2003, 2004), is a fruitful approach to exploring the links between identity and image. Theirs is one of the weaker versions of organizational identity that we referred to earlier, since it tends to view it as the summary of the shared beliefs of those individuals who make up the organization. Nevertheless, for us, it has high practical value. Davies *et al.*'s starting point, in contrast to our plural view of reputations, is that corporate reputation is 'the collective term referring to all stakeholders' views of corporate reputation' (p. 62), including internal identity and external image, which they define as the views of the company held by external stakeholders, especially customers, and the views of employees.

Gary Davies' and his colleagues' principal argument is that employees and customers' perceptions of the reputation of an organization will influence their behaviour towards it, reminiscent of the service–profit chain we discussed in Chapter 2. In service businesses such as retailing, in which most of their research has been conducted, the perspectives of employees and customers towards the organization and its services are seen as interdependent and form part of the reputation chain (see Figure 3.5). Their model proposes an ideal, rather than typical, relationship between satisfied employees, high level of organizational identification, strong brand reputations, customer satisfaction, loyalty and increased sales.

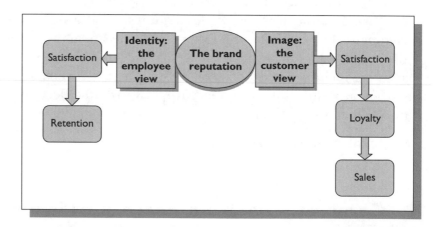

Figure 3.5
The reputation chain (adapted from Davies *et al.*, 2004, p. 76).

The core link in the model is the alignment of identity and image. If a misalignment develops with obvious gaps between internal and external views, these are seen as potential causes of crises. So far, this is unremarkable stuff, but the most novel and useful aspect of their model is their way of assessing the reputation of an organization and measuring the gaps between identity and image. As far as we are aware, there are no reputable and tested measures that ask the same question of employees and customers when assessing the identity–image– reputation links. There are good and obvious reasons for this, since the criteria and weighting employees use to evaluate 'who we are' and those used by customers to judge the image of the company are likely to be different in some important respects. As Hatch and Schultz have pointed out, the starting point for identity is the internally driven culture, while image is more likely to be outsider-driven by sources such as the media and communications channels. Nevertheless, all authorities on this topic recognize that there is a two-way interaction between employees' and customers' views of the organization, which Davies *et al.* (2003, 2004) now define as 'corporate character'.

They have spent a number of years researching a corporate character scale to assess the reputation of an organization from the perspectives of employees and customers. Drawing their ideas from existing literature and from primary survey research of 2061 employees and 2565 customers in 49 different business units of 13 organizations, they have developed five major and two minor dimensions of corporate character that employees and customers can use to evaluate an organization's identity, image and reputation. The major dimensions are agreeableness, competence, enterprise, ruthlessness and chic; the minor dimensions are informality and machismo. The dimensions can be broken down into 16 facets and measured by the strength of agreement with 49 items (see Table 3.1).

Since much of the research took place in retail stores with employees, managers and customers, the results and some of the items (such as chicness) reflect the context. Their findings showed that *agreeableness* was the factor most highly correlated with employee and customer satisfaction among all three groups of respondents; employees, however, showed greater concern for all seven dimensions and store managers showed less concern for enterprise than the other two groups. All three groups were dissatisfied by ruthlessness.

The second and third most highly correlated dimensions with satisfaction were enterprise and competence, though both were more important to employees, which might be expected since

Table 3.1

The Seven Pillars of Corporate Character.

Major and minor dimensions	Facets	Scale items associated with facet/dimension
Major Dimensions		
Agreeableness	Warmth	Friendly, pleasant, open, straightforward
	Empathy	Concerned, re-assuring, supportive, agreeable
	Integrity	Honest, sincere, trustworthy, socially responsible
Enterprising	Modern	Cool, trendy, youthful
	Adventurous	Imaginative, up-to-date, exciting, innovative
	Bold	Extravert, daring
Competent	Conscientious	Reliable, secure, hardworking
	Driven	Ambitious, achievement-oriented, leading-edge
	Technocratic	Technically competent, corporately competent
Ruthless	Egotistical	Arrogant, aggressive, selfish
	Dominant	Inward-looking, authoritarian, controlling
Chic	Elegant	Charming, stylish, elegant
	Prestigious	Prestigious, exclusive, refined
	Snobbish	Snobby, elitist
Minor Dimensions		
Informal		Casual, simple, easy-going
Machismo		Masculine, tough, rugged

Source: Based on Davies *et al.*, 2004, pp. 152–156

these are more obviously relevant internally. Chicness came fifth, most probably because that is an important factor in retailing to employees and customers. Informality and machismo were minor factors, not correlating strongly with satisfaction, but Davies and his colleagues have chosen to retain them as they are likely to be important in other contexts. For example, in some research we conducted in a voluntary organization with a largely female management, machismo was negatively correlated with employee satisfaction (see Box 3.3).

However, being highly correlated with a phenomenon does not mean that you can say anything statistically about what causes what. For example, there is a well-known debate in organizational behaviour over the 'happy worker – productive worker' relationship: high levels of performance may cause employees to feel satisfied just as much as employee satisfaction can cause high levels of performance (Harter *et al.*, 2002). So, the final stage of their research was to ascertain the main drivers of satisfaction from this list of dimensions, which they did using a statistical technique known as stepwise regression for all three groups. The results showed that *agreeableness* was the most important driver, accounting for 48%, 35% and 32% of the variation in satisfaction levels among staff, customers and managers respectively. The second, and only other, factor that explained variation in satisfaction levels was enterprise; when combined with agreeableness, they explained 52% and 39% of the variation in employee and customer satisfaction levels respectively. They also attempted to find out if there was a significant link between satisfaction and financial performance. Here the results were more tentative, as might be expected, but they found a relationship between customer satisfaction and year-on-year sales growth, which in turn was correlated with agreeableness, enterprise and chicness. Employee satisfaction did not correlate with financial performance, but did so with agreeableness, informality, enterprise and was negatively correlated with ruthlessness. They concluded that image is associated with performance (as measured by sales growth), but only via customer satisfaction.

The practical implications of this work are that employee satisfaction and customer satisfaction may not be necessarily linked; managers have to want to create these links through concerted actions. Thus harmonizing image and identity has three aspects to it:

■ **Achieving symmetry.** This is achieved by using a similar framework and set of dimensions to measure identity and image, e.g. the corporate character approach.

- **Achieving affinity.** It is not enough for customers and employees (and other stakeholders) to see the corporate character in the same way; what satisfies them must be the same to achieve the emotional links, e.g. they must both value agreeableness or enterprise, and place a negative value on ruthlessness.
- **Achieving connection.** Connections are the logical reasons why employees would want to see satisfied customers through, for example, seeing a connection between their attitudes and behaviours, satisfied customers (and other stakeholders) and the financial performance of the company.

We would certainly recommend that organizations wishing to explore gaps between organizational identity and how outsiders view an organization's image (its reputations) might want to develop a more contextually sensitive adaptation of this approach. We have begun to do this in a range of contexts, including a financial services company, a political party and a voluntary organization (see Box 3.3).

Box 3.3   Corporate character in a voluntary organization

We undertook a piece of research in 2003 for Age Concern North Tyneside, a charitable organization in the North of England. The organization provided a range of services for older people, including sheltered housing, day care and drop-in centres so that elderly people could get advice and training on insurance, life-skills, computing etc. The organization was part of a larger, well-known national network that had developed a mission and values framework, but operated relatively autonomously. Like all charitable organizations, it had to compete for funding with other charities; it also had to secure competitive contracts with the local government authority in the area for the provision of services for the elderly, based on negotiated service-level agreements. Thus, in many respects, it was subject to market-style conditions on pricing and costing, and on promoting itself as a worthwhile recipient of donations. It also had to operate in a highly competitive labour market for good quality care

workers, nursing staff and administrators to ensure that the service standards agreed with the local authority were met. However, it had to do
so without the capacity to offer competitive wages and salaries, even at
median local market conditions, since it was poorly funded in comparison to nursing homes run directly by the local authority.

The senior management team, comprising a CEO, who was also
on the Board of the national parent organization, Age Concern England,
the finance and operations managers, and the HR manager, were a
well-qualified, enterprising and committed team, who, interestingly, were
all women. Given their problems, they wished to understand more about
the identity-image problem to (a) devise a strategy and set of practices
that would help them ensure that staff were aligned with the values of the
parent group, and (b) help them compete in the local labour market for
good quality staff so that they could achieve better levels of service and
enhance their image with potential funding agencies.

The first stage of the investigative work involved surveying all 120 full-
time employees in groups during working hours, which returned a very
high response rate. We developed a questionnaire based partly on the
corporate character dimensions and items suitably amended for the context. Despite not being able to survey the 'customers', many of whom were
too old to complete questionnaires, this approach was deemed highly
appropriate because the values framework mapped directly onto certain
of the corporate character dimensions. The other section of the questionnaire examined the state of psychological contracts, leadership styles
and communications, and individual identification, which we shall look
at in more detail in Chapter 4.

The results showed that staff as a whole viewed the organization's
character as competent and agreeable, followed by enterprising, which
mapped onto the parent values of being expert, caring and dynamic,
and which could be treated as proxies for what clients sought. It also
showed, as might be expected, that the organization was neither ruth-
less nor macho. Nor was it seen as particularly informal. However, the
extent of perceived competence and agreeableness among staff was
not particularly high, nor was it universal, since staff at the three different 'sites' rated the character of the organization differently. Closer
examination of the state of psychological contracts – what employees
valued about work, what was perceived as 'promised' by the organization and what was actually delivered in practice – helped shed light on
some of the likely causes, as did this next topic – leadership.

Organizational action: governance, leadership and engagement

Governance and leadership

To recap on our introduction to these issues in the opening chapter, we argued that organizational identity deals with the 'Who are we?' question and how such conceptions influence the corporation's autobiography – its image – cannot be sustained without supportive organizational actions. Two of the most important dimensions of organizational action are governance and leadership. Consider the case of Hurricane Katrina in Box 3.4.

Box 3.4   Lessons from failure

At the end of August 2005, Hurricane Katrina devastated the city of New Orleans and much of the Gulf Coast of the USA killing more than 1000 people and exposing to the rest of the world the inability of America to act when faced with a crisis that many claimed was foreseeable. Pictures of a bemused President Bush caught like a rabbit between the lights, and a disengaged local police force were brought into the living rooms of billions of people through TV reports and other news media. The disaster provoked a bitter debate about the (lack of) leadership and governance displayed by government officials before, during and after the hurricane, with an array of leaders at various levels of national and state governance coming in for severe criticism, including President Bush, Kathleen Babineaux Blanco, the Governor of New Orleans, Mayor Ray Nagin of New Orleans, Homeland Security Secretary Michael Chertoff and former Federal Emergency Management Agency director Michael Brown, who took part of the formal blame for lack of action.

In a discussion at Wharton Business School, the following comments were made by prominent US academics in response to a question on whether this was a failure of leadership, or a natural consequence of the governance structure of the USA, which is split between federal, state and local officials and the formal protocols that have to be observed between them, e.g. the state has to formally request Federal assistance.

Morris Cohen: [Bush] was very reluctant to [send in troops]. He would have been roundly criticized. But in hindsight I think he should have. The resources were sitting there within miles … He, or someone, made the wrong decision. And yet it's an uncertain process. If the President had been too aggressive, that would have engendered all kinds of criticism. The next time that leader had to make a decision, he would be more careful.

Robert Mittelstaedt: Despite all the laws about what a president can or can't do – or what approval you need from state governors – when the chips are down, leaders step up and take action and worry about the consequences later. Bush should have declared martial law on Tuesday [30 August, one day after Katrina swept through the city], sent troops in there and started to marshal resources. Bush's later statement [in which he took responsibility for any shortcomings on the part of the Federal government] was a halfhearted answer. The picture that comes to mind is Bush reading the little goat book [to schoolchildren when White House Chief of Staff Andrew Card informed the president of the terrorist attacks on September 11, 2001]. On Monday [August 29], Bush was in Phoenix talking to people in an old folks home about his Medicare prescription plan. In both instances, he ends up with a dumb look on his face. I have never seen him as a leader. He's just a politician managed by his handlers. And I'm a Republican. Imagine if Bush had stepped up on Tuesday [30 August] and sent massive troops in there to evacuate people and offer medical aid. Suppose afterward you had a congressional investigation into whether he should be impeached for violating the *posse comitatus* law [an 1878 statute prohibiting Federal troops from being used for law enforcement on US soil]. Would he rather have his people in front of the commission saying, 'Didn't you understand how bad this crisis was?' rather than sitting by while people drowned? I'd much rather be in that position than where he is now. Leaders don't worry about consequences. Leaders are born, not made. He has amazing power but inherently doesn't have much leadership ability. There is no leadership test to be elected.

Lawrence Hrebiniak: Our government is decentralized, but only to a point. We have both centralized and decentralized resources. If that system is to work, both sides must be well prepared for action. There should be some integration between the local and the central level. Bush should have had the right people in Homeland Security or FEMA contact these [local and state] people and say, 'We've got a hurricane coming. Who should respond first? What resources do you need?' You talk to them and you find out where they are short of capabilities and you make up the slack.

In direct response to the question, 'Was any leadership exhibited in New Orleans?', the following comments were made.

Robert Mittelstaedt: Where did leadership show up? The Coast Guard. They had deployed helicopters to the area, so they were able to move resources in right behind the storm. That's why choppers were all over the place rescuing people. People at the middle level in the Coast Guard knew it was their responsibility and they just did it. They understood their mission and they were there and they saved thousands of lives.

K@W: Did the political culture of New Orleans contribute to the failure of local leadership?

Robert Mittelstaedt: One of my relatives, a judge, once ran for mayor of New Orleans and lost. The only explanation I had for his loss was that he was politically connected but not corrupt. It's a place with a long history of political corruption and a lack of concern for the broader public good. Even with somebody like Nagin, who has made some attempts to try to improve that environment and go after the corruption, it's still far down on the list of cities that have things under control. The poverty level is horrible. Crime is terrible. The public school system is terrible. I don't believe the response [to the aftermath of the storm] was related to racism; you have seen white flight out of New Orleans for decades. All of that contributes to an environment where there are no leaders who can effectively deal with the bulk of the problems, many of which go back to Huey Long [the corrupt former governor of Louisiana]. It's been an anti-business state in many ways. The economy is totally dependent on shipping and tourism. If you don't have leaders who want to solve these things, you get what you saw on TV.

Source: Reprinted with permission from 'A Month After Katrina', Knowledge @Wharton, available online at http://knowledge. wharton.upenn.edu

In the opening chapter, we discussed work that showed how governance and its problems are embedded in the multiple identities of organizations (Golden-Biddle and Rao, 1997). The directors in this study not only experience role conflict resulting from competing expectations from their legal and fiduciary obligations but 'conflicts of commitment' as they struggled to reconcile incompatible expectations ensuing from their desire to uphold different identities. Golden-Biddle and Rao have developed a very useful framework to analyse problems such as Hurricane Katrina, or, indeed, any situation that relates the actions or inactions of boards of directors and senior managers to organizational identity and individual's identification with their organizations (see Figure 3.6).

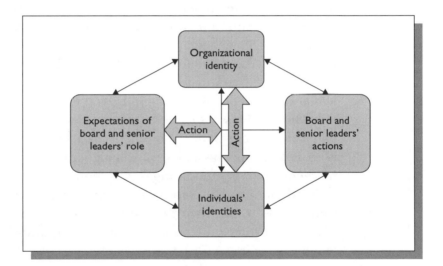

Figure 3.6
How identity shapes the role of directors and other senior leaders (adapted from Golden-Biddle and Rao, 1997).

Their framework sets out the four mutually interdependent elements – organizational and individual identities, and senior managers' expectation of how they should act and how they do act which are linked by two processes of identification and action. So, first of all, individuals will identify most strongly with the organization when they believe that preserving the organization's identity will satisfy their own needs, a process we shall examine more closely in the next chapter. Second, and most importantly for this section, the actions of leaders are based on expectations of how they should act and expectations concerning the result of their actions. Thus, when senior leaders act in ways consistent with their expectations and those of others, these actions maintain strong degrees of integration between individuals' and organizational identities. However, when they don't act in accordance with expectations, or experience role conflict or conflicts of commitment to multiple identities, the process of identification is weakened, especially among employees. Applying this analysis to the Hurricane Katrina case, President Bush's initial failure to act, along with those others indicted, certainly failed to meet the expectations for the American presidency to show decisive leadership and may have led to a decline in identification among voters and many employees of the New Orleans Police Force with the Bush presidency (which reached an all-time low during the early stages of the disaster), the state and city government. Moreover, it may have confirmed the impression among some that Bush was a weak leader controlled by his aides and given to appointing 'cronies' like Michael Brown to important appointments for which he had no real background. Another, perhaps kinder, interpretation is that Bush and his aides were caught in a conflict of commitment, between upholding the Federal government's organizational identity that embraced the spirit of September 11 and upholding the identity of individual states for independence, which are protected by statute from having uninvited federal troops on their soil for law enforcement.

This type of analysis is consistent with the earlier comments on leadership *styles* in Chapter 1, in which we highlighted the failures of senior leaders to 'walk the talk' by acting out the mission and values statements. For example, both views expressed in the Hurricane Katrina case are consistent with the need to hold an individual to account rather than the more diffuse and fractured structure of governance. Moreover, as we noted, there are few more powerful explanations for lack of identification by employees, often manifested in scepticism and cynicism, than the failure of senior leaders to act in ways consistent with organizational identity (Pate *et al.*, 2000). More positively, we also noted that when leaders act to preserve an organizational identity that employees perceive to be in their best interests, high levels of individual identification ensue. For example, following President Bush's decisive actions after September 11, his personal ratings went up markedly. And during the next disaster to hit the US coast, Hurricane Rita, the Bush administration acted well before the event, one might speculate as much to restore identity of the Bush presidency for decisive leadership and Bush's personal ratings, as for protecting the citizens of Galveston from the storm.

This process was also brought home to us most recently during a recent piece of research at Agilent Technologies, discussed earlier, when senior managers did everything they could to preserve the organization's identity as an employer of choice, even when they were ordered by headquarters to take their fair share of employee layoffs. Consistently throughout the period of layoffs and beyond, individual identification, as measured by attitude surveys, remained high. However, when senior managers, faced by ever-mounting pressure to change the contracts of those remaining, breached the old 'deal' on employment, identification levels plummeted. Jeff Pfeffer (1998), in his book *The Human Equation*, cites this process as one of the worst sins of US organizations, especially those that follow a 'hire and fire' policy.

Conclusions

In this chapter, we have drilled down a little further into the core of our model and argument, which focuses on the relationships between image, organizational identity and organizational actions, including governance and leadership. We have also touched on how these interrelationships are justified by the desire of organizations to secure greater identification with employees, having them think and behave as individuals in ways that support these organizational-level conceptions and actions.

We examined a number of practical frameworks, including Balmer and Stuart's AC^{3}ID identity alignment. However, the two most useful from our perspective are Gary Davies' Corporate Character approach and the insights provided by Golden-Biddle and Rao's analysis of how identity shapes the role of directors and senior leaders. The former is best applied to assess gaps between employees' understanding of an organization's identity and how outsiders view its image, and can be adapted to specific organizational contexts without radical alteration. The second shows how the actions of collective leadership, probably the most important influence on external and internal perceptions of the organization, are linked. We applied this analysis to a major case of leadership failure in the context of a crises of national identity and follow up the implications of this for individuals in the next chapter.

References

Albert, S. and Whetten, D. (1985) Organizational identity, in L. L. Cummings and B. M. Staw (eds), *Research in organizational behaviour* 7. Greenwich, CT: JAI Press, pp. 263–295.

Balmer, J. T. and Greyser, S. A. (2003) *Revealing the corporation: perspectives on identity, image, reputation, corporate branding and corporate-level marketing.* London: Routledge.

Balmer, J. T. and Stuart, H. (2005) *The changing identities of British Airways: implications for communicating corporate social responsibility.* Paper presented to the annual conference of the Reputation Institute, June, Madrid.

Davies, G., Chun, R., da Silva, R. V. and Roper, S. (2003) *Corporate reputation and competitiveness.* London: Routledge.

Davies, G., Chun, R., da Silva, R. V. and Roper, S. (2004) A corporate character scale to assess employee and customer views of organization reputation, *Corporate Reputation Review,* **7** (2), 125–146.

Golden-Biddle, K. and Rao, H. (1997) Breaches in the boardroom: identity and conflicts of commitment in a nonprofit organization, *Organizational Science,* **8**, 593–611.

Gouldner, A. (1954) *Patterns of industrial bureaucracy.* New York: Free Press.

Groysberg, B., Nanda, A. and Nohria, N. (2004) The risky business of hiring stars, *Harvard Business Review,* May–June, pp. 92–100.

Harter, J. M., Schmidt, F. and Hayes, T. L. (2002) Business unit level relationships between employee satisfaction/engagement and business outcomes: a meta-analysis, *Journal of Applied Psychology,* **87**, 268–279.

Hatch, M. J. and Schultz, M. (2001) Are the strategic starts aligned for your corporate brand?, *Harvard Business Review*, Jan–Feb, pp. 129–134.

Kellerman, B. (2004) *Bad leadership: what it is, why it happens and why it matters*. Boston, MA: Harvard Business School Press.

Pate, J., Martin, G. and Staines, H. (2000) The New Psychological Contract, cynicism and organizational change: a theoretical framework and case study evidence, *Journal of Strategic Change*, **9** (1), 481–493.

Pfeffer, J. (1998) *The human equation: building profits by putting people first*. Boston, MA: Harvard Business School Press.

Pfeffer, J. (2005) Working alone: whatever happened to the idea of organizations as communities?, *Research Paper, 1906*. Stanford, CA: Stanford University Press.

Rindova, V. P., Pollock, T. G. and Hayward, M. L. A. (2006) Celebrity firms: the social construction of market popularity, *Academy of Management Review*, **31**, 50–71.

Schein, E. (1985) *Organizational culture and leadership*. San Francisco, CA: Jossey-Bass.

Sparrow, P. R. and Cooper, C. L. (2003) *The new employment relationship*. Oxford: Butterworth–Heinemann.

Whetten, D. and Mackey, A. (2002) A social actor conception of organizational identity and its implications for the study of organizational reputations, *Business and Society*, **41**, 393–414.

The quality of individual employment relationships and individual employee behaviour

Introduction

In the previous chapter, we focused on how organizational identity and actions shape image. We also indicated, in turn, how the identification process can influence the individual identities (or self-concepts) of employees. Using two examples, we illustrated how this apparently academic distinction between organizational and individual identities has important practical consequences, since the latter is rooted in how employees perceive themselves, and not how they see their organizations. That said, there are processes at work in which individuals may, *under certain circumstances*, come to incorporate elements of their organization's identity into their self-perceptions, drawing on what academics describe as social identity and self-categorization theories (Hatch and Schultz, 2004). So, the core message for practitioners is that changing employees' identities – their self-concepts of who they are – is a more difficult and uncertain task than many of the more basic culture management and communications-driven, customer relationship texts would have you believe, leaving aside the ethical issues associated with 'brandwashing'. We will deal with this issue when we discuss the effectiveness of employee branding in Chapter 8, which is an attempt to use communications techniques to achieve greater levels of identification with existing employees, as well as recruiting new ones in the so-called 'war for talent' (Barrow and Mosley, 2005). Just how effective employer branding and HR communications can be is open to question, and will depend on their understanding of this identification process, psychological contracts and other key individual–organizational linkages.

Acknowledging these notes of caution and ethics for the moment, to which we shall return, there is little doubt that how individual employees see themselves, how they behave and the kinds of connections they have with their organizations will shape organizational identity and actions. To repeat our core message, this is one of the main premises of this book, that reputations and brands are driven from the inside. We refer to this interest in employee perceptions and behaviours as *the quality of individual employment relationships*; we use it to encompass a set of distinctive, but overlapping, processes at work, all of which are slightly different in conception and effects but, in combination, link employees to their organizations. These processes are *psychological contracting*, and the main individual organizational linkages of *identification, internalization, psychological ownership* and *commitment* (e.g. Pierce, 2001, and Sparrow and Cooper, 2003, among others). Such a list is often confusing for practitioners, and that is probably why the idea of *engagement* has become so popular in recent years, since it promises to tap into or overlay all of the others as a form of temperature check for HR managers (see Figure 4.1). However, like any idea or piece of equipment (in this case, survey tools) that claims to do everything (especially on the cheap), it may result in doing nothing particularly well. And, as we will argue, there is more than a hint of this problem in the consultancy-based reworking of engagement. So, we take a more detailed look at these ideas in this chapter to reveal their similarities and differences and to provide you with a necessarily more complex picture of an undoubtedly complicated problem: how do people come to relate to their organizations and how can we help them realize their aspirations through work? (We use 'necessarily' because 'complexification', rather than simplification, often serves everyone's interests, including those busy managers who look for simple answers. This is based on the premises that the social world isn't a simple place and one-size-fits-all solutions rarely work without some grounding in context). To do this we will make use of two ideas that are popular in the human resource management literature. The first, the psychological contract, is supported by research for the Chartered Institute of Personnel and Development (CIPD, 2003a, 2004). The other is engagement, a bit of a catch-all term for more complicated individual–organizational linkages, including identification, internalization, commitment and psychological ownership, though, as we shall see later, it does bring something extra to the party.

Finally, it almost goes without saying, how individuals behave at work is one of the major influences on reputations and brands. Such workplace behaviour depends on the outcomes of knowledge, skills and abilities – the human capital pool which, in turn, relies on organizational investment in knowledge stocks and knowledge flows. This is one of the key messages of the RBV and strategic human resource management (SHRM) (Wright *et al.*, 2001), which we shall also touch on in this chapter and take up in Chapters 5 and 6. Let's begin by examining a case we researched with close colleagues to show how our organizing framework for this chapter (Figure 4.1) might be applied.

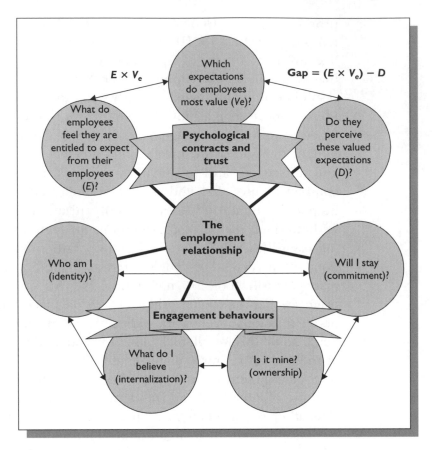

Figure 4.1
A framework for understanding the employment relationship.

Box 4.1 'Psychological contracts' among oil workers in the UK offshore drilling industry

The offshore drilling industry

In 1999 the industry comprised 14 companies employing some 6000 men and a limited number of women in onshore and offshore operations. The work of the offshore drilling employees is usually depicted as hazardous, involving long hours in shifts and working away from home. The majority of employees on the drilling rigs are semi-skilled roustabouts, supervisors and drilling technicians and technologists, most of whom have worked in the industry for a number of years. Despite the contracting nature of employment conditions, some employers and many employees tend to treat the industry as a source of a traditional career rather than as a pure wage-for-work relationship with limited job security and no career progression. Though mobility between companies was a feature of employment in the industry because of the contract nature of the work, many of the employers had an implicit policy of retaining good employees because of their personal knowledge of particular drilling rigs. Consequently, it was common practice in the industry to attempt to offer a degree of security during slack times by standing down men for a period on limited pay until new contracts became available. Such work protection practices, however, were not a feature of all companies, and this became a source of difference among employers, from the perspective of both employees and of clients, who were the oil 'majors' operating in the North Sea, including companies such as BP, Shell and Exxon. These client companies regarded a degree of employment continuity among the contractors' workforces as sufficiently important that they would sometimes 'foot the bill' to keep good workers on the books of drilling contractors, especially if a new contract was imminent. Traditionally, these workers had also been highly compensated in relation to comparable jobs onshore, though through time the differentials had been eroded to a point where recruitment had become difficult in 2000.

The UK offshore oil and gas industry as a whole had been traditionally hostile to unions and union representatives. As a consequence, in the drilling industry, unionization was actively discouraged and no company gave any form of recognition to the unions with members in the industry. In 1998, however, the UK government's White Paper on *Fairness at Work* was introduced with provisions to re-introduce the rights of unions to pursue recognition claims if they could be justified in terms of union membership.

The UK offshore drilling contractors, which operated drilling rigs on behalf of the oil and gas majors in the North Sea oil and gas fields, immediately saw themselves at risk to predatory unions because they had been subject to attempts by a hostile union called OILC to organize members on the drilling rigs. So, when the employers became aware of the union recognition provisions of the White Paper, they perceived the threat of OILC for disruption as 'mission critical', particularly if the union was able to recruit sufficient members and gain recognition under the legislation.

As a consequence, the drilling companies combined themselves into a consortium, with the help of consultants, to decide what their stance should be. The first step the consultants recommended was that they should undertake an attitude survey of all employees in the industry to assess their general perceptions of what they wanted from work, what they saw as the key obligations of their employers and whether these obligations were being met by their employers. The consultants also wanted the firms to understand the attitudes of workers to trade unions, so that they could advise the companies on how to proceed with union recognition. This survey involved all employees in the industry and achieved a relatively high response rate of more than 60%.

The employee survey phase as a means of intervention

The survey data provided a wealth of information on employee perceptions. Tables 4.1 and 4.2 provide a selection of these data, which were presented to the drilling contractors' HR managers.

Table 4.1

Selected data from the Employee Survey on key elements of the psychological contract.

(SCALE: 1 = strongly agree; 3 = neutral; 5 = strongly disagree)

(For the purposes of interpreting these mean average responses, you should treat any result lying outside the range 2.4 to 3.6 as statistically significant. Any figure lying within this range should be treated as similar to the mean average, given the sample size)

Question	Mean average response of all employees on a 5-point Likert Scale
As far as could be expected the company has provided me with a reasonably secure job	2.55
The company has provided me with fair pay for the work I do	3.06
The company has provided me with good career opportunities	2.94
The company has provided me with interesting work	2.54
The company has ensured my fair treatment by managers and supervisors	2.67
The company has helped me with the problems I have encountered outside work	3.14
The company always provides me with a safe working environment	2.33
The company provides me with good training for the job	2.43

Table 4.2
Selected data from the Employee Survey on the need for union representation
(SCALE: 1 = strongly agree; 3 = neutral; 5 = strongly disagree).

Question	Mean average response of all employees on a 5-point Likert Scale
Employee relations in this company would be improved by having an employee representative who could speak to management on our behalf	2.20
Management in this company usually consult employees on issues that affect them	3.01
Management in this company usually give employees plenty of opportunity to comment on proposed changes at work	3.16
Having an employee representative would generally be beneficial in securing fairer terms and conditions of employment	2.31
There is definite need for better representation in this company to give voice to employee wishes and grievances	2.18

Based on these data and other findings and forms of analysis from the
survey, the headline conclusions from the study, which were reported to
the HR managers and their senior managers, were as follows:

■ The standard predictors of why employees in non-union companies
  show little interest in joining unions are: (1) high levels of job satisfaction; (2) positive beliefs about existing communications, consultation
  and grievance-handling procedures; and (3) negative instrumental
  beliefs about the ability of unions to improve pay and conditions.
  From Tables 4.1 and 4.2, it could be seen that job satisfaction was not
  significantly high, and that positive beliefs about existing communications were not high. Furthermore, unions were seen positively as a
  means of providing a voice on key issues and, of lesser significance, in
  improving terms and conditions of employment.
■ Employees did not perceive that they were well managed, particularly
  in relation to supervisors treating people poorly and to perceptions of
  a lack of trust in supervisors to work in employees' best interests.
■ Employees were particularly interested in future employability, and
  the perception of a lack of career development by employees was

strongly associated with positive attitudes to unions as a means of representation and participation in decision-making.

■ The lack of interactional justice (perceptions of fair treatment by the company and the lack of trust in managers) and the lack of effective commitment (attitudes towards the companies) were associated with positive attitudes to unions as a means of representation and participation in decision-making.

■ Expectations of job security were relatively low and, at the time of the survey, were worsening.

Source: Adapted from Martin *et al.*, 2003

The psychological contract

The case in Box 4.1, on first reading, is not obviously about reputations and branding, but on closer examination says a great deal about the overall external and internal reputation (or lack of it) of an industry-based consortium of employers and the reputations of individual firms in the consortium for good human resource management and leadership – essential elements of an employer brand. It also contains a great deal of information about the importance of psychological contracts, employees' attachments to work and the importance they placed on skills and career development. Consequently, we want to use the case to introduce these ideas. First, however, we need to define what we mean by psychological contracts, look at how they are formed and how they are transformed.

Defining and forming psychological contracts

Psychological contracts and contracting could well be used as an organizing concept for this chapter as they touch on many dimensions of individual–organizational linkages. Nevertheless, we will not use the idea in this way, but in a more specific sense as follows. Psychological contacts describe the expectations and beliefs that employees hold about the mutual obligations and 'promises' between themselves and their organizations, such as expectations and promises about fair pay or career opportunities provided by their companies, or the amount of effort they might reasonably be expected to exercise in performing their work (Conway and Briner, 2005). Therefore, the psychological contract mirrors the explicit legal contract by focusing on the largely implicit and unwritten reciprocal obligations; though certain writers have included written 'promises' by employers, such as those evident in mission statements, for example, to treat people with dignity and fairness. Peter Herriot (2001) has provided a basic but useful definition of psychological contracts as:

> The perception of the two parties, employees and employer, of what their mutual obligations are to each other.

This definition needs some elaboration to tease out the key features of such contracts. To help us, we can draw on the insights into psychological contracts and the employment relationship provided by Paul Sparrow and Cary Cooper (2003), who have produced an excellent book dealing with this whole field. They have highlighted four key aspects of psychological contracts and how they come to be formed and changed:

- They are *subjective, unique and idiosyncratic*: (1) they are based on the subjective expectations and perceptions of employees (and employers); (2) every individual has his or her own interpretation of these expectations and perceptions; and (3) they vary from one person and organization to another. Therefore you can gain an insight into psychological contracts by questioning only one party to the relationship because the contract 'is in the eyes of the beholder'.

- They are *reciprocal*: they emerge in the context of a *specific* mutual employment relationship. As there are two parties to this relationship, they each have their own psychological contracts about the specific employment relationship (but not employment relationships in general).

- They are not objective 'facts', but are based on *beliefs and perceptions* held by individuals. However, because people act on their subjective perceptions, they are no less real in their consequences than if they *were* fact.

■ They arise from beliefs and perceptions of *obligations* that, in the case of employees, are what they believe they are entitled to as a consequence of perceived *promises*, either explicit or implicit, made by the employer (Conway and Briner, 2005). In that sense, a psychological contract is more than just a set of expectations that can arise in the absence of a promise. Only expectations relating to perceived promises are entitled to be considered as part of the psychological contract. Just what these promises look like in practice and how they arise are illustrated in Box 4.2. You can see how these promises relate to official communications of the organizational identity and to leadership and governance.

Box 4.2 'Promises' in the employment relationship that create obligations

'Promises' arising from spoken and written communications:

■ strategic documents, employer commitments to certain courses of action, mission and values statements, agreements, pledges, speeches

■ corporate brand values, ethics statements and social responsibility policies, e.g. the kinds of statements on social responsibility and safety made by companies such as BP and Shell, the client companies of the offshore drilling contractors

■ employer branding/employer of choice policies (see Chapter 6)

■ financial statements or employer reporting statements

■ statements made on application forms, etc., by employees, and employers' advertisements, websites, etc., e.g. GE's ecoimagination, the drilling contractors' promotional materials to employees

'Promises' arising out of behaviour and actions of leaders and managers:

■ observations of senior leadership, management or employee actions, e.g. how managers and employees act in relation to one another in treating each other with respect (see Box 4.1 for the perceptions of how employees saw management style)

■ interactions with senior leaders, managers or employee representatives, such as how recruiters behave during the interview process, or as in the Offshore drilling case in Box 4.1, custom and practice on standing men down during slack periods, or retaining people who had been 'good employees' in the past

Breach and violation of psychological contracts

Like legal contracts, psychological contracts can be breached or violated if employees feel that the significant terms have been broken, or that perceived obligations are unmet. The distinction between breach and violation is largely one of degree; breaches are treated as minor, usually short term and less significant, whereas violations are seen as more serious, more long term and significant in terms of outcomes. As an example, you might want to reflect for a moment on whether employees in our off-shore drilling industry survey saw elements of their psychological contracts with the companies as met, breached or violated, and what actions might help repair any damage.

It is to the violation of psychological contracts that many researchers attribute major breakdowns in employee relations, or failures in organizational change programmes. For example, violation of psychological contracts has been used to explain

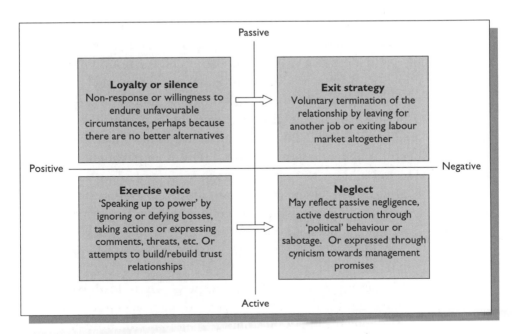

Figure 4.2
Range of employee responses to psychological contract violation (based on Turnley and Feldman, 1998; Sutton, 2002, and others).

strike action and rises in absenteeism and employee turnover; at the same time, violation has been used to explain rising levels of cynicism about never-ending 'programmes' of organizational change and lack of trust in managers to 'walk the talk' (Pate *et al.*, 2000).

One way of thinking about employee responses to contract violation is to distinguish between active and passive 'actions' on the one hand and positive and negative 'actions' on the other (see Figure 4.2). Note how apparent loyalty or silence by employees may occur as a response to management actions that breach, or even violate, expectations regarding promises. In one sense, this can be treated as a positive response to changes managers may make in the psychological contract because they have built up a store of trust and a reputation for integrity in the past. But it may also be seen as negative because employees endure what they perceive as unfair treatment as they are unable to foresee alternatives to their current employment. When the employment situation changes, however, they are very likely to adopt an exit strategy if the breaches continue, as frequently happened in the North Sea offshore drilling industry. A further implication of this framework is that managers should do all they can to encourage employees to 'speak up to power', rather than suppress discontent. Robert Sutton (2001) in an excellent account of 'weird ideas that really work' promoted the notion that innovating organizations should hire people that make them feel uncomfortable and encourage others to ignore and defy their superiors. By encouraging such actions, managers are not only able to encourage innovation but can rebuild trust where it has been broken, an essential component of employment relations. This rebuilding of trust through sharing control with employee representatives is one of the main justifications for encouraging new forms of partnership agreements with trade unions. One of the consequences of not doing so is the risk of employees adopting a negative, 'neglect' strategy, or even resorting to sabotage (Pfeffer, 2005).

Predicting why and what happens when leadership and management actions that, through design, accident or miscalculation, lead to breaches being treated as violations has been studied by Conway and Briner (2002) and others (Martin *et al.*, 1998). They point to four characteristics of perceived promises that can have a major impact on employee responses to breach or violation. They are:

- the degree of explicitness of a perceived promise – the more explicit the promise, e.g. communicating in mission statements, 'people are our most important asset'; the greater the sense of injustice and the more active – positively or negatively – the employee response
- attributions of personal responsibility for contract breach or violation – the more personally responsible a leadership team or individual managers' reputations are held to be for the perceived breach, the more intense will be employees' reactions, especially in trusting them to act in employees' best interests in the future
- the unexpectedness or infrequency of the breach – the more unexpected or infrequent the breach/violation (a break with past behaviour), the more intense or active the response will be from employees; again this relates to what we learned about expectations of leadership in Chapter 3 in the cases of HP and Agilent, and Hurricane Katrina
- the degree of importance the party attaches to the goal or relationship breached – the greater the attachment to the goal/relationship that is breached, the more likely it will be treated as a significant violation and, hence, provoke a negative response, for example the Hurricane Katrina case.

Types of psychological contract

Though psychological contracts are individual in nature, resulting in as many contracts in an organization as there are employees, psychologists have tried to classify some of their more general features. Three such classifications have emerged in the extensive research in this area (e.g. Rousseau, 1995; Thompson and Bunderson, 2003). These are set out in Table 4.3 and reflect changes taking place in organizations and the wider economy.

During the 1990s in the USA, it was argued that the traditional, relational contracts that many, mostly white-collar, employees

Table 4.3

Different types of psychological contracts.

Dimension	Transactional	Relational	Ideological
Organizational obligations	Degree of job security, safe work and a 'fair day's pay'	To provide a career with training and education, promotion opportunities, interesting work and long term employment prospects	Demonstrate credible commitment to a valued cause
Individual obligations	'A fair day's work'	Go beyond contract by doing excellent work and demonstrating high commitment and identification with organization	Participate fully in the organizational mission/cause by being a good organizational and societal citizen
Beneficiary	Self	Mutual interest between self and organization	The organization and employee share same passion/cause
Based on beliefs about human nature, which are:	Self-interested, instrumental worker who works for money	Socialized employee, who is collectively oriented and finds satisfaction in work itself	Principled involvement
Characteristics of violation	Black and white	Grey areas which are negotiable	Grey (negotiable) but also non-negotiable, moral 'hot-buttons'
Typical response to violation	Leave organization	Withdraw commitment and revert to a transactional exchange	Principled organizational dissent
Basis of attachment to work and organizations	Compliance and focus on the job	Identification with organization and career	Work as a calling

Source: Based on Thompson and Bunderson, 2003, p. 575

held with their employers – based on commitment in return for job security and career prospects – could no longer be sustained because of increased global competition. Consequently, it was suggested that this traditional, relational contract was being replaced by a more transactional contract; this time, however, one with a slight twist on the model highlighted in Table 4.3. Organizations recognized that they could no longer offer stable employment to all, nor could they guarantee careers to all, even though they wished to retain the benefits of relational contracting from employees working 'beyond contract' and showing high levels of commitment and identification as long as they remained in employment. As a result, the notion of *employability* came into common usage: employers sought temporary commitment from employees as long as they remained in the job, but offered in return the opportunity to employees for self-development and to hone their skills on interesting and demanding projects. This employment proposition, which was a form of 'come and work for us, learn and do enjoyable work', was attractive to many mobile, knowledge-based employees in high-tech, computing and software development, and in the creative industries, such as arts, media, science and some managerial jobs, because it made them more employable for their next job (Cappelli, 1999; Florida, 2002). In effect, their career paths became boundaryless, because they moved in and out of organizations and even occupations. This notion of employability, however, was much less widespread than much of the literature would have had you believe, especially outside the 'new economy' organizations based in the American high-tech conurbations of the San Jose Valley, Cambridge and Raleigh–Durham, and the research-based, 'creative' cities, such as San Francisco, Boston, Austin, San Diego, Seattle and Minneapolis. Nevertheless, according to the excellent book by Richard Florida (2005) on the 'Flight of the Creative Class', there is reason to believe that these new careers are likely to be realized in the near future in the conurbations of countries such as Finland, Sweden, the UK, France, Germany, India and others noted for their high-tech and creative centres, perhaps at the expense of the aforementioned American regions.

Many organizations, however, are seeking through their reputations and branding statements to go beyond even relational contracts and create ideological relationships with individual employees. Most mission-driven organizations aim to captivate employees by having them believe that they are working for a greater or higher-level purpose, even in those basic industries such as retailing. For example, Wal-Mart, the world's largest retailer, tries to engage employees by convincing them that they have the opportunity to 'give ordinary folks the chance to buy the same things as rich people'. Tesco, which we examine in Chapter 6, is another, albeit with a more sophisticated, segmented approach to HR. However, it should be obvious to most readers that ideological contracts are more likely to be found amongst higher-level professionals in occupations with a sense of vocation, such as medicine, teaching, religion and even politics, or in voluntary organizations such as Save the Children or Cancer Research.

The nature of psychological contracts

From an HR manager's point of view it is clearly useful to gain insights into employee perceptions of perceived promises because they have extremely important consequences for understanding the effectiveness of people management strategies and management actions. Table 4.4 shows the relationship between

Table 4.4
Inputs, content and outputs of the psychological contract.

Key factors that shape psychological contracts	The content of psychological contracts	Key outcomes
Employee characteristics and expectations of perceived and important 'promises' ⇨	Perceptions of fair treatment by the organization ⇨	Employee behaviour and attitudes, including identification with work and the organization, employee commitment, employee citizenship behaviour ('going the extra mile')
Organizational characteristics	Trust in management to do the best for employees	⇕
The employment value proposition and HR policies and practices on recruitment, career development, training, rewards, employment security, etc	The extent to which employees perceive to have been promised is actually delivered	Employee performance, including work effort, absenteeism, leaving, etc

Source: Based on Martin *et al.*, 1998; Guest and Conway, 2002; CIPD (2003a)

what some researchers have found to be the important factors that shape psychological contracts, the key components or content of psychological contracts themselves and positive and negative outcomes associated with the way in which psychological contracts are managed.

What most employees appear to expect from employers and what they regard as the most important employer obligations have been identified by a number of researchers (see Herriot *et al.*, 1997; Sparrow and Cooper, 2003; CIPD, 2004). These items are often used in surveys to determine the health of psychological contracts in organizations (Box 4.3).

Box 4.3   Items commonly used to measure the 'content' of psychological contracts

- To provide an adequate procedure for induction into the job and training to make people more effective and safe
- To ensure that the procedures for selection, appraisal, promotion and layoffs are fair
- To provide justice, fairness and consistency in the application of important rules and on discipline and dismissal
- To provide equitable treatment on pay and rewards in relation to market circumstances and to be fair in the allocation of non-pay benefits to individuals and groups
- To provide interesting work where possible
- To provide fair pay for taking on responsibility in the job
- To provide career development and support for employees to learn new skills
- To allow people reasonable time off and flexibility to meet family and personal needs
- To consult and communicate effectively on matters affecting employees
- To allow employees reasonable autonomy in how they *do* their jobs
- To act in a personally supportive way to employees
- To recognize loyalty and reward special contributions
- To provide a safe and friendly work environment
- To do what they can to provide employment security
- For managers to act in such a manner that they keep promises and commitments and do their best for employees

Employers, on the other hand, seem to expect that employees will work extra hours when needed, take on work outside their responsibilities when circumstances dictate, look for better ways of undertaking the job and suggest improvements, be flexible, save costs and adapt to changes in the work environment.

Psychological contracts and trust

Permeating nearly all discussions of psychological contracts is the notion of trust (Rousseau, 1995; Herriot, 2001; Pate *et al.*, 2003), and ours is no different. Trust is one of those ideas that are progressively accepted as a key to unlocking good employment relations and organizational design, especially in the light of developments in new, networked forms of organization (see Chapter 9). Indeed, in Table 4.4, we have defined it in terms of the strength of trust that an employee has in management to 'do the best for employees', though this is a rather circular and weak definition. So, in line with our view that definitions are important, let's look at trust for a moment to tease out its essential features.

One of the best attempts to provide a formal definition sets out four themes of how trust is viewed and used, all of which have important practical implications for psychological contracting and engaging employees (Bhattacharya *et al.*, 1998). Drawing on earlier views of trust as involving the expectations we hold about managers' or leaders' motives when placed in risky situations, they set out the following characteristics:

- Trust becomes an issue in employment relationships in *uncertain* and *risk-laden situations*, for example, where employees are subject to capricious leaders, during downturns in economic activity, or where there are no rules regarding governance or action.
- Trust is based on a *reasonable expectation* of organizations providing something important to employees since they need some idea of how much they can trust

managers to deliver what is important, for example, the content of items in the psychological contract in Box 4.3 such as career development.

■ Trusting someone must involve an *important expectation*, as we have already made clear in our approach to psychological contracts. Employees have to value what is being promised or (not) delivered. We also have to be able to account for the *strength of that expectation*, in the sense that we can say that in approximately 90% of similar situations, employees in a company might reasonably expect managers to deliver what has been promised.

■ Finally, to trust and be able to trust is *good*: we use it in the positive sense that we can trust our organizations to deliver, not in the negative sense that 'HR managers can always be trusted to foul up around here'.

Measuring and managing psychological contracts

The implications of these features of trust combined with other elements of psychological contracting should be relatively clear. If we accept the points raised by the previous discussion, managing the individual–organizational relationship through effective psychological contracting requires HR to provide answers to the three questions, and regularly measure how well the organization has addressed all or some of the commonly used content items of psychological contracts (Box 4.3). Consequently, one of our main points in this book is that we believe that most organizations would want to know, or, indeed, need to know: (a) what individual employees feel they are entitled to expect from their employers (E) arising from promises made to them; (b) relatively speaking, the rating of these expectations in terms of their importance/value to individual employees (Ve); and (c), whether they see these values expectations being delivered (D). In simple algebraic terms, HR should attempt to measure the gap between what employees perceive being delivered against what they feel they are entitled to expect, weighted by their importance/value to employees.

$$\text{The psychological contract gap} = (E \times Ve) - D$$

We regard this weighting element to be important because it is of little use to employees or employers to have expectations satisfied that are not important to them, a topic we will return to in Chapters 5 and 6 when discussing workforce segmentation. Some organizations spend a great deal of wasted time and effort in meeting or even over-delivering on employee expectations that are not particularly valuable to certain individuals or groups, while under-delivering on ones that are. The consequences, as Huselid *et al.* (2005) have pointed out, can be very important for strategy execution, as we have discussed when examining the employability thesis.

Engaging employees

We will look at engagement in its more specific sense in the last part of this chapter; first, however, we want to focus on the notion of engagement in a more general sense (see Figure 4.1). From our perspective, employee engagement and its associated behaviours in an organization depend on four key processes:

- individual identification and identities (who am I?)
- internalization (what do I believe?)
- psychological ownership (is it mine?), and
- commitment (will I stay?).

These four components of individual–organizational relationships have been the subject of intense research and speculation, and are at the core of modern human resource management. As Sparrow and Cooper (2003) have argued, the *individualization of the employment relationship* has been one of the most important developments of recent times among organizations in most developed countries, especially where the influence of trade unions has decreased and the use of non-standard forms of employment contracts has increased. Such developments towards individualization can be seen in two ways. On the one hand, some writers and critics have highlighted the negative side by pointing out how modern nation-states and large organizations have rejected their responsibilities for providing employment security and passed the onus on to individuals to make themselves employable through calls for self-development and displays of flexibility. On the other hand, proponents of these changes have argued that many employees are increasingly motivated by the need for autonomy, actively seeking more career flexibility and the opportunities to follow rather different, boundaryless career and work patterns from those of their predecessors, a point discussed in the previous section. Many such individuals tend to work in knowledge-intensive and creative occupations and organizations, business and financial consultants, professional engineers, entertainment, education and healthcare. Because these people have such different orientations to work and because they tend to be in short supply, organizations and nations increasingly find themselves competing for talent and having to devise new ways of managing them (Davenport, 2005; Florida, 2005).

Measuring and managing identification, commitment, psychological ownership and internalization

In our attempt to review this complicated field of individual–organizational linkages, we have come across a plethora of terms associated with engagement, including those we discuss below and others, such as organizational citizenship, culture, climate and so on. The volume of words, academic articles and books spilled out on these topics over the past thirty or so years would stun the average lay reader, as would the complex and often bitter arguments that different camps prosecute (Henry Kissinger, a well-known, former US Secretary of State, once opined that academic arguments were so bitter because they had so little to argue about). For HR managers, however, it is important they understand the differences between these terms since many employee surveys conducted by 'blue-chip' organizations fail to distinguish between them, or, even worse, confuse them. As a consequence, HR managers often have to rely on measures for A (e.g. commitment) while hoping for B (e.g. organizational identification).

Individual identities, identification and internalization

We have made the point repeatedly in the past few chapters that organizational identity and individual identities, while linked through the process of identification, are not the same thing; nor can we assume that individuals will necessarily identify with the organization's values, even if they understand why they are necessary and form part of the wider interests of everyone in the organization. So, managing change at the organizational level does not mean changes will occur in the self-concepts of individual employees, though this may be what organizations are really attempting to achieve. Most of us will recognize this in the tensions of our own careers, in achieving a balance between self interest and the interest of others, which is often played out in the work–life balance issues, e.g. will I write this book or spend more quality time with my children? If you don't recognize it in your own careers, you will see it frequently exhibited in the political behaviour of others in leadership and management positions.

The link between individual identity and identification with organizations is best explained by social identity theory (SIT) and the related notion of self-categorization (Ashforth and Mael, 1989; Dutton *et al.*, 1994; Hatch and Schultz, 2004). Though there are variations on the theme, SIT sees the individual and organization as potentially linked through a process something like the following:

1   Individuals develop a **personal identity**, which is made up from idiosyncratic personal features, including personality traits, physical features, abilities and interests, e.g. extroverted, physically fit, soccer player, often with few other interests or abilities, except a desire for

celebrity status (take your pick from a number who appear on British television!). A key component of personal identity is a need to preserve or enhance self-esteem, which is often equated with a healthy or unhealthy degree of narcissism (Brown, 1997).

2   Individuals begin to develop a **social identity**, the first stage of which is to *self-categorize* the different, salient groups that they wish or do not wish to belong to, e.g. let's say in the case of one of us, our understanding of the categories of man, father, academic, HR practitioner, Scotsman, etc. Self-categorization involves a process of having knowledge of these reference groups and understanding something of their values.

3   Personal identity and self-categorization interact to begin to form a **self-concept**, a self-definition and understanding about oneself that is continuously tested out by rounds of impression management. This self-concept is conditioned by the likely and actual reactions of salient others or groups they aspire to identify with (in-groups) to enhance their self-esteem. A self-concept is also formed in relation to groups the person does not wish to identify with (out-groups). To continue with our soccer player example, their in-groups might be the pop world, media celebrities and even (usually self-made) business people and politicians with an eye for the main chance (increasingly such in-groups are seen to hang out together as their world blurs into one of celebrity); out-groups might be political activists or intellectuals. In essence, this is a theory about oneself, involving actual or imagined agreement about what you are like (Scott and Lane, 2000).

4   **Social identification** occurs when an individual's self-concept is seen to be at one with, or belonging to, a particular social group one aspires to, i.e. by psychologically accepting the values and norms of the group as an integral part of themselves. This can occur either symbolically (e.g. dressing like an academic, or flying a Scottish flag, which, incidentally, neither of us do) or actually becoming one (e.g. prioritizing the academic, then the HR professional identity in the case of one of

us, and reversing that prioritization in the case of the other).

This process helps answer the question 'Who am I?'. For those of us with an interest in talent management, SIT provides one of the best ways of forecasting whether someone will fit the organization and be able to become an effective performer in it. Projections about a recruit's 'future self-concept' have been shown to be one of the best predictors of what people will eventually do for a living (Herriot, 2001). Note, we have not said anything as yet about individuals incorporating a corporate, organizational identity into their self-concept (see Box 4.4), which is why we have emphasized the distinction between individual and organizational identities and suggested the latter is not just the sum of the former, though this process does imply a possible connection.

Box 4.4   Self-disclosure, identity and (lack of) organizational identification

To continue in the spirit of self-disclosure (but, hopefully, not self-aggrandizement) and, in the process, learning about yourself through writing (Clegg *et al.*, 2005; Grey, 2005), let's use one of us as an illustration (readers and students often tell us it is a help to provide a personality behind the words). He is a full-time business school academic, who was by no means an extrovert but had a healthy(?) need for self-esteem, and whose early interests and abilities lay in understanding people and business studies, and competitive sports, e.g. football and athletics.

His career 'anchors', those underlying features that have shaped his work life (at least according to assessment guides) are the need for autonomy, developing expertise and being entrepreneurial/creative. After trying early, failed, 'careers' in football and art (a little, but not sufficient, talent/motivation for both), he did a degree in business because it was the only programme available in the vicinity that taught applied social sciences in which he had developed an interest. Following graduation, he became involved in personnel management, but soon began to think about an academic career because of his, rather romantic, view of academics in higher education, and in business schools in particular (since he had studied in one as an undergraduate, which helped him self-categorize what it meant to be an academic, and had a high regard for some of the, rather bohemian, people who taught him).

With the passing of time and other degrees, he progressively came to value the independence and intellectual aspects of academic life, and sought through research, teaching and writing the esteem of his professional colleagues, which is institutionalized in the UK by the peer-reviewed Research Assessment Exercise (your work is judged by peers in relation to everyone else's to help provide your institution – and, indirectly, you – with a score). The idea that he could also do something useful to help managers and employees work together to make the Scottish economy more effective also began to figure progressively in his referents (although English by origin, he had come to identify himself as a Scot, based on what he understands an educated Scot to be, and identify with the economic and social development of Scotland). All along, he had continued to identify himself with the HR profession because he valued what reflective, influential HR practitioners and consultants could do to improve industrial and economic life. Note, we have not said anything about him identifying with a particular university or organization; indeed, his current portfolio career, which involves him in teaching in a number of different ones in various parts of the world (exporting people and ideas is what Scotland seems to do best) and consulting for different companies, suggest that a single organizational affiliation is not something that he would feel at one with. Besides, he had already spent 23 years with one university, which he outgrew and it outgrew him.

You might say that this is his autobiographical image; others will author his biographical reputation(s), including his wife, kids and mother-in-law in due course, as he struggles to cope with other aspects of his identity.

This attempted self-disclosure is not mere self-indulgence (though there may be a degree of (healthy?) narcissistic rationalization) but an example of what Denise Rousseau (1995) terms an idiosyncratic career and what Richard Florida (2002, 2005) would see as an increasingly important component of the 'creative class'. Increasingly, organizations are faced with managing such people, which is one of the most difficult challenges they face, and one that requires quite different solutions to conventional 'talent' management, as we shall see in the next chapter.

There are several rather subtle, but important, implications that emerge from this version of social identities. The first is that to identify with an organization does not require someone to expend effort in doing so; a person only needs to see themselves as 'psychologically intertwined' with the organization (Ashforth and Mael, 1989). So organizationally focused behaviour and loyalty (or affective commitment) are rather different ideas and, according to different theories, are either causes or consequences of identification. We will return to this point when discussing the contribution of engagement to understanding individual–organizational linkages. The second is to emphasize that this is a relative process. We tend to highlight the similarities between our own self-identity and those of the group we aspire to relate or belong to, and play up the distinctiveness between ourselves and those groups that don't fit in with our self-identity (Sparrow and Cooper, 2003). So, for example, this may be the reason many people do not define themselves as belonging to their organization; it also fits into our earlier analysis of cosmopolitans and locals. Third, the question 'Who am I?' is not the same as 'What do I believe?'. This latter question is addressed by the process of internalization.

Internalization is the process of incorporating the goals and values of an organization into one's identity or 'as part of themselves' (Mael and Ashforth, 1992; Dutton *et al.*, 1994; Pierce *et al.*, 2001). Getting employees to internalize the organization's identity is what most organizations seem to be striving for, reflecting the idea of ideological psychological contracting cited earlier and the oneness between individual and social identity in the original formulation of SIT. It reflects employees' motivations to be on the side of right and not wrong – there can be few shades of grey here – and is based on a need to believe in the virtues of the organization. The results are pride in membership and positive inclinations to the organization and its leadership (Reade, 2001), as well as behaviours such as remaining with the organization and performing 'beyond contract'.

Some of the original work on internalization in relation to organizational identities was carried out on alumni of US universities, a number of whom, you might expect, have fully internalized the values of their alma mater, and have put their hands in their pockets to ever-increasing degrees to make endowments of the size that universities in other countries can only dream of. There are cynics among us, however, who would question the degree of internalization and suggest that such giving may be attributable, in certain cases, to the kinds of unhealthy narcissism, ego-defensive and self-aggrandizing motivations and behaviours associated with 'semi-detached' leadership (Brown, 1997) or, more prosaically, tax breaks. Part of the problem with these ideas is that you cannot really look into someone's head for motives; you can only examine what they do and what they say, which is why questionnaires are often a poor test of internalization.

You may have guessed that there is an important qualification in what you have read: social identification and internalization are changeable over the course of employment and subject to constant negotiation and re-negotiation. The identification process is a continuous round of iterations, confirmation and disconfirmation of self-identity, which is often associated with re-inventing one's career. The idea of an increasingly boundaryless career, in which employees are believed to not only move in and out of organizations but also occupations during their employment history, often having second and third careers, is one illustration of these processes (Arthur *et al.*, 1999). Both of us, for example, have had three careers and three professional identities, sometimes simultaneously, as HR practitioners, academics and consultants. These three identities can lead to tensions and, at various times in our careers we have emphasized one more than the other in the process of our career re-inventions.

The social identification and internalization processes are also dependent on continuous positive evaluation of the organization's image by its employees; such an evaluation also takes into account what employees believe important others (e.g. customers, close friends, etc.) think about its image. This last element is one of the most important features of how images are incorporated internally (Dutton *et al.*, 1994). Finally, how leaders behave in their governance and day-to-day actions can influence this continued identification enormously; we are now witnessing calls for more and better feedback evaluations of individual and collective leadership at the boardroom level (Goffee and Jones, 2005). This is a role in which HR can play an important part, as we shall discuss in the final chapter of this book.

Psychological ownership

Jon Pierce and colleagues (2001) have argued that, although identification and internalization are important constructs for understanding the relationships and attachments between individuals and their organizations, neither is a complete nor even necessary explanation of one of the most important individual–organizational connections, namely psychological ownership. They define this idea as follows:

> As a state of the mind, psychological ownership ... is that state in which individuals feel as though the target of ownership (material or immaterial in nature) or a piece of it is 'theirs' (i.e., 'It is MINE!'). The core of psychological ownership is the feeling of possessiveness and of being psychologically tied to an object. (Pierce *et al.*, 2001, p. 299)

Rather slickly, they contend that 'mine' is a small word, but one with enormous consequences for organizations. Ownership, they argue, arises because people have a built-in need to possess, or because it satisfies certain human motives, which are either socially derived or genetic. These include:

- the need to **control** our lives; ownership confers on us certain rights and abilities to shape our work environment so that we can become more effective – for example, the degree to which we can determine our working times and places through flexible working
- **self-identity**, which is formed partly through our interactions with what we possess, and our reflections on what they mean – for example, company cars and the way we personalize our computer equipment
- the need to have a **place**, or 'home', that we can call our own, which is not only a physical but also a psychological space. For example, employees not only seek office or work spaces they can call their own, but also look for 'soul mates' they can metaphorically set up a 'home' with at work. This is an argument against the current fashion for saving costs and forcing communications through open-plan offices and 'hot-desking'.

Ownership is achieved by three 'routes', involving:

- having a strong degree of control of the object of our ownership, such as the job or the organization and its performance
- coming to know the object of our ownership intimately by having a 'living' relationship with it, for example the metaphorical gardener who comes to feel the garden belongs to him/her after a certain time of working in it
- investing the self into the object of our ownership. Through time, as we expend effort into shaping, creating or making something, we feel that we come to own what we have shaped, created or made, such as machines, ideas and even people, e.g. our projects, protégés and apprentices.

The consequences of psychological ownership are to create among employees a set of perceived rights and responsibilities that help explain why individuals promote and resist change. So, change that is self-initiated by employees who have high levels of psychological ownership is more likely to be promoted and accepted because it enhances feelings of self-efficacy and control. Likewise, imposed change is likely to be resisted because it diminishes feelings of self-efficacy and self-control. This concept is extremely important in understanding the success or otherwise of stock or share ownership in organizations, often given as a form of reward to individuals and as a way of creating organizational identification. As Sparrow and Cooper (2003) point out, providing employees with share or stock options without building in the routes to psychological ownership will not produce the hoped-for benefits in terms of greater organizational identification and motivated behaviour.

Finally, however, it is also worth noting that high levels of psychological ownership can also create pathological responses among those people who become separated from the objects of their ownership. For example, many years ago one of us worked as a personnel manager in a construction company. Some senior managers in that company proposed laying-off a large number of young electricians who had spent many months installing electrical wiring in a new and high profile building, on which many of these apprentice electricians were naturally proud to have worked. On hearing of the proposed layoff, in a deliberate act of sabotage these apprentices systematically removed all the cabling and equipment they had installed. Pfeffer (2005) argued that this response to leadership was becoming more common in the USA.

Commitment

In our case on the North Sea oil industry (Box 4.1), our measures of employees' relationships with their organization focused mainly on commitment, a term that is used to refer to a number of different attachments to work, including commitment to work itself, to specific jobs, to a union or workgroup, to a career or professional calling, or to the employing organization(s). It is the last of these that has received most attention because it has promised much in measuring, a little like engagement, nearly all important aspects of the employment relationship and desired organizational outcomes, such as loyalty, 'going the extra mile' (organizational citizenship behaviour), low absenteeism and good performance. However, for the same reason we criticized engagement as a rather blunt instrument, commitment (at least some versions of it) also falls into that category (Reade, 2001). This is the reason we prefer to use the additional measures of psychological contracts, identification, internalization and ownership.

Organizational commitment is sometimes thought to have three components, which are set out in Box 4.5. An individual's commitment can be made up of one or more of these types of commitment, and usually a composite measure of all three is provided in general surveys.

Box 4.5   Three types of organizational commitment

■ **Affective (or attitudinal) commitment**, which is based on a willing acceptance of the organization's goals and an identification or emotional attachment with the organization and its values. Measures include items like 'I really feel as if this organization's problems are my problems.'

- **Continuance commitment**, which refers to the extent to which employees are bound to the organization in terms of their intention to remain or leave. This may result from a weighing up of the costs and benefits of staying or leaving, such as perceptions of alternative jobs, or the financial hardship associated with leaving. Measures include items like '*I would continue to work for this organization even though I received a better offer from another employer.*'
- **Normative commitment**, which refers to an individual's perceptions of obligation or loyalty to the organization. Measures include items like '*This organization deserves my loyalty.*'

Source: Based on Meyer and Allen, 1991

There are several problems, however, with the notion of organizational commitment that render it a less useful concept in describing the strength of the relationship between individuals and their organization, especially in contemporary contexts (Swailes, 2002). First, it is used as both an explanation and an outcome of individual–organizational linkages. Since it aggregates a number of different ideas, it is not easy to develop a sound explanation of what may cause commitment (Reade, 2001). As an illustration, what may cause people to remain with an organization (continuance commitment) may be different from what causes people to identify with it or be loyal to it, e.g. lack of opportunities elsewhere. Second, the notion that employees may be committed to only one organization, especially in the light of recent changes towards networking in organizations and in the light of boundaryless careers discussed earlier, may be becoming outmoded. Third, the goals and values of a large organization are likely to vary from one part to another, such as in those organizations that have strong lines of business brands, and rejection of one specific value (or line of business brand) may coexist with the acceptance of other values (or other lines of business). This could be the case, for example, with organizations that have ethically dubious products such as cigarettes as part of their portfolio.

Perhaps more than anything, however, the reason to be a little wary of the concept of commitment is its promised relationship with desirable organizational outcomes. Although high levels of continuance commitment have been shown to be related to lower labour turnover and absence, and affective commitment has been shown to be associated with job performance, the links between organizational commitment as a whole and performance are really quite weak (Sparrow and Cooper, 2003). Also given the changes in the nature of employment discussed in the previous paragraph and throughout this course, even this weak relationship may diminish over time. So, we prefer to define and use commitment as the reasons underlying people's wish to remain with an organization (Pierce *et al.*, 2001).

Bringing them altogether

Pierce *et al.* have compared and contrasted the four concepts of commitment, identification, internalization and ownership, the outcomes of which are highly relevant to managers who hope to manage psychological contracts and individuals' attachment to their organizations. We have adapted their table to highlight the most important practical implications (see Table 4.5).

Engagement and supportive behaviours

As Table 4.5 shows, identification, internalization, ownership and commitment are really causes of what employers are usually looking for, which are competent and relevant behaviours that translate these emotions, attitudes and understandings into *action*, e.g. satisfying customers, sharing knowledge and increased effort. Over the past few years, HR professionals and consultants have begun to use the concept of employee engagement as a way of adapting these well-known psychological concepts to the practical concerns of aligning HR with the business agenda. Like any other immature idea that promises a lot to managers, engagement has caused some controversy over what it means and, as we have shown in our discussion of commitment, fuses a number of different ideas together, not always successfully. Until recently, there has been very little academic research on this largely consultancy-driven

Table 4.5

The differences between commitment, identification and psychological ownership.

Criteria for distinctiveness	Organizational commitment	Organizational identification	Internalization	Psychological ownership
Core proposition or concept	Desire to remain with organization	Use of organization's identity to define oneself	Oneness with the organization's goals and values	Possession of the 'organization', job or area of work
Questions answered for individuals	Should I remain?	Who am I?	What do I believe?	What is mine?
Motivational bases	Security Belongingness Beliefs and values	Attraction Affiliation Self-esteem	Need to distinguish between right and wrong Moral and ethical	Control Self-identity Need for place
How it develops	Decision to remain with organization Self Affiliation	Incorporating organizational values into self Affiliation Emulating organizational characteristics	Integration of organization's values and goals	Active imposition/investment of self on organization
Main consequences for practitioners from research findings	Organizational citizenship behaviour ('going the extra mile') Intention to leave or remain Attendance and absenteeism	Support for organizational values and participation in its activities Intention to remain Frustration/stress Alienation Lack of integration into organizational values/culture	Organizational citizenship behaviour Intention to leave or remain Engagement behaviours	Development of employee rights and responsibilities Promotion of/resistance to change Frustration, alienation and sabotage Integration of employees with work Organizational citizenship behaviours

Source: Adapted from Pierce et al., 2001, p. 306

concept, perhaps because it overlaps with other, more established ideas in the psychological and management literature, such as the ones we have already discussed and others like organizational climate and citizenship. Given that it has caught the imagination of practitioners, however, it is worth examining to see what it can offer us in terms of a more complete picture of the identity–image relationship and its links to reputations, brands and performance outcomes.

To make our position clear on this issue, our view is that engagement, or certain versions of it, is helpful because it offers an insight beyond emotions and attitudes such as those typically measured by conventional surveys. There are two reasons for this judgement, both identified by Robinson, Perryman and Hayday (2004) in their UK-based Institute of Employment Studies report. First, it invokes the idea of specific behaviours associated with identification, internalization and commitment that demonstrate business awareness and a willingness to promote the interests of the business. Second, like psychological contracts, it invokes the idea of a two-way employment relationship; engagement does not occur in a managerial vacuum, employers have to work at engaging employees just as employees have to work at being engaged.

Like most of the models we've discussed in the previous two chapters, the justification for engagement lies in one version or another of the people–performance link, or even directly in the service–profit chain. A close examination of the various consulting tools and the ideas that underpin them reveals some simple but powerful messages that are increasingly supported by their own research or by those independent academics who have been given access to their data. Towers Perrin, one of the major HR consultancy organizations, is a good example, with its linkage framework showing how engagement relates to business performance (see Figure 4.3).

Gallup Consulting, another major player in promoting engagement, has developed the Gallup Path, tracing a causal link between: (1) the identification of employee strengths; (2) the right fit between the person and the job; (3) great managers; (4) engaged employees; (5) engaged customers; (6) sustainable growth; (7) real profit increase; and (8) stock increases. Based on many years of survey research undertaken for companies

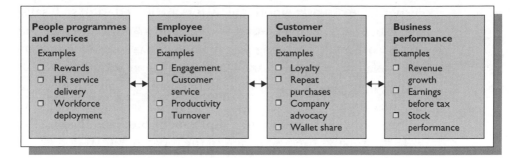

Figure 4.3
The Towers Perrin Linkage Framework (reprinted by permission from Towers Perrin).

throughout the world, they have shown a plausible connection between improvements in the first five of these and improvements in the last three. This connection has been supported by US academic researchers using the Gallup data; they found that aspects of well-being at work, including job satisfaction but especially 'engaged employees, on average, do a better job of keeping employees, satisfying customers, and being financially productive and profitable' (Harter *et al.*, 2002, p. 16). It should be noted, however, that these researchers were a little more circumspect about the lines and direction of causality and the role that might play in this relationship.

Defining engagement

Various consultancy companies and writers on this subject define engagement in different ways, as the preceding discussion has implied. For example, Harter *et al.*'s (2002) more academic approach sees engagement as an element of a broader category of ideas known as well-being at work, which embraces emotional and cognitive (knowledge acquisition) elements. They view engagement as a driver of intermediate outcomes such as job satisfaction, commitment, fulfilment, caring and positive behaviours. However, most consultants stress behavioural-related dimensions to work as well as the cognitive dimensions. For instance, Towers Perrin (2003) see engagement as invoking emotional and rational factors relating to work and the overall experience of work: emotional factors are linked with 'staff satisfaction, a sense of inspiration and the affirmation they get from their work and from being part of an organization'. Rational factors relate to people's understanding of their job, the unit for which they work and how their performance relates to business performance.

Similarly, the Institute of Employment Studies (IES) in the UK, in probably the best review of the topic to date, reflect these emotional, cognitive and behaviourally related dimensions in their definition and approach to engagement (Robinson *et al.*, 2004). Rather unhelpfully, however, they have defined engagement as a 'positive attitude held by the employee towards the organization and its values ...' (p. 9). More usefully, they also define an engaged employee as one who has an understanding of the business context in his or her organization and works with colleagues to behave in a performance-enhancing manner for the benefit of the organization. In return, the organization has to work with employees to engage them in more than a transactional relationship.

Measuring engagement

Given the range of definitions, not surprisingly there are different items used to measure engagement. Table 4.6 below sets examples from three sources – Gallup Consulting, Hewitt Associates and the IES – in a little more detail, analysing them into items most closely related to (a) emotions and feelings connected with identification, commitment and ownership, (b) understanding and beliefs about their organizational roles and its image, and (c) behaviours and behavioural intentions. Each approach has items in all three categories; probably the main difference between them is that Gallup is more inclined to include behaviours that stress the obligations of employers to employees in fulfilling psychological contracts, whilst the IES lays more stress on employees demonstrating organizational citizenship-type behaviours. Hewitt Associates have less of a focus on behaviours and more on emotions, feelings and understanding.

Table 4.6
Items used to measure engagement and different approaches.

Items used to measure engagement	Gallup	Hewitt	IES
Emotions and feelings			
Closely identify with values of organization			[x]
Trust senior leaders to balance employee interests with those of company		[x]	
Proud to tell others I am part of company		[x]	[x]
My opinions at work count			
The purpose/mission of organization makes me value my job	[x]		[x]
Feel confident about future success of organization	[x]	[x]	
Have a best friend at work	[x]		
Feel confident that organization is making appropriate changes for future		[x]	
Feel products/services provide real value/benefits to customers		[x]	
Understanding and beliefs			
Colleagues committed to quality	[x]		
Know what is expected of me	[x]	[x]	
Have right materials/information to do job	[x]	[x]	
Given opportunity to do my best at work everyday	[x]		
Organization known as good employer			[x]
Organization has a good reputation			[x]
Understand organization's goals		[x]	
Behaviours			
Regularly receive recognition and praise for doing good work	[x]		
Supervisor or mentor takes care of me as a person	[x]		
Receive encouragement to develop myself	[x]		
Have received recent opportunities to develop	[x]		
Have received recent appraisal	[x]		
Would recommend organization's products and services		[x]	
Speak highly of organization to friends			[x]

(continued)

Table 4.6

(*Continued*)

Items used to measure engagement	Gallup	Hewitt	IES
Frequently make suggestions to improve team/department performance			[x]
Always do more than is required			[x]
Try to help others in organization			[x]
Try to keep abreast of current developments in my area			[x]
Volunteer to do things outside of job requirements to contribute to organization			[x]

Like most work on engagement, all three approaches show impressive degrees of correlation with performance measures, as illustrated by our earlier discussion of the Gallup approach and the validation work by the US academics. The IES study shows why this might be the case in mapping their engagement measures with what they present as the characteristics of an engaged employee (see Table 4.7).

Table 4.7

Mapping of employee engagement with the characteristics of an engaged employee.

	Characteristics	Statement
The Engaged Employee	Looks for and is given opportunities to improve organizational performance	The organization really inspires the very best in me in the way of job performance
	Is positive about the job and organization	I speak highly of this organization to my friends The organization has a good reputation I would be happy for my family and friends to use the organization's products and services
	Believes in the organization	This organization is known as a good employer
	Works actively to improve things	I frequently make suggestions to improve the work of my team/department/service

	Characteristics	Statement
	Treats others with respect and helps colleagues to perform better	I try to help others in this organization whenever I can
	Can be relied on, and goes beyond contract	I always do more than is required
	Sees the bigger picture, even at personal cost	I volunteer to do things outside my job that contribute to the organization's objectives
	Identifies with organization	I find my values and the organization's are very similar I am proud to tell others that I am part of the organization
	Keeps up-to-date with developments in their field	I try to keep abreast of current developments in my area

Source: Adapted from Robinson *et al.*, 2004, p. 15

Let's look at another case we researched for the book that used a measure of employee engagement in its attempt to re-brand itself. Before we conclude this chapter, you may wish to reflect on the strengths and weaknesses of their approach in the light of our discussions in this and previous chapters.

Box 4.6   Linking branding and HR at Standard Life Investments

Standard Life Investments, which is headquartered in Edinburgh, Scotland, was launched in 1997 as an autonomous organization within the Standard Life group of companies with the aim of becoming a major international investment house. Since then it has achieved impressive results and has major offices in London, Montreal, Boston, Hong Kong and Dublin and representative offices in Beijing and Seoul, and currently employs around 650 staff. Part of the company's success has been based on establishing a strong corporate brand in the investment market, which has been fully supported by the HR team in Edinburgh in their combined efforts with the 'business' managers to build high levels of employee engagement and a strong employer brand. Such has been their contribution to the creation of the external brand image since 1997 and the development of a strong internal identity, that they won a prestigious HR Excellence award in 2001 for the company with the most innovative HR practices.

The key driver for HR's contribution to the establishment of such a corporate reputation has been the need to recruit and retain talented people, particularly the highly paid investment fund managers who are at the core of the business and acknowledged to be the most important competitive differentiator between investment houses. These people are the equivalent of the stars in Premier League soccer or men and women's professional tennis and can earn salaries to match. Recruiting, engaging and retaining these 150 'stars', and the 500 or more people that support them, has been a critical issue, especially since Standard Life is committed to its Edinburgh base, outside of the main labour market in London. Sitting alongside this 'talent management' driver has been the desire of the company to create a more 'professional', team-based culture, based on 'adult' relationships and high levels of trust, instead of the previously hierarchical culture which they inherited from their mutual assurance heritage. So, for example, the previous 20-graded jobs structure has been eliminated, as has payment for overtime and detailed job descriptions and evaluations. These have been replaced with an output and high trust regime in which there is very little close monitoring of work but individualized pay, in which the variable pay element ranges from 15% of base salary for junior administrative staff to 200% for the investment fund managers.

The HR team has worked with business colleagues in investment and marketing since 1997 to create a strong 'internal' or 'employer' brand, which is treated as the key to matching client experiences and expectations with the company's promotional and advertising strategy and its external image. This began with focus group interviews with customers on determining the external brand values, which were fed back to employees in numerous workshops to help them understand how clients saw the organization, how they wanted to see it and what employees would need to do differently to support the brand. Early on in this process, they realized that achieving this aim would require a heavy investment in promoting 'engagement', which they defined in terms of loyalty and psychological commitment to the company. Following some early investigative work, they commissioned the Gallup organization to conduct an investigation into the levels of engagement amongst employees. A survey tool called Q12 was amended by the HR team to include eight of their own questions, which subsequently became known as Q20 internally and has been the principal means of measuring progress in employee engagement since 1998. This measure has the added advantage of allowing the company to benchmark its employees against other organizations in financial services and against similar companies worldwide. Since the first survey Standard Life have shown a steady improvement in those employees defined as 'actively engaged' from 12% in December 1999 to 33% in February 2003, with those defined as 'actively disengaged' declining from 14% to 7% over the same period. According to Gallup external benchmarking figures for the financial services industry, this has moved Standard Life Investments from around the 50 percentile to the top quartile of companies in terms of employee engagement. In addition, the company reduced turnover levels from 12% in 1999 to 5% in 2002, and calculated they have saved £0.5 million.

Senior HR staff saw these measurements as a critical element in helping them make their case for continued inclusion in the corporate reputation process with business managers who are used to financial measurement. However, these measures are only the starting point in the conversation about how to develop further the team-based culture and individuals, all of whom undergo a 'strength-finder' career development review and a 360 degree appraisal. HR staff stressed the importance of integrating the internal and external image of the organization in these interviews and the role of continuous communication in developing a positive corporate reputation. They also stressed the importance of senior management involvement in this process, with Sandy Crombie, the head of Standard Life Investments in 1998 and now CEO of the main board of Standard Life, taking an active role in the external and internal brand-building process.

Conclusions

To bring this chapter to a conclusion, we have tried to set out a necessarily more complex view of what it takes to connect people to their organizations, hopefully in a readable way. This is best summarized by the processes and formulas in Figure 4.1. In our view, organizations that really want to understand and manage the quality of individual employment relations to create greater organizational identification and positive outcomes such as customer loyalty, positive reputations and brands need to adopt a more *evidence-based* approach to HR (Pfeffer, 2005). This evidence base may need to go beyond the current fashion for engagement surveys, which are a rather blunt, but nevertheless useful, instrument for tapping emotions, understanding and behaviours in employment. For example, in our case, Standard Life Investments have, wisely in our opinion, added additional questions to the standard engagement survey. However, they, like many organizations, may not have gone far enough.

Our main recommendation from this chapter is that organizations wanting to know about their employees and wanting to engage in more sophisticated HR practices, such as segmentation and high performance work practices (see Chapter 5), need to understand the nature and variation of psychological contracts in their organizations, the key individual–organizational linkages of identification, internalization, psychological ownership and continuance commitment, and the levels of engagement behaviours claimed by employees in their day-to-day work. This need not involve enormous questionnaires that employees are reluctant to complete because of being over-surveyed, but will necessarily be longer than the typical, 12-question engagement survey. Good examples of standard questionnaires used to identify the state of psychological contracts are contained in the book by Conway and Briner (2005). Besides, in our experience, so long as employees find the questionnaires interesting and relevant in giving them a voice on matters that are important to them, they will complete longer and more in-depth surveys on a fairly frequent basis. Now, however, we move onto the core HR processes that help drive these employee relationships.

References

Arthur, M. B., Inkson, K. and Pringle, J. K. (1999) *The new careers: individual action and economic change.* London: Sage.

Ashforth, B. E. and Mael, F. (1989) Social identity theory and the organization, *Academy of Management Review*, **14**, 20–39.

Barrow, S. and Mosley, R. (2005) *The Employer Brand®: bringing the best of brand management to people at work*. London: Wiley.

Bhattacharya, R., Devinney, T. and Pilluta, M. M. (1998) A formal model of trust based on outcomes, *Academy of Management Review*, **23**, 459–472.

Brown, A. D. (1997) Narcissism, identity and legitimacy, *Academy of Management Review*, **22**, 643–686.

Cappelli, P. (1999) *The New Deal at work: managing the market-driven workforce*. Boston, MA: Harvard Business School Press

CIPD (2003a) *Managing the psychological contract*. Factsheet, May. Wimbledon: Chartered Institute of Personnel and Development.

CIPD (2003b) *Living to work*. CIPD Survey, October. Wimbledon: Chartered Institute of Personnel and Development.

CIPD (2005) *Employee well-being and the psychological contract*. Wimbledon: Chartered Institute of Personnel and Development.

Clegg, S., Kornberger, M. and Pitsis, T. (2005) *Management and organizations: an introduction to theory and practice*. London: Sage.

Conway, N. and Briner, R. B. (2002) A daily diary study of affective responses to psychological contract breach and exceeded promises, *Journal of Organizational Behaviour*, **21**, 25–42.

Conway, N. and Briner, R. B. (2005) *Understanding psychological contracts at work: a critical evaluation of theory and research*. Oxford: Oxford University Press.

Davenport, T. H. (2005) *Thinking for a living: how to get better performance and results from knowledge workers*. Boston, MA: Harvard Business School Press.

Dutton, J. E., Dukerich, J. M. and Harquail, C. V. (1994) Organizational images and member identification, *Administrative Science Quarterly*, **39**, 57–88.

Florida, R. (2002) *The rise of the creative class*. New York: HarperCollins.

Florida, R. (2005) *The flight of the creative class*. New York: HarperCollins.

Goffee, R. and Jones, G. (2005) Individual and collective leadership in the boardroom: why feedback is vital even at the top, *Ivey Business Journal Online*, September/October. http://www.iveybusinessjournal.com/article.asp?intArticle_id=581 (28 February 2006).

Grey, C. (2005) *A very short, fairly interesting and reasonably cheap book about studying organizations*. London: Sage.

Guest, D. and Conway, N. (2002) Communicating the psychological contract: an employer perspective, *Human Resource Management Journal*, **12** (2), 22–38.

Harter, J. M., Schmidt, F. and Hayes, T. L. (2002) Business unit level relationships between employee satisfaction/engagement and business outcomes: a meta-analysis, *Journal of Applied Psychology*, **87**, 268–279.

Hatch, M. J. and Schultz, M. (2004) *Organizational identity: a reader.* Oxford: Oxford University Press.

Herriot, P. (2001) *The employment relationship: a psychological perspective.* Hove: Routledge.

Herriot, P., Manning, W. E. G. and Kidd, J. M. (1997) The content of the psychological contract, *British Journal of Management*, **8**, 151–162.

Huselid, M. A., Becker, B. E. and Beatty, R. W. (2005) *The workforce scorecard: managing human capital to execute strategy.* Boston, MA: Harvard Business School Press.

Mael, F. A. and Ashforth, B. E. (1992) Alumni and their alma mater: a partial test of the reformulated model of organizational identification, *Journal of Occupation Behaviour*, **13**, 103–123.

Martin, G., Staines, H. and Pate, J. (1998) The New Psychological Contract: exploring the relationship between job security and career development, *Human Resource Management Journal*, **6** (3), 20–40.

Martin, G., Pate, J. M., Beaumont, P. B. and Murdoch, A. (2003) The uncertain road to partnership: industrial relations in the UK North Sea drilling industry, *Employee Relations*, **25** (6), 594–612.

Meyer, J. P. and Allen, N. J. (1991) A three-component conceptualization of organizational commitment, *Human Resource Management Review*, **1** (1), 61–79.

Pate, J., Martin, G. and McGoldrick, J. (2003) The psychological contract, trust and violation: a conceptual model and some case study evidence, *Employee Relations*, **25**, 557–573.

Pate, J. M., Martin, G. and Staines, H. (2000) The new psychological contract, cynicism and organizational change: a theoretical framework and case study evidence, *Journal of Strategic Change*, **9** (1), 481–493.

Pfeffer, J. (2001) Fighting the war for talent is dangerous to your organization's health, *Organizational Dynamics*, **29** (4), 248–259.

Pfeffer, J. (2005) Creating a performance culture. Presentation at University of Strathclyde, 23 September.

Pierce, J. L, Kostova, T. and Dirks, K. T. (2001) Towards a theory of psychological ownership in organizations, *Academy of Management Review*, **26** (2), 298–310.

Reade, C. (2001) Antecedents of organizational identification in multinational corporations: fostering psychological attachment to the local subsidiary and the global organization, *International Journal of Human Resource Management*, **12**, 1269–1291.

Robinson, D., Perryman, S. and Hayday, S. (2004) *The drivers of employee engagement.* IES Report no 408, Brighton: Institute of Employment Studies.

Rousseau, D. (1995) *Psychological contracts in organizations: understanding written and unwritten agreements.* Newbury Park, CA: Sage.

Rousseau, D. M. (2001) The idiosyncratic deal: flexibility versus fairness, *Organizational Dynamics*, **29** (4), 260–273.

Scott, S. G. and Lane, V. R. (2000) A stakeholder approach to organizational identity, *Academy of Management Review*, **25**, 43–62.

Sparrow, P. and Cooper, C. (2003) *The employment relationship: key challenges for HR.* Oxford: Butterworth–Heinemann.

Sutton, R. I. (2001) *Weird ideas that work: 11½ ways to promote, manage and sustain innovation.* London: Allen Lane, Penguin Press.

Swailes, S. (2002) Organizational commitment: a critique of the construct and its measures, *International Journal of Management Research*, **4** (2), 155–178.

Thompson, J. A. and Bunderson, J. S. (2003) Violations of principle: ideological currency in the psychological contract, *Academy of Management Review*, **28** (4), 571–586.

Towers Perrin (2003) Working today: understanding what drives employee engagement. http://www.towersperrin.com/hrservices/webcache/towers/United_States/publications/Reports/Talent_Report_2003/Talent_2003.pdf (18 February 2006).

Turnley, W.H. and Feldman, D. C. (1998) Psychological contract violations during corporate restructuring, *Human Resource Management*, **37** (1), 71–83.

Wright, P. M., Dunford, B. B. and Snell, S. A. (2001) Human resource management and the resource based view of the firm, *Journal of Management*, **27**, 701–721.

CHAPTER 5

Four lenses on HR strategy and the employment relationship

Introduction >

In this chapter and the next one we discuss what the HR function can contribute to branding, reputations and performance through its impact on the lived experience of employees and the quality of their individual employment relationships. As we have already pointed out, however, this is not a one-way process. Just as HR can drive reputations, brands and performance, in turn, these outcomes help attract and retain talented people, one of the major challenges facing most organizations (see Figure 5.1). What people on the inside think about organizational identity and image is informed by how they think relevant outsiders see them, for example from the views of professional colleagues, potential employees, the financial press, customers, CSR ratings, environmental activists and the public at large. So, employees' views of positive perceptions are likely to influence their willingness to remain with the company; furthermore, talented people are attracted by high performing and reputable companies, one of the reasons underlying an employer of choice strategy (see Chapter 7).

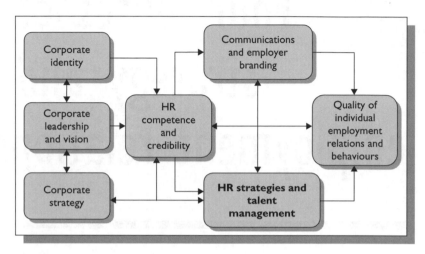

Figure 5.1
Linking HR and talent management to strategy and the quality of individual employment relations.

The connections between HR drivers, however, and these other variables are not as clear-cut as many of the more prescriptive HR texts would have you believe, nor as simple as Figure 5.1 would imply. How HR fast-forwards into individual employment relations and interpenetrates with corporate strategy is a rather more complex process; it is not just a question of aligning HR with the business strategy and pulling the right levers to generate positive psychological contracts and engaged employees. If life were so easy, there would be little point in writing yet another 'how to' book on the subject, since the market is awash with them. Most of these, researched and written with varying degrees of sophistication, are of the 'one-best-way' variety, with a basic but compelling message (not always intended but often read as such): search for best practices among 'best-in-class' firms on a range of HR variables, benchmark yourself against these firms and implement those practices that fit your needs, sometimes in a 'pick-'n-mix' fashion. Some of these works are naïve in the extreme; others are exceptionally good. We would include in the good category Jeff Pfeffer's (1998,

2005) works, discussed later in this chapter, especially in providing 'evidence-based' practices and in simplifying and communicating complex realities.

The very idea of best practices, however, has been roundly criticized by writers and practitioners who argue that 'context matters'. This has resulted in another school of thought in strategic HRM, which focuses on the 'fit' between bundles of practices and organizational contexts. This 'it-all-depends-on-the strategic-environment' approach is based on a few simple ideas. The first is that HR has to address the key strategic drivers of an organization, though these may vary according to competitive circumstances. The second is that there is no sustainable competitive advantage in doing what everyone else is doing, especially if you are one of the late-comers. The third is that there is little sense in treating all employees the same, in terms of their added value to an organization's key strategic drivers, their abilities and what they want from work. These are the messages of a number of influential books and articles, including one by Huselid *et al.* (2005), which we shall also examine in this chapter and when discussing segmentation approaches to people management and HR in Chapter 6.

As important as the best practice/best fit debate is for our understanding of HR, reputations and brands, under-girding it is another level of analysis with even more profound consequences for HR and its connections to outcomes, ethics and change models. To paraphrase the title in the excellent strategic management book by Richard Whittington (2001), we really should be asking the questions: 'what is HR strategy and does it really matter to reputation management and brand performance?'. The answers, according to Whittington, in his more general discussion of business strategy, depend on what the *outcomes* are/should be and how we should/do go about *devising and implementing* such strategies (see also Legge, 2004, who also adopted Whittington's model to explain HRM).

Concerning the first of these questions on the outcomes of strategy – the goals to which strategy is (or should be) directed – we have to ask ourselves: are we trying to achieve a unitary goal such as increased shareholder value, or are we looking to balance this with other outcomes such as public good, good governance and a socially and environmentally responsible reputation (see Figure 5.2)? Or, to take another example, is our current strategy and organization aimed at exploiting old ways of working by driving out variance among the workforce and generating high levels of cooperation around a core theme of making money now; or is it/should it be about exploring new ways/ideas by enhancing variance and initiative around a core theme of achieving results in the long term – the 'innovate or die' argument (Sutton, 2001; Roberts, 2004)? We will return to this question later in this chapter. The second question is concerned with how strategy is, or should be, devised and implemented: is strategy best devised and implemented in a top-down, big bang fashion, exemplified by the headline-grabbing, CEO-envisioned and driven, programme of change; or are we better to follow a more middle-emergent and incremental approach that involves as many people as possible and addresses the politics of change all of the way through the process (see Figure 5.2)?

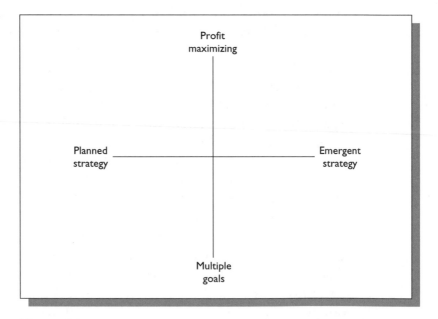

Figure 5.2
Answers to Whittington's Two Questions on the nature of strategy (based on Whittington, 2001).

Though we acknowledge that there is a 'both – and' answer to these questions, we will use them in their simple form to provide a framework for our analysis of HR strategy, reputations and brands. This approach may be less clear-cut than accepting the dominant views of the best practice or best fit schools, and we will be treading on some big toes in the process, but part of our role is to evaluate received wisdom, even that which appears on the pages of the Harvard Business School Press and is frequently 'endorsed' by the UK-based CIPD and the Society of Human Resource Management (SHRM) in the USA. So, the rest of this chapter will address the following two questions on HR strategy:

- To what uses should HR strategy be put?
- How should HR strategies be developed in practice?

HR strategy: why does it matter?

HR strategy and best practice

Let's look at a case that helps illustrate many of the points we wish to address in this chapter and the importance of the two questions.

Box 5.1   HRM at Paragon

Many of the cases in this book have been based on a best practice approach in which high performance HR strategies have been aligned with the strategic vision of an organization to produce strong organizational identities, reputations and brands. One of the problems, however, with using evidence from headline cases of best practice in high performing companies is that you don't always know if best practices were the causes of high performance if you don't test them out in other situations – most importantly, the use of the self-same practices in companies that were low performers (Joyce *et al.*, 2003). This was one of the criticisms of the 'In Search of Excellence' companies, so influential in the 1980s, nearly half of whom were no longer excellent five years after Peters and Waterman reported that excellent companies were excellent because of seven practices. The best practice literature, which is so easily digested, is widely available on airport book shelves; and the pressures to 'follow the pack' are so strong that it is very likely that many firms that continue to perform poorly use the same high performance practices. Even worse, what's the betting on best practice leading to total failure?

Here is a case of one company that exemplifies the best practice approach. The rise of the Paragon company is the stuff of legends among the business press. It was attributed with inventing radically new business concepts in the 1980s, with re-inventing itself many times during the 1990s and described in one of the major business publications as one of the 'Most Innovative Companies' five years in a row, was 24th on *Fortune*'s Best Companies to Work For, number 2 on Reputation of Employee Talent, and number 1 on the Reputation of Quality of Management. So, on any test of reputation management, this company was up there with the best. How had it achieved such adulation?

Paragon's credo of innovation and high performance

Paragon was attributed with re-defining the rules of the previously highly regulated industry in which it became a dominant player by (1) embracing a free market philosophy; (2) repeatedly developing new business models to earn superior revenues in a rapidly changing industry and market environment; and (3) re-defining its mission and strategy – it had been a well-known producer of specialist products and services with large amounts of capital assets but during the 1990s became a trading company only, not only in these products and services but in related ones. In doing so, it reflected the general trends in industry to focus on its specialist competence in transforming itself into a new-economy, knowledge-based company trading on its intellectual capital. As its CEO repeatedly said, 'assets were bad, intellectual capital was good'.

Paragon's people management strategy: supporting reputations and the brand through talent management and high performance HRM

1   **Talent management and rewards:** The CEO and HR director recognized that in creating a trading company they had to compete with the best in the financial world and elsewhere. They decided to recruit the best MBA graduates they could hire, at the rate of 250 a year. As one senior manager commented, 'We had these things called Super Saturday. I'd interview some of these guys who were fresh out of Harvard, and these kids could blow me out of the water. They

knew things I'd never heard of.' The main attraction for these new recruits was the reputation Paragon had created for itself as 'hip, dynamic, new-economy company'. Bright young graduates in astrophysics and science were turned into trading specialists who could do fast and creative deals in the performance-oriented culture. These 'A' players were placed in these 'A' jobs of making deals, and were rewarded appropriately by being paid as entrepreneurs, with a salary package that embodied four elements: base salary, high performance bonuses, additional perks and stock options. The main criteria for bonuses were how they contributed to shareholder value. Top performers were rewarded inordinately and promoted without regard for seniority or experience. As the CEO said, 'The only thing that differentiates [this company] from our competitors is our people, our talent ... We hire very smart people and we pay them more than they think they are worth.'

2   **Human resource development:** The company lived out the CEO's credo of building on smart people rather than assets, with HR given a large budget for career development and to create an open market for internal transfers. This was aimed at creating knowledge transfer and flexibility among the many operating units and allowing free movement across previously sacrosanct divisions. The rewards policy supported such free movements by allowing people to retain titles, even though they may be doing rather different jobs (and thus not entitled to the previous title). The stock options were also designed to give people the focus on the business, rather than identification with their own units. Performance management was carried out on the basis of segmenting jobs and people into A, B and C categories, with A referring to the most important jobs and best performers, B to supporting jobs and promising people, and C to marginal jobs and marginal or poor performers. Each year, every unit was required to put people into a forced distribution ranking and identify the bottom 15% performers who were usually 'named, shamed and fired'.

3   **Design of work:** The way in which work and jobs were designed reflected the needs for innovation, entrepreneurship and high performance. Work teams were provided with 'phantom equity' to provide them with a sense of responsibility and involvement for running autonomous projects. This equity could be swapped for real stock once the teams had realized a profit from their ventures. This way

of encouraging innovation provided Paragon with a steady stream of business ideas, one of which was an award-winning e-business development, which reduced transaction times by huge amounts. The company benefited from many such developments.

4 **Values:** Paragon, in line with its name, promoted a value system of communication, respect, integrity and excellence, which the CEO used all avenues to promote. The communications and public relations function in the company, along with the CEO, used many avenues to have people live the values in their day-to-day interactions. However, this aspect of HR was probably the least successful, since employees tended to live the unwritten value of finding new ways to make money. From a shareholder value perspective, however, was this emphasis on revenue generation such a bad thing?

Many readers will have picked up important messages regarding linking strategy to good HR practice from this case, which could well have come straight from the pages of many US texts that follow an essentially prescriptive approach to HRM, strategy and performance. But even companies that have adopted a 'classical', design approach to HR, beginning with the business strategy and implementing a set of state-of-the-art HR practices, can fail. Even worse, HR can, as Spector (2003) insightfully argued, be the 'un-indicted co-conspirator' in helping a company 'crash and burn'. For, as some readers will have guessed, not only did Paragon fail spectacularly, but its HR talent management and reward practices helped it on its way – Paragon, of course, being a pseudonym for Enron.

Consequently, the Paragon/Enron case should serve as a warning to HR practitioners. How they answer the first question concerning the outcomes to which strategy, especially HR strategy, should be put can cause immense damage to companies. It also serves as a warning to those advocating a design approach to strategy: many of the problems of Enron seem to be attributable to its CEO, Jeffrey Skilling, who drove a top-down, talent management and reward strategy that helped Enron make bad strategic decisions, become a victim of 'irrational exuberance' and develop a leadership of 'bad apples', three of the usual explanations for the failure of Enron (Spector, 2003). So, if leadership can be a source of failure as well as success, we should be asking ourselves: how should HR strategies be developed in practice? So much for a best practice approach to HR strategy, you might say?

We think not. Though our book is also written with a view to helping HR practitioners make a more relevant contribution to their organizations, hopefully our more discursive, analytical approach does not fall into the trap of emphasizing a one-best way, or giving HR the centre-stage in management decision-making. Clearly, as the formidable US HR academic George Strauss (2001) has pointed out, British writers often misunderstand the US approach to HRM by elevating it to a level of importance that it rarely achieves among US firms or in the US university business school community. HR practitioners, because of their 'trained incapacity' to think from the perspective of their specialism, tend to look first inside the company for HR strategy by focusing on people and people-related outcomes rather than business and environmental issues (Wright *et al.*, 2003).

Strategy surely matters in the general sense of what is important to organizations and so, we believe, does HR strategy; though both have to be viewed from different perspectives about what aspects of strategy matter. You can often look at HR strategy through different lenses to get a more complex 'reading'. In this chapter, we have chosen to look at it through four different lenses, all of which shed light (and, unfortunately, some heat) on what it is and whether it matters. For, as Gareth Morgan (1997) has pointed out, what you see depends on where (and when) you stand; managers, including HR specialists, need to be able to work with a number of different and even competing ideas simultaneously to be able to understand and manage the complicated situations often found in managing people and organizations.

Four lenses on strategy and HRM explained

Whittington organized the two dimensions in Figure 5.2 to produce four explanations of strategy. We have adapted these to show how HR strategy can be seen through four different lenses, each one of which help us understand HR and evaluate its links with reputations and brands (see Figure 5.3). All four views are characterized by different assumptions and offer unique answers to the questions of 'what is strategic HRM and does it matter?'. Note, however, the boxes and callouts have purposely not been drawn the same size because some of these lenses are more important than others in HR, at least in terms of their impact on practice.

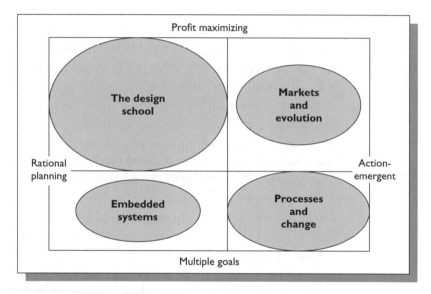

Figure 5.3
Four lenses on HR strategy (based on Whittington, 2001).

These four lenses or perspectives on HR strategy are: the **design** perspective, classic in the sense that it is the most important and dominant one; the increasingly important **process and change** perspective, which is the basis for casting HR specialists as change agents (Ulrich and Brockbank, 2005); a **market or evolutionary** view, which reduces the role of HR strategy to cost reduction, managing downsizing and flexibility; and the **embedded systems** approach, which focuses on how HR strategy and practices are rooted in particular contexts or business systems, making their transfer to other organizations, industries and national cultures much more difficult than is usually imagined.

Let's explain just how these four views have been arrived at before we examine them in more detail in this and the next chapter. There is a long tradition in the literature on HR and employee relations (Fox, 1974) that addresses the first question concerning the outcomes of HR strategy – whether practice or thinking emphasizes *unitary, profit maximizing* outcomes such as shareholder value or *pluralist, multiple* outcomes such as satisfying diverse stakeholder interests. Answers to the second question have tended to divide according to those people favouring rational choice and planning as a way of making strategy and those favouring the emergent, political and action-oriented nature of strategies (Mintzberg *et al.*, 1998). Karl Weick (2001), a well-known US scholar, rather provocatively set out this second question in the form: do we think our way into action or do we act our way into thinking? He argues for the latter, that strategy-making is more like improvisation than design, with managers using whatever materials/knowledge they have at hand to fashion or craft strategy, the first step of which is to examine these materials/knowledge to see what they have previously been used for and what has been achieved with them. So, having an intimate understanding of what human capital and resources you have and recombining them in novel ways is what makes good HR strategy from an improvisation perspective. Sutton (2001) has talked about such an approach as 'seeing old things in new ways', for which he adopts the term '*vuja de*'. This is equivalent to inventing new combinations of existing ideas.

Therefore, according to Whittington, the design school and what we have called the embedded systems lens share one key assumption – that planning and rational choices are important. They differ, however, because the design school increasing shareholder value is seen as the only legitimate claim on their activities, while the embedded systems approach takes into account multiple demands and pulls in formulating and implementing strategies, such as the CSR agenda, which we shall discuss more fully in Chapter 9. This is very similar to the competing interest problems facing leadership we discussed in Chapter 3. For example, the design school has focused on profit maximization and business drivers whilst embedded systems stress the entrenched nature of managerial actions in organizational, industrial and national cultures, including the social backgrounds, education and professional orientations of managers. This focus may still result in rational choices, but this time, rational choice is exercised as a balancing act, satisficing or optimizing between competing claims rather than maximizing outcomes.

A good example of this balancing act would be how strategic HR decisions are often taken in Sino-foreign joint ventures where market forces and the profit motive have to be understood in the context of overt political influence (Zhang and Martin, 2003). Another example from our research concerns the international recruitment consultants, Hudson International, who were in the process of implementing an employer branding project across their subsidiaries in a number of European countries. Implementing the new values framework and reviews of HR practices is being achieved through a major consultation exercise with employees in the various companies. In Europe, with its overlay of national cultures and institutions, this has meant taking into account not only language differences but also the contestable notion of values. As the European HR Director explained:

> certain words we use mean very little in Germany, with no equivalent translation. And even the notion of values itself has different meanings in the different countries. For example, speaking to the Italians, and telling them you have these values that you would like to implement causes them real problems. They look at you and say, well what were you before? Didn't you have values before? We never had to do that with TMP (the American-owned previous parent company) – these were the words and that was what you would have to use. So each country will look at the notion of values and make them meaningful in their context.

In contrast, the *evolutionary* and *market-based* assumptions associated with so-called popular ecology views on organizations rest on the relentless and unpredictable nature of the market environment for managers, and predict their helplessness and inability to make much of a difference to their organization's chances of success. In effect, this economics-dominated perspective sees the hidden hand of markets selecting out those firms that will survive in the increasingly competitive global economy and has little time for human agency and managerial choice. As Whittington suggested, there is a cruel paradox at work since only those firms that are fit for such competition will survive but managers have very little ability to help shape their firms for survival other than make them cost-effective and fast and flexible enough to respond to market signals of what is required to compete.

From a very different perspective, the assumptions of those holding a *process and change* perspective on HR strategy are at odds with the dominance and rationalism of markets and the processes of natural selection. Instead they point to the many imperfections in market forces, the power of large firms to create virtual monopolies through global branding and the importance of human agency in new, highly creative firms that are able to become major players in existing and new industries by learning faster and better. Furthermore, reflecting the idea of Weick (2001) and ideas drawn from complexity and chaos theory (Stacey, 2001), some writers have argued that managerial attempts at long-term planning had little effect on organizational outcomes because strategic change was a much messier, emergent and politically influenced process than rational planners assume to be true. These change writers have given much greater emphasis to building organizational coalitions, bargaining and learning as a way of producing incremental strategic change. The cumulative effect of small increments in strategic change, as Morgan (1993) has pointed out, can result in *quantum* or radical change over a longer time period.

The classical approach to strategic HRM, the focus on planning, best practice and strategic fit

As we have already explained this school assumes that unitary goals such as profitability or maximizing shareholder value are the natural state of affairs or, at least, should be – to paraphrase the US president, Calvin Coolidge, the 'business of business is business' argument in which social responsibility and ethical behaviour are not objectives that business can, or should be, concerned with. Its adherents also hold strong beliefs that the rational planning and design of strategy, structure and human resource systems are the best means to achieve such unitary goals. The key problem for these people is how to build an organizational design and HR systems that allow managers to focus on strategic responsibilities and to attain simultaneously cost advantages, differentiation of their products and services and, increasingly, to leverage learning from one part of the organization to another (see later discussion on developments in the architectural approach). In the field of strategy, the classical approach has been dominated by the military metaphor and by industrial economics. The translation of such strategic thinking into the field of HRM, however, has been influenced by US industrial and organizational psychologists who have moved into business schools (Strauss, 2001). These psychologists have in common with their economics colleagues a belief in the power of rational choices and science to produce useful knowledge on HR principles. As a consequence, much of their writing is heavily prescriptive rather than a description of how strategy and HRM relate to each other in practice. At its best, it can be very useful – witness the application of games theory to economics and management, which has helped two economists win Nobel prizes (*Economist*, 2005b); at its worst it can be almost otherworldly, either because the messages are so simple as to not be worth recording, or because they are so complicated and written in such obscure jargon that few practitioners could be bothered reading them.

The two schools of strategic HRM that best exemplify this tradition are the best practice and strategic fit schools and it is to these schools we now turn.

Best practice HRM

As Boxall and Purcell (2000) have argued, the ideas of best practice HRM have received most enthusiasm from American practitioners and academics. Best practice models come in three different guises (Wood, 1999). The first is **high commitment management**, developed by Walton (1985) and others to refer to a set of HR practices on job design, team working, problem solving and minimum status differentials which were associated with a managerial orientation of treating people as assets rather than costs and aimed at securing commitment rather than compliance. The second, **high involvement management**, is usually associated with the work of Lawler *et al.* (1998). It is broadly similar to high commitment management but with a greater emphasis on developing skills and knowledge and on paying people for performance and skills development. The third is **high performance management or high performance work systems.** The work of Huselid (1995) and Becker and Huselid (1998) is best known for attempting to demonstrate strong statistical links between HRM and financial outcomes. The focus of their work, which was conducted throughout the 1990s, is on the links between targeted performance management, work restructuring, skill development and contingent pay practices, and organizational performance, this time not working through attitudes and values but on how these practices directly influence behaviour.

In the UK, David Guest's writing (e.g. Guest, 1987) is best known for his beliefs in the superiority of high involvement HR and the importance of integrating HR systems into the broader business strategy of the organization. Another major study, by Patterson *et al.* (1997) in UK manufacturing industry linked the use of (a) the comprehensiveness of the selection, appraisal and development systems, (b) the extent of factors such as job flexibility and team working and (c) the use of quality improvement, high pay, performance-related pay and harmonized conditions of employment to positive changes in profitability and productivity over time. They also demonstrated the greater power of such HRM practices to affect these outcomes than changes in other practices, such as quality management, the adoption of advanced manufacturing, R&D and strategy.

Two of the most accessible and best-researched exemplars of this best practice tradition are by Jeffrey Pfeffer (1998), who wrote seven practices of successful organizations, and the UK-based, high performance work practices study (Sung and Ashton, 2005 – see Box 5.2). Turning to Pfeffer first, his second book became something of a standard introductory text on MBA courses in the US for a period of time. Rather controversially, however, Pfeffer's work was (and remains) critical of US current practice and he frequently looked to Europe for inspiration. The recently up-dated list of best practices of high performing cultures are (Pfeffer, 2005):

- Employment security
- Selective recruiting for talent
- Self-managed teams or team working
- High pay contingent on company performance
- Extensive training
- Reduction of status differentials and the tall poppy syndrome
- Shared information and the building of communities.

The CIPD in the UK often sponsors such research to help practitioners learn from other companies, with one of the most recent attempts being the high performance work practices project, co-sponsored with the Department of Trade and Industry (see Box 5.2). This work has identified three sets or 'bundles' of practices that were related to positive outcomes, though these were found to be slightly industry-dependent (Sung and Ashton, 2005) and which is more resonant with the best fit approach discussed next.

Box 5.2   High performance work practices (HPWPs) in the UK

This study was carried out for the CIPD and UK government's Department of Trade and Industry on good HR practices (HPWP) employed in cases drawn from a sample of *The Sunday Times* 100 best companies to work for and a survey of 294 organizations facilitated by the CIPD.

HPWPs were defined as a set of complementary practices covering three areas. In total, 35 HR work practices were allocated to so-called 'bundles of practices' on the following basis:

- **High employee involvement practices**, e.g. self-directed teams, quality circles, sharing access to company information, continuous improvement teams, internal engagement surveys etc.
- **Human resource practices**, e.g. sophisticated recruitment and selection, competency assessment, induction, performance appraisal, coaching and mentoring, work re-design, etc.
- **Reward and commitment practices**, different types of financial rewards, including performance pay for all or some, stock options, family-friendly practices, flexible hours, job rotation, etc.

The key findings were:

1   The level of HPWP adoption, as measured by the crude number of practices adopted, is linked to organizational performance. This is especially true for the adoption of employee involvement in delivering more effective training, motivating staff, managing change and careers, having more people earning in excess of £35 000 a year and fewer people earning less than £12 000 a year is also linked to organizational performance.

2   The cases illustrated a relationship between the objectives of the organization (its strategic goals), the industry sector it operated in, how product market strategy is used to achieve goals, and the range of HPWPs used. For example, innovative organizations used different bundles from others.

3   There was also some evidence that some bundles of practices worked better than others in generating specific outcomes, e.g. to enhance organizational competitiveness, reward and commitment practices seemed to fit better than others.

4   Different bundles of practices were associated with different sectors, e.g. financial services made more use of financial incentives, whereas manufacturing and business services with a more quality-oriented strategy made more use of high involvement practices.

5   Training and development was taken as a given, the 'table stakes', and not a differentiating factor.

6   Leadership was 'crucial in creating, shaping and driving practices'; HPWP organizations tended to be leaders in their industry and to be consistently re-inventing practices to refresh themselves.

Source: Based on Sung and Ashton, 2005

As we have noted, much of this literature has a good grounding in evidence-based practice. Furthermore, it is difficult to argue against the idea that there are some practices with near universal relevance from which most organizations would benefit, such as selective hiring of talent and training, and others that would be desirable under favourable conditions, such as guarantees of employment security (Boxall and Purcell, 2003). Such practices, though, deserve little more than a label of 'promising' or good practice (the CIPD's preferred term) rather than best practices, since context is very important in determining the success of practices, as the embedded systems perspective points out (Leseure *et al.*, 2004). For example, the question has to be raised, 'best practice in whose interests?'. Clearly, the answer to this will depend on whether you are asking employees who have experienced frequent layoffs in the past, managers whose bonuses and stock options are based on increasing shareholder value, as in the case of Enron, or on increasing employee identification with the business, as is increasingly the case in firms valuing their brands. It will also vary according to whether you value individualism, as is the case in the US and, to a lesser extent, the UK, or whether you value collectivism and high levels of employee representation in decision-making, as is currently the case in Germany and the Nordic countries.

An equally damaging criticism of the best practice solution is the implied answer to the question, 'if the medicine is so potent, why isn't everyone taking it?'. The answer to this lies in the lack of competitive advantage in following the herd, which is the problem to which the 'best fit' school addresses itself.

Best fit HRM

Best fit approaches have tended to dominate the academic, rather than practitioner, literature on HRM, reflecting the portfolio planning/life cycle approaches in marketing during the 1970s and the competitive positioning work in the emerging field of strategy in the 1980s. Perhaps the best known of these best fit approaches was Schuler and Jackson's (1987) attempt to locate appropriate HR strategies and their behavioural implications in the competitive strategy framework developed by Porter (1985). This approach suggested that quite different bundles of HR practices would be relevant to the strategies of differentiation, focus and cost leadership. For example, encouraging innovative behaviour in firms following a differentiation strategy would require distinctive motivational policies from those that invoked the kinds of behaviours required for cost reduction.

However, best fit is not only concerned with this external fit between HR systems and strategy, but also with internal fit.

Internal fit comes in two varieties. The first is the degree of coherence among HR policies and practices themselves, to create powerful combinations and avoid deadly paradoxes. For example, in attempting to develop an external fit with the CSR agenda, a potentially deadly cocktail of HR practices would be team working and rewards based on individualized, performance-related pay. The illustration of the bundles of practices in Box 5.2 is an attempt to map internal fit. The second kind of fit we shall examine in a moment. Before doing so, let's look at some of the criticisms of fit approaches.

Schuler and Jackson's work is still influential but, naturally enough, has suffered from the same criticisms levelled at Porter's rather static, outside-in and either/or approach to strategy. Thus whilst few would claim that innovation and cost leadership require different role behaviours and HR policies, these tend to be a little more complicated than a simple reading-off exercise as implied by the Schuler and Jackson model. Using our framework in Figure 5.3, at least two lines of criticism can be made, which tend to apply to most strategic fit approaches. The first is that by locating HR policies and role behaviours in rather static models of competitive positioning, if followed to the letter, these are likely to become self-fulfilling prophecies. So, for example, if cost reduction HR strategies are followed, there is a possibility at least, if not the certainty, of creating a vicious circle that limits future innovation. First, vital knowledge resources may be made redundant (see the evolutionary, market perspective); second, the reputation of a firm as a good employer may be damaged, doing little for its ability to recruit in the future (Cascio, 2005). Nor are differentiation HR strategies without their negative consequences. For example, by increasing variance into the organization through recruiting innovative people, some companies have found to their cost that it is difficult to establish control when the nature of the market changes. This was one of the problems associated with Apple in the mid-1980s, though it is interesting to see how Stephen Jobs, the founder and originator of this policy, has had to re-invent Apple as a digital music producer to become a more creative company. It was also one of the causes of the demise of Enron: remember the approach to talent management and rewards which, some would say, caused a culture of greedy individualism.

As this last example shows, these kinds of models tend to neglect the changing nature of organizations, reflected in dynamic and reciprocal relationships between strategy and HR, and the dangers of confusing static 'maps with territories' (Weick, 2001). Devising and implementing HR strategies on the basis of crude maps, without regard for the subtleties and variations on the ground (e.g. different businesses within businesses, variations among employee competences, desires, needs, etc.), can be a recipe for failure. It is for these reasons that more recent thinking on strategy and HRM has turned to 'local' segmentation or architectural approaches (Paauwe and Boselie, 2005), which we shall now explore in discussing the second type of internal fit.

Segmentation approaches

This second type of internal fit focuses on creating synergies between HR policies and practices themselves and between HR systems and other organizational systems. One of the most recent of these is the 'architectural' approach associated with some academics based at Cornell University's well-known Center for Advanced Human Resource Studies (CAHRS). Though the ideas have been around for a long time in the labour economics and management literature on the flexible firm, the HR architecture approach (Lepak and Snell, 2002; Kang *et al.*, 2003) is, perhaps, the most thorough of the best fit arguments for HR strategy and provides the intellectual basis for current practice in segmenting internal employee labour market (Huselid *et al.*, 2005).

This framework is based on the RBV discussed in Chapter 2 and on two central propositions. The first is that different kinds of human capital are more or less valuable to an organization, e.g. people with specialist skills who have to be trained in an organizationally specific way of doing things versus people who may have specialist skills but these skills are not specific to the organization. The second is that managing human capital stocks (the supply to the firm) and flows (through a firm over time) is at the heart of everything an organization does. The architectural metaphor is used to connote a potential for designing organizations by identifying bundles of HR practices, employment modes and employment relationships for different employee cohorts, based on the degree to which their human capital is strategically valuable to the organization. This is a bit of a mouthful, but can be summed up in three propositions:

1   The value and uniqueness of human capital to organizations differ, i.e. talent matters. Value refers to the benefits that such people can add over their costs to customers. So, for example, good HR people can create lots of added value if they can address the key strategic drivers of the organization by contributing to external reputations and brands. Uniqueness refers to the idea that human capital is more or less firm-specific; organizations may have to make significant investments in recruiting, developing, engaging and retaining certain people while being able to secure the services of others on the open market, e.g. HR strategists and business partners who have an intimate knowledge of the business versus valuable, but generalist HR consultants in selection, training and development, employment law, etc.

2   Cohorts of human capital can also be distinguished by their employment modes, which can be either internally focused on a contract of service, or externally focused, usually on a contract for services.

3   Cohorts of human capital can also be distinguished according to the different psychological contracts with the organization. For the sake of simplicity, we can point to transactional versus relational contracts, discussed in Chapter 4.

Combining these three dimensions and reworking the original model a little (see Figure 5.4), we can create a picture of segmented human capital in organizations fitting into at least four different modes, with different implications for reputations and branding:

■   **Core knowledge/creative employees,** who add high reputational value (e.g. senior managers, financial analysts and fund managers, senior design engineers, senior medical staff, etc.) have both uniqueness (high firm-specific talents) and create high added reputation/brand value/celebrity status (or pose significant reputation/brand risk) to their organizations. They are also likely to be central to innovation, knowledge generation and flows agenda. The typical employment relationship is based on either relational or even ideological psychological contracts, high levels of organizational identification and strong individual – organizational linkages/trust relations. The mode of employment is internal, focused on a long-term career, job security and based on benefits that are likely to keep employees inside the organization and committed to its cause, such as stock options, continuous development, flexible benefits and working, and family-friendly policies, etc. It is mainly to such employees that organizations look to help them create (or avoid damaging) reputations and brands, and to whom they direct their employer of choice/employer branding policies and risk management efforts.

- **Compulsory, traditional human capital** (e.g. maintenance workers, technicians, software engineers, mid- to low level managers, administrators, core operations employees, including new-style call centre sales staff, etc.). These people are similar to core employees because they are important for adding high value beyond their costs and enhancing reputation, but are not unique because the types of skills can be readily bought on the external labour market and transferred in from other organizations, nor are they central to innovation, knowledge generation and flows agenda. The employment relationship tends to be more transactional, with less emphasis on organizational identification, commitment and the need to invest in high trust relations, though the mode of employment is usually of a full-time contract of employment variety. The focus of rewards and relations is on short-term productivity, performance-related pay, with appraisal and development emphasizing short- and long-term results.

■ **Idiosyncratic human capital/alliance of business partners:** these people have highly unique skills and, often, are important in bringing in new ideas; consequently, they are difficult to find on the open labour market. However, they are not consistently core to the reputations and branding of the organization, e.g. certain kinds of HR professionals in recruitment and employment law, accountants, financial engineers, etc., though this idea may be changing as companies increasingly compete on the basis of leveraging partnerships or business ecosystems beyond the firm, e.g. Nike, Microsoft and Cisco. The employment relationship tends to become externalized through high investment in building relationships with individuals in these functions across the business, but does not extend to investing in their skills/careers. Such employees are prime candidates for outsourcing, but usually as long-term strategic partners since they have unique talents. Examples, here, might include consultants, project managers, engineers and even academics. Sometimes, such people are self-selecting, with careers that follow a highly idiosyncratic pattern, often in the form of portfolios of contracts, where they will work for more than one employer (Barley and Kunda, 2006). They tend to have a professional (cosmopolitan), rather than firm (local), orientation to careers.

■ **Ancillary human capital/contract workers:** in situations where human capital is not unique and creates less added-value, reputation capital or poses little reputation risk to the core business, employees are increasingly employed on a contract for services basis, either through outsourcing or, if remaining on a contract of employment, on a strict basis of payment-for-work done. Work tends to be standardized, with little discretion and with performance management limited to ensuring that employees meet targets. There is little investment in human resource development beyond that which is essential to meet basic job and legal requirements. Such employees tend to be located in relatively low skilled, production, service or administrative roles, and are prime candidates for reductions in numbers through the application of information and communications technology (ICT). Low level call centre staff are one example; mid- to low-skilled HR specialists are another, given the advances of ICT in e-HR.

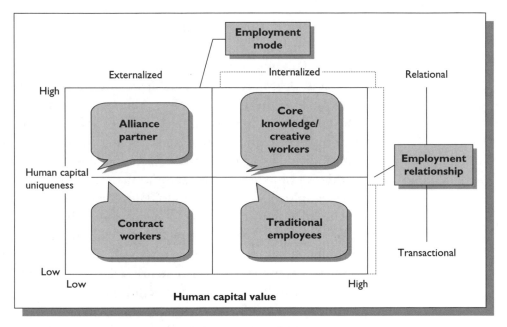

Figure 5.4
The basic architectural model.

To help make sense of some of the material on the importance of context in HRM, let's finish off this chapter by looking at a case of diversity management, one of the shibboleths of politically correct, best practice HRM.

Box 5.3   The Glass Ceiling: diversity management, best practice and best fit

An *Economist* article in July 2005 reported an interesting conundrum. Despite years of effort by companies to develop diversity policies, based on best HR practice, little had changed in terms of numbers of women in top management jobs in Fortune 500 companies (8%), with only

0.7% of CEOs being female. This is despite nearly half of jobs in the US economy being held down by women and women being as well educated as their male counterparts (as measured by Masters-level degrees) (*The Economist*, 2005b). The problem is well known and quite well understood, following the *Wall Street Journal*'s coining of the term the 'Glass Ceiling' in 1985 and a US government commission on this topic in 1995. However, it seems the success numbers are low and not getting any bigger over time. Yet, as the report pointed out, companies are doing more and more to address the issue with companies that were once the bastions of male-domination, e.g. IBM, GE and BP, now making a 'business case' for diversity; i.e. that diversity pays because the market is diverse in terms of tastes, with women and racial minorities becoming increasingly important consumers. Such increased differentiation on the outside, so the argument goes, has to be matched by equivalent differentiation on the inside. Moreover, given the 'war for talent', organizations need to increase the potential pool by including as many diverse groups as possible.

There is evidence that some North American company programmes are beginning to work, with IBM reporting 14% of its senior executives being women, and the Canadian company, Alcan, reporting that three out of its four main businesses are managed by women at the top. Part of what has been behind this has been to change the 'tone at the top' from long hours to more of a work–life balance culture. Yet, despite these well publicized cases and the application of best HR practices, the more things change, the more they remain the same in the USA and the large European economies.

This picture, however, is not quite the same the world over. Look at this table, which shows the proportion of female directors in different countries in 2004.

Country	Female directors as a percentage of total (approx.)
Norway	21.0
Sweden	17.0
USA	12.0
Australia	9.5
UK	7.0

(continued)

Country	Female directors as a percentage of total (approx.)
Germany	6.0
France	5.5
Singapore	5.0
Hong Kong	4.5
Spain	3.5
Italy	2.5
Japan	0.3

What does this table tell you about the importance of context, in this case national context, to the application of best practices?

Conclusions

In this chapter we have introduced the notion of HR strategy and four lenses on strategic HRM, all of which contribute to our understanding of how HRM can influence reputation management and corporate branding. We also discussed the merits of best practice versus best fit strategic HRM. We concluded that, since context matters a great deal in strategy, a contingency approach to HRM is more likely to be appropriate in guiding managers in the design of HR strategies. One of the most useful of these contingency approaches is the architectural metaphor developed by researchers at Cornell in the USA, which we reworked a little to show its relevance to reputation management and branding. The key implication of this architectural approach and of other recent developments in HR segmentation is that there is little sense in treating all employees the same because they differ in their potential to add value, reputation advantage, or risk to an organization's key strategic drivers; they also differ in their abilities. Different bundles of HR practices are required for each segment, especially for those employees whose jobs help build reputations for innovation, differentiation and entrepreneurship (reinforcing the initiative agenda) and those who help exploit existing knowledge and/or maintain social legitimacy (the cooperative agenda).

As the Enron case has shown, some so-called best practices can lead to disastrous results, when pushed to the limits. Consequently, the idea of external fit with the organization's environment and internal fit with each other – bundles of practices – is important in shaping employment relationships and, therefore, reputations and brands. The above case on the Glass Ceiling shows how embedded certain practices might be in different cultural and institutional settings. One of the questions it raises is: would it ever be possible to transfer Norwegian diversity schemes to Japan, or even Italy?

References

Barley, S. R. and Kunda, G. (2006) Contracting: a new form of professional practice. *Academy of Management Perspectives*, **20**, 45–66.

Becker, B. E. and Huselid, M. A. (1998) High performance work systems and firm performance: a synthesis of research and managerial implications, in G. Ferris (ed.), *Research in personnel and human resource management*, **16**, 53–101.

Boxall, P. and Purcell, J. (2000) Strategic human resource management: where have we come from here?, *International Journal of Management Reviews*, **2** (2), 183–203.

Boxall, P. and Purcell, J. (2003) *Strategy and human resource management*. Basingstoke: Palgrave Macmillan.

Cascio, W. F. (2005) HRM and downsizing, in R. J. Burke and C. L. Cooper (eds), *Reinventing HRM: challenges and new directions*. London: Routledge.

Economist (2005a) The conundrum of the glass ceiling, *Economist*, 23 July.

Economist (2005b) War games: a big payoff for two games theorists, *Economist*, 15 October.

Fox, A. (1974) *Beyond contract: work, trust and power relations*. London: Faber.

Guest, D. (1987) Human resource management and industrial relations, *Journal of Management Studies*, **24** (5), 503–521.

Huselid, M. A. (1995) The impact of human resource management practices on turnover, productivity and corporate financial performance, *Academy of Management Journal*, **38**, 635–672.

Huselid, M. A., Becker, B. E. and Beatty, R. W. (2005) *The workforce scorecard: managing human capital to execute strategy.* Boston, MA: Harvard Business School Press.

Joyce, W., Nohria, N. and Robertson, B. (2003) *What really works: the 4+2 formula for sustained business success.* Boston, MA: Harvard Business School Press.

Kang, S.-C., Morris, C. S. and Snell, S. A. (2003) Extending the human resource architecture: relational archetypes and value creation. *CAHRS Working Paper series, 03-13.* Ithaca, NY: Cornell University.

Lawler III, E. E., Mohrman, S. A. and Ledford, G. E. (1998) *Organizing for high performance: employee involvement, TQM and reengineering programs in Fortune 1000 corporations.* San Francisco: Jossey-Bass.

Legge, K. (2004) *Human resource management: rhetoric and realities* (Anniversary edition). London: Palgrave.

Lepak, D. and Snell, S. A. (2002) The strategic management of human capital: determinants and implications of different relationships, *Academy of Management Review,* **24**, 1–18.

Leseure, M. J., Bauer, J., Birdi, K., Neely, A. and Denyer, D. (2004) Adoption of promising practices: a systematic review of the evidence, *International Journal of Management Reviews,* **5/6**, 169–190.

Mintzberg, H., Ahlstrand, B. and Lampel, J. (1998) *Strategic safaris: a guided tour through the wilds of strategic management.* New York: Free Press.

Morgan, G. (1993) *Imaginization.* London: Sage.

Morgan, G. (1997) *Images of organization* (2nd edition). London: Sage.

Paauwe, J. and Boselie, P. (2005) HRM and performance: what next?, *Human Resource Management,* **15** (4), 68–84.

Patterson, M., West, M., Lawthorn, R. and Nickell, S. (1998) *The impact of people management practices on business performance.* London: Chartered Institute of Personnel and Development.

Pfeffer, J. (1998) *The human equation: building profits by putting people first.* Boston, MA: Harvard Business School Press.

Pfeffer, J. (2005) *Creating a performance culture.* Presentation at University of Strathclyde, 23 September.

Porter, M. (1985) *Competitive advantage: creating and sustaining superior performance.* New York: Free Press.

Roberts, J. (2004) *The modern firm: organizational design for performance and growth.* Oxford: Oxford University Press.

Schuler, R. and Jackson, S. (1987) Linking competitive strategies and human resource management practices, *Academy of Management Executive,* **1**, 207–219.

Spector, B. (2003) HRM at Enron: the unindicted co-conspirator, *Organizational Dynamics,* **32**, 207–220.

Stacey, R. (2001) *Complex responsive processes in organization, learning and knowledge creation.* London: Routledge.

Strauss, G. (2001) HRM in the US: correcting some British impressions, *International Journal of Human Resource Management,* **12**, 873.

Sung, J. and Ashton, D. (2005) *High performance work practices: linking strategy and skills to work performance.* London: Department of Trade and Industry in association with the Chartered Institute of Personnel and Development.

Sutton, R. I. (2001) *Weird ideas that work: 11½ ways to promote, manage and sustain innovation.* London: Allen Lane, Penguin Press.

Ulrich, D. and Brockbank, W. (2005) *The HR value proposition.* Boston, MA: Harvard Business School Press.

Walton, R. E. (1985) From control to commitment in the workplace, *Harvard Business Review,* **85** (Jan–Feb), 77–84.

Weick, K. E. (2001) *Making sense of the organization.* Oxford: Blackwell.

Whittington, R. (2001) *What is strategy and does it matter* (2nd edition). London: Thomson.

Wood, S. (1999) Human resource management and performance, *International Journal of Management Reviews,* **1**, 367–413.

Wright, P. M., Gardner, T. M. and Moynihan, L. M. (2003) The impact of HR practices on the performance of business units, *Human Resource Management Journal,* **13** (3), 21–36.

Zhang, H. and Martin, G. (2003) *Human resource management practices in Sino-foreign joint ventures.* Nanhchang: Jiangxi Science and Technology Press.

CHAPTER 6

New developments in HR strategy and the employment relationship

Introduction

In this chapter, we follow up our discussion on segmentation to examine a range of interesting developments that should help HR practitioners create better external and internal reputations, and brands. As part of this discussion, we also introduce the ideas underlying talent management, one of the growth areas in strategic HR because it is one of the major problems facing businesses and public sector organizations, especially in the knowledge sectors and creative industries. We also evaluate these ideas using the lenses introduced in Chapter 5 to reveal their strengths and weaknesses. Finally, we discuss some of the international issues of reputation management, branding and HR, concluding with a case of Wal-Mart in Germany. For those readers involved in multinational companies, we develop these international issues in Chapter 7.

To give readers an insight into the problems certain organizations are facing in this field, we will use a consulting case we were asked to work on. Confidentiality is important here so we have changed the name and location of the company to protect its identity.

Box 6.1   Business and HR issues at Banco (South)

The strategic drivers

Banco (South) (the Company), part of the Banco Group, has under-gone a great deal of change over the past decade, including a recent strategic re-positioning and re-branding exercise that has attempted to differentiate the bank from competitors as a 'local', regional bank but with access to all of the advantages and resources of a major, 'global' financial institution. This positioning and re-branding exercise has been accompanied by the development of a group-wide internal values and behaviours framework, drawing on ideas, research and material from head office. Banco (South) takes part in a group-wide engage-ment survey carried out by a major survey consulting organization. This survey provides a temperature check in the form of quarterly results on employee identification (including internalization of group values, feedback on management style and career development) and engagement with the Group values, as demonstrated by engagement behaviours. The results of this survey are used to provide feedback to senior managers on how people management is supporting the key business drivers, including sales performance and revenue generation, and is used to calculate the performance bonuses of managers in the region.

The Company benchmarks itself against Group norms on all per-formance indicators, and against performance norms for the financial services industry as a whole. As part of this exercise, it uses consulting data to benchmark against engagement norms for the industry, shown it to be in the top quartile for all companies in the relevant group. However, the Company norms on certain key indicators, particularly engagement, are lower than the Group mean norms, even though the South region performs well overall in revenue generation. A further issue raised during discussions with HR staff was the South region's needs to put into place a fresh initiative for IIP re-accreditation (Investors in People[1]), due in 2006.

[1]Investors in People (IIP) accreditation is a quality standards exercise for HR that many UK companies seek to use as a means of guaranteeing the quality of their HR provision. Gaining and retaining accreditation is an exacting process used in setting performance objectives for HR departments and as part of an employer of choice policy.

Initial diagnosis

In discussions with senior HR staff, the following problems were identified as potential causes or factors underlying the Company's performance problems:

1   There was perceived to be no clear line of sight between employees' understanding of the values and behaviours framework and the external image and positioning of the organization. It was felt that this might be a consequence of using a 'global' values framework created by Head Office, which might have had less resonance with the 'local' situation of employees of the Company in the South region.

2   Although there were various sophisticated HR initiatives in place, there was a perception of lack of coherence among them and that they might not be addressing the key strategic drivers of the new strategy and brand. It was felt that there was a morale problem among substantial elements of the Company workforce who were either actively disengaged or apathetic. Without fully understanding the reasons for this, there was a suspicion that leadership and management style, and the basis of rewarding managers for short-term sales performance may be part of the problem. Though leadership style and the basis for rewarding managers may have been linked, this was not always clear and could vary over the regional network; in any event, changing rewards policy was a Group function and not something that could be altered locally by Company HR staff.

3   Whilst the new survey dealt with general levels of engagement and employees' understanding of the values, it was not sensitive enough to provide the information to allow Company HR staff to develop 'locally sensitive' HR policies that would help drive the positioning and branding strategy and improve the benchmarking performance. This applied to Banco (South) and its 10 districts, which form the South region retail banking network. It also applied to its wholesale banking, private banking and regional head office services (including HR, marketing, finance and IT).

4   Senior HR staff also believed that delivery on psychological contracts by the Company of what employees *want, value and* expect may be part of the problem: they may be over-delivering in key areas on the needs of certain groups of employees and under-delivering to others, with the knock-on consequences for attraction, retention,

> motivation, performance and in 'living the brand'. Unless data were made available to HR, senior managers and line managers on these issues, there is no way of knowing if this was the case, nor of tackling what had come to be regarded as an employee segmentation problem.

We have already discussed, in Chapter 4, some of the issues of data collection and analysis that were part of the problem we were faced with in tackling the case. More importantly, however, the case also raises the 'so what?' question: what do we do with the data to improve matters? To help us address this question, we examine some developments in segmentation theory and practice that proved useful in thinking about the real-life problems of the case.

Developments in segmentation approaches

As discussed in Chapter 5, the evidence for the architectural approach is quite convincing, though just because firms manage different groups in the same company differently does not always point to an intended, coherent and effective design strategy. Indeed, according to a wide-ranging review of research on the links between HR and performance, the evidence points in the opposite direction (Marchington and Zagelmeyer, 2005). Moreover, in some cases, it leads to invidious comparisons and endemic employee relations problems because 'losers' in the war for talent resent the success of 'winners'. However, among many practitioners, there are consistent calls for organizations to manage their human resource strategy according to 'architectural' principles. There have been at least three recent important contributions in that direction, all of which are relevant to the Banco case in Box 6.1:

1   Modifications to the original architectural framework by Lepak and Snell, to consider knowledge flows as well as knowledge stocks (Morris *et al.*, 2005).

2   Understanding different employees' lifestyles, wants and expectations to create segments.
3   Workforce segmentation and talent management (Huselid *et al.*, 2005).

Developments in HR architecture

Turning to developments in HR architecture, how human capital and knowledge are combined and managed across an organization over time is an extremely important source of reputational capital and branding. For example, the Swiss–Swedish multinational company ABB, which was the darling of the business press for much of the 1990s and a model for so-called transnational firms, achieved its reputation on the basis of being able to transfer knowledge between different parts of its global empire more rapidly than its competitors through management and leadership development, so creating future sources of value (Martin and Beaumont, 1998; Belanger *et al.*, 1999). Indeed, this ability to transfer and leverage knowledge flows is probably one of the main sources of reputation and value of innovative companies, whether large or small.

The basis on which such firms operate is so-called *social capital*, which is dependent on high levels of organizational identity and individual identification. Social capital is based on (a) the strength of interpersonal networks among employees in and outside of an organization, (b) levels of trust and knowledge sharing between them and (c) the kinds of shared mental models and mindsets of employees, including their sense of organizational identity, which allow them to communicate with each other more or less economically and effectively. We shall meet this concept again when discussing CSR in Chapter 9.

High levels of social capital are necessary to help bring all four groups of employees described in the previous chapter together – core knowledge workers, alliance partners, contract workers and traditional employees – to assist knowledge flows in any organization that employs such a model. However, knowledge flows can be put to two rather different uses, which will have an important influence on HR strategy and organizational design. These are *exploratory* learning (developing something new) and *exploitative* learning (refining and recombining existing knowledge). Combining them we create two HR archetypes – the *entrepreneurial* and *cooperative* modes (Morris *et al.*, 2005). You may have noticed that we have already met these two archetypes in this book under various guises. They include: initiative *vs* cooperation (Roberts, 2004); the idea that reputations are about competing on differentiation, while the CSR agenda focuses on meeting (high) standards of socially legitimate and responsible behaviour (Boxall and Purcell, 2003; Deephouse and Carter, 2005), and increasing variance in an organization as opposed to driving out variance (Sutton, 2001).

These ideas are all variations on the well-established balancing act in organizational studies between a firm's need to *differentiate* and to *integrate*. The key point here is the metaphor of a balancing act; no organization can do without some degree of integration for control purposes or without differentiation for its very existence (why would it exist if it provided exactly the same goods or services as any other in the same place, time, price points, etc.?).

Irrespective of how you label the two types – the use of knowledge flows and different type of learning seems to be as good as any – they are associated with rather different bundles of HR practices, which help us develop the conversation on segmentation quite well (see Table 6.1). You may wish to reflect on how these different bundles of practices might apply to the problems in the introductory case.

Understanding employees' lifestyles and psychological contracts

Many surveys of the links between strategic HR and performance focus on what HR professionals intend should happen and the practices they put into place. However, they rarely examine how employees actually experience HR in practice (Kinnie *et al.*, 2005). Understanding employee's lifestyles and their perceptions of psychological contracts is essential not only to making

Table 6.1

Appropriate HR practices encouraging knowledge flows and reputations for consistency *vs* encouraging 'disruptive' innovation.

	Bundles of HR practices	
	Cooperative/exploitative/ social legitimate behaviours for knowledge flows and reputations for consistency	Cooperative/exploratory/ differentiation behaviours for disruptive innovation
Work design	■ Team-based, to enhance interaction, cohesion and trust ■ Job rotation to strengthen ties and knowledge transfer ■ Bringing in partners from outside to enhance trust	■ Flexible work design to help create diversity and facilitate temporary, sometimes creatively abrasive project teams ■ Cross-functional teams to help learning transfer, new ideas/mindsets ■ Keeping knowledge in-house with no outsourcing of core business
Rewards and motivation	■ Group-based incentives for fostering organizational identification ■ Selection based on fit with values ■ Multi-rater feedback/appraisal ■ Communities of practice to foster working together	■ Individual incentives to encourage initiative ■ Paid on basis of unique and valuable knowledge (high levels of economic rent for knowledge) ■ Pay for creative abrasion/friction and ideas, rather than social cohesion
Human resource development	■ Long-term, relational psychological contracts to foster identification and internal networks ■ Extensive internal branding activities/values ■ Career development and mentoring for building identification	■ Boundaryless careers inside organization (and outside) to develop new ideas ■ Contributions to organizational memory through knowledge banks and sharing of such knowledge ■ External development to bring in new ideas ■ Encouragement of professional identities and networks to learn

Source: Adapted from Morris *et al.*, 2005, p. 70; Davenport, 2005; Hagel and Seely-Brown, 2005

the connections between HR strategies and reputations, but also to refining such strategies to meet differing expectations and wants.

One writer who has popularized the idea of understanding employee lifestyles and how employees experience HR is

Lynda Gratton (2004). She has called for the need to build *individual autonomy, organizational variety* and *shared purpose* as the necessary conditions for building a democratic enterprise. Since these characteristics form the goals of most companies concerned with their long-term reputations and brands, her interests mirror our own in reflecting on the relationships between individual identification, organizational identities and performance. The central propositions of her book are that democratic enterprises will perform better than others for five reasons:

1   They are more likely to engage employees.
2   They create win–win solutions, by balancing individual and organizational needs.
3   They enjoy a reputation for fairness and justice, which helps attract and retain talent, as well as being an end in its own right.
4   They are more flexible and agile because they help people make choices, innovate and create diversity, so essential for the kinds of incremental changes that can turn into longer-term transformational change.
5   They are more able to integrate different parts of an organization to create a shared sense of identity.

Reflecting on our discussion of individual–organizational linkages in Chapter 4, Gratton points to a number of cases in which companies have taken steps beyond the typical engagement survey to learn about employees. An excellent example is Tesco, one of the world's largest and most successful retailers (see Box 6.2).

Box 6.2   Segmenting employees by lifestyle at Tesco

Tesco is the second largest retailer in the world and is growing fast. It is also one of the UK's most admired companies. The CEO challenged the organization to learn as much about its employees as it did about its customers. Tesco has a reputation for being able to have an individual relationship with customers based on the mass of data it collects and analyses through its Customer Insight Unit (CIU), established in 1995. However, it became obvious to the CEO, Sir Terry Leahy, when he was appointed in 1997, that the company did not know nearly as much about its employees. He immediately set about a programme to establish a set of employee values, which was launched in the same year. Feedback, however, in the form of 'Viewpoint', a survey designed to tap into employee identification with the values, showed that only around 40% of staff felt they were valued by the company and their direct manager, with roughly the same, low number reporting that their opinions were listened to. Given these poor results, an appointment was made of a Values Manager, and the values programme was re-addressed through the development of an employer brand proposition (see Chapter 7). Leahy and his Resources Director, David Fairhurst, challenged HR and the values team to work with the CIU and use their marketing expertise internally to learn more about employees.

What emerged was a People Insight Unit (PIU) in 2001. This group built on a range of qualitative and quantitative research techniques to gain insight into their employees. They used focus groups to develop a survey, entitled 'Your Life … Your Future', to understand more about psychological contracts in the company. These survey data were fleshed out with insights from annual and bi-annual engagement survey data from the previous seven years. From this exercise they developed a 'Steering Wheel', balanced scorecard, an important component of which were four key drivers of employee commitment – supportive management, the opportunity to get on, interesting jobs and trust and respect among colleagues.

What also emerged from the data analysis were five segments, each with distinctive expectations, values and perceptions of what had been delivered:

- **Work–life balancers:** mainly older women, with or without children, who most of all wanted flexible hours or part-time employment. They were not particularly interested in challenging work or responsibility.
- **Want it all:** typically aged 25–34, degree holders, working in Head Office, who wanted challenge, careers and high pay, but were prepared to internalize the company values and work for the company's success. They were the most mobile and were most likely to leave if the deal was not delivered.

■ **Pleasure seekers:** many of these were part-time students, single, male but with service of five years. They worked long hours but lacked commitment; their ambitions lay in overseas travel and enjoying themselves outside of work. This group was the most mobile and likely to leave if competitors paid higher. Interestingly, the CIU predict that this group will form a much higher proportion of the working population in the future.

■ **Live to work:** typically young married men or older full-time managers with 10 years' service and working in head office or in distribution. The most ambitious and committed, working long hours and seeking challenging jobs and promotion. For them work was not a social place, and they were willing to sacrifice their home life for the company.

■ **Work to live:** mainly women over 35, with or without children, with long service of around 10 years or more. They were not interested in long hours or challenge, and were willing to do repetitive tasks. Their main desire was to be able to work close to home. Forecasts for this group show a decline in the future.

Forecasts of these different groupings showed different rates of expected commitment and retention.

The second stage of the project has been to design customized employment propositions for each of these groups, e.g., by offering cheap flights as part of the package to pleasure seekers. Their aim is to provide different groups with what they value in terms of employment, and not to waste effort, time and money in providing people with what they do not value. It is not aimed at becoming an employer of choice by providing every kind of benefit to all, but by being selective. The results have been impressive. In 2004, Tesco recorded the lowest staff turnover rates in the grocery retailing industry, of 18% for store staff, 17% for distribution staff and 8% for head office staff, which are much lower than average in an industry notorious for its poor retention rates.

Coupled with these HR initiatives, Tesco has recorded some of the most impressive growth and profitability figures in British industry, making the national news on more than one occasion in 2005.

Source: Based on Gratton, 2004; Barrow and Mosley, 2005; http://www.tescocorporate.com/insidetesco.htm

Tesco is not alone. Another example of this approach is the Royal Bank of Scotland (RBS). Like Tesco, it has grown rapidly, showing one of the fastest recorded growth rates in the global financial services sector to become the world's fifth largest bank and the UK's seventh largest company. RBS has used its technologically advanced human capital system to create up-to-the-minute data on its 137 000 employees in 27 countries. Using a range of databases and survey tools, including its global people data, joiner survey, leaver survey, regular pulse surveys and employee opinion survey, it can build dynamic pictures of its workforce based on different responses to questions on work–life balance, performance and development, leadership, recognition, relationships, the nature of the work itself, reward packages and what employees think of its products, brands and reputation. The output from these data collection exercises is used to create business metrics to support line managers and a range of human resource initiatives, including tailored employee propositions.

It is also worth noting the work of market researchers Taylor Nelson Sofres (TNS), who have carried out major cluster exercises on employee commitment data from 2002 and 2004. They use measures along two axes: *commitment to the organization* and *commitment to career* (see www.tnsofres.com). Combining these two axes to create a two by two matrix produces four clusters of employees. These aggregate-level data produced by TNS can be used as basic benchmarks for organizations wishing to understand how they compare against the working population as a whole in the UK. The emerging clusters are **Ambassadors** (41% of the sample), who are committed to their organization and their career; **Career-orientated** (20%), whose commitment is more to their profession and career than the company (see cosmopolitans in Chapter 4); **Company-orientated** (8%), whose commitment to the organization is greater than to their work or career (see locals in Chapter 4); and **Ambivalents** (31%), who show low commitment to either the company or career.

The Global Employee Commitment Report carried out by TNS surveyed 20 000 employees in 33 countries. Its main finding was that more than a third of the world's companies were failing to get the most out of their employees. According to one commentator, these findings confirmed that Britain's employers have a significant problem on their hands if they want to win the respect and trust of their employees. Though only about half of UK workers feel any loyalty at all to the company they work for (being classified as either Ambivalents or Career-oriented), the picture was even bleaker in Japan, Korea and Bulgaria. Fifty-nine per cent of employees in Japan, 58% in Bulgaria and 55% in Korea were uncommitted to both the work they do and the company they work for. Contrast these findings with the picture in Israel and Norway and you may understand something of the international variation of these segments. Fifty-nine per cent of Israeli and 57% of Norwegian employees fell into the Ambassador category, significantly above the levels found in the other countries.

Some older readers may be thinking, a little like us, that none of this kind of work is entirely new. Indeed, there is a long history of sociological studies on orientations to work that produced similar clusters and segments. Gouldner's work on cosmopolitans and locals, discussed in Chapter 4 was one of the first, followed by the landmark 'Affluent Worker' studies in the UK during the 1960s, and the repeat performances by Michael Mann on the 'Working Class in the Labour Market'. These studies informed later American work on segmenting labour markets and the highly influential ideas of *the flexible firm* proposed by John Atkinson and his colleagues in the 1980s. Similarly, career development studies in organizations have also provided equivalent insights into what employees wanted from work, especially in terms of career orientations and anchors.

Much of the data collected and the types of analysis used in these academic studies were the same as the Tesco and RBS studies. The surprising element to us in all of this activity is that many organizations have been so slow in systematically collecting and using such data, though in one sense we should not be surprised since understanding employees has always been treated as an expense (usually an unnecessary one) rather than as an investment – unlike spending on market research. Barrow and Mosley (2005) pointed out how only a tiny proportion of expenditure in market research is allocated to understanding labour markets and employees. What is different, however, and may explain the recent upsurge in employee data collection, is the relative ease and speed with which such data can be collected and analysed, using online surveys to achieve high response rates. This drastically reduces the expense element, and coupled with innovative insights into what can be done with these data to achieve significant business results, employee surveys have now begun to address the 'hot buttons' of many businesses. Our examples of designing individualized employment propositions and reducing turnover help provide evidence for this business case; so do the examples of Tesco and RBS. These examples also serve as a good introduction to the last of our segmentation approaches.

Workforce segmentation and talent management

There has been a noticeable change in the recommendations in the strategic management literature from the 'global to local'. This change represents a move away from a rather simple world of monolithic organizations pursuing generic strategies, such as low cost, focus and differentiation, to an altogether more complicated scenario, made up of increasingly differentiated multinational companies and new-style, networked forms of organizations turning towards strategies that are, or have to be, more localized, and relevant to tightly defined geographical markets or product/service segments (Hagel and Seely-Brown, 2005; Paauwe and Boselie, 2005) (see Chapter 7). What works in one set of usually localized and mostly short-lived competitive conditions, will not often work in others for any length of time (Greenwald and Kahn, 2005a). This is because the three main sources of competitive advantage, customer captivity, proprietary forms of technology and knowledge, and economies of scale, are either temporary or must be combined with one or both of the others to have any lasting advantage in globalized markets. Competition usually ensures that customers have plenty of options in the long run, since technology and knowledge becomes obsolete or widely available, and even economies of scale only hold good for restricted markets (many fixed costs are tied to a specific product-market or geographical area). We will look at an example of Wal-Mart's entry into Germany later in this chapter to illustrate the problems of global strategies, and follow up this global–local problem in the next chapter.

As a result, dynamic localism and decentralization of strategy compete with the benefits of a more corporatist agenda in the new strategic HR literature. One of the best examples of this is the strategic workforce segmentation approach developed by Mark Huselid, Brian Becker and Richard Beatty (2005). They have chosen the terms, '*differentiating the workforce strategy*' to '*drive effective strategy execution*' as their strap line for new approaches to HR segmentation. In a similar fashion to our discussion of the four lens framework on which this chapter is based, they argue that just as strategy can be analysed in terms of content (the goals to which it is put) and execution (the process of implementing strategy), so can its workforce strategy. This they define as the systems used to select, develop and reward the workforce.

Reflecting the trajectory of thinking in the strategic management literature, they make an initial distinction between organizations that use *generic best practices* to drive strategy execution (which are low on workforce differentiation and low on strategic impact) and *core workforce differentiation* (which is akin to some of the internal fit approaches we have considered, such as the HR drivers of generic innovation, cost and focus strategies in Table 5.1 in the previous chapter). This trend to core workforce differentiation is regarded as a move in the right direction but not one that goes far enough in identifying the *elements* of those generic strategies that drive strategy execution. Thus the second, and arguably more important, trend they identify is towards *strategic customization* (see Figure 6.1), the elements of which are likely to vary across an organization on the parts of a generic strategy for which individual managers have direct responsibility. Borrowing from Michael Porter, Huselid *et al.* noted these elements provide the key *strategy activity systems*, which are operationalized by *strategic performance drivers*.

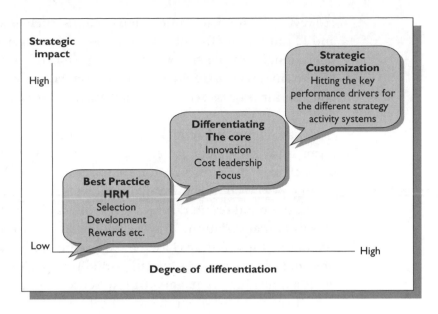

Figure 6.1
Customization of workforce strategy (based on Huselid *et al.*, 2005, p. 35).

There is a lot of complicated business-speak here, so let's use an example of what it could mean in practice. In any organization there is likely to be more than one generic strategy in operation. For example, in our Banco example, the core strategy seems to be one of differentiation by providing the complete range of financial services offered by an international bank but tailored to a local (South) regional market to reflect its distinctive wants and needs. Such a strategy is, rather inelegantly, known in 'the trade' as 'glocalization'. This is likely to require high levels of (i) *local customer intimacy solutions* to capture and retain customers and (ii) *global operational excellence* to achieve economies of scale. Customer intimacy depends on behaviours that demonstrate flexible responses to local customer problems and high levels of cross-selling of products and services, such as financial advice, insurance and mortgages (which usually form the main sources of revenue generation in retail banking) They also require HR systems to support these behaviours, e.g. those aimed at generating high levels of flexible responses and knowledge sharing across different parts of the business.

However, certain 'back office' departments, such as accounting and IT, and even HR, may have strategic goals that emphasize operational excellence, which is based more on continuous improvement, waste reduction, risk averse behaviour and a high concern for process accuracy rather than on external customer focus.

Consequently, the retail branch managers will have quite different strategic performance drivers for selling products and services and providing customer solutions from back office managers who control information flows across the bank. Even within the retail branch banking network itself, there may well be substantial variations in types and levels of customer intimacy among those regions based in large cities and those in rural or semi-rural areas, and thus rather different performance drivers for individual managers. In one sense, this is just another way of saying that all strategy is local, as we have suggested, because there is rarely such an entity as a global consumer or global employee. Local differences matter! – though this is not a truism that some companies recognize (see the Wal-Mart case at the end of the chapter).

One of the most important points made by Huselid *et al.* is that, although competitors (in this case, competitor banks) may have a similar generic strategy, the source of their competitive advantage will lie in either:

■ addressing different strategic activities (e.g. organizing and managing the product/service mix of the bank) in different ways, or
■ addressing the same strategic activities (e.g. the same product/service mix provided by bank branches to others) in different ways.

Devising and executing HR strategies that assist in either source of advantage is one of the best ways of ensuring that these strategy activities are performed in a manner that is not easily imitated by competitors.

So, the lessons for our case study of Banco (South) are to:

■ Set out the key strategic activities that will lead to successful strategy execution. This process will help define the key performance drivers (see Table 6.2 for an example of strategic activities and performance drivers for retail managers)

■ Identify the unique human capital demands (knowledge, skills and attitudes) of each performance driver, and

■ Develop differentiated workforce strategies to meet the human capital demands of each strategic activity.

Table 6.2

Examples of strategic activities and performance drivers for retail bank managers

Performance driver	Strategic activity
Maximize reliable service to customer Manage attrition rates of existing customers Develop effective marketing programmes for new/existing customers Continue developing products and service range	Grow and retain the number of high value customers and high potential customers
Cross-selling of banks' branded products and services Grow revenue from non-branded products and services Increase fees to customers and balances in accounts	Increase revenue per customer
Transfer customers to online banking Increase customer use of online banking Reduce transaction costs per customer	Reduce cost per customer to the bank

HR's role in developing differentiated workforce strategies depends on two features of strategy.

■ **Content:** How well they are able to use innovative bundles of HR practices to impact directly on the human capital demands of each performance driver. This addresses the content aspects of strategy in much the same way as our earlier examples of innovation, cost and focus, but this time, developing HR strategies that support innovation where it is needed in the business (e.g. growing high value customers through creative marketing and product design), cost leadership (e.g. reducing transaction costs per customer), or focus (addressing the specific needs of high value or 'wealthy' customers).

■ **Execution:** How well they implement workforce strategy through effective talent management as the focus for their activities. Huselid *et al.* argue that too much current activity of HR is spent on dealing with employee performance problems – especially low performers – and not enough time is spent on helping line managers address high performance problems, especially recruiting, motivating and retaining high performers to perform high value jobs, which is the core of the so-called talent management problem.

Since this notion of talent management is so important to modern HR practice and workforce segmentation – the CIPD in the UK identified it as one of their three major research objectives for 2005/6 – we need to spend a little time discussing it and how it applies to reputation management and branding.

Managing talent

The term 'talent management' has become popular as a result of a major study by North-American-based McKinsey consultants Ed Michaels, Helen Handfield-Jones and Beth Axelrod, who undertook their original work in 1997 on the impact of how companies managed their leadership talent on corporate performance, and have subsequently followed this study up with further research (Michaels *et al.*, 2001). Prior to the bursting of the dot.com bubble in the USA in early 2000, the recruitment of talented people was seen to be the biggest single issue facing US business. Based on some in-depth research among business leaders, these writers concluded that the 'war for talent' was, and would continue to be, one of the most important problems facing industry and commerce in developed countries. The changed labour market circumstances following the downturn in economic prosperity in the USA associated with the dot.com collapse did nothing to diminish their beliefs; subsequent research by them has provided strong support for their thesis in a number of industrial sectors and countries. Their work showed that only a small proportion of senior managers believed their organizations: (a) recruited talented people (their A-class high performers); (b) did all they could to identify and retain these talented performers, and to develop performers with potential (the B class); or (c) undertook to remove or replace low performers (whom they called C-class performers).

Key definition: Defining talent

Talent is seen in individual terms comprising 'a sharp strategic mind, leadership ability, emotional maturity, communications skills, the ability to attract and inspire other talented people, entrepreneurial instincts, functional skills and the ability to deliver results' (Michaels *et al.*, 2001, p. x).

Talent management, they argued, required a new talent mindset among business leaders because it was so 'mission-critical', and therefore could not be left to HR departments. Instead, it required the direct support of the organization's board of directors and needed to be made a core element of the work of business leaders (see Table 6.3).

These authors proposed that organizations that sought to become top performers should implement three elements of a talent management approach. There should be:

- disciplined talent management, through rigorous and continuous assessment, development of managers and matching them with jobs
- creative recruitment and retention through refined and meaningful employee value propositions (EVPs), which we shall discuss more fully in Chapter 8 on communications and employer branding; and
- thoughtful executive development, using coaching, mentoring and on-the-job experiences at key points in managers' development.

Table 6.3

The new talent mindset

Old HR mindset	New talent mindset
The vague leadership and HR rhetoric of 'people being our most important asset'	A deeply held conviction that talented people produce better organizational performance
The responsibility for people management lies with HR	The responsibility for managers to do all they can to strengthen the talent pool
Small-scale and infrequent programmes for succession planning and training managers in acquiring and nurturing people	Talent management as a central component of the business and part of the ongoing role of senior leaders
Managers have to work with the people they inherit	Managers constantly taking active and bold steps to attract and develop their talent pool and actively manage low performers

Source: Adapted from Handfield-Jones *et al.,* 2001

Handfield-Jones has turned this approach into a useful consulting tool, summarized in Table 6.4.

Table 6.4

Elements of a talent management approach

Danger signs	Signs of progress	Signs of achievement
Disciplined talent management		
A focus only on obvious successors in succession planning exercises	Some discussion of incumbents performance	Clear identification of A, B and C performers in each talent pool
Lists of high potential people, but little action	Consultation of list when vacancies occur	Written action plans for each high potential's development and retention
Belief that there are no poor performers	Admit that there are likely to be some, but avoid doing much about it	Act decisively on poor performers by improving or replacing them
Hold no one accountable for talent management, except for HR	Evaluate managers on how well they manage their staff	Hold leaders directly accountable for developing their talent pool

Danger signs	Signs of progress	Signs of achievement
Creative recruitment and retention		
Empty rhetoric about being a good employer to work for	Think about the EVPs for each type of talent	Understand the strengths and weaknesses of the EVPs for each type of talent and plan to strengthen them
Hire only at entry levels and grow only from internal hires	Occasionally bring in senior or specialist people from outside	Recruit a steady flow of talent at all levels
Go to the same sources for recruiting talent	Experiment with new sources, but look for similar backgrounds	Creatively tap new pools of talent, looking for essential capabilities
Have high and consistent attrition rates among managers	Analyse attrition data by department and type	Know the attrition rates of A, B and C performers and understand why they are leaving, performing or underperforming
Thoughtful executive development		
Leave the job assignments of managers to the manager who hires them	Suggest some candidates from the high potential list or job posting system	Involve leadership teams on every assignment decision, seeking to optimize these across the company
Recruit most qualified candidate with no discussion of development	Stretch people, but not in the context of any development plan	Thoughtfully consider the development needs of each assignment and the development needs of each candidate
Assume that the best way to develop people is by throwing them in at the deep end	Provide formal feedback through appraisal once a year	Embed candidate feedback and coaching into the routines of the organization and the jobs of leaders
Invest in training driven by top-down assessments of candidates and then only in response to immediate needs, threats or crisis	Offer regular but basic programmes for management development and leadership, usually off-the-job	Offer integrated management/ leadership learning programmes for each transition point of managerial careers

Source: Adapted from Handfield-Jones, www.handfieldjones.com/diagnose/index.html
(28 February 2006)

Another, similar approach to talent management is found in the four categories of employees that make up a 'talent value chain' (Rosen and Wilson, 2005; Zingheim, 2005):

■ The **Superkeepers**: the 3–5% of employees who consistently demonstrate the 'what and how' of superior performance in ways that reflect the core organizational values, and help others to do so.
■ The **Keepers**: the 25–30% of the organization who make a continual difference; they have demonstrated leadership capabilities and exceed normal expectations for job performance and skills.
■ The **Solid citizens**: the 65% or so of people who meet normal expectations for job performance and skills, and may be able to exercise leadership in some situations.
■ The **Misfits**: the 3–5% of people who continuously fall below normal expectations for job performance and skills, are unable to exercise leadership in some situations, and do not fit with the organizations' core values.

This kind of differentiation mirrors the language of psychological contracting by recognizing the individual nature of psychological contracts and the different types of contracts. Moreover, there are various ways in which marketing ideas have been incorporated. First, internal marketing is implied in organizational price segmentation through rewards strategy. Second, given that talent, by definition, is in short supply, its price has risen markedly over the past few decades in many countries. So organizations, it is argued, will have to become used to 'paying for the person', rather than having fixed rates and bands for staff. Differentials between high performers and average performers will gradually increase to reflect market values, providing people with high levels of *economic rent*, the additional levels of rewards beyond those necessary to keep people working when they are in short supply, e.g. star football players, who most probably would continue to play for much lower wages than are paid for playing in the English Premier League or the top male and tennis players who earn enormous rewards on the international tennis circuit.

Zingheim poses six questions she claims organizations need to address (which could also form the mantra for successful Premier League football clubs):

1   What are the absolutely necessary skills and capabilities needed to be successful?
2   Who possesses these Superkeeper skills in the company?
3   Can you identify and find potential Superkeepers outside the company?
4   What total rewards package (career development, compelling vision, workplace environment, and total pay) are Superkeepers looking for?
5   What changes do you need to make to your total rewards package to put your company in the market for top talent?
6   Is your company ready to embrace such a talent management philosophy, and adapt its rewards packages?

There is certainly evidence of this last question having been answered in the affirmative since the 1980s, with ratios of salaries between the top-paid managers and the average salaries of employees increasing significantly in most countries (Wolf, 2002). For example, CEO salaries rose by an average of 8.3% per year during the period 1993–2003 in the USA, whereas the pay of the average employee barely rose at all during the same period (Sparrow and Cooper, 2003; Conyon, 2006).

The third use of marketing is in the strategies for dealing with different 'portfolios' of performers. The traditional Boston Consulting approach to the growth-share matrix uses language like investing in potential 'stars' (the As or Superkeepers) and 'putting down the dogs' (the Cs or Misfits). Such language and approaches to individualizing talent, however, have not captured the imagination of all commentators and practitioners. The case of Enron points to problems that can arise when individual talent management is over-emphasized, especially at the expense of other members of the organization. The Banco Group, like many other organizations which have embraced a talent management approach, is aware of the problems, but may be driven to follow the industry recipe of the Financial Service sector of paying excessively for performance (see Chapter 9).

If you are beginning to form an opinion that all of this rationalism is either all right in theory but wouldn't work in practice, is really little more than old wine in new bottles, or, to put it more kindly, it's a bit of '*vu jade*', then you are still with us. We have nothing against 'how to' books, but, to repeat our take on these matters, 'life ain't that simple'. We have already introduced the three other lenses in Chapter 5, which offer a fresh perspective on the answers to the HR strategy question. They also help point out the strengths and weaknesses of the design school and some of the new developments in architecture and segmentation.

Evolutionary perspectives, the focus on markets and the 'new deal in employment'

As we suggested earlier, evolutionary perspectives rest on assumptions that all markets in the long run are perfect, with few or no significant barriers to entry; also that these all-powerful markets can select out the fittest companies for survival in competitive market environments. What such markets need is a ready supply of firms willing to enter the selection process to drive the forces of competition to a point where they become overpopulated. Only those who have managed to achieve a fit with the competitive dynamics of the industry by maximizing profits and minimizing costs will survive in the long run. The dot.com boom in the 1990s and 'dot.bomb' decline in the early part of this current decade illustrates this point quite well. It is also likely that many of the numerous firms entering the rapidly expanding e-business and e-trading markets in the USA, Asia and Europe will also suffer the same fate – Yahoo!, Amazon, e-Bay are exceptions that prove this rule.

As a result, strategy doesn't matter in such competitive circumstances, especially HR strategy! Moreover, they have little faith in the capacity of managers and leadership to do other than contain costs for short-term competitive advantage and ensure their firms are flexible enough to respond to rapidly changing market circumstances. Consequently, this has not been promising ground for HRM scholars and practitioners. This evolutionary view is worth taking seriously because it explains the reactions by many organizations to difficult market circumstances (i.e. when barriers to entry are low) and provides a rationale for HR cost-cutting, even while simultaneously claiming 'people are our most important assets'. The case of Agilent in Chapter 3 is a good example of a firm with a once proud record for job security having to operate in changed market circumstances of increased competition; and, we are sure, you can name many more.

One of the few HR thought-leaders to embrace such a position is Peter Cappelli (1999). He pointed to evidence of change in the American economy during the last decade including changed work organization to empowered teams and reduced hierarchy, downsizing and delayering, lower levels of training, decreased employment security and lower employee expectations of jobs and conventional careers, reduced job tenure, increased outsourcing and a higher incidence of contingent pay. These trends, he argued, had a serious message for firms that tried to deny the logic of market circumstances, often cast in the form of a proposition – 'change-or-die'. Gone were the days of relational contracts and job security; instead he proposed that firms would have to renegotiate changes in psychological contracts to transactional/exchange-based contracts. Of course, such changes were not without costs, especially when labour markets became tight, as they did in the late 1990s. Employees had learned the lessons of new deals only too well and began to exhibit much less commitment to employers and to traditional careers. Coupled with the increased evidence of new organizational forms, such as the so-called flexible firm based on a sharp distinction between core and peripheral employees, project organizations, networked and cellular organizations, some commentators were forecasting the 'end of career' thesis. Managing HR in such circumstances had fundamentally different implications than in the past, with employers offering and employees seeking new deals based on employability – training and development for the next job (Martin *et al.*, 1998).

There is little doubt that Cappelli's argument has been influential, and downsizing has been one of the trends over the past decade or more that has caught on not only in its natural home, the USA, but also in the UK and continental Europe. In December 2005, Angela Merkel was elected as the first woman Chancellor of Germany, partly on a ticket reminiscent of Margaret Thatcher to restructure German industry by reducing guarantees of job security. Moreover, HR has largely bought the message by looking to technology in ever-increasing doses to reduce its costs and its own headcount (Martin *et al.*, forthcoming).

What Cappelli may have failed to take into account were the rather different circumstances of the knowledge economy and creative class, which has made the management of talent, particularly knowledge workers so critical and difficult; critical because they are essential to the longer-term reputations and brands of companies, especially in innovative organizations; difficult because they refuse to be managed in the patronizing ways of traditional HRM. This is the message of Gratton's democratic enterprise; it is also the message of Thomas Davenport (2005), who has argued that knowledge workers need to be managed in very different ways from traditional workers, e.g. from overseeing work to doing it; from organizing in hierarchies to organizing in communities, from hiring and firing to recruiting and retaining talent, from evaluating visible job performance to assessing invisible knowledge achievements; and from supporting the bureaucracy to fending it off (see Chapter 9).

Wayne Cascio (2005) has been researching into downsizing for more than a decade. He began his studies in a paper published in 1993 by concluding that 'the presumed economic benefits of employment downsizing, such as lower expense ratio, higher profits, increased return on investment, and boosted stock prices, often fail to materialize' (p. 171). Neither, he argued, did overheads decline proportionately; nor was there evidence of greater innovation and productivity. Revisiting the evidence in 2005, he has seen little to change his mind, though, he admits downsizing does work in certain circumstances. These are when employees are let go as part of a systematic business planning process, rather than a reaction to short-term market signals.

Part of the reasoning underlying the failure to realize benefits from downsizing is the effect on talent: those people who remain often bear the brunt of increased workload but also show less commitment and lower morale than previously; talent 'walking out of the door' also reduces the extent of existing networks, the quality of relationships with customers, business forgone and potential innovation. These outcomes have a negative effect on reputations and brands, but if that were not enough, downsizing also affects the ability of organizations to recruit talented people in the future, as we shall see in Chapter 8.

Yet, despite this evidence, even organizations with the best of intentions and long histories of best practice HR, including guarantees on job security, cannot avoid the imperatives of markets, especially if they are caught up in the ineluctable logic of manufacturing decline among developed countries. *The Economist* reported the statistic, as at September 2005, of only 9% of the US workforce employed in the manufacturing sector, with the UK likely to reach such low levels in the near future. Such logic makes segmentation strategies more necessary but, as companies such as Agilent have found out, more difficult to implement.

Processual approaches, the focus on change and HRM

Processual approaches take a contrary view of the power of markets to determine how organizations succeed and question the notion that, in practice, organizations pursue unitary goals. Processual approaches are also united in the belief that a rational planning approach to strategy that is realized as intended is a rare occurrence in an increasingly chaotic and unknowable world. Griffin and Stacey (2005), for example, have set out eight conditions for strategic control concerning the capacity of managers for rational action. Most importantly, these include: (1) that set goals remain stable over time, (2) that managers are capable of setting specific and clear goals, (3) that these goals are anchored in some future reality, (4) that managers share the same goals and (5) that they have the necessary foresight to plan in advance the actions necessary to achieve future states. Of course, put like this, there are few situations in modern industry where such conditions are likely to apply.

For processualists, strategic planning, organizational and HR strategy are little more than a good story that helps managers make retrospective and plausible sense of a series of previous, usually unplanned and sometimes random actions (Weick, 2001; Kinnie *et al.*, 2005). What is important about such strategic sense-making is that managers are able to provide accounts to themselves and to others that are socially acceptable and credible (an important insight into some recent CSR initiatives by organizations?). After all, senior managers are supposed to be the organizational architects, planning our way into action through their unique foresight; it is exactly those functions that we are conditioned to expect from leadership in the western world and it is how enormous salary differentials between senior managers and average employees are often justified.

Instead of employing this, rather different use of an architectural metaphor, Weick calls for *improvised* design in organizations. This is quite distinct from the conventional and linear design, planning and implementation process rooted in the architectural metaphor, both in explanation and in prescription. Improvisation, according to Weick, is a focus on the process of continuous craft-like activity, in which the responsibility for redesign is distributed throughout the organization and is based on the notion of *resourceful humans* (to be invested in) rather than *human resources* (to be cut). Thus, from Weick's perspective, planning as part of the improvisation process performs a number of roles, the first of which is to help managers interpret and justify past behaviours, hopefully so that they can learn to make sound judgements from these actions. Second, he argues that the planning process and strategic 'maps' are useful only to the extent that they help energize and galvanize people into future public and irrevocable actions, because it is through a commitment to action that future sense-making and improvisation can take place. Tom Peters' old quote of 'ready, aim, fire' is an attempt to popularize this idea (not surprisingly, since he cites Weick as one of his greatest influences). Third, such improvisation becomes more plausible when we assume that people act their way into meaning rather than mean their way into acting.

> When people improvise and then look back over their action to see what they might have meant, they often discover decisions that they apparently made, although they didn't realize it at the time ... Thus action is decision-interpreted,

> not decision-driven. Actions are crucial because they
> constrain meaning and structure and organizational form. It
> is these constraints that people seem to lose sight of when
> they assume decisions affect action. (Weick, 2001, p. 77)

So, acting your way incrementally into strategy is preferred because it leads to learning (and to the basis for rationalizing incremental changes as a strategic campaign after the event). Critics of incrementalism have pointed to the limited usefulness of small-scale changes, arguing that radical transformations in culture and human resource management are sometimes required for organizational survival (Stace and Dunphy, 2001). However, as Morgan (1993) has pointed out, incrementalism can produce quantum change through constant iterations. Indeed, he goes further by arguing that transformational change is only possible through incrementalism. Drawing on a number of cases, he has shown how successful 'quantum' change unfolds through a series of highly leveraged 15% initiatives (small-scale, targeted changes) that create 'new contexts in which radically new things can happen'. Each new context provided a decision point at which managers could either learn and go forward, or unlearn and return to previous states (http://www.imaginiz.com/provocative/change/success.html).

Thus processualists focus on the internal complexity of organizations, the limited capacity of managers for rational action, satisficing, the importance of micro-politics in shaping action and small-scale decisions during action. The emphasis in this literature is on organizational coalitions, bargaining and learning as a means of producing strategic change. Some of the seminal work on the role of HRM from this perspective was the research by Pettigrew and Whipp (1991). Their longitudinal case research pointed to the importance of managing the processes of change and the role of intense communications, learning and the layering down of competences over many years in producing long-term competitive success, including building reputations for competence. Other writers from this perspective have also evidenced the messy and accidental nature of changes and human resource management actions that are subsequently rationalized as 'strategic' rather than opportunistic (Dawson, 2003).

The positive message on learning underlying the processual perspective has been most notably taken up by the RBV writers on HRM because they reject the dominance of markets and the ease with which human resources can be bought and sold in the marketplace. Instead, resource-based theorists have focused on the importance of intangible assets and their long-term development as the real source of competitive advantage.

The key message of this processual school for reputation management and HR is that strategic implementation matters! Multiple goals and plural reputations are the natural order of things and HR must learn to manage the politics of changing reputations and understand that reputations and brands are built through continuously leveraged, small-scale changes made during the course of action. It also highlights the problems of top-down programmes of reputation and brand management. A number of years ago, Michael Beer and his colleagues (1990) wrote a well-known paper on why change programmes did not produce change, which was largely put down to their top-down, big-bang nature. Senior managers in their study attempted to change structures, systems and abstract notions such as culture, instead of making ad hoc and relatively small-scale changes to concrete business problems that have immediate payoff. This was one of the messages we tried to put forward in the AT&T case in Chapter 1, and it is certainly a message worth bearing in mind for those responsible for brand management and reputation management.

The embedded systems perspective

We have already made much of the idea that strategy is essentially local, often in geographical terms, and that leaders and managers are deeply embedded in the densely interwoven business system and institutions of their home country. Even among companies that claim multinational status, evidence suggests that they generate their revenues from one dominant location. As Greenwald and Kahn (2005b) wisely counsel:

> For all the talk of the convergence of global consumer demand, separate local environments are still characterized ... by

> different tastes, different government rules, different
> business practices, and different cultural norms ... The
> more local a company's strategies are, the better the
> execution tends to be. (p. 103)

As a result, such companies and their managers are embedded in a relatively local network of institutional characteristics, social relations, professional and educational backgrounds, ethnic backgrounds, cultural norms and value systems.

These historically embedded *institutional differences* among countries (Whitley, 1999), point to strategy and HRM being institutionally and culturally specific phenomena. Institutions refer to the social, political, economic, business and labour market features of a country or region that have historically interacted to create distinctive national business systems. So, for example, we often talk about a distinctive American business system or an Asian business system.

The idea of unique national business systems has become influential in the management literature since the 1990s. It encompasses the idea of differing national cultures but is a much broader concept and has focused on the difficulties in borrowing and diffusing best practices from overseas countries. Though competition among national business systems at the international level has led to borrowing and copying of practices, this process of diffusion does not necessarily result in convergence because the embedding of such practices has to occur in pre-existing and nationally distinctive configurations of business practices. The consequences of this line of thinking for organizations seeking to export their values and practices are threefold: (1) they need to be aware of the historical and institutional configuration of the business system in which they seek to operate; (2) they are likely to meet with institutional resistance to such 'foreign' practices; (3) even if companies are initially successful in implanting their home-grown practices, they can never be sure how these transferred practices will interact with the existing systems to produce anything like the originally intended outcomes.

We have already met a number of examples of this, the first being the case of AT&T in Chapter 1; but because it is so important to the corporate reputation and branding debate, we devote

Chapter 7 to it. For the moment, however, read the short case in Box 6.3 of the world's largest retailer, and some of the mistakes it made in entering the German market, to get an idea of just how important embedded systems are to the debate on strategy, HRM and reputation management.

Box 6.3   Wal-Mart and Overseas Expansion in Germany

Traditionally, retailers are not very good at going abroad. Wal-Mart is no exception. It has done well in America's border countries. It has been successful in Canada, for instance, and in Mexico, where Wal-Mart is the biggest private employer. It has also done quite well in the UK with its takeover of ASDA.

But, in Germany, Wal-Mart ended up with 'egg on its face'. Wal-Mart entered Germany, the third-biggest retail market after America and Japan, in 1997–98 by buying two local retail chains, Wertkauf and Interspar, for $1.6 billion. Whereas Wertkauf was well known and profitable, Interspar was weak and operated mostly run-down stores. Wal-Mart has lost money in Germany ever since. Problems have included price controls preventing below-cost selling, rigid labour laws and tough zoning regulations that make it extremely difficult to build big stores.

Wal-Mart also faced well-established rivals in Germany, such as Metro, and hard discounters such as Aldi and Lidl, already comfortable with razor-thin profit margins. Many retailers in Germany are owned by wealthy families whose business priorities are not always the maximization of shareholder value.

But there was more to it than that. Wal-Mart's entry was 'nothing short of a fiasco', according to the authors of a 2003 study at the University of Bremen. At first, Wal-Mart's expatriate managers suffered from a massive clash of cultures, not helped by their refusal to learn to speak German. The company has come to be seen as an unattractive one to work for, adds the study. In part, this is because of relatively low pay and an ultra-frugal policy on managers' business expenses.

As we suggested, this contrasts with Wal-Mart's much smoother expansion into Britain, where it bought ASDA for $10.7 billion in 1999. ASDA already had a strong business competing on price, and it has since overtaken struggling Sainsbury to become the second-biggest supermarket chain after Tesco. But that may say more about Sainsbury's difficulties in overcoming its problems than ASDA's successes. Unlike Tesco, Sainsbury was slow in responding to Wal-Mart's expected arrival in the British market. In particular, it was late in expanding into non-food goods, the source of much of Tesco's growth.

Wal-Mart's growth ambitions beyond its natural home in the south–central region of the USA have been accompanied by a historical decline in relative profitability since the 1980s, like all US grocery retailers (Greenwald and Kahn, 2005b). Although noted for its purchasing power advantages and logistical advantages based on technology, these did not travel to Germany, which demonstrates the limited impact of operating advantages and the local nature of strategic success.

Questions for reflection:
1   What institutional features of the German system have prevented Wal-Mart from making a successful entry into that country?
2   What could they have done to overcome these problems?

Conclusions

We began this book by examining the case for a corporate agenda but have now come to accept that there are limitations on this process arising from the notion that context matters! These limitations have important implications for our discussion of reputations and branding. So strategy, understood as what is really important about a business, is, to all intents and purposes, local. This idea is reflected in the notion of the strategic turn to a focus on activity systems, customer segmentation and other local concepts introduced in this chapter. It is also reflected in the increasingly sophisticated attempts to segment HR strategies, which we have discussed and applied to a case. However, none of this is particularly new, but has become more in vogue because technology and knowledge about segments has made the business case for understanding employees more affordable; we seem to live in an age when HR strategy reflects marketing strategy in enjoying the epithet of mass customization.

That said, there are important qualifications about HR strategy, whether it matters and how we should best implement it, which has been the subject of our last section. The next chapter takes up this issue of localization and embeddedness in more detail.

References

Barrow, S. and Mosley, R. (2005) *The Employer Brand®: bringing the best of brand management to people at work.* London: Wiley.

Beer, M., Eisenstat, R. A. and Spector, B. (1990) Why change programs don't produce change, *Harvard Business Review,* **68** (6), 158–166.

Belanger, J., Berggren, C., Bjorkman, T. and Kohler, C. (1999) *Being local worldwide: ABB and the challenges of global management.* Ithaca, NY: Cornell University Press.

Boxall, P. and Purcell, J. (2003) *Strategy and human resource management.* London: Palgrave Macmillan.

Cappelli, P. (1999) *The new deal at work: managing the market-driven workforce.* Boston, MA: Harvard Business School Press.

Cascio, W. (2005) HRM and downsizing, in R. J. Burke and C. L. Cooper (eds), *Reinventing HRM: challenges and new directions.* London: Routledge.

Conyon, M. J. (2006) Executive compensation and incentives. *Academy of Management Perspectives,* **20**, 25–44.

Davenport, T. H. (2005) *Thinking for a living: how to get better performance and results from knowledge workers.* Boston, MA: Harvard Business School Press.

Dawson, P. (2003) *Understanding organizational change: the contemporary experience of people at work.* London: Sage.

Deephouse, D. L. and Carter, S. M. (2005) An examination of differences between organizational legitimacy and reputation. *Journal of Management Studies,* **42**, 329–360.

Economist (2005) Industrial metamorphosis: factory jobs are becoming scarce. It's nothing to worry about. *Economist* Online edition, 29 September.

Gratton, L. (2004) *The democratic enterprise: liberating your business with freedom, flexibility and commitment.* London: Financial Times/Prentice Hall.

Greenwald, B. and Kahn, J. (2005a) *Competition demystified: a radically simplified approach to business strategy.* New York: Portfolio/Penguin.

Greenwald, B. and Kahn, J. (2005b) All strategy is local, *Harvard Business Review,* Sept–Oct, 94–107.

Griffin, D. and Stacey, R. (2005) *Complexity and the experience of leading organizations.* London: Routledge.

Hagel III, J. and Seely-Brown, J. (2005) *The only sustainable edge: why business strategy depends on productive friction and dynamic specialization.* Boston: Harvard Business School Press.

Handfield-Jones, H., Michaels, E. and Axelrod, B. (2001) Talent management: a critical part of every leader's job, *Ivey Business Journal*, Nov./Dec., http://www.iveybusinessjournal.com/article.asp?intArticle_ID=316 (20 February 2006).

Huselid, M. A., Becker, B. E. and Beatty, R. W. (2005) *The workforce scorecard: managing human capital to execute strategy.* Boston, MA: Harvard Business School Press.

Kinnie, N., Hutchinson, S., Purcell, J., Rayton, B. and Swart, J. (2005) Satisfaction with HR practices and commitment to the organization: why one size does not fit all, *Human Resource Management*, **15** (4), 9–29.

Marchington, M. and Zagelmeyer, S. (2005) Foreword: linking HRM and performance – a never-ending search, *Human Resource Management*, **15** (4), 3–8.

Martin, G. and Beaumont, P. B. (1998) HRM and the diffusion of best practice, *International Journal of Human Resource Management*, **9** (4), 671–695.

Martin, G., Staines, H. and Pate, J. (1998) The New Psychological Contract: exploring the relationship between job security and career development, *Human Resource Management Journal*, **6** (3), 20–40.

Martin, G., Alexander, H., Reddington, M. and Pate, J. M. (forthcoming) Using technology to transform the HR function and the function of HR.

Michaels, E., Handfield-Jones, H. and Axelrod, B. (2001) *The war for talent.* Boston, MA: Harvard Business School Press.

Morgan, G. (1993) *Imaginization.* London: Sage.

Morris, S., Snell, S. A. and Lepak, D. (2005) An architectural approach to managing knowledge stocks and flows: implications for reinventing the HR function, in R. Burke and C. Cooper (eds), *Reinventing human resources.* London: Routledge.

Paauwe, J. and Boselie, P. (2005) HRM and performance: what next?, *Human Resource Management*, **15** (4), 68–84.

Pettigrew, A. M. and Whipp, R. (1991) *Managing change for competitive success,* Oxford: Blackwell.

Roberts, J. (2004) *The modern firm: organizational design for performance and growth.* New York: Oxford University Press.

Rosen, A. S. and Wilson, T. B. (2005) Integrating compensation with talent management, in L. A. Berger and D. A. Berger (eds), *The talent management handbook: creating orgnizational excellence by identifying, developing and promoting your best people.* New York: McGraw-Hill, pp. 351–365.

Sparrow, P. and Cooper, C. (2003) *The employment relationship: key challenges for HR.* Oxford: Butterworth–Heinemann.

Stace, D. A. and Dunphy, D. C. (2001) *Beyond the boundaries: leading and creating the successful enterprise* (2nd edition). Sydney: McGraw-Hill.

Sutton, R. I. (2001) *Weird ideas that really work: 11½ ways to promote, manage and sustain innovation.* London: Allen Lane.

Weick, K. E. (2001) *Making sense of the organization.* Oxford: Blackwell.

Whitley, R. (1999) *Divergent capitalisms: the social structuring and change of business systems.* Oxford: Oxford University Press.

Wolf, A. (2002) *Does education matter? Myths about education and economic growth.* London: Penguin Books.

Zingheim, P. (2005) Compensating superkeepers: talent your company needs to thrive, in L. A. Berger and D. A. Berger (eds), *The talent management handbook: creating organizational excellence by identifying, developing and promoting your best people.* New York: McGraw-Hill, pp. 365–383.

Corporate reputation and branding in global companies: the challenges for people management and HR

Introduction

Both of us have substantial experience of working and research-ing in multinational enterprises (MNEs), so the kinds of mistakes that Wal-Mart seems to have made in Germany (see Box 6.3) are well-known to us. Nevertheless, we still find them surprising, espe-cially given the insights provided by the huge volume of literature in the popular business press and experience of expatriate man-agers concerning international differences. So, in this chapter we want to share some of our experience and personal research in MNEs with you (see, for example, Hetrick, 2001), as well as highlight the most important findings from research on international HRM, reputation management, corporate branding and CSR.

In Chapter 6, we introduced the idea of embedded systems and the all-important lesson that context matters in transferring practices. This is supported by the general drift in the strategic management literature and practices of many MNEs from global to local solutions to meet increasingly differentiated markets. Workforce segmentation, discussed in the previous two chapters, is merely a manifestation of this general trend. At the same time, however, this book has stressed the trend towards corporateness, reflecting the simultaneous needs for these organizations to balance integration (a strong corporate identity and image) and differentiation (local identification and responsiveness). Global companies are also required to transfer their knowledge and learning rapidly between the parent company headquarters (HQ) and its subsidiaries, among subsidiaries and, increasingly, from subsidiaries back to the parent (HQ). How well they achieve this knowledge transfer often determines their long-term success and depends on the nature of the balance between corporateness and differentiation. Yet, as we have seen, operating in international environments adds levels of management complexity to MNEs, especially when dealing with the problems of differences in national cultures and institutional frameworks. These problems have been graphically labelled, the 'liability of foreignness'.

Key concept: The liability of foreignness

This has been defined by Zaheer (1995) as 'the costs of doing business abroad that result in a competitive disadvantage for a multinational enterprise (MNE)'. These costs broadly refer to all of the additional costs a firm operating in a market overseas incurs that a local firm would not incur. Four such categories of costs are likely to arise: (1) costs directly associated with distance, such as the costs of travel, transportation and coordination over distance and across time zones; (2) firm-specific costs based on a particular company's unfamiliarity with and lack of roots in a local culture and business system; (3) costs resulting from the host country environment, such as the lack of legitimacy of foreign firms and economic nationalism among governments and people; (4) costs imposed by home country governments on doing business overseas, such as the restrictions on high-technology or weapons sales to certain countries. The relative importance of these costs and the choices firms can make to deal with them will vary by industry, firm, host country and home country. Regardless of its source, the liability of foreignness suggests that, other things being equal, foreign firms will have lower profitability than local firms and, perhaps, a lesser chance of survival.

Reputation management and corporate branding are even more essential strategies for MNEs than for large domestic businesses, especially when addressing the inherent profitability problems raised by the liability of foreignness. Economists argue that information asymmetries are one of the most important constraints preventing the efficient working of free markets. Why, for example, would you want to buy British education if you live in the USA, especially since you are unlikely to have the equivalent knowledge of, or access to information about, a remote British university as you would about an American one based in New York or Boston. Perhaps naturally, you would be unlikely to have as much confidence in their degrees, or place as much trust in their ability to deliver personal service as you would with your local university. It is for just this reason that university education has traditionally remained a largely domestic business, though this changed during the 1990s when the major university celebrity brands began to export their services overseas, with Harvard being the best example. University business schools, in particular, have been at the forefront of investing in reputation management and corporate branding since they are the most powerful market mechanisms for dealing with such information asymmetry over trust and confidence issues. And, in line with the central thesis of this book, universities are also investing heavily in HRM because they realize good reputations and strong corporate brands rely on their talent and on how well and how sensitively they manage their people and overseas affiliates. This is a lesson that Wal-Mart apparently failed to learn in Germany.

In this chapter we will discuss the additional problems faced by MNEs in global reputation management and branding, since they make up a substantial element of world trade. We will examine the different HR strategies they commonly adopt and illustrate these with our research. As you will see, there is a strong element of 'best practice' in the proposed solutions, which focus on balancing the needs for integration and differentiation. However, readers should be aware that best practice always has to be qualified by the question: in whose interests? For, as we shall see in Chapter 9, there is a major difference of opinion in whose interests companies should be run – shareholders or the wider communities in which MNEs operate?

Globalization >

The general trend to so-called globalization and a world dominated by MNEs has become a fact, at least according to some influential commentators (Friedman, 2005). Globalization, however, is an over-used and ambiguous concept that variously means (1) a smaller world resulting from communications, (2) convergence of economies along the lines of the American Business Model, or (3) Americanization of cultures, tastes, politics and products – the so-called 'McDonaldization of Society' thesis. We will use it in a more specific sense to refer to the internalization of markets and the dominance of such markets by international companies, many but not all of which are American. More than half of world trade occurs within and among these corporate giants (Yeung, 1998). Some of the world's largest MNEs hold total assets and generate income comparable to the wealth of a number of national economies. Over the course of a few decades some MNEs, such as Daimler–Chrysler, Fords, Toyota, Wal-Mart, GE, Citigroup, Mitsubishi, Siemens, IBM, Exxon and BP (and Microsoft, which is ubiquitous but not seriously large) have evolved to highly sophisticated networks transcending national boundaries and becoming household names in virtually every corner of the global economy, so-called transnational companies.

MNEs also probably employ more than one-fifth of the world's workers outside the agricultural sector in the industrialized countries. Estimates in 1999 suggested that there were 53 000 multinational companies, controlling about 450 000 subsidiaries and selling goods and services worth an estimated $9.5 trillion (Edwards *et al.*, 1999). The total number of workers employed by MNEs worldwide was also thought to be around 70 million with some 29 million working for foreign subsidiaries (Royle, 1997).

These companies typically share some key characteristics. Some of these characteristics, as we have seen, embody a careful balancing act between the needs of integration and differentiation, including:

1   The need to pursue a degree of uniformity in areas such as branding, manufacturing processes, core services such as IT and HR, and increasingly image and reputation to support their business strategy.
2   'Best practices' in the form of knowledge and learning to reap the benefits of being large.
3   A degree of decentralized decision-making to reflect local markets and idiosyncratic tastes, and cultural and institutional differences, whilst simultaneously centralizing many 'best practice' human resource processes on recruitment, talent and performance management to build a global corporate reputation.
4   Employee mobility through expatriate assignments and short-term secondments, and cross-border management to instil company practices and values.
5   The development of core business processes and the move away from country-based operations towards line of business or product/service divisions. For example, when Shell changed its business from oil extraction to retailing and re-focused on centres of excellence around the world, HR had to arrange the staffing, the procedures and the policies to help implement the change in place and embed it within the company.

Do MNEs differ in the ways they operate?

What is special about the strategies of MNEs from, say, equally large, domestic operators, or firms with only a limited international exposure through exporting or franchising? One way of answering this question is to refer to the well-known model in Figure 7.1 for balancing the integration–differentiation problems (Perlmutter, 1969). This framework has been used to analyse different approaches to international management, especially HR management (see Figure 7.1).

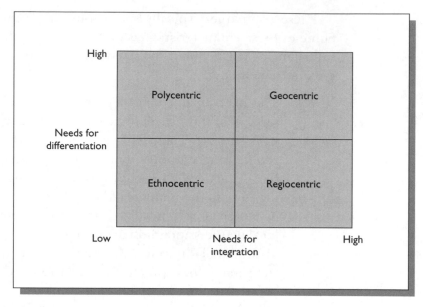

Figure 7.1
Classifying approaches to international management development and deployment.

- **Ethnocentric** approaches are characterized by organizations that have little interest in either developing a strong corporate culture across subsidiaries/markets or in establishing a strong local identity. Often they have a strong belief in the virtues of their own culture and institutions and seek to export them overseas. The approach to staffing, deployment and development is focused on head office interests and its predominant need to maintain financial control. 'Exporting' home managers to run local subsidiaries with little or no thought given to the role and training of local managers is the usual approach to management 'development'. They may even see educating local managers as a dangerous strategy (too much knowledge!). This resonates with political or economic colonial/imperialist styles of management.
- **Polycentric** approaches are characterized by firms that have little knowledge of local product and/or labour markets, or believe in the importance of differentiation above all else. Such an approach is evident in the hiring of local managers, developing them locally, and 'letting them get on with the job' with minimal interference.

■ **Regiocentric** approaches are characterized by a strong emphasis on regional integration, such as having a strong regional brand, or a regional corporate culture that reflects product and or labour market features. Japanese firms setting up in Europe were good examples. Managers tended to be recruited from home office, deployed in a particular region and educated into a regional mindset.

■ **Geocentric** approaches are characterized by a belief that nationality has no place to play in modern business and that home office 'imperialism' is bad for business because it promotes monocultures and inhibits change. High needs for integration and differentiation are thought to be reconcilable but such organizations are relatively rare. They believe in recruiting managers from inside or outside the company, regardless of nationality, and in developing them to have a global mindset through education in international (academic and/ or corporate) business schools and through frequent assignments in different countries.

As you might expect, the geocentric strategy has been held up as the ideal model because it attempts to combine and balance the theoretical ideals of integration and local responsiveness (see Box 7.1 on UBS). However, there is rarely a one best way of doing anything, whether it is governing world affairs, organizing economies, playing football or managing international businesses. Like all 'metanarratives', at various points in time and space, they have been found wanting, even the American Business Model which has been exported to much of the rest of the world by the International Monetary Fund (Kay, 2004). Usually, it is better to think in terms of 'small stories' (see Chapter 8), which are embedded in the institutions and cultures of parent company nationality and the idiosyncratic features of the host country. For example, even the ethnocentric approach has advantages and still dominates the HR strategies of many internationalizing organizations. It has some historical justification since it was the basis of the British Empire's strategy for most of its 200-year dominance of world affairs (although there have been periods and places when Britain pursued a more polycentric strategy, for example, in North America). It has also been a strategy employed by many US

MNEs as part of the USA's 'economic imperialism' at various points in recent history and in certain regional contexts with particularly good effect (though not in the case of AT&T in our opening chapter and Wal-Mart in the previous chapter). So, like all two-by-two forms of 'boxology', these categories are an oversimplification of the strategies employed by MNEs, which are often more complicated in reality, reflecting an intricate web of influences (Tayeb, 2003).

Box 7.1   Geocentric HR practices at UBS and Unilever Polska

UBS: UBS, now the sixth largest financial services group, operates on a global basis. The organizational structure reflects this with country managers representing the business and functional areas, such as HR. For example, the Global Head of Resourcing, based in London, reports to the Global Head of Talent Management, based in New York. UBS has around 80 000 employees, with 6–7000 based in the UK. According to interviews, globalization had been a major issue for the business for many years. The drivers were based on a desire to integrate the company across borders, efficiencies of scale and demands from clients for a 'one-stop shop'. The challenge for the HR teams was to use 'global principles' to govern processes. As an example, the following principles are used as part of a global governance framework for employee resourcing:

- Vacancies are always advertised internally before commencing an external search
- HR manages relationship with head-hunters, not the line manager
- Head-hunters are only used for jobs above a certain grade

One of our interviewees commented that 'the more you look for areas of commonality, the more you find them'. This approach means that when employment policies are adapted or created, there is an immediate engagement with country managers from design through to implementation. The challenges for the HR function within UBS are less on developing a 'global mindset' and more on the role and capability of the HR function and its relationship with the business as a strategic partner.

Unilever Polska: According to the National Personnel Director of Unilever Polska, 'Unilever Polska is very much a reflection of the global thing, with certain different shading. The fact that it is called "global" does not mean at all that what is available worldwide must be applied in Poland. Not at all. Anything that is predominately best practice … if you don't find it relevant you don't take it. It is as simple as that. Now having said that, there are, of course, as in any other international company, certain guidelines, or framework, within which we have to stay. Things like job evaluation, remuneration guidelines, management development guidelines. I think that would be it. Anything else is up to the National Chairman, i.e. up to me to suggest to the Board to approve or disapprove. If we are talking job evaluation, it's a kind of "lingua franca". If you go to Malaysia and I say "job class 20", and I took somebody who is job class 20 with us, and in Malaysia they tell you he's job class 20, [the] experience, the skills, the expertise will be more or less the same. That's why I call it a lingua franca. If I say we recruit people by a selection board, what we have in Poland is more or less available in South Africa or Argentina. If I say there are certain restrictions on remuneration that means there are certain guidelines which we have to follow here as well as in Hungary, US and UK, providing this does not break local rules.'

The geocentric strategy closely resembles the *transnational* strategy described by Bartlett *et al.* (2004). A transnational strategy rests on facilitating learning among subsidiaries, developing high flexibility and local responses to problems and building an interdependent and integrated culture. Companies seeking to develop a transnational company are advised to pay great attention to their corporate culture and organizational identity as a means of achieving global integration, since it is the company's values, organizational culture and identity that are seen as the common language or 'corporate glue'. HR policy tends to be specific and influential with numerous guidelines, procedures and guiding corporate values. It is argued that employees in foreign subsidiaries learn and internalize the values, behaviours and norms of the global company. The intent is to de-emphasize national cultures and identities and replace them with the company's culture and organizational identity.

Examples of geocentric HR procedures are global policies regarding recruitment and promotion criteria; 'single status' policies, a uniform stance towards unions; standardized procedures for performance evaluation; global compensation policies; uniform monitoring of human resource management through opinion surveys; a code of corporate values guiding the indoctrination of newly hired recruits; and policies on ethics and CSR.

The geocentric company uses an integrated framework of HR policies and practices as a basis for adaptation to local regional or global circumstances. The strategy is a conscious attempt to mix local approaches with global policies. For example, a set of universal competencies might be identified as part of a global performance management scheme, using particular rating scales to ensure consistent standards. However, the actual practice of appraisal interviewing and how ratings are arrived at may differ from country to country.

Can corporate HR practices be transferred across national boundaries?

In Chapter 6, we introduced the idea of embedded systems, based on the important institutional and cultural differences among countries. MNEs are often thought to be a force for convergence but these differences are still important and influence strategy, people management and HR practices. We have already seen this in a number of cases throughout this book.

The extent to which HR practices, intended to reinforce corporate identities, images and brands can be transferred is often thought to be a reflection of the 'institutional distance' between the parent company's country of origin and the host company's country of origin (Martin and Beaumont, 2001). But what exactly are embedded systems and the institutions on which they are based? And how have they come to be formed? How, for example, do the laws, customs and industrial relations history of a country or region constrain brand-building?

National cultures

Sociologists often refer to *institutions* in their analysis of societies, by which they typically mean the key 'pillars' of society such as the family, religion, education, the mass media, business and financial institutions, labour movements, the state and its agencies, and so on. These key institutions both shape and are shaped by national cultural beliefs, assumptions and values (Tayeb, 2003). You will see in Box 7.2 a well-known example of describing differences in national cultures.

Box 7.2   National cultural values

Generally speaking, in the management literature at least, culture refers to 'systems of meanings – values, beliefs, expectations and goals – shared by a particular group of people that distinguish them from members of other groups' (Gooderham and Nordhaug, 2003, p. 131; Schneider and Barsoux, 2003). Ed Schein, one of the founding fathers of cultural studies in management, has defined culture as:

---

a set of basic assumptions – shared solutions to the universal problems of external adaptation (how to survive) and internal integration (how to stay together) – which have evolved over time and are handed down from one culture to another. (Schein, 1985)

One of the best-known attempts to distinguish countries according to the differences in national cultural dimensions is by Hofstede (2003). He identified five such dimensions:

- **Power distance:** High and low power distance refers to the extent to which the less powerful members of organizations and institutions, such as the family, accept and expect that power is distributed unequally. This bottom-up view suggests that a society's level of inequality is endorsed by the followers as much as by the leaders. France and Spain are often cited as examples. Power and inequality, according to Hofstede, are fundamental facts of any society, and experience of living in different societies will lead anyone to the conclusion that all societies are unequal, but some are more unequal than others.
- **Individualism:** This dimension is defined in contrast to *collectivism* and refers to the degree to which individuals are integrated into groups. In individualist societies the ties between individuals are loose: people are expected to look after themselves and their immediate family. The USA is seen as a highly individualist society. In collectivist societies, people from birth onwards are integrated into strong, cohesive groups, more often than not in extended families, which provide

protection and a level of identity in exchange for unquestioning loyalty. Chinese societies are good examples. It should be noted that Hofstede did not intend the notion of collectivism to have a political meaning, such as occurred in the old USSR. It refers to the group, not to an official state ideology.

- **Masculinity** versus its opposite, *femininity*: Hofstede attracted much criticism for his use of terms here, especially from writers concerned with gender studies. However, he claims that he has been misunderstood or misinterpreted. His argument was that different societies distribute roles between the genders in different ways. His studies revealed that (a) women's values differ less among societies than men's values; (b) men's values from one country to another contain a dimension from very assertive and competitive (and very different from women's values in a country), to modest and caring (and similar to women's values in that country). The assertive pole he called 'masculine' and the modest, caring pole, 'feminine'. The women in feminine countries he described as having the same modest, caring values as the men; in the masculine countries they are somewhat assertive and competitive, but not as much as the men, so that these countries show a gap between men's values and women's values. Sweden is often used as an example of a feminine society.

- **Uncertainty avoidance:** This refers to a society's tolerance for uncertainty and ambiguity and how it deals with these issues. According to Hofstede, it refers ultimately to a society's search for and belief in a universal Truth and indicates the extent to which a country's culture mentally programs its members to feel comfortable in unstructured situations. Unstructured situations refer to new and perhaps surprising ones, which are different from those usually experienced. Uncertainty avoiding cultures try to minimize the possibility of such situations by imposing laws and rules, safety and security measures, and on the philosophical and religious level by a belief in absolute truth. Germany is often cited as an example.

- **Long-term *vs* short-term orientation:** This fifth dimension was brought to public notice by one of Hofstede's colleagues, Michael Bond, in a study among students in 23 countries around the world, using a questionnaire designed by Chinese scholars. Values associated with long-term orientation are thrift and perseverance; values associated with short-term orientation are respect for tradition, fulfilling social obligations and protecting one's 'face'. Both the positively and the negatively rated values of this dimension are found in the teachings of Confucius, the influential Chinese philosopher who lived around 2500 years ago. However, the dimension also applies to countries without a Confucian heritage.

Hofstede's work, like a number of writers who have adopted a cultural differences approach, has a number of shortcomings, which practitioners should be aware of when using such research:

- He generalized about the culture of national populations on the basis of a small number of questionnaire responses of one organization in particular countries. Small sample research is prone to error. In addition, attempting to describe national variables while undertaking research at the level of the firm is always dangerous. The corporate culture of the firm is always likely to influence respondents' answers.
- He did not acknowledge the variation in cultures within countries, as noted earlier, which can often be greater than the variation between countries, e.g. the former Yugoslavia and USSR.
- Questionnaires are not a good means of identifying deep-rooted concepts like culture. Many academics claim that survey methods tap the surface of culture, which can be fully understood by more in-depth qualitative research, or by living in a culture.

Nevertheless, Hofstede's research is still the standard work against which all other studies of international management compare themselves; and his ideas have been replicated and validated, at least partially, in numerous studies[1]. Both of us have found it a useful starting point to think about the practical implications of operating in different national cultures. Like any framework, however, it has limitations that have to be addressed by other ideas, through which the institutional approach comes into its own (as Hofstede himself has come to realize in his more recent work).

---

[1]A more recent and ambitious study of comparisons in global leadership drawing on Hofstede's work is the GLOBE project (Global Leadership and Organizational Behaviour Effectiveness). The website is certainly worth consulting, see www.thunderbird.edu/wwwfiles/ms/globe/.

Institutions and business systems

It is possible to make an analytical distinction, at least, between the more abstract notion of national culture, with its emphasis on values, assumptions and beliefs, and the more concrete notion of institutions, which refer to the particular organizational forms and structures of behaviour that define a society (which influences cultures and are, in turn, influenced by them). In the business literature, institutional analysis, along with some of the ideas about national cultures, has been used to describe the variety of national or regional models that provide alternative and often competing modes of operating in the global economy (Whitley, 1999). As we have suggested, competition between national systems has led to much borrowing and diffusion of best practices, but these cross-border developments have not resulted in the wholesale convergence predicted by the proponents of globalization. Yes, institutionalists accept that national systems are increasingly interlinked and interdependent and that we are witnessing greater mutual influence between such national systems, but they also point out that the picture is of a more complex pattern of simultaneous *convergence* and *divergence* in any system (Ferner, 2000). These writers have introduced the concept of national (or regional) 'business systems' to describe complex patterns of institutions and behaviour that have become an accepted way of comparing and contrasting business and management issues in countries and regions of the world. We can get a better idea of what a business system might comprise by examining the following definition.

Key definition: A national business system

National Business Systems comprise the interlocking institutions that shape the markets, nature of competition and general business activity of a country (or region). These institutions include the industrial relations system; the systems of training and educating of employees and managers; the typical structure of organizations, the typical relationships among firms in the same industry, typical firms' relationships with their suppliers and customers, the nature of financial markets of a society; the conceptions of fairness and justice held by employers and labour; the structure of the state and its policies for business; and a society's idiosyncratic customs and traditions as well as norms, moral principles, rules, laws and recipes for action.

Based on Hollingsworth and Boyer, 1997, p. 2

As you can see, this definition refers to the cultural features of society, such as assumptions about fairness and justice, norms, moral principles and recipes for action, but it also highlights the specific organizational forms, relationships and systems that both reflect and give rise to these cultural features of a nation or region's business system. We believe that this wider conception of business systems and how they develop provide additional insights for practitioners that make the approach indispensable for a deep understanding of how to manage in specific countries; the kind of understanding that might have served Wal-Mart well in Germany. There are at least four characteristics of a business system approach that make it useful for practitioners wanting to understand the potential for creating strong corporate brands:

- The importance of a historical perspective
- The systemic and enduring nature of business systems
- The role of critical turning points in changing systems
- The basis for comparing business systems.

The importance of a historical perspective

The first of these insights is the emphasis on the *historical development of business systems*, an area which organizational behaviour specialists interested in international comparisons and cultures have either neglected or played down. To those of us who have lived and worked in different countries, this neglect of history may seem strange, since people in everyday situations are often proud of their history when describing their countries' distinguishing achievements. For example, ask Scots, Swedish or Dutch people, all inhabitants of small countries with a tradition of good education, what they have done for the modern world.

They will often point out a long list of mainly historical inventions, ideas and people they have 'gifted' to the 'New World'. Thus Scotland claims 26 US presidents as being of Scottish descent, as well as the inventors of the telephone (Alexander Graham Bell), the steam engine (James Watt), the television (John Logie Baird), the science of economics (Adam Smith), branches of philosophy (David Hume) and sociology (Adam Ferguson), penicillin, interferon, Dolly the Sheep and many other, well-known engineering and scientific applications (Herman, 2001). Scottish firms also had an enormous influence on the development of modern financial services companies and in financing industrial development in places such as Hong Kong, Canada and the USA. So, to stick with these countries for the moment, it seems inconceivable that we could truly understand how international firms with origins in Scotland (like RBS, Standard Life or Scottish & Newcastle Breweries, three major Scottish MNEs mentioned in this book), Sweden (ABB or IKEA), or the Netherlands (Philips or ABN-AMRO) operate in practice without a historical perspective on the relationships between education, innovation and export of people for which these countries were noted, especially to the New World.

To widen the discussion a little, we might ask the question: why is it that two countries as geographically (and, in some respects, as culturally) close as the UK and Germany have developed distinctively different forms of economic organization, industrial relations and attitudes to management, particularly managing people? For example, Wal-Mart was relatively successful in its UK acquisition of ASDA, but much less successful in Germany. Frustratingly for those managers who look only to the present and the future, part of the answer requires insight into the timing of industrialization in these two countries, their relationship to the development (or absence) of political parties that supported the working classes, the development of trades unions, approaches to the development of managers and the legacy of major events such as the two world wars during the 20th century. As some researchers have pointed out, trade unionism in the UK developed prior to mass industrialization in the 18th and 19th centuries to provide support for craft-based workers and pre-dated, by many decades, the political party (the Labour party) created to support mass working class interests.

Consequently, the structure of trade unionism in the UK has been complex, with large numbers of unions pursuing different aims and often competing with each other for members and for pay. Historically, many of these unions have had a strong political agenda because they were formed before the Labour party, the result of which, according to some commentators, has only served to increase the conflict between management and labour for most of the 20th century in Britain. Strike activity, particularly unofficial strike action by small groups of workers, became a marked feature of industrial conflict after 1945, at least in the minds of the popular press, and gave birth to the phenomenon known as the 'British disease'.

Overlaid on these political and labour factors was a traditional approach to recruiting and developing business leaders and managers in the UK (predominantly England) who were not experts in the task they were managing (witness the previously described attitudes to vocational education), but were more noted for social skills and graces for which their education and social class backgrounds partially equipped them. It is not surprising that these 'gifted amateurs' defined their roles predominantly in terms of people management and external networking rather than as technically proficient experts, except in the field of accounting information. What might be more surprising, given the people-management bias of the traditional British manager, is that so much industrial conflict resulted. This can be partly explained by the historically marked differences in social class values that permeated UK management and labour, and which furthered the 'arm's-length' relationship created by the relative inability of British managers to relate to their workers in terms of expertise or the task (Stewart *et al.*, 1994).

By contrast, much of German industry and its labour movement had to be reconstructed from scratch, following the demise of Hitler and the Nazi party and the devastation caused by the Second World War. The German trade unions were purposely reorganized, with British help, along industrial lines, so that the competition between unions for members and pay never developed to the same extent that it did in the UK. These factors, coupled with the return to a supportive system of labour legislation that had been developed by the social democratic political party prior to the 1940s and the new capital formation associated with

much of German industry, resulted in a relatively peaceful industrial relations system for many decades. This state of relatively
harmonious industrial relations provided the stability that was
necessary for rapid German economic development since 1945
and consensus between management and labour has continued
to be a feature of German industry even when economic development slowed down during the late 1990s.

Supporting these industrial relations factors and the effects
of the Second World War is the traditional German attitude to
education, particularly engineering education, and the beliefs
of German managers in expertise and the importance of the
task. German managers are noted for not distinguishing technical work from managerial work. Management is necessary to
get things done, is not 'over and above' technical work and is best
done by managers taking action themselves, rather than necessarily working, at one remove, through other people (Lawrence,
1992). This attitude, coupled with the much higher technical
education of many German managers, meant that they were able
to define their jobs less as people managers and more as technical experts. So, given a more harmonious context, higher level
of technical capability and the greater respect from workers for
this ability, it is not difficult to explain why the German business system might be quite different, though there are signs that
the reputation for technological superiority may be declining
and that the education system, as presently constructed and once
vaunted, is holding back German progress. According to an
Economist survey of Germany published in February 2006, the
rigid school system has produced the 'PISA shock', named after
the OECD programme that produces research on international
comparisons of mathematics and other abilities. Germany came
21st out of 31 countries assessed in 2001 in maths and science
competences for schoolchildren, though there has been recent
improvement (*Economist*, 2006). Moreover, Germany's renowned
system of producing high quality apprentices by attending a
Hauptschule is also under threat, as German firms recruit fewer
apprentices and potential students look elsewhere for education
and training.

Geoffrey Jones, a British-born Harvard Business School
Professor, has made an important point about the lessons of history, comparisons with the American business system and, by

implication, the problems that American managers might experience when managing outside of the USA. He has argued that there has never been 'one best way' of achieving business success:

> Historical experience stands as a powerful corrective to over-simplistic management fads and fashions, and to slavish transfers of management systems and practices that might work well in one country but can be disastrous in another ... Generations of British business historians explained their country's economic 'failure' by establishing what it did 'wrong' compared to US or German business ... We maintain that comparisons which use the United States as a benchmark can be misleading. The United States is an idiosyncratic country by virtue of its size and growth, high levels of entrepreneurial energy, legalistic culture, and a number of other unusual features. (Interview with Geoffrey Jones, available online at http://hbswk.hbs.edu/item.jhtml?id=4106&t=bizhistory&nl=y; accessed 12/5/04)

The systemic and enduring nature of business systems

A second feature of business systems is the *interlocking and enduring nature of business-related institutions* in any country or region over time. Often we find that new industries develop in a particular country or region, and call for new kinds of skills and work patterns. Good examples of such developments during the latter part of the 20th century include call centres and software development in India, electronics manufacture in Malaysia, China, Taiwan and South Korea, and motor vehicle manufacturing in the southern states of the USA. These new industries and the typical kinds of employment policies and practices associated with them were necessarily overlaid on the existing, dominant system of older industries and human resource management patterns. Although changes occurred in the business systems of the affected areas of India, China, Malaysia and the southern USA, these changes were constrained by previous institutional frameworks, such as the dominant patterns of worker organizations, including trade unions, legislation and patterns of business ownership (e.g. the importance of family-owned firms in Malaysia and the state ownership of traditional Chinese firms). For example, foreign companies wishing to set up in China were required to form a relationship with a local partner to form a joint venture. Such joint ventures are governed by a system of regulations on employment practices regarding contracts, union recognition and safety that continue to reinforce the role of national and regional governments and the control of the Communist party on economic development (Zhang and Martin, 2003). Thus, it has often been the case that the rise of new industries and associated employment practices may herald some significant changes in certain aspects of the business system, but because these changes do not fit closely with the previously dominant business institutions, the interlocking and conservative nature of these previously dominant institutional arrangements means that the existing system remains largely intact, albeit in a modified form.

Some companies have understood this problem of institutional inertia only too well when setting up new facilities overseas. For example, most Japanese car manufacturers which entered the US market during the 1980s set up their production facilities in southern locations to avoid many of the institutional constraints associated with typical US vehicle manufacturing in the northern states of the USA. Indeed, some researchers have pointed out that these Japanese firms tended to locate not in the major centres of population in these southern states but in formerly rural small towns to source employees without previously formed expectations of a manufacturing environment and without a previous history of trade union membership. Such was the case with Toyota, which set up its major American production plants in small towns in Kentucky, Southern Indiana and West Virginia, far removed in distance and 'mentality' from the major centres of vehicle manufacture in Michigan and Ohio.

The role of critical turning points and changes in systems

A third feature of a business systems approach is the importance of aptly named *critical turning points* in bringing about radical change (Hollingsworth and Boyer, 1997, p. 267). These turning points include wars, economic crises and political upheavals, often revealing severe problems in previously dominant systems and resulting in transformational institutional change. The new institutional frameworks that were imposed following these upheavals often redefined the pre-existing relationship between employers and employees. As a consequence, the changes in management–employee relationships became embedded in institutional arrangements (e.g. laws, bureaucratic systems, lobbying bodies, etc.), which persisted long after the upheavals that gave rise to them. We have already discussed the impact of war on Germany. Another excellent example is from the USA during the New Deal era, which followed the critical turning point of the Great Depression in the 1930s and led to a new industrial relations framework, based on a highly codified system of collective contracts and trade union recognition, which exists to this day in the northern US states. As the inwardly investing Japanese car manufacturers attempted to point out in their location decisions, the New Deal institutional arrangement may have been appropriate during an era of mass production with an emphasis on a standard and limited product range and cost containment, but was not suited to their novel 'lean production' strategy of providing high levels of quality, a wider product range and even lower costs.

In the UK, the radical transformation of politics and industrial relations brought about by the election of the Thatcher government in 1979 put Britain on a road very different from the European corporatist consensus between government, big business and the trade unions that still forms the ideology of the EU. The legacy of Thatcherism is still at the heart of the divisions between Britain and many member states over economic policy. Moreover, the decline in trade union density in the UK, from 52% in 1979 to only 29% of the working population in 2005, is a consequence, in part, of the radical policies pursued by the Thatcher government, and in part of the more sophisticated HR strategies designed and implemented in the UK from the mid-1980s. Such strategies include the focus on anti-discrimination, family-friendly policies on job sharing, childcare provision, coupled with performance-related pay, all of which have impacted on the traditional role of the trade union.

A more complex basis for comparing and contrasting international business systems

A fourth feature of the business systems approach is to allow comparisons of different national systems on a more complex range of key dimensions than national cultural characteristics and, at the same time, to reveal their unique nature. These key dimensions for comparison cover major institutional arrangements such as the nature of *product, labour and capital markets,* the organization or *clustering* of firms, the role of the *state and legal regulation,* systems of *vocational education and training,* and *industrial relations.* However, the unique character of any one system is guaranteed by the particular configuration of what dimensions are important and their interaction over time. For example, in the development of the US business system the 'path-dependence' or 'what came before what' of each of the key features of the system meant that it turned out to be unique (Jones, 2003), even though it might be possible to compare countries as close as America and Britain on any one of these dimensions by itself.

The evolution of the MNEs

In the preceding sections we have set out the national cultural, institutional and historical constraints on companies' attempts to develop strong corporate identities and cultures among those MNEs that seek to become geocentric. This has led some writers to suggest that the truly geocentric organization is more myth than reality or is an ideal rarely achieved in reality. Firms seeking geocentrism have been described as moving through four stages related to the life cycle of the firm (Adler and Ghadar, 1990):

■ Stage 1: Managers make brief visits or have short assignments to assist the overseas units with any technical or product needs.
■ Stage 2: HQ acknowledges that local markets require a differentiated approach where products and business methods are adapted to local circumstances. Home

country nationals (HCNs) are recruited to sales, marketing and HR roles as they are perceived to have a greater understanding of local circumstances.

■ Stage 3: When the company seeks to exploit integration and cost advantages. One of HR's most important tasks would be to focus on integrating employees through management courses and training and by expanding the same corporate identity, values and norms of behaviour through performance management techniques. Additionally, the use of sophisticated HR tools such as succession planning might be used to integrate employees resulting in subsidiary units comprising a mixture of parent company nationals (PCNs), HCNs and third country nationals (TCNs).

■ Stage 4: This is reached when there is a balance between global integration with national responsiveness. At this stage, recruitment of managerial staff is based on the best person for the job rather than any consideration of nationality or links to HQ. Extensive use is made of cultural diversity training and programmes.

The expatriation of parent company managers is a key element in this process, especially during stages 1–3. All MNEs exert a degree of control over their subsidiaries to ensure certain patterns of behaviour on the part of local management, workforce representatives and employees. Such control can be either *direct* or *unobtrusive*. Direct control is defined as the degree of involvement in local activities, i.e. direct involvement in decision-making; international guidelines on the selection and promotion of employees would be viewed as an overt means by which managers are expected to comply. Unobtrusive control is defined as the way in which HQ shapes and constrains decisions made at subsidiary level through controlling the premises underlying decision-making. Good examples of this process are management training or management exchanges designed to reinforce corporate identities.

Expatriating managers to host country subsidiaries is more than a mechanism of direct control, sometimes described as the equivalent of 'gun-boat' diplomacy. Expatriate managers bring with them the values, attitudes and ways of doing things that embody the corporate culture and identity. As such, researchers have argued that they are the transmitters of corporate culture and identity, boundary spanners, cultural or identity carriers. They also provide a more pervasive means of unobtrusive control through the diffusion of values and attitudes in their day-to-day work practices. Because of this pervasive influence, companies such as Unilever and ABB, which are sometimes described as geocentric, relying heavily on a cadre of international managers to diffuse cultural and identity practices across the company (Martin and Beaumont, 1998). Ferner and Edwards (1995, p. 241) see the physical movement of staff 'as a key means of disseminating cultural understanding and ways of doing things'.

The case of the Mars Corporation in Box 7.3 illustrates some of the stages and complexity involved in the evolution of one MNE.

Box 7.3   The evolution of Mars

The Mars Corporation has 65 factories in 60 countries worldwide. The company produces sweets, ready to serve meals, pet foods and drinks, as well as electronic payment systems, with a range of household names for brands, including M&Ms, Twix, Mars Bars and Snickers in snackfoods, to Pedigree, Whiskas, Cesar and Sheeba in petcare, and Uncle Ben's in foods. The annual turnover of the Mars Corporation amounts to over $18 billion with a global workforce of over 28 000 people (http://www.mars.com/About_us/The_Mars_story.asp; 28 February 2006).

Mars is an American family-owned company, which began with the invention of the well-known Mars chocolate bar in 1923. According to Brenner (1999), the company's success has been mainly due to the founder's son, who moved to England in the 1930s when his father refused to allow him to have one-third control of the company. The son was given the foreign rights to produce a chocolate bar in Europe. He was so successful that he bought out his father's company in the US soon after the latter's death. The company began by producing chocolate bars, later diversifying into producing pet food and other food products in the 1940s. Ownership of the company resides with the Mars family, one of the richest in the United States. The company is still managed on a day-to-day basis by the two sons who attempt to visit each Mars unit at least twice a year (Brenner, 1999).

The company's history is of expansion, nationally and globally. This desire is at the heart of its corporate strategy. This is encapsulated by the founder's somewhat grandiose comments: 'I wanted to capture the whole goddamn world' (Brenner, 1999, p. 59). Despite the fact that an American family owns the company and that it is US-based, Britain remains Mars' leading market.

Mars opened a subsidiary in Poland in 1990, largely because confectionery is one of the most profitable and competitive industries. It is often said that chocolate and sweets are among the first things people buy when their incomes rise. Poles have long had the highest per capita chocolate consumption in Central and Eastern Europe and figures suggest that this consumption has risen five-fold since 1990, to about 2 kg of chocolate and 3 kg of sweets per annum. However this is well below Western European averages of more than 5 kg in chocolate alone, suggesting that there is much greater market potential in Poland.

To build its company culture and overcome the problems of buying a state-owned factory, with 'bloated' workforces, complex distribution systems, huge product ranges and outdated plants scattered arbitrarily around a single city or region, Mars built its factory and market presence from scratch. In 1991 it acquired land about 50 km west of Warsaw and installed machinery to make dry pet food. The market in pet foods was at this time non-existent. The company ensured that it took only a small risk by installing previously used machinery from various European companies and drafting ten expatriate managers to manage this new operation. By December 1992 it was clear that the market was growing. The company employed 120 people and was producing 15 000 tonnes of pet food, with a turnover of around $US 30m. Other product lines were added to production: snack foods (e.g. Mars bars) in 1995; and wet pet foods (e.g. canned dog food) in 1996.

In 1995 a new factory was opened, producing confectionery products such as Mars bars, Milky Way and Galaxy. By this time there were 1000 people employed by the company with 700 on-site and the rest operating as a national sales force. By the end of 1997 the turnover had reached circa $US 200m with expectations of continued substantial growth over the next 4–5 years, with a total number of 1400 employees. By 2001, Mars had around 90% of the pet foods market and around 12% of confectionery.

Mars defines its culture explicitly in the form of five principles: *quality* for customers and value for money, individual *responsibility* and responsibility for others, *mutuality* in sharing benefits, *efficiency* in using resources and doing only what can be done efficiently, and *freedom* to shape the future with profits to remain free. These were developed 20 years ago by the Mars family, who desired global expansion but wanted to maintain unity and integration.

The founder, by explicitly stating his vision and values, and continual reinforcement through regular visits and active participation, is central to Mars culture. As one British manager commented: 'Culture is strictly defined by members of the family, who have a very, very direct influence.' The central tenets of the culture are reinforced through the artefacts, atmosphere and office layout. Brenner (1999) succinctly encapsulates the working culture at Mars:

Everyone has the same size desk, everyone answers his own telephone and everyone is awarded a 10 per cent bonus for punctuality. To encourage communication, managers sit in a wagon wheel fashion in the centre of a large room, encircled by junior associates. The sales dept is right next to the marketing dept, which is right next to manufacturing and accounting. There are no offices, no partitions and no privacy. That way, the founder reasoned, everybody in the company would know what everyone else was doing ... (Brenner, 1999, p. 189)

At Mars there is little regard for status and formality is frowned upon; everyone is referred to by his or her first name. Personal communication is the normal state of affairs.

Global companies use the corporate identity and culture as a unifying force to overcome issues of nationality, with Mars being a classic example.

Most workers are dressed in their starched whites, uniforms provided by the company and laundered daily. Some are wearing hard hats and everyone has their first name emblazoned on their coats. There is no way to tell who is in charge – who is an executive and who is a janitor. There is no way to tell you that you are in a factory located in the former Soviet Union, just 120 km outside Moscow. (Brenner, 1999, p. 284)

I often used to say that I didn't really live in Poland as the Mars unit was just like any other. (Former expatriate British manager working in Poland)

Mars also has a policy of using the informal aspect of any language irrespective of culture or country. In Poland, traditionally the formal means of addressing a colleague is used as a sign of respect. The usage of the informal means of address meant that the culture often had to be explained to outsiders such as suppliers.

Yet Mars encountered significant problems in transferring its values to Poland. The company communicated the Mars values in the first few years through training workshops. Competitions were held to reward employees who could demonstrate that they were able to demonstrate the Mars values at work or home. However, as the responses from the local managers demonstrate, the Mars values were perceived negatively and as a form of brandwashing. The communist legacy meant that the five Mars principles were perceived as anachronistic propaganda. The five values were used as fundamental truths, which Polish managers viewed uncomfortably. For instance, one respondent recounted that at a meeting in the UK one of the attendees had quoted the 'principle' of responsibility as a way of supporting a particular business strategy. The respondent said that this action was reminiscent of management activities in the former communist era. For this reason, the emphasis of the Mars Company on its stated values was perceived to be anachronistic propaganda by Polish respondents.

> Polish people don't want to hear five principles … People still remember the communist times and the propaganda. The values do not need to be made explicit in Poland because it is a different environment. In the West there is greater stability, so managers can concentrate on maintaining relationships. But we need to improvise and be more spontaneous. Therefore the values are seen as limiting, perhaps suffocating and need to be adapted. (Interview with a Polish manager)

Consequently, in 1998 the management team decided to adapt the five principles to the Polish culture. The adapted values, whilst different from the original values, share similar ambitions. They are now far more prescriptive, with a greater range of examples aimed at assisting meaning and understanding. For example, the value of 'mutual respect' itemises six meanings or codes of conduct. These include:

> We are fair and sensitive. This should not be confused with unthinking generosity but rather refers to the concept of understanding different point/requirements and making decisions, which are mutually beneficial. (Company Handbook)

The role, philosophy and activities of HRM within the Mars Corporation aim to develop, define, communicate, maintain and enforce the parent company culture across all units. This status may be the reason why the Personnel Director in Poland was the only expatriate HRM manager in the Mars Corporation encountered during the research. Mars placed great emphasis on entrusting the HR function of a foreign unit to an expatriate manager. By so doing the company seeks to ensure its parent culture is diffused. The Mars Corporation seeks to operate a geocentric strategy by overlaying national differences with a strong corporate identity, but to what extent has it got the balance right?

Conclusions

In this chapter we have discussed the added complexity experienced by MNEs in creating strong corporate reputations and brands and the importance of HR in that process. MNEs follow different strategies with respect to their global ambitions; these we discussed at length and illustrated with some of our case study research. They include ethnocentric, polycentric, regiocentric and geocentric strategies, all of which present a different answer to the perennial problem of balancing the corporatist integration agenda and the more responsive, local differentiation agenda. Although current thinking suggests that the geocentric response is the most appropriate, there are plenty of examples of successful organizations following the other agendas. Moreover, most organizations seem to move through four stages en route towards geocentricity; though, as we suggested, this is more of an ideal than something achieved in reality.

One of the other main themes of the chapter has been the added complexity of national cultural and institutional differences in transferring practices across borders. While the cultural difference school has been the most discussed in the literature, it is increasingly recognized that institutions and institutional distances often provide the best explanation of why practices remain 'sticky' and do not transfer well. We have made the point that any organization wishing to fully understand the potential for transferring practices should have a thorough understanding of these institutional differences and of business systems. The Mars case illustrated this point vividly, with the difficulties it had in establishing a presence in Poland. In Chapter 10 we will also look at the case of Scottish & Newcastle Breweries, which raises similar questions concerning the tensions between global and local brand building, and HR policies.

References

Adler, N. J. and Ghadar, F. (1990) Strategic human resource management: a global perspective, in *Human Resource Management in International Comparison* (ed. R. Pieper). Berlin/New York: de Gruyter, pp. 235–260.

Bartlett, C. A., Ghoshal, S. and Birkinshaw, J. (2004) *Transnational management: text, cases, and readings in cross-border management* (4th edition). Boston: Irwin/McGraw-Hill.

Brenner, J. G. (1999) *The Chocolate Wars*. New York: HarperCollins Business.

Economist (2006) Wasting brains: Germany's school system fails to make the most of the country's human capital, *Economist*, 11 February.

Edwards, T., Rees, C. and Coller, X. (1999) Structure, politics, and the diffusion of employment practices in multinationals, *European Journal of Industrial Relations*, **5** (3), 286–306.

Ferner, A. (2000) The embeddedness of US multinational companies in the US business system: implications for HR/IR, *Occasional Papers no. 61*, De Montfort University, Leicester Business School.

Ferner, A. and Edwards, P. K. (1995) Power and the diffusion of organizational change within multinationals, *European Journal of Industrial Relations*, **1** (2), 229–257.

Friedman, T. L. (2005) *The world is flat: a brief history of the twenty-first century*. London: Penguin/Allen Lane.

Gooderham, P. and Nordhaug, O. (eds) (2003) *International management: cross-boundary challenges*. Oxford: Blackwell.

Herman, A. (2001) *How the Scots invented the modern world*. New York: Three Rivers Press.

Hetrick, S. (2001) Globalisation, convergence and divergence. Unpublished PhD thesis, City University Business School, London.

Hofstede, G. (2003) *Culture's consequences, comparing values, behaviors, institutions, and organizations across nations* (2nd edition). London: Sage.

Hollingsworth, J. R. and Bower, R. (eds) (1997) *Contemporary capitalism*. Cambridge, MA: Harvard University Press.

Jones, G. (2003) Multinationals, in F. Amatori and G. Jones (eds), *Business history around the world.* Cambridge: Cambridge University Press, pp. 353–371.

Kay, J. (2004) *The truth about markets: why some nations are rich but most remain poor.* London: Penguin.

Lawrence, P. (1992) Management development in Europe: a study in cultural contrast, *Human Resource Management Journal,* **3** (1), 11–23.

Martin, G. and Beaumont, P. B. (1998) 'HRM and the diffusion of best practice', *International Journal of Human Resource Management,* **9** (4), 671–695.

Martin, G. and Beaumont, P. B. (2001) Transforming multinational enterprises: Towards a process model of strategic HRM change in MNEs, *International Journal of Human Resource Management,* **10** (6), 34–55.

Perlmutter, M. V. (1969) The tortuous evolution of the multinational corporation, *Columbia Journal of World Business,* **4** (1), 9–18.

Royle, T. (1997) Globalisation, convergence and the McDonalds Corporation. Unpublished PhD thesis, Nottingham Trent University.

Schein, E. (1985) *Organizational culture and leadership.* San Francisco, CA: Jossey-Bass.

Schneider, S. C. and Barsoux, J-L. (2003) *Managing across cultures* (2nd edition). Harlow: Financial Times/Prentice Hall.

Stewart, R., Keiser, A. and Barsoux, J-L. (1994) *Managing in Britain and Germany.* London: St Martin's Press.

Tayeb, M. (ed.) (2003) *International management.* Harlow: Pearson Education.

Whitley, R. (1999) *Divergent capitalisms: the social structuring and change of business systems.* Oxford: Oxford University Press.

Yeung, H. W-C. (1998) *Transnational corporation and business networks – Hong Kong firms in the ASEAN Region.* London: Routledge.

Zaheer, S. (1995) Overcoming the liability of foreignness. (Special Research Forum: International and Intercultural Management Research), *Academy of Management Journal,* **38** (2), 341–364.

Zhang, H. and Martin, G. (2003) *Human Resource Management Practices in Sino-Foreign Joint Ventures.* Nanhchang: Jiangxi Science and Technology Press.

CHAPTER 8

Corporate communications and the employment relationship

Although we have been a little sceptical of the more overblown claims of communications specialists regarding their contribution to reputation management and branding, few managers, especially in HR and marketing, would disagree with the view that communications are at the heart of creating positive organizational images and identities. Indeed, the business press has recorded a catalogue of communications and public relations failures to do so, including during the

Exxon Valdez oils spill disaster, problems with Farley's and Gerber's baby milk and baby foods, Perrier's benzene contamination of its bottled water (Haig, 2001), and British Airways' repeated crises at Heathrow following the series of summer strikes (see, for example, *People Management*, 2005). These failures of communications (but also of content) not only have cost companies many customers but have also damaged employees' trust and identification with their brands, and hindered the ability of these firms to compete in the market for talented people.

One result of this growing awareness of communications in business is a recent turn in strategic management to seeing 'strategy-as-narrative' (Barry and Elmes, 1997), which claims the essence of organizational strategy, in sharp contrast to earlier planning perspectives, is in authoring a *credible, compelling* and *novel* story. Drawing on our earlier metaphor of self-authored and other-authored biographies, usually this narrative is part-biographical, co-authored with customers, clients, employees and other stakeholders. If it is not co-authored, research shows that official corporate stories tend to be counterbalanced and negated by insiders' and outsiders' unofficial biographies with potentially damaging consequences in the long term (one of the dangers we referred to in the discussion of Google in Chapter 1) (Boje, 2006).

So, in this chapter we will focus on the role of corporate-level communications in shaping the experience of employees, organizational identities and images. To do so, we will examine some of the newer ideas in corporate communications and then focus on internally focused communications strategies, including employer of choice programmes and employer branding. A few years ago, one of us developed a model of strategic HR change in multinational organizations that drew heavily on strategic narratives (Martin and Beaumont, 2001). This model, with just a little modification, helps provide an integrating framework for academic and consultancy writing in this field, as we hope you will see later in this chapter.

First, however, to help you understand some of the issues involved, let's examine a recent case we researched with a colleague of ours, Annette Frem, Culture Change Manager of Orange.

Box 8.1   Opening case: Orange in Denmark

Introduction

Orange in Denmark developed from a company called Mobilix A/S. It was established in March 1998 as a subsidiary of France Telecom, which had acquired local licences in a number of countries for mobile phone companies. Initially, these companies were largely left alone and operated as independent brands, without any real attempt to create a sense of corporateness. Nevertheless, Mobilix became a success in Denmark, achieving the third largest operator-status in terms of market share and brand awareness.

Just as BT in the UK had created the O_2 brand to distinguish its mobile communication arm from the main line of business, France Telecom recognized that they needed to establish a strong brand image for their own venture into this product market. Consequently, they acquired the UK-based Orange, which had a strong brand image in mobile communications. France Telecom immediately embarked on a re-branding exercise to help subsidiaries leverage the Orange brand. This included re-branding Mobilix A/S as Orange A/S in May 2001.

'Orange on the Inside'

'Orange on the Inside' was launched as a culture change process to help Mobilix employees and managers identify with the external Orange brand image. French-born, lifetime France Telecom employee Monique Muller-Zetterstroem had been CEO of Mobilix from its inception. She was seen as the 'mother' of the company, and personally led the change process. The changes were intended to align with the Orange vision, to make a difference to people's lives by creating simple and innovative services that help people to communicate and interact better, expressed by the brand values of being straightforward, honest, friendly, dynamic and refreshing. One of the biggest challenges was building confidence in the new management team. This required their profiles to be raised among existing Mobilix employees and to help build employees' confidence and trust in them.

Note here the use of process rather than programme to describe Orange on the inside, which was intended to avoid the cynicism associated with previous Mobilix employee initiatives and to demonstrate to employees that management understood that changing a company's culture wasn't a quick fix, but a process in which they were willing to invest time and money.

A project team was established, covering internal communications, HR and branding to put together a plan to drive the process internally. The project leader was given a reporting role to the monthly Chief Operating Officers meeting of Orange to track progress. The 'Orange on the Inside' process comprised the following elements:

- Launch events of the 'Orange on the Inside' process
- An ongoing employee survey process to establish where the company was starting from and to assess its progress against goals. This comprised:
  - ❐ A culture questionnaire
  - ❐ Focus groups, and
  - ❐ One-to-one management and key influencers' interviews
- Management seminars to keep management actively involved
- Division meetings to share survey findings and action points
- Brand workshops
- Culture workshops

The process in operation

1 **Launch events:** The CEO, Monique Muller-Zetterstroem, invited all employees to the launch of the 'Orange on the Inside' process, giving them a chance to meet her in person and to be able to ask her directly all of the questions they may have had concerning the process. She toured the country to meet all employees in person, telling them about the background for the change and the steps involved in the process. She also asked all the employees to fill in a culture survey to assess where the company was in respect of Orange's values framework, and gave personal guarantees to employees to take action on the basis of the findings. In total, she met about 1000 employees during a nine-day period, covering 17 events in Denmark.

2 **The survey process:** The questionnaire used at the launch events drew on the Orange 'Culture Blueprint' which was provided from the Orange Group. The questionnaire was based on the brand values to make the experience of completing it part of an exploration of the Orange brand. The survey process was also intended to signify to employees that the management wished to hear their views. In addition to the questionnaire, ten focus groups covering a sample of 10% of employees and managers, were held over a concentrated period of five days to add qualitative data to the questionnaire data. Every attempt was made to ensure that these focus groups included

sceptics as well as those employees more likely to have bought into the Orange message. All senior managers and staff identified as key influencers had one-to-one interviews to ensure all views and levels of the business were taken into account. These interviews were intended to create an element of 'management buy-in' and to begin coaching them in their new roles and responsibilities associated with the new ways of doing Orange business.

3   **Management seminars:** These data collection exercises were used as the basis for day-long management seminars, which were designed to analyse the problems and initiate improvement projects. Each seminar was designed as an interactive session and played on the Orange values of being refreshing and dynamic. For example, instead of straight reporting back of the survey results, the management team was divided into small groups competing over whether they could guess the results of the survey. The evening session was an interactive workshop session which will be covered later on in this case study.

4   **Division meetings:** Senior managers were made responsible for feeding back the information to their own employees. Again this approach forced them to be personally involved in the process and served as a trust-building exercise, during which managers provided personal stories about action points which they had committed to progressing as a result of the management seminars.

5   **Brand workshops:** Throughout the process the centrality of the brand to Orange's success was communicated to all staff, though for many the concept of a brand was quite new to them. Consequently, it was important that employees were given the opportunity to explore and familiarize themselves with the brand values and culture of Orange. So, all employees were asked to participate in two workshops, a half-day brand workshop and full-day culture workshop. Few excuses for non-participation were permitted.

6   **Culture workshops:** The aim of the culture workshops was to rebuild the psychological contracts between the employees and Orange and challenge employees to make a conscious or unconscious choice about whether or not they wanted to be part of the new company. Like the brand workshops, they were interactive learning sessions to explore six themes:

   ❏   Their common heritage with Orange ('Where were we coming from'?).

   ❏   The strategy of Orange ('The future's bright, the future's Orange'), and the key business drivers.

❏ The relationship between the brand and customers ('Orange on the outside').

❏ The relationship between how employees behaved and the brand promise ('Orange on the inside').

❏ Critical opportunities in day-to-day life that employees would meet in making decisions on how to implement brand values ('Noticing and acting').

❏ Role modelling the new brand values and what employees could do differently to support the brand ('How we behave').

7   **Brand ambassadors (change agents):** The workshops were facilitated by skilled and enthusiastic local employees, not trained Orange facilitators. The reason for doing so was because the company believed that employees would be more willing to listen to 'one of their own' rather than an Orange employee who may not be a source of credible information about the company. It was also believed that employees would be more willing to voice concerns if it was not to Orange facilitators.

Outcomes

The survey process revealed some serious issues that the management had to deal with, including the need for more information about strategy, establishing ways of communicating and rewarding bright ideas to support the values, the motivation of managers, expectations and communication of desired behaviours, the need for employee 'get-togethers' and the need to focus on employee well-being.

Unfortunately, as is often the case in such examples, Orange in Denmark changed dramatically and the Danish company went through a number of re-organizations and redundancies. However, the 'Orange on the Inside' process was seen to be successful and integrated into a new corporate workstream, called the 'Renaissance' project. This process has been widely used in other parts of Orange globally.

Corporate communications, HR and branding: towards a definition

This case provides a contemporary account of how one company is using communications to integrate overseas acquisitions and subsidiaries into a high profile and, increasingly, global corporate brand. The early evidence points to success in Denmark, though, as Orange managers admit, this is no guarantee it will work elsewhere and in another timeframe. However, most of the elements of modern corporate communications good practice are there to see; indeed the case has been used in a number of presentations as an exemplar for others to follow.

So, what can we learn about corporate communications from a 'local' case that can be transferred 'globally'? There are at least two ways of answering this question: the first is by comparing traditional views of communications with newer ones to examine the role of changing context; the second is to see it as part of a strategic narrative of change *through, and in,* communications. This latter perspective is the one we shall concentrate on in this chapter, but first, how have communications changed in the past couple of decades?

Old vs new views on corporate communications

The field of corporate communications has become prominent since the early 1990s in most organizations, but even now is recognized to be quite different from when corporate communications departments first began to appear. Table 8.1 shows how things have changed to reflect the changing contexts of the present decade, which, according to Don Schultz and Philip Kitchen (2004), will make corporate communications much more important than previously was the case. Most of these changes we have met before, but are worth re-stating and re-locating in a communications perspective.

Seen in this light, the Orange case, especially the 'Orange on the Inside' process, is very much a 21st century approach, especially with its emphasis on dialogue and interactivity, involvement of all functions and people, and focus on branding and communications as key drivers. However, the process has not been in operation long enough to make a good assessment, since, as both of us can testify to from experience, it takes a number of years to change a culture. Journalists often conclude their stories with an 'only time will tell' qualifier; it will be well after this book has been published that Annette Frem will be able to know

Table 8.1

Changing corporate communications.

	Traditional corporate communications	21st century corporate communications
Basis and direction of communication	Everything is outbound, reflecting needs of corporation	Dialogue and interactivity among stakeholders
Channels	Specialist people and departments using a plan–develop–implement model	Focus on 'customer' needs and integration of functions using a sense–adapt–respond model
Focus of communications	Need to address national markets	Need to address global markets
Content of communications	Focus on how well corporation is employing tangible assets, e.g. finance, plant etc.	Focus on how well corporation is employing intangible assets, e.g. values, brands, people, knowledge, CSR
Basis of differentiation	Products and services unique selling propositions	Customer value or customer captivity
Structural drivers	Communications reflect corporate monolith	Communications reflect alliances, partners and context
Importance of communications	Corporate communications as optional	Corporate communications as a core strategic driver
Importance of corporate message	Corporate brand as optional	Corporate brand as a key strategic aim

Source: Based on Schultz and Kitchen, 2004

the outcomes of 'Orange on the Inside' or the Renaissance project in Denmark and elsewhere.

Strategy and communications as a narrative of change

The other way of analysing this case is to see it as a compelling, novel and credible strategic narrative for change. This approach to corporate communications is based on the so-called post-modern or 'linguistic turn' in management studies during the 1990s; a turn helped by companies such as GE, whose reported dissatisfaction with planning and hard analysis in strategic management was well documented during the 1980s. Instead, numbers and positioning gave way to 'strategy as perspective'. This involved looking into the heads of strategists, their values and aspirations, for the 'vision thing' and the search for the 'organization's soul' (Mintzberg *et al.*, 2004). More of this in the final two chapters; the point to note for now is that this turn has certainly added to our understanding of the links between HR, corporate reputations and branding. Strategy as perspective, or as we prefer to call it, 'strategy as communications', is basically concerned with strategists telling and selling a *compelling, novel and credible story* to different audiences (Barry and Elmes, 1997). If you reflect on your organization's public pronouncements, these are the essential qualities and functions of all good vision, values and mission statements; they are also essential elements of how effective and ethical leadership relates to followership, and to the change processes underpinning reputation and brand-building (see Chapter 9). Such stories have to be new or refreshed to inspire followers; they have to incorporate a compelling, aspirational view of the future; and they also have to be credible in relation to the history and context of the organization, and the lived experience of employees (Boje, 2006). Successful change management also incorporates these qualities: we can think of few cases where these were not part of what effective leaders did in 'theorizing the need for change' through aspirational and credible stories (Martin and Beaumont, 2001), as we shall see later in this chapter. The Orange experience in Denmark embodies all of the elements of a successful narrative for change, which could have formed a leitmotif for how they approached the Mobilix acquisition.

In the field of reputation management, Cees Van Reil (2003), who works with Charles Fombrun at the Reputation Institute, is the writer most associated with this perspective. He has described corporate communications as the 'orchestration of all the instruments in the field of organizational identity (communications, symbols and the behavior of organization's members) in such an attractive and realistic manner as to create or maintain a positive reputation for groups with which the organization has a dependent relationship' (p. 163). Such communications, as he points out, can be of three types:

- Management communication, which focuses on how leadership communicates externally and internally, and how they bring about a positive communications climate
- Marketing communication, which focuses on advertising, personal sales, sponsorship, direct mail, sales support, etc., and
- Organizational communication, including public relations, investor relations, environmental communication, corporate advertising and internal employee communications.

For Van Riel, the critical points are that all such types need to be coordinated to create positive reputations in the sense that they need to have a common starting point, but, most importantly, they need to be based on a sustainable corporate story (SCS). The idea of an SCS is an interesting one which we have incorporated into our model in Figure 8.1. The four key criteria against which an SCS should be judged reflect the narrative perspective on strategy. These are as follows:

1 Realism: all stakeholders see it as typical of their organization as a whole and as differentiating it from others
2 Relevance, to all members' interests
3 Responsiveness: the style of narrative and communications should be part of an ongoing, dynamic conversation between internal and external stakeholders, and
4 Sustainability: reconciling the competing demands of stakeholders and organizational members over time.

Sustainability, however, is difficult to achieve in practice. Research in this field has shown that stories that adopt a 'single voice', even one that has 'buy in' from the majority of employees, quickly become the object of less flattering narratives and the object of a dynamic process of refinement (Bjoe, 2006). This dynamic nature of sustainability needs to be taken into account by HR and communications specialists, a point to which we shall return later in this chapter.

Change as communications narrative

As we noted in the introduction to this chapter, we developed a model of strategic change, based on extensive research into the problems of change and change agents in multinational organizations (Martin and Beaumont, 2001). This earlier model, drawing on communications narratives and the idea of strategy as a perspective, can be adapted to incorporate the ideas of Van Riel and some of the consulting work in this field to provide a new, comprehensive framework for 'strategic change through communications' (see Figure 8.1). The initial model set out the relationships between a complex set of events, activities, language practices, emotions and reactions that help explain two key questions in change management:

■ What is needed for sustainable strategic HR change to occur in organizations? and

■ Why is it that most strategic HR change initiatives are rarely successful in creating sustainable change in organizations?

Sustainable change has been defined as when new ways of working and the attainment of improved outcomes become the norm in organizations (Buchanan *et al.*, 2005). Mirroring Van Reil's SCS, the value of this model lay in seeing strategy as a convincing narrative or storyline that managers and employees often co-construct, 'buy into' and use to give a sense of mission and purpose to their organizational lives. The notion of strategic discourses and change conversations plays a major part in the model (see Box 8.2) and helps flesh out the idea of sustainable corporate stories.

Box 8.2   Strategic discourses and change conversations

A strategic discourse is a set of communicative practices that are closely linked to specific purposes of powerful groups. Discursive practices in management include strategic conversations that managers use to promote change. Four types of strategic conversations have been identified that good leaders and managers use in promoting their change initiatives:

■ Initiating conversations that are used to get the change process under way, which include assertions, directives, promises, etc. that engage employees and outline what is needed.

■ Understanding conversations to test the reality of the change propositions and to generate involvement. These conversations focus on claims, evidence, 'theories' of cause and effect (if we do this, we shall achieve this ...) to help employees understand what is needed and what will result for the organization and for them.

■ Performance conversations, used to generate action, which focus on conversations, promises and directives that are intended to produce results.

■ Closure conversations, which are assertions and declarations used to signify the successful (or unsuccessful) completion and 'celebration' of the change process.

Source: Based on Ford and Ford, 1995

One of the advantages of this framework over most of the communications approaches lies in locating the processes of change through communications in receptive contexts. The model sets out four stages in the strategic change process – conception, transition, embedding and feedback – in four levels of context for change. In the case of Orange, for example, the social context, which refers to the social distances between the cultures and institutions of the parent country and its subsidiaries (see Chapter 7), would be important in understanding the transfer of a 'global' Orange culture to countries such as Denmark.

The key features and stages of the model are as follows:

1 **Receptive contexts for change.** These contexts are especially important for successful HR change to become embedded in complex organizations. We can identify four such levels of context: the social, the outer-organizational, the inner-organizational and the relational context. The social context we have already described as

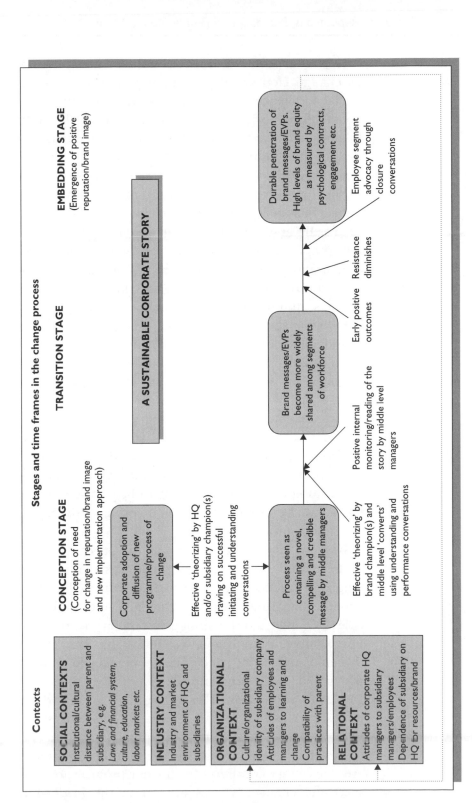

Figure 8.1

Strategic change-through-communications in multinational/division organizations (based on Martin and Beaumont, 2003).

having an important influence on the process of strategic change. However, the nature of the industry in a particular locality or country and its environment is also potentially important. For example, the relatively youthful and high-tech nature of the global mobile telecommunications industry, other things being equal, was more likely to help the development of a global Orange culture than traditional telecommunications. This industry has been dominated by major national players, such as BT and France Telecom, which may have had a tendency towards ethnocentricity in the past. The inner-organizational context, which in a multinational environment refers to the differences in organizational cultures, attitudes to learning, change and compatibility of practices between corporate headquarters and its subsidiaries, can have a great bearing on the effectiveness of change initiatives. These intra-organizational differences are potentially relevant in explaining the success or failure of corporate-wide initiatives such as branding and culture change programmes. Finally, the attitudes of local managers and their relative power in relation to the parent company or head office will shape the reception of change programmes. Orange clearly understood this issue in working to help raise the profile of local Danish managers and incorporate them into the change process.

It is also important to note that the process aspects of the model (the various stages, patterns of events and language practices) are embedded in these changing contexts over time. This is particularly relevant in the case of Orange and the 'Orange on the Inside' process. For example, Orange sought to brand the changes as a dynamic, sustainable process rather than a programme with a fixed beginning and end.

2   **The conception stage.** This is the stage during which new strategies and new strategic HR discourses are developed. High-level corporate support, adoption and sponsorship of the change discourse and programmes are a necessary condition for further progress towards successful change, as was evident in the leadership

exercised by Monique Muller-Zetterstroem. However, it was not a sufficient condition. So, our process model allows for two-way development of the strategic changes, in which the ideas are just as likely to come from middle managers, HR specialists and internal/external change consultants, which was also reflected in the Orange case. This feature mirrors Van Riel's important point about the need for a responsive, dynamic conversation between the organization and its stakeholders.

3   **The transition stage.** For the key messages of change to progress to the transition stage, credible and novel organizational identity changes and HRM initiatives (occurring in, and through, effective communications) have to be read positively by all levels of management, including main board, subsidiary and middle-level operational managers. In a study we conducted on ABB, it was evident the managers in certain subsidiaries of one of the company's major divisions became 'highly skilled' at denying the need for change, using many examples of why such changes in culture were unnecessary and difficult to implement in their specific circumstances. Chris Argyris (1993) has labelled this process of using skilled communications to deny problems as *skilled incompetence.* This is one of the principal reasons for organizational resistance to change, because managers, often for the first time in years, are asked to question the very assumptions on which they have always operated. Goss *et al.* (1993) have argued that one of the main reasons for the failure of many programmes of change is because employees are subject to a constant stream of unfinished managerial fads and fashions. Employees become adept at ignoring these programmes of change, most of which have little impact and regularly fail to become embedded in the organization. However, incomplete programmes, often based on fads and fashions in management, result in increased levels of cynicism towards future change initiatives and to change 'fatigue' (Pate *et al.*, 2000), again features of typical change programmes that Orange in Denmark sought to avoid.

4   **The embedding stage.** For the message of change to progress towards the embedding stage, in which a new strategic HR discourse of change has taken root, the communication of early positive outcomes, supported by evidence of its benefits, is necessary to overcome continued resistance; or, as is often more likely, to overcome the 'benign neglect' by employees that can accompany change programmes, i.e. hoping these changes will go away by ignoring them. The notion of 'early wins' is one of the most important and enduring in change management; it suggests that small-scale experiments and initiatives rather than wholesale, top-down programmes are the best way forward, as discussed in the previous chapters. One of the few near-certainties in business is that 'big change invokes big opposition', so it is critical to identify the groups that you 'trial out'. We also refer to measures of just how deeply the messages of change are embedded in an organization. Excellent examples of such ongoing measures are the state of psychological contracts over time and the extent of commitment, internalization, identification and psychological ownership of the changes, as discussed in Chapter 4.

5   **The feedback stage.** This stage is critical for continuous change in the organization, during which the outcomes of strategic innovations are fed back into the organizational contexts – particularly new employee attitudes and behaviours, the capacity of employees to unlearn, change and innovate, and positive attitudes towards the ways in which changes were implemented. Positive feedback is likely to set the tone for how future change initiatives will be received. In a study we conducted of a Scottish-based textile company (Martin *et al.*, 1998), we noted how previously negative experiences with change programmes had led employees to develop strong feelings of cynicism towards senior managers and their efforts to introduce continuous changes in work practices. Such cynicism made future change initiatives almost impossible to implement.

> ## Using internal corporate communications to tell a sustainable corporate story to employees and potential employees

In the preceding sections, we have outlined some general principles about effective corporate communications relevant to the HR, reputation management, branding process In these next sections, let's home in a little more closely on some of the current communications ideas that put the spotlight on employees – employer of choice initiatives and employer branding. Both of these ideas have been incorporated into our strategic change-through-communications model, to which we shall return later in this chapter.

Employer of choice

As we have discussed in previous chapters, the importance of talent management has increased in proportion to the numbers of people employed in knowledge-based and creative industries in the developed world. It is also likely to become critical to the economic development of countries such as China and India. For example, a McKinsey report in October 2005 forecast huge shortages of graduates in China over the coming decade, which, if not matched by an increasing supply, would hold back its progress. Consequently, companies worldwide, including some Chinese and Indian companies, have turned to employer of choice programmes to attract and retain talented people. However, as we shall see, these programmes are not without their critics (Huselid *et al.*, 2005).

According to consultants such as Ahlrichs (2000) and Ashby and Pell (2001), becoming an employer of choice is a deliberate business strategy, which has driven some large, medium and small American and British employers to benchmark themselves against others in rankings such as the Best Place to Work, published by *Fortune* magazine in the US, and *The Sunday Times* list of

Best Companies to Work for in the UK. Another British organization prominent in these exercises is the Great Place to Work®
Institute, which has compiled data from the USA, Europe and
the UK to develop a Trust Index© survey and benchmarking
against the '100 Best Places to Work in Europe'.

For some organizations, following an employer of choice
strategy means little more than more sophisticated and sensitive
recruitment practices, such as improving recruitment design,
online recruitment, sensitive induction, retention analysis, cafe-
teria compensation and benefits, and 'growing your own' talent
(Ahlrichs, 2000; Konrad and Deckop, 2001; Tarzian, 2002). For
others, it means a new, more contextually sensitive, version of
the old-style, relational psychological contract in which long-
term commitment from employers, demonstrated through the
organization's goals, values and trust initiatives, is matched by
high commitment and low turnover or separation rates from
employees. As we have already discussed, such a psychological
contract is characterized by highly competitive remuneration
and benefits, often including elements of contingent pay, interesting, challenging and varied projects, a commitment to training
and development tailored to individual needs, flexible working
arrangements and a motivating work environment.

The UK-based 'Best Companies' organization is one of the
most sophisticated examples of employer of choice approaches
(Leary-Joyce, 2004). This organization runs an annual competition, sponsored by the CIPD, the UK-government Department
of Trade and Industry and *The Sunday Times* newspaper. Its mission is to help improve the quality of employment or workplace
relations through its discussion forum, benchmarking trend
analysis and competition, and research of good and bad HR
practices. Their annual survey is based on validated survey data
of 180 000 employees, factor-analysed to produce the following
eight criteria on which employees believe to be the most important in influencing their experience of work:

- Quality of leadership – how employees feel about the
  head of the organization, senior managers and the
  extent to which they identify with the company's values and principles
- Direct supervision – feelings about and communication with their direct manager

■ Opportunities for personal growth – feelings about training, career development and prospects

■ Well-being – feelings about work stress and pressure, and work–life balance

■ Team and colleagues – feelings towards their immediate colleagues and how well they work together

■ Giving something back – feelings about their organization's positive impact on society

■ Engagement with company – the level of engagement employees have for their job and organization

■ The deal on pay and benefits – how happy employees are with their pay and benefits.

These are all factors that would typically figure highly on anyone's list of good practices and reflect much of what we have argued for in this book. It is interesting to note, given the focus of much of Chapter 9, that both the Best Companies and Great Place to Work® Institute have included among their criteria the CSR agenda, with the former having 'giving something back' as part of their list, while the latter has special awards for CSR. Both are also keen on the nature of communications being a two-way, responsive, dynamic dialogue. The Great Place to Work® Institute even has a special award for companies that establish a 'Whistleblowing Friendly Culture', which encourages employees to speak up to power.

This consultancy-driven recipe for an employer of choice strategy is reminiscent of the best practice work of Pfeffer (1998), discussed in Chapter 5, and his more recent calls for dialogue and community in organizations. Contrary to the ideas associated with the evolutionary, market-based perspectives on strategic HR (e.g. Cappelli, 1999), which advocated changes to a new, employability contract, Pfeffer made it a central element of his argument that employment security provided the necessary table stakes for implementing other high performance work practices. He reviewed a number of studies showing the negative consequences of downsizing, including important connections between downsizing and negative impacts on organizational performance, with strong, negative correlations between high employee turnover and positive assessments of customer service, the latter of which is a vital factor in establishing and maintaining strong brand identities. If downsizing had to be undertaken, Pfeffer agued that it could be accomplished sensitively and sensibly, retaining the morale of those surviving and minimizing the impact on the company's image in concurrent and future recruitment campaigns.

In 2005 the list of UK-based companies that ranked in the top ten were Nationwide Building Society (financial services), ASDA (part of Wal-Mart's retailing group), KPMG (business consulting and financial services), Carphone Warehouse (mobile communications retailer), Cadbury Schweppes (food and drink manufacturer), Compass Group (contract caterer), Pfizer (pharmaceuticals), Severn Trent Water (utilities) and W. S. Atkins (engineering consultants). There are similar lists of the top 100 medium and small organizations, including many public sector, voluntary sector and services companies. In 2005 the list was headed by W. L Gore, the Gore-Tex manufacturer, St Ann's Hospice, Beaverbook the Jewellers, Pannone, a legal firm, Data Connection in computer software and Sandwell Community Caring Trust, personal care and support – a varied array of organizations.

Like all best practice approaches, however, they 'fail' the test of differentiation, discussed at length in Chapters 5 and 6. Huselid *et al.* (2005) produce two telling scenarios that make this point graphically. The first is the existing narrative of most employer of choice policies, which run along the following lines: *we wish to communicate to potential and existing employees this is a great place to work, providing extensive benefits to all, including security, career development and good pay, for which we are well known. As a consequence, we attract lots of people to apply and few ever want to leave.*

Huselid *et al.*'s argument is that such a strategy results in little differentiation between good and poor performers, attracts people who are less interested in performance and more interested in benefits, attracts too many people for HR to make good judgements about their worth and 'locks in' poor performers by over-compensating them. The results are that the organization provides some people and groups with what they don't deserve, while under-rewarding 'A' performers, who may leave. In the long run, they contend, employer of choice policies are a potential recipe for bloated, unresponsive, mediocre organizations.

In its place, a strong case is made for a more differentiated, talent management-based narrative, based on employee self-selection: an *employee of choice* rather than an employer of choice message. The communications storyline recommended is as follows: *we are not an employer of choice because we don't want high numbers of unsuitably qualified applicants that increase our selection costs; nor do we want people staying if they don't perform and we make this clear in the operation of our performance management policies. Instead, we wish to communicate that this is a high performance culture, requiring high levels of ability, motivation and effort, for which people will be rewarded. Not everyone will be able to match our requirements, so only apply if you are able to meet these exceptional requirements.*

This is a very different message, but the question remains: is it one, if taken to excess, that could result in an Enron situation? In other words, to return to the point of the Paragon case in Chapter 5: can organizations overrate talented people? Perhaps the answer lies somewhere in between employer of choice and employee of choice strategies. Which, in some respects, is why employer (or internal) branding has become so popular in recent years.

Employer branding

These ideas are the ones that most obviously have brought marketing into HR; when HR specialists are asked to think about their links with marketing, inevitably, but myopically in our view, they will use the term, 'employer branding' or a variation on that theme. We say myopically because, as we have argued throughout this book, there is much more to the crossover between the two functions than employer branding; nevertheless, the ideas associated with this new approach to HR are highly relevant and practical.

As we have suggested, over the past few years the concept of employer branding has certainly entered into the lexicon and practice of HR specialists, particularly as a result of consultants such as Versant in the US and People in Business in the UK offering 'toolkits' to engage employees by creating compelling employee value propositions. Perhaps the most extensive study to date of employment branding is the US Conference Board's work (Dell and Ainspan, 2001), which surveyed and undertook follow-up interviews with executives in 137 major US companies. This research found that employees were becoming a much more important target for corporate image-makers, although they did not necessarily use the term 'employer branding'. Forty per cent of respondents reported using the methods of corporate branding in their attempts to attract, retain and motivate employees. A further, unpublished study by the *Economist* in 2003 showed high awareness of employer branding among HR specialists, especially in brand-conscious American and Asian companies.

Europe, however, was not far behind. We have presented at a number of practitioner conferences in the UK since 2003, at which a host of other organizations in the private, public and voluntary sectors have given their versions of employer branding. To name only a few: Virgin, Vodafone, British Gas, Nationwide Building Society, Diageo, Reuters, the Royal Mail, Standard Life Investments, Ealing and Westminster Councils, the London Stock Exchange, the Crown Prosecution Service and Cancer Research. In addition, case study evidence has reported a fast-growing interest among continental European companies, such as Nokia, Philips, Siemens, Saab, Fiat and Deutschebank, in the idea of employer or internal branding (Bergstrom *et al.*, 2002; Sparrow *et al.*, 2004). So, taken together, it seems that European companies are following the lead of American companies in this direction.

Employer branding has been defined as the 'company's image as seen through the eyes of its associates and potential hires', and is intimately linked to the 'employment experience' of 'what it is like to work at a company, including tangibles such as salary and intangibles such as company culture and values' (Ruch, 2002, p. 3). Like the minimalist version of employer of choice, much of the content of employer branding programmes is often little more than the communication of the internal, HR equivalent of the 'marketing mix' – attraction, recruitment, motivation and retention (see Table 8.2). For example, Mitchell (2002) has set out three marketing principles and five communications messages for 'selling the brand inside'.

Table 8.2 compares examples of practical advice from the consulting literature, most of these expressing similar sentiments to the advice in Box 8.3 on p. 281.

Table 8.2

Comparing employer branding advice

MacKenzie and Glynn (2001): Ten recommendations for communicating an employee brand	Govendik (2001): Engaging employees to define the brand	Ruch (2002) (Versant Consulting): Guide to building loyalty in your organization	Bergstrom et al. (2002): Why internal branding matters: the Five Cs
Get consistent – build a layer of a few key messages that can be reinforced by facts	Find the company from within, by surfacing the brand image through the eyes of employees	Assess your company culture, using the cultural elements survey	*Clarity*: know what the message is that you want to send depends on: ■ Knowing your internal audience intimately ■ Deciding on the language and symbols that are the 'face' and 'voice' of the brand
Recognize what is not part of the message to be communicated	Create a brand vision and brand attributes or values that will ring true with brand ambassadors	Construct an appropriate employer brand identity that can be marketed externally and internally	
Understand the key moment of truth in the recruitment process, especially the point at which people would accept an offer. Make this as early as possible	Roll out the brand by compelling employees to understand the brand, their responsibilities in making the brand live and by getting them excited and engaged in the brand roll-out	Develop an employer brand promise, which describes the value proposition to employees	*Commitment*: Building consensus around the brand through shared understanding and on-going education, which is woven into the life of the brand
Know whats compelling about the organization, especially for high performers	Gain employee buy-in through consistent education and training	Develop an employer brand voice, a tool for ensuring consistent communications with associates	*Communications*: Use communications that employees approve of. Leaders have to be involved; high frequency; multiple channels; and attention to detail for consistency of message

(continued)

Table 8.2
(Continued)

MacKenzie and Glynn (2001): Ten recommendations for communicating an employee brand	Govendik (2001): Engaging employees to define the brand	Ruch (2002) (Versant Consulting): Guide to building loyalty in your organization	Bergstrom et al. (2002): Why internal branding matters: the Five Cs
Understand the 'brand promise', particularly which elements are non-negotiable	Reinforce key brand attributes by giving employees first crack of the whip in giveaways, gifts, etc., associated with the roll-out of the brand	Implement the brand promise, using the brand voice and integrated communications tools	*Culture*: Understand the culture so that you can anticipate resistance, and use techniques that will help people buy into the new story
Work *with* employees to ensure that there is consistency in the story	Define the brand as part of the organizational culture by creating a constant stream of stories and events designed to support the key brand attributes	Measure the employer brand effectiveness, using a specially constructed index in key areas such as recruitment, retention and motivation	*Compensation*: Offer a strong payback to those who deliver the brand
Design collateral information to make the truth compelling
Ensure that intermediaries have the same story and work on your behalf
Do not allow any intervention to pass without reinforcing the message of the employment brand
Ensure that your internal change efforts are in line with your emerging employment brand			

Source: Adapted from Martin and Beaumont, 2001

Box 8.3   Selling the brand inside (based on Mitchell, 2002)

The marketing principles are:

- **Choosing the moment:** capitalizing on critical receptive contexts for change, usually when a fundamental revisiting of the values, direction and structure of the company is taking place.
- **Linking internal and external marketing:** ensuring alignment in the messages internally and externally, enabling employees to deliver on the external message and ensuring that the external message is a credible one with employees.
- **Bringing the brand alive for employees:** creating an emotional connection between employees and the brand by drawing on key values and attitudes of different segments of the labour force and extensive participation in the design and roll-out of the employer branding messages.

The five communications messages for selling brands are:

1   Don't preach, but listen to employees and use their language.
2   Emphasize beliefs rather than intentions, because beliefs capture the brand essence and are more inspiring to employees.
3   Make the medium part of the message, using surprising and innovative media rather than the traditional presentations.
4   Design material fit for purpose; this broadly refers to ease of use.
5   Have fun, because humour goes a long way in carrying a campaign.

None of this work is particularly new and likely to take HR specialists in a direction they were not already travelling. However, our understanding of the application of marketing techniques to HR is getting more sophisticated. Two recent contributions demonstrate this progress, one from academia, another from the consulting world.

US marketing academics Miles and Mangold (2004, 2005) have developed a model of what they have called *employee branding*, which, in some respects, resembles our introductory framework in Chapter 1 (see Figure 8.2). They have applied this model to the case of Southwest Airlines (see Box 8.4), which is well known for its use of sophisticated HR techniques.

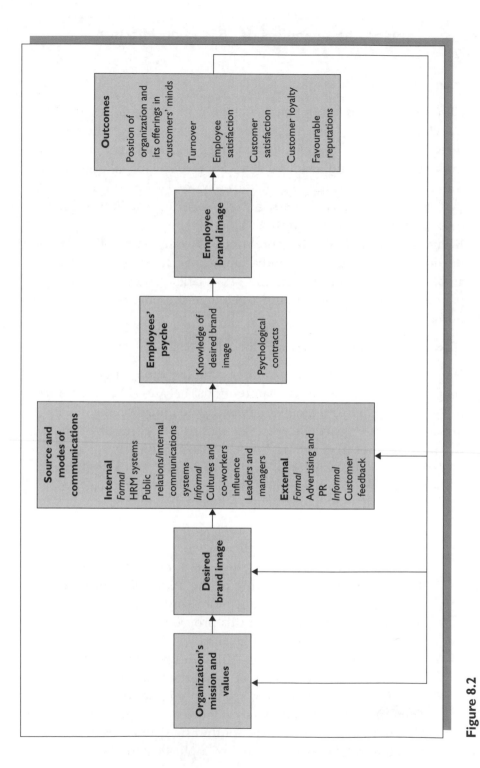

Figure 8.2
The employee branding process (adapted from Miles and Mangold, 2005).

The definition they apply to employee branding is 'the process by which employees internalize the desired brand image and are motivated to project the image to customers and other organizational constituents' (2005, p. 535). Their model is essentially prescriptive in stating that the organization's mission and values are the starting point for understanding and implementing a brand image. This image has to be conveyed through a range of internal and external, formal and informal communications media to shape employees' understanding and psychological contracts. Most of the usual qualifications apply concerning the nature of communications, including the coherence and credibility of the message and medium, and the need for leaders and managers to act as they say in reinforcing the message. The qualifications fit well with our strategic narrative approach. The resulting employer brand image will lead, they argue, to a range of favourable outcomes, including positive organizational reputations, customer loyalty and satisfaction, positive brand and organizational positioning, employee satisfaction and turnover (see Figure 8. 2).

Box 8.4   Employer branding in Southwest Airlines

Southwest Airlines in the USA is one of the most quoted cases of best practice in HRM and it should come as no surprise that it has won many practitioner awards, one of the most recent being for employee branding (note the change in terminology they used). Miles and Mangold (2005) have produced a full account of this process, which we have summarized to give a flavour of good practice in this leading-edge case.

The cornerstone and distinguishing feature of Southwest Airlines is its corporate mission and values framework, based on 'dedication to the highest level of Customer Service delivered with warmth, friendliness, individual pride' and 'Company Spirit'. Interestingly, Miles and Mangold, who are marketing academics, suggest the foundation of this mission is that *employees come first* because it is they who deliver exceptional levels of customer service.

The constant transmission of the mission and values is a key success factor in external and internal communications, and in the organization's success. First, it helps create the desired brand image, which is the message that it wants its customers to receive, and one which employees are made aware of on a daily basis. It is also sufficiently detailed in expressing what happens when things go wrong, so that customers and employees know what to expect and how to behave. Employees, for example, are asked to deliver 'positively outrageous service' in fulfilling the mission and brand promise.

Communication is at the heart of Southwest Airlines' strategy. Their 'people department' (not HR department) use the recruitment and selection process to recruit 'team players' whose values and attitudes fit the brand; they also use the human resource development process to clarify and reinforce the values, culture and 'Southwest Spirit', using a range of media such as 'Keeping the Spirit Alive' videos and other collateral. The performance management and rewards systems are also used to communicate the brand through incentive pay, including stock options and profit sharing. Interestingly, by linking pay directly to flights, they ensure pilots understand the need for cost efficiency. Pfeffer (2005) reported that Southwest Airlines have by far the lowest costs per mile of any comparable airline in the world because pilots have a clear line of sight between how they fly the plane, where they park it, customer service and profitability.

Finally, the company is prominent in using the public relations media to communicate to employees the importance of the mission, and by entering nearly every competition available that reinforces the message of people driving customer service (e.g. Top Performing companies awards, Fortune's most admired companies, most socially responsible company awards etc.). It is also noted for its advertising to potential employees (and customers) through its 'Southwest is a symbol of Freedom' campaign, which is translated into eight individual freedoms for employees, including learning and growth, to be themselves, etc.

In addition to formal communications, Southwest recognize the importance of informal communications between employees, managers, colleagues and customers. How employees act and talk about the company helps create its culture, which is made more formal through its Culture Committee structure. These committees operate in each Southwest location to examine the problems of culture management and develop solutions. Like many US companies, Southwest has an 'open-door policy' to enable rapid communications between managers and the workforce, which sits alongside the more formal union–management bargaining structures. Employees are also invited and expected to share letters from customers about good and bad service, and to provide solutions where required. However, as Miles and Mangold point out, these solutions are not expected to be delivered at the expense of employees' freedoms.

According to Miles and Mangold, an employee's psyche is where the knowledge and willingness to project a brand image resides, which Southwest recognize in their use of a covenant between the company and its employees. This covenant (similar to our use of the psychological contract) provides a clear understanding of what employees can expect and what is expected from them. The extent to which there has been a delivery on the 'deal' from the employees' perspective is determined not only through the appraisal systems, but through informal conversations and lunches with the CEO, Colleen Barrett, for randomly selected employees.

The employee brand image – the image that employees project to other employees and potential recruits – is determined by communicating the brand image consistently and frequently to all employees using the methods previously outlined. Second, Southwest makes every attempt to deliver its covenant to employees. All communications, formal and informal, are expected to be 'on-brand' to align the employee brand with the desired brand image, both of which stem from the mission and values of *putting people first.*

Source: Based on Miles and Mangold, 2005; Pfeffer, 2005

From the consultancy sector, among the most insightful contributions to the field is by Simon Barrow and Richard Mosley (2005), directors of People in Business. They have been credited with inventing the term 'employer branding' and have long experience in applying marketing expertise to HR. The core proposition of their approach is the integrated brand model, which closely resembles the one by Gary Davies and his colleagues on reputation management (see Chapter 2). Figure 8.3 offers a summary of their ideas.

Employer brand positioning, according to Barrow and Mosley, depends on creating a realistic analysis of the external and internal brand propositions, only aligning them if there is a broad agreement between the two through a core proposition. Reflecting what we have discussed so far, they argue credibility is at the heart of all good external and internal communications,

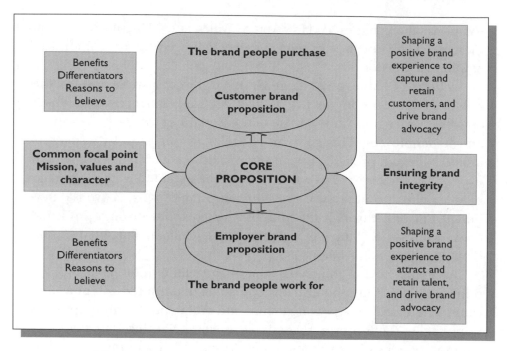

Figure 8.3
An integrated brand model (adapted from Barrow and Mosley, 2005, p. 111).

but the messages also have to be aspirational, embracing a distinctive focal point and 'big idea'. And, following our initial discussion of old versus new communications and sustainable corporate stories, they have to be consistent and enduring throughout.

Also reflecting our discussions of new developments in strategic HR architectures and workforce segmentation, they advocate targeting customer and employer brand propositions for different audiences (see Figure 8.4). One of the main arguments for doing so is to strike a balance between conformity and diversity; between fitting people to values and fitting values to people. This is the same argument raised in Chapter 6 in our discussion of segmenting by lifestyles, exemplified in the Tesco case. So while it is necessary to define the overall position of an employer brand, it is also necessary to build in flexibility into the workforce by having distinctive employee value propositions for different types of employees with customized messages and packages for each career segment.

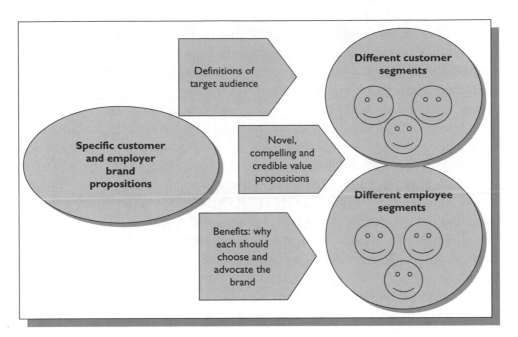

Figure 8.4
Employee value propositions and segmentation (based on Barrow and Mosley, 2005).

The example they use to illustrate this customization is drawn from the Microsoft website, which has distinct employee value propositions for each career group, though all reflect the core employer brand logo 'realize your potential' (http://www. microsoft.com/uk/careers/peoplefirst.mspx). You might want to explore this site to understand how employee value propositions work in practice. What might happen if the balance between conformity (to the corporate message) and diversity (in fitting employer value propositions to the needs of the business) is illustrated in the little example in Box 8.5 concerning talent management in the British Army.

Box 8.5   Talent management in the British Army

Consider this example from the British military, which provides evidence of a potential problem in striking a balance between a strong corporate message and targeted employee value propositions. In 2004 the UK Ministry of Defence and Army chiefs announced their intentions to rationalize the British Army for operational reasons to turn it into a more streamlined fighting force. In doing so, they proposed a merger of a number of regiments that had a long and distinguished history. These included merging a number of well-known Scottish Regiments, which had formed a significant part of Britain's fighting force for two centuries and which would form the largest single regiment in the British Army.

Supporters of these regiments, including many existing and former officers and Scottish politicians, put up spirited resistance to the proposed mergers, at one point describing them as an 'act of lunacy'. Part of their argument was based on the strong emotional ties between these regiments and the regions that they were drawn from, which formed their traditional recruiting grounds. They argued that the strong family ties between these regiments and the local region would be damaged irreparably. Despite these arguments, the Scottish regiments were merged to form the Royal Regiment of Scotland. In October 2005, however, the news media broadcast a story, based on research, which showed recruitment to the army in Scotland was at dangerously low levels, some 10% below target and 18% lower than in previous years. These poor recruitment figures were forecast to have an important impact on the fighting potential of the British Army at a period when it was being called on to support a number of conflicts in different parts of the world, including Iraq and Afghanistan. One Scottish politician summarized the argument against the merger:

> What the Government and defence chiefs fail to appreciate is that there is no affinity nor goodwill towards the Royal Regiment of Scotland from the people of Scotland – that is amply demonstrated with the collapse in recruiting …
> (Peter Duncan, MSP, quoted in the *Dundee Courier*, 2 November 2005)

Army officials were beginning to recognize that these historically low levels of new recruits in Scotland could be attributed in part to the failure to attract young people from the traditional regional recruiting grounds. They also believed it was due to other reasons connected with image, including an unpopular war in Iraq, poor image of the British generally following well-publicized incidences of bullying and mysterious deaths at Deepcut Barracks, and competition from private sector security companies that have been 'poaching' SAS, Marines and Special Forces troops with offers of much higher pay. Their response has been to create a 147-strong recruiting team, with its headquarters in central Scotland, to mount a 'charm offensive'.

Employer brand equity

Creating employers brands requires organizations to make estimates of how successful they have been, just as they would in creating customer brands. In Chapter 2, we explained how understanding strong brands requires a measure of relative value and used the ideas of brand equity to identify the potential of a brand to add value. We can apply this idea to measuring the relative employer brand equity comprising four similar components. Measuring brand equity in this way can provide evidence of how deeply embedded and sustainable the corporate story is in the organization (see Table 8.3).

Table 8.3

Measuring employer brand equity.

	Components	What is it?	Creates value by:
Employer brand equity	Perceptions of psychological contract and engagement	An emotional link between the brand and employees that cause them to be attracted to and remain with the organization	Reducing costs of gaining new employees Creating brand 'ambassadors' Gives breathing space when the organization is undergoing change
	Awareness of brand propositions	Employees and potential employees' familiarity with brand	Potential employees prefer the familiar/well-known over the unknown Enables people to compose a quick mental shortlist of potential employers
	Perceived quality of the employer brand	Assessment of expected quality that an employer brand will deliver	People more likely to work for an organization they believe to be of higher quality and recommend to others Launch-pad for

(continued)

Table 8.3
(*Continued*)

	Components	What is it?	Creates value by:
Employer brand equity	Associations	The images and ideas connected with the employer brand – what it means to employees and potential employees	asking employees to work in new ventures/projects, e.g. overseas Creates interest and relevance to employees Helps differentiate from competitor employers Sends signals to employees' significant others – says something good about the employee to others

Conclusions

In this chapter we have attempted to show how corporate communications can help produce change in the quality of employment relationships by shaping psychological contracts and increasing levels of individual identification and internalization of the corporate messages on reputations and brands. We have used a model of strategic change through communication applied to multinational or multidivisional companies to show how the processes of change are linked to more or less receptive contexts for change. We have also evaluated some of the ideas connected with employer of choice and employer branding programmes, concluding that, in line with our argument in Chapter 6, corporate messages usually need to be accompanied by a more segmented approach through employee value propositions to different target audiences to be effective.

These conclusions are very much in line with research on the distinctive role of communications in managing psychological contracts (Guest and Conway, 2002). They found that three categories of corporate communications were associated with different outcomes for psychological contracts. Job-related communications, which refer to the ongoing interaction between the employer and employee in the job, e.g. during appraisal, career development etc., and communications during the recruitment process were associated with 'contract explicitness, lower levels of breach, fairer exchanges and management perceptions of the impact of the psychological contract on employee-related outcomes' (p. 35). Top-down communications from management, for example mission and values statements, were rated the least effective by managers in the study, which is consistent with other evidence and with the arguments in this chapter.

The study also showed that senior managements were well aware that their organizations quite frequently were unable to keep their promises and commitments, and were aware of the potential impact such breach may have on psychological contracts. Yet, they recognized the importance of communications and psychological contracts to the success of their organizations. Such an apparent contradiction raised the question of why they make such promises in the first place.

One answer is that they do not have a good enough understanding of the communications process, and the role of sustainable corporate stories in creating better reputations and brands. We hope the model and discussion on employer branding, segmentation and employer value propositions may have helped.

References

Ahlrichs, N. S. (2000) *Competing for talent: Key recruitment and retention strategies for becoming an employer of choice.* Palo Alto, CA: Davis-Black Publishing.

Argyris, C. (1993) *Knowledge for action.* San Francisco, CA: Jossey-Bass.

Ashby, F. and Pell, A. R. (2001) *Embracing excellence: become an employer of choice to attract the best talent.* Hemel Hempstead: Prentice Hall.

Barrow, S. and Mosley, R. (2005) *The Employer Brand®: bringing the best of brand management to people at work.* London: Wiley.

Barry, D. and Elmes, M. (1997) Strategy retold: toward a narrative view of strategic discourse, *Academy of Management Review,* **22** (2), 429–452.

Bergstrom, A., Blumenthal, D. and Crothers, S. (2002) Why internal branding matters: the case of Saab, *Corporate Reputation Review,* **5** (2–3), 133–142.

Boje, D. (2006) Pitfalls in story-telling: advice and praxis, *Academy of Management Review*, **31**, 218–224.

Buchanan, D., Fitzgerald, L., Ketley, D., Gollop, R., Jones, J. L., Saint Lamont, S., Neath, A. and Whitby, E. (2005) No going back: a review of the literature on sustaining change, *International Journal of Management Review*, **7**, 189–205.

Cappelli, P. (1999) *The new deal at work: managing the market-driven workforce*. Boston, MA: Harvard Business School Press.

Dell, D. and Ainspan, N. (2001) *Engaging employees through your brand*. Conference Board Report, No. R-1288-01-RR, April, Washington, DC: Conference Board.

Ford, J. D. and Ford, L. W. (1995) The role of conversations in producing intentional organizational change, *Academy of Management Review*, **20**, 541–570.

Goss, T. and Pascale, R. (1991) *Managing on the edge*. London: Penguin.

Goss, T., Pascale, R. and Athos, A. (1993) The reinvention of the rollercoaster, *Harvard Business Review*, **71** (Nov–Dec), 97–108.

Guest, D. E. and Conway, N. (2002) Communicating the psychological contract: an employer perspective, *Human Resource Management Journal*, **12** (2), 22–38.

Haig, M. (2001) *Brand failures: the truth about the 100 biggest branding mistakes of all time*. London: Kogan Page.

Huselid, M. A., Becker, B. E. and Beatty, R. W. (2005) *The workforce scorecard: managing human capital to execute strategy*. Boston, MA: Harvard Business School Press.

Konrad, A. M. and Deckop, J. (2001) Human resource management trends in the USA: challenges in the midst of prosperity, *International Journal of Manpower*, **22** (3), 269–278.

Leary-Joyce, J. (2004) *Becoming an employer of choice: make your organization a place where people want to do great work*. London: Chartered Institute of Personnel and Development.

Martin, G., Beaumont, P. B. and Staines, H. J. (1998) 'Managing organizational culture', in C. Mabey, T. Clark and D. Skinner (eds), *Experiencing HRM*. London: Sage.

Martin, G. and Beaumont, P. B. (2001) Transforming multinational enterprises: towards a process model of strategic HRM change in MNEs, *International Journal of Human Resource Management*, **10** (6), 34–55.

Miles, S. J. and Mangold, W. G. (2004) A conceptualization of the employee branding process, *Journal of Relationship Marketing*, **3** (2/3), 65–87.

Miles, S. J. and Mangold, W. G. (2005) Positioning Southwest Airlines through employee branding, *Business Horizons*, **48**, 535–545.

Mintzberg, H., Ahlstrand, B. and Lampel, J. (2004) *Strategy bites back.* London: Financial Times/Prentice Hall.

Mitchell, C. (2002) Selling the brand inside, *Harvard Business Review,* Jan–Feb, pp. 34–41.

Pate, J. M., Martin, G. and Staines, H. (2000) The New Psychological Contract, cynicism and organizational change: a theoretical framework and case study evidence, *Journal of Strategic Change,* **9** (1), 481–493.

People Management (2005) British Airways and Gate Gourmet sign a new in-flight catering contract, *People Management,* 21 October, p. 7.

Pfeffer, J. (1998) *The human equation: building profits by putting people first.* Boston, MA: Harvard Business School Press.

Pfeffer, J. (2005) *Creating a performance culture.* Presentation at University of Strathclyde, 23 September.

Ruch, W. (2002) Employer brand evolution: a guide to building loyalty in your organization. http://www.versantsolutions.com.

Schultz, D. and Kitchen, P. (2004) Managing the changes in corporate communications and branding, *Corporate Reputation Review,* pp. 350–366.

Sparrow, P. R., Brewster, C. and Harris, H. (2004) *Globalizing human resource management.* London: Routledge.

Tarzian, W. (2002) Linking the hiring process to brand management, *Strategic HR Review,* **1** (3), 22–25.

Van Riel, C. B. (2003) The management of corporate communications, in J. M. T. Balmer and S. A. Geyser (eds), *Revealing the corporation: perspectives on identity, image, reputation, corporate branding and corporate-level marketing.* London: Routledge.

CHAPTER 9

Corporate strategy, corporate leadership, corporate identity and CSR

Introduction

In this penultimate chapter, we focus on the corporate-level drivers of people management, reputations and brands in our introductory model from Chapter 1. These are *corporate strategy*, *leadership* and *governance*, and *corporate identity*. Although we have touched on these drivers throughout the book, there are a number of important points still to be considered since HR strategy does not and cannot be constructed in a vacuum. HR strategies are often portrayed as second- or even third-order strategies that follow rather than drive business or corporate strategies though, as we have seen in Chapter 2, the resource-based view of strategy (the RBV) and the importance of intangible assets such as knowledge, reputations and brands, have changed that picture a little.

So, first, we will examine in more depth the RBV to show its value to our central thesis that reputations and brands are driven from the inside out. This is especially so in knowledge-based and creative industries. While many senior managers espouse such sentiments in claiming that 'people are our most important assets', only those that act on such rhetoric will place faith in the practices of HR and good people management to deliver quality reputations and brands. This relationship between rhetoric and action in strategy sometimes requires an act of faith on their part. Thus, we will examine that idea of *strategy as a perspective* or world-view, since it is often what goes on in senior leaders' heads that is all-important in shaping the future direction of organizations, which we hope to influence. We will also look at developments in strategy-making in creative and knowledge-based industries, which rest on building core competencies and leveraging partnerships and networks to produce innovation (Hagel and Seely-Brown, 2005), as it is in such industries that reputations and talent probably matter more than in traditional ones. It is also in these industries that we are likely to find most difficulty in pursuing a corporate agenda. This is because they are more likely to be populated by new forms of organizations, such as networks and virtual forms, which are, by definition, fragmented and thus pose new problems for HR, reputation management and branding.

Second, we need to engage in a deeper discussion about corporate governance and leadership, which we have so far only touched on. Increasingly, these issues are shaping the reputation management and branding agendas. In particular, we examine three different models of governance: shareholder value, stewardship and stakeholder approaches. This discussion provides a necessary backdrop to the third of our themes in the chapter – creating a corporate identity as a social responsible corporation. Reputation management and the CSR (corporate social responsibility) agenda have become intertwined over the past decade because CSR is one of the fastest growing areas of interest in business and the basis on which a large number of organizations are beginning to construct corporate identities and compete in product and labour markets. We analyse the notion of CSR and the claims made for it, including the business case; we also look at the attempts to create measurable standards for CSR, including the so-called 'triple bottom line' (3BL). The CSR agenda, however, is not without its critics. These critics come from the right in the shape of neo-classical economists and proponents of shareholder value, supported by writers on business ethics. They are also from the left, who regard CSR as nothing more than a public relations fig leaf, which does little to alter fundamental power relations in society. Some of the most interesting criticisms, however, come from within, including critics of the 'doing well by doing good' business case and the idea of a measurable bottom line.

A key theme of this chapter is that the basis on which the leadership of an organization constructs its governance model will ultimately determine its approach to people management, reputation management, CSR and brand-building. Increasingly, it is to responsible leadership that we will look for more socially responsible policies. Leaders, however, will need advice from a broader-based and more knowledgeable HR function, schooled in the debates over strategy, governance and CSR, since it is on the basis of effective people management that strategic success, governance, CSR, reputations and brands ultimately depend.

We begin the chapter by examining the UK Financial Services Industry, which is experiencing problems with its reputation, along with many of its member companies. These reputation problems are rooted in assumptions about strategy, leadership and governance and the values of its key opinion leaders and employees. Though the industry is vital to the future of the British economy and to all savers and investors, including the rapidly growing population that will rely on pensions and investment income for a living, it is among the least respected by its UK consumers. Expectations of it are high, but customers' perceptions of delivery against these expectations are low. This poor reputation among the general public hurts it financially because of a lack of trust in its products and services. Furthermore, it has negative consequences for its ability to attract talented people to apply for jobs, with the insurance sub-sector being a good example (Goldsmith, 2005). As a consequence, it relies more than any other industry on high levels of financial incentives to attract and retain staff (Sung and Ashton, 2005). Such an approach to talent management is arguably unsustainable in the long run (Groysberg *et al.*, 2004), though the principle of tying pay to performance is one of the classic dictums of neo-classical economists and many US HR specialists. We end the chapter with an example of a firm that may be getting it right because they have treated CSR seriously as a main board issue and because of the benefits of CSR in building social capital among employees and improving employee engagement.

Box 9.1   Unfit for the future?: The UK financial services industry

On 8 November 2005, we took part in a major conference in London on the future of the financial services industry, comprising firms providing products and services for savings, loans and investments, including banks, insurance companies, asset managers, securities companies, mortgage lenders, intermediary brokers, finance companies, financial consultants, etc. This conference provided an excellent illustration of the problems of an industry facing up to a poor reputation among consumers, government, the media and the general public. The questions addressed by speakers and in the group discussions focused on what could be done as an industry and by its individual companies to make it fit for the future by improving its reputation. Two keynote presentations highlighted the general problems faced by the industry. We summarize these, and some of the discussions with senior marketing, communications and HR managers that ensued.

According to one principal speaker, Anna Bradley, formerly a member of the regulatory body, Financial Services Authority (FSA), the industry was 'unfit for future challenges' unless it offered customers greater value by changing its business model from one that prioritized new customer sales to one that provided expert advice and value for money to existing, as well as new, customers. Her main argument was that the legacy of past strategies had resulted in a poor industry image, a view supported by the other keynote speaker, Ian Stewart. Bradley evidenced the history of mis-selling of pensions, payment-protection insurance on loans and individual mortgages, which she argued still continues, along with contemporary problems concerning equity release schemes, individual savings schemes and long-term care insurance as evidence of uncompetitive products and poor customer value. She also flagged the relatively lack-lustre performance of many financial services companies in providing returns to shareholders, a point supported by recent evidence on the financial performance of some of the largest UK banks. For example, during 2005, the UK banking sector was the 'least loved' of the three big sectors dominating *The Financial Times* top 100 companies – banking, pharmaceutical and oil – performing poorly, especially the big four banks (*Scotland on Sunday,* 11 December 2005). The net result of these problems was a lack of confidence and trust among consumers, and a perception that many companies in the industry 'fleeced customers' over savings and investments products and services. Moreover, there seemed to be a lack of understanding by company managers that problems existed: in one survey 75% of customers expressed a lack of trust in the industry and failure to do a good job, while 75% of managers in the industry thought they were doing a good job.

Further evidence for poor image was provided by Ian Stewart, Research Director for Mintel, a market research agency, and a former senior manager in the industry. Drawing on a Mintel survey conducted in 2004, he pointed out that only 15% of customers claimed their banks understood their needs, despite one-third regularly visiting their branch. This situation was not helped by a challenging social and economic environment, comprising: (a) an ageing population and potential pensions crisis; (b) an increased emphasis by government on individual responsibility for healthcare and education; and (c) a generally poor financial understanding and capability among the population at large, which had resulted in high borrowing and an over-reliance on property for investment. Stewart cited the Mintel survey evidence in which only 27% of customers rated themselves as having a good understanding of financial products and 74% claimed to learn about them through trial and error.

To balance the picture a little, both presenters argued that some of these criticisms applied only to certain sectors of the industry. Evidence supporting this was provided by an *Economist* article in December 2005, showing the mortgage market in the UK seemed to be working well, according to an independent study carried out for the UK Office of Fair Trading. However, the same article pointed to evidence of market failure in the retail banking sector, especially in respect of consumers and small businesses, where despite banking charges being generally low in European terms, other evidence pointed to excessive fees being charged to individuals and small firms by the larger banks (*Economist,* 2005a).

As a result of numerous UK government reviews and reports from the Office of Fair Trading of market failure, the FSA had attempted to regulate the industry through a number of interventions over enhanced disclosure, new responsibilities in insurance, changes in advice and an enhanced complaints procedure. However, according to Bradley, changes had been 'largely piecemeal and slow', which was not likely to help the industry or consumers, especially given the opening up of cross-border markets in Europe.

The analysis of both keynote presenters pointed to long-term and fundamental causes, the most important of which was the 'myopic' industry focus on short-term sales and profits. Bradley focused on the lack of connection between producers and consumers; the industry over-emphasized sales of products to new customers, supported by extremely high levels of incentives to customers and sales staff that rewarded the acquisition of new business, rather than servicing existing customers. This situation was most noticeable in the insurance and credit sectors in which competition among wholesalers, resellers and retailers for customers had resulted in the practice of offering 'golden hellos'. She also highlighted advice that was confused with sales: sales of new business were rewarded by high levels of fee-based incentives, which resulted in brokers and sales staff masking the sales of particular products as neutral advice; however, she did recognize the unwillingness of customers to pay for advice as a 'plea in mitigation'.

Stewart continued with this theme by focusing on the changing nature of consumers. He pointed out there were many more customer segments today than previously and that customers were more demanding. His argument was that customers were 'growing old disgracefully', in comparison to previous savings-oriented, more careful generations, because they had to pay for increased mortgages, higher education for children, weddings, increased leisure and more varied lifestyles. As a consequence, old certainties no longer existed. Yet the industry continued to sell old products in old ways, despite the widespread dislike among consumers of high pressure selling through financial advertising and continuous direct mailing. Again, this was redolent of an old-fashioned sales-dominated strategy based on products rather than on solutions, which are based on customer wants and needs, and in offering high value services through expert, committed and trustworthy employees.

Coincidentally, two days after this conference, a report was carried in the *London Evening Standard* on figures newly published by the Office of National Statistics on the average earnings in London postcodes. The headlines pointed out the average earnings of males living in the postcode of Poplar and Canning Town, once one of the poorest areas of London, was £101 032, nearly 40% more than the City and Westminster at £66 969, the nearest London postcode to it in terms of earnings, and nearly three times the London average male earnings of £361 442. Nowadays, however, Poplar and Canning Town boasts Canary Wharf as part of its constituency, home of many of the UK's largest financial services companies (the City and Westminster is another area dominated by financial services companies). According to this newspaper article, these earnings in Poplar and Canning Town reflected the high levels of bonuses being paid to staff in the financial services industry. The negative consequences on high house prices in London were, according to the article, a potential cause of social conflict in the capital.

The conference was asked to tackle the problems of the industry in a series of facilitated group discussions and feedback sessions. End-of-conference summaries of these discussions and general conclusions were characterized by blaming government and the FSA for over-regulation and consumers for their lack of understanding and 'failure to acknowledge' the benefits provided by the industry as a whole. High on the list of solutions were the need for more effective communications and public relations, highlighting the benefits of the industry to the economy and customers, the need to charge for advice, and educating customers and society at large on the needs for savings and investment. Low on the list of solutions was the need to address corporate governance in the industry, the need to examine incentives and rewards strategies and the need for more sustainable, socially responsible policies. Even lower on the list of solutions was the willingness of any of the marketing directors present in the room to suggest their own company would be willing to break with the industry recipe of going for sales growth and changing the nature of incentives to sales staff and other key managers, though a number recognized that these were fundamental (but intractable) problems.

This case reveals some of the problems of strategy, governance and social responsibility in an industry and many of the firms in it. When reading the rest of this chapter, you should think about the financial services case to ground your thoughts. Also, you may wish to reflect on how an understanding of the following concepts might be applied to the case. Financial services is not unique, but is at the forefront in using financial incentives to motivate people (Sung and Ashton, 2005), which, as we shall see, is a critical issue in governance and responsible leadership.

Corporate strategy: the importance of an inside-out perspective

As we noted in Chapter 2, the RBV has provided an important source of justification for the focus on strategic human resource management, on the management of people as a source of competitive advantage, and for expenditure on attracting, retaining, developing, rewarding and motivating talented people. To recap on the RBV, it came about because of the changing emphasis in competitive strategy away from external factors, such as the attractiveness of an industry and how firms should position themselves in an industry, to a concern with capitalizing on internal resources that were *rare, valuable, inimitable* (not easily copied) and *non-substitutable.* High on anyone's list of such resources are people; but these also include reputations, brands and knowledge. Indeed John Kay, a leading British economist, has questioned the relevance of the joint stock company and a shareholder value-model of corporate governance in the 21st century:

> The distinction between the role of shareholders and employees was clear when shareholders had bought the plant and employees worked in it. But the principal assets of the modern company are knowledge, brands and reputation, which are in the heads and hands of employees. What can it mean to say the shareholders 'own' these things? (2004, p. 58)

This quotation calls into question one of the main premises of outside-in approaches to strategy, which is that it is easier to re-arrange and fit assets and complementary resources to match a choice of strategy than to change strategy to match the inherent assets and resources of the company (Dunford *et al.*, 2001). Although this matching of people to strategy is a core assumption underlying the design school of strategy, it is also one of its greatest failings, since strategy unconnected to implementation is a major problem facing many organizations (Pettigrew and Whipp, 1991; Joyce *et al.*, 2003).

Early work on links between the RBV and strategic HRM suggested that it was how firms put together bundles of HR practices that were a source of competitive advantage. We discussed this view in relation to best practice and bundles of practices in Chapter 5. However, later writers saw the flaw in this argument because best practice could be easily copied; instead they suggested that it was *systems of HR practices*, including their complementarities and interdependencies (internal and external fit), that were a more significant source of advantage.

Yet, at least according to some writers, even these are not enough to create unique, valuable, rare and inimitable resources. What was more important is how these practices relate to individuals – their identities, attitudes and behaviours – which has been one of the main arguments of this book. Perhaps the best case for this argument is the distinction made between a firm's *human capital pool* (its stocks and flows of people in, through and out of the organization) and its *human resource practices*, which we have discussed previously. The main point is that it is probably more important to focus on how the human capital pool – skilled and potentially willing people – are managed *by line managers* to produce key behaviours that create value than to focus on systems of HR practices. This distinction is at the heart of SHRM models and provides the basis for the architectural and segmentation models discussed in Chapter 6.

Returning to the quote from John Kay, a basic premise of this human capital approach is that firms do not own human resources in the same sense that they own financial or material resources; people possess an important degree of free will in how they engage with an organization, often summed up in the phrase 'discretionary behaviour'. So it is how strategists face up to the unpredictable problem of engaging people, individually and collectively, to behave beneficially for an organization that is their principal focus, and is one of the main issues for leaders' and senior managers' day-to-day attention. It is in this sense we can talk about *people management* (of the human capital pool) being important rather than human resource management, since, as we have shown in this book, it is factors beyond the control of typical human resource departments that influence identities, identification and behaviour.

A problem of the RBV, however, is the difficulty in providing evidence to support its central tenets, at least according to proponents of outside-in approaches to strategy (Wright *et al.*, 2001). Though there have been some attempts to do so, the ideas underlying the RBV do not lend themselves to easy proof, especially using the kinds of large-scale surveys that seem to be required for widespread acceptance of such ideas. For example, the RBV contention that strategic HR variables create inimitable competencies and capabilities in organizations, key influences of reputations and brands, requires that we can observe this process in action; yet only longitudinal, observational studies of cases could hope to do this. These types of studies require years to complete and are extremely resource-hungry. Moreover, inimitable competences and identities may result from more complex sets of causes and not just HR variables. Indeed, in some cases, these combinations can outweigh reputations for poor people management. Arguably, this has been the case with the renowned combinations of logistical, supply chain and information processing competences of Wal-Mart or Nike's combinations of brand management and supply chain management which have been at the heart of their success in spite of negative press for labour management. They may also be a consequence of little more than 'time-compression diseconomies', which result from the time it often takes for follower firms to catch up innovative organizations, an idea related to first-mover advantage.

Allowing for such difficulties in proving the RBV and these more complex causes, it seems inconceivable that the kind of organizational competencies, capabilities and reputations of most firms are not closely tied to the people, individually and collectively – to their skills, self-identities and collective identities, and the behaviours they display. It is also inconceivable that organizational competencies, capabilities and reputations will remain constant over time, as we have already touched on in Chapter 4 in our discussion of changing organizational identities and the example of how IBM has managed to re-invent itself consistently. Changing environments, especially market changes, require *dynamic capabilities* from organizations to constantly integrate, reconfigure, acquire and divest themselves of key resources, including competencies and reputations. Again, as Wright *et al.* (2001) pointed out, it is the human architecture of the firm – its people management and HR policies – that will be central to such dynamic capability-building.

Strategy in knowledge-based and creative industries

As we have consistently argued throughout this book, the RBV is especially relevant in organizations and industries that rely on innovation and creativity for success, sectors increasing in importance in most developed economies (Florida, 2005). Knowledge and creative workers, who are most capable of exercising discretionary behaviour, often require to be managed in quite different ways from traditional workers. For example, Tom Davenport (2005) has argued that knowledge workers do not like to be told what to do and necessarily enjoy more autonomy than other workers because much of their work is invisible and difficult to measure in any meaningful sense. Yet, his research, based on more than 600 knowledge workers in a hundred companies, has led him to conclude that you cannot merely hire talented people and leave them alone; this, he argues, is a recipe for low productivity because organizations tend to treat them as a homogenous group and manage all types of knowledge workers in the same way. Organizations that are more effective in managing knowledge workers have adopted a segmented approach, creating specific *knowledge environments* for particular groups and, sometimes, individuals. Such environments are adapted for different kinds of learning communities and learning styles, and also specific measures of productivity. Extending Davenport's argument, however, we believe that it is more than knowledge environments that are important; the employment environment should also embrace different kinds of employee value propositions, psychological contracts and engagement approaches to ensure that appropriate behaviours align with an organization's innovative intent.

For example, Davenport suggests there are several ways of distinguishing among knowledge workers. One of these is to distinguish between employees whose work is mainly concerned with *knowledge creation*, such as research scientists, development engineers, writers and other creative employees, etc.; *knowledge transmission*, e.g. journalists, software writers, teachers, etc.; and *knowledge application*, e.g. many doctors, managers, software developers, consultants, etc. People working in these different categories are likely to value different elements of the employment offering and be motivated by different aspects of the psychological and material deal. Knowledge creators may, for example, value flexibility in the times and places of work and in being rewarded for outcomes such as patent creation, discoveries of new products or applications, original books, articles and other creative media written or produced, whereas knowledge transmission requires people to be in greater touch across and outside the organization, placing a greater emphasis on an organization facilitating learning communities and on rewarding such people for sharing knowledge. Knowledge applicators, on the other hand, need to have constant access to high quality knowledge and people, organizations, products or processes to practise their trade on. Such people are likely to value working on high profile projects to enhance their careers and to be rewarded for keeping up with and applying state-of-the art knowledge to create added value.

Strategy in virtual organizations

Nowadays, however, managing innovation and creativity is less likely to take place in a single organization over which senior leaders can exercise even a degree of corporate control. Increasingly, innovation is the result of networks of organizations producing goods and services, and more often than not, these will cross international boundaries. We have already discussed such networked or, as some call them, virtual organizations (Galbraith, 2002), with Nike and Cisco being good examples. Two theories of strategic advantage underpin these new organizations: one is the *core competency school*, the other is the *leveraged school* (Hamel and Prahalad, 1996; Hagel and Seely-Brown, 2005). The core competency school is synonymous with the RBV

and has stressed the importance of mobilizing internal competencies or capabilities as the key sources of strategic advantage.
These competencies or capabilities can be *tangible* resources
such as people, finance, technology, processes or materials, or
intangible, such as brands and reputations, talent, knowledge,
intellectual property and networks. The argument has turned
on how much an organization should invest in these resources
and outsource others that are necessary, but not core, to their
business, however defined (Hamel and Prahalad, 1996). Again,
we can use IBM as an example, which divested its computing
business to Denovo, the company's Chinese business partner,
so that it could change focus to being more consistent with
IBM's projected image as a solutions company, rather than one
that sold hardware.

One of the criticisms of the core competency school is that it
has been too firm-centric, even in its business partner variant.
Instead, the leveraged school has emerged in recent years,
based less on organizations relying on internal competencies
and outsourcing to business partners and more on gaining
leverage by mobilizing and orchestrating resources outside of
the firm to create *value nets* or *ecosystems.*

Hagel and Seely-Brown have advocated merging these two
approaches to accelerate capability-building across organizations. Core competencies provide the necessary specialization
and deepening of knowledge to extend their knowledge and to
innovate further; leveraging complementary competencies or
capabilities outside of the organization, increasingly working
with international partners, expands the potential for innovation
if they collaborate over common business problems. One example
from manufacturing is the problem of building a world-class
aircraft to compete with Boeing, which resulted in the European
collaboration to create Airbus Industries. Another example is
from education, one of the world's largest creative industries.
Universitas 21 Global is a consortium of leading, research-led
universities from the UK, Europe, Asia, Australasia and North
America that has been developed to create a virtual e-learning
academy. It is orchestrated by a near-virtual network integrator
in Singapore, which provides marketing, the course programmes
and a small academic staff, but nearly all of the teaching material and faculty come from the partner universities. Building

such a competitive edge requires strategists to engage in *dynamic specialization* (focusing on core competences to create platforms for growth), *connectivity and coordination* (learning how to access the resources of other specialized companies) and *leveraging capability-building* (learning how to collaborate through a productive friction in which each company or partner pushes the others to become better and faster).

And yet, here lies a paradox. Such an approach to strategy and organization is inimical to monolithic corporateness; but, at the same time, building *shared meanings, identities* and *dynamic trust* in such networks of organizations is at the heart of their success. These strategies place enormous importance on the *network integrator* to connect and coordinate the system, the basis on which an increasing number of companies are likely to see themselves as adding value, rather than by providing this service in addition to producing their own products. Building shared meanings and identities in these networks requires HR and people management to work iteratively to a common understanding, rather than to engineer one at the outset. This incremental process of identity- and image-building requires a rather different set of skills than those of corporate designers, since negotiating, compromise, openness and learning are at the heart of such ambitions.

Similarly, building dynamic trust requires a different approach to HR and managing people than is evident in traditional trust relations between contractors and sub-contractors, which has tended to look backwards. The question in such traditional relationships has been: have you been trusted in the past to deliver against my expectations? Given the needs to operate in rapidly changing environments across different international cultures and business systems, the more appropriate question is likely to be: can I trust you in the future to help us to build our capability together? Usually this is without the comfort zone of hindsight and past records to go on. Such a problem faced one of our case study companies, Standard Life Investments, in attempting to set up businesses in China and India. Senior managers explained that it would only do business with partners that could match their culture and focus on sound business processes. For them, India was a more natural target because of a common business language and a UK-based legal and business system. Conversely, they saw their progress in China had been slow because of the slow pace and 'exotic' nature of the negotiation process, learning the language, ambiguities in the regulatory environment and in finding a partner willing to accept Standard Life Investments' business model.

Instead, trustworthiness is likely to arise from mutually defining the outcomes and sharing views and resources on the 'skill and will' of the different parties to deliver. HR's role in creating skills across enterprises through learning and development initiatives is likely to be critical in this process. Equally, creating motivation (the will) of organizations lacking the necessary skills may be improved by thoughtful incentives to acquire them rapidly. The process and atmosphere is one of *integrative bargaining* (a focus on mutuality and increasing the size of total resources available to the system so that all parties gain something of their aims), rather than *distributive bargaining* (a focus on sharing out a fixed sum in an 'I win, you lose' scenario) (Kochan and Lipsky, 2002; Cox, 2004).

Leadership and governance

The RBV is consistent with the notion of strategy as a perspective, which, as Mintzberg (1987) pointed out, is a way of linking the idea of strategy to what goes on in the heads of strategists. Outside-in approaches to strategy focus on positioning an organization in its environment, usually in relation to competitors. However, ideas such as an environment and positioning are perceptions or social constructs, located inside the minds of strategists and leaders, rather than concrete facts. So, what you see depends on where you stand, and through our collective perceptions and definitions of the situation we socially construct our environments. In that sense, all strategy is idiosyncratic, a product of the specific mindsets of a group of leaders or strategists, with both positive and negative aspects to it. For example, leveraging partnerships, which we discussed in the previous section, is really an act of faith in which partners have to believe that the parties are going to act in a trustworthy manner to work together for each other's benefit. Of course, this assumes that all parties know where their best interests lie and that they are able to detect exploitation by others, which is not always the case (Cox, 2004).

Mintzberg points out that strategy is to organizations what personality is to individuals. As a consequence, reputations and brands are a product of the minds, personalities and identities of leaders – what they want to be known for as much as a product of any analytical thinking, which, in any event, is often used to rationalize leadership vision (Mintzberg *et al.*, 1998). One excellent example of this is GE's 'greening' of its business, which we raised in Chapter 3 (see Box 9.2).

Box 9.2   GE and corporate social responsibility

In December 2005, *The Economist* carried an article on the CEO of GE (one of the world's largest companies), Jeffrey Immelt, 'betting his future on environmental technologies'. Such a strategy is by any definition a U-turn from GE's earlier manoeuvres that involved huge cost-cutting and divestment exercises, incremental, rather than radical, innovation and a willingness to pollute the US environment to maintain its cost and revenue targets.

Immelt's stated strategic aims are to have every GE business cut its greenhouse gas emissions by 2012 by a much greater degree than that required by the UN's Kyoto protocol, at least as measured by what GE might be forecast to produce on its current business plans. He has also promised to double revenues from 17 clean-technology businesses and to double research spending on clean products. These are significant enough targets, but what is more telling is that GE, unlike many US companies or even the US government, has accepted that global warming is real and that they have a role to play in leading America and American business to do something about it. The article made the key point:

> Mr Immelt is ... convinced that clean technologies will be the future of GE ... If he is right, then not only will GE benefit, but businesses everywhere will have to follow in its tracks in one form or another. If he is wrong, [he] will have led one of the world's biggest and most powerful companies down a dead-end, and the cost to its reputation, if not its financial performance, is likely to be huge.

Of course, there are critics who see this socially responsible strategy as public relations spin; others who believe GE's own culture of cost control and incremental innovation will prevent radical transformations; and yet others, including a sceptical investment community which forecasts that shareholder pressures will lead the company to tone down or change its strategy (and management team). However, GE's senior management team members have spent considerable time 'listening to their customers' who have told them that rising fuel costs, the regulatory environment and changing consumer expectations will result in demand for greener technologies in the energy industry.

Source: *Economist*, 2005b

If Immelt and his management team continue (or are allowed to continue by their investors) with their course of action, the outcomes of this strategy will only be evident in the next decade. However, this visionary strategy in the context of corporate America tells us a lot about the nature of strategy-making and leads us nicely into a discussion about different assumption of governance and social responsibility held by leaders, and their implications for HR, reputations and brands.

Corporate governance, HR and reputations

We have made the point that reputation management and HR fit more closely with a stakeholder theory of corporate governance than a shareholder value model. Our two case studies so far, the reputation of the UK Financial Services Industry and the changes at GE, have highlighted how strategies, HR, reputations and brands cannot be divorced from an organization's assumptions and stance on governance. It remains to justify that position by outlining the central principles of theories of governance. In doing so, we will rely heavily on the work of

Thomas Clarke (2004), one of our close colleagues and an expert in corporate governance.

Different approaches to corporate governance

Governance as an issue has a long history but came to the fore with advances in industrial capitalism during the early part of the 20th century as a consequence of the rise of the joint stock company, large-scale enterprises and the separation of ownership by shareholders from control by professional managers. The classic works on these developments pointed to a managerial 'revolution' and the beginnings of an early stakeholder theory of the firm, in which managers held effective control over the different interests represented within it. Managers were thought to act in such a way as to 'hold the ring' between the competing claims of shareholders, customers, employees, government and the general public in a pluralist theory of industrial government.

Since then, there have been a number of interesting developments, all of which have tried to answer the question: what is the best means of controlling the supposed controllers (i.e. managers) to protect shareholders and other stakeholders? According to Clarke, three of these theories stand out:

- Agency theory
- Stewardship theory, and
- Stakeholder theory.

Agency theory was the response of neo-classical economists to this question in positing a contractual view of the firm. Basically they argued that there was a legal and metaphorical contract between owners (the financiers of the business and thus the principals) and managers (their agents). Managers raised funds from financiers to operate the business; financiers, in turn, needed managers to generate returns on their investments. In essence, the contract that ensued specified what managers would do with the funds and what the division of returns would be between the principals and agents. The main problem lay in the unforeseeable future contingencies, leaving open the question of residual control rights – the rights to make decisions not foreseen by the contract. In reality, managers ended up with substantial control over these residual rights and could exercise great discretion over how to allocate funds. So, agency theory concerned itself with the central problem of how to constrain managers from misallocating funds and acting in their own interests rather than those of the principals.

For neo-classical economists, it is shareholders whose interests should dominate the corporate agenda and for whom the corporation should be run; it is they that bear the residual risk whereas managers effectively get paid whether or not the firm makes a profit or loss and are simply a charge on the business in the same way as other preferred creditors. Investors, however, only get paid if the firm makes a profit and do not get paid if the firm makes a loss. Consequently, investors have the greatest inherent interest in ensuring that the firm makes the greatest amount of profit and are the party in whose interests the firm should be run. According to agency theorists, maximizing shareholder value leads to superior, overall economic performance for the firm and for the economy at large as short-run interests in securing adequate earnings and long-run interests in increasing the capital value of the firm converge (Roberts, 2004).

Agency theory assumes efficient markets, including markets for corporate control, for management labour and for corporate information. Efficiency results from many buyers and sellers, all of whom have perfect information on which to base their interactions. To the extent that efficient markets in these areas exist, managers will bear the costs of any misconduct and, therefore, are much more likely to exercise self-control in awarding themselves excessive pay increases and in conducting business affairs. In essence, a firm is depicted as a market made up of many contractors – owners and managers – negotiating and re-negotiating their interests. In case the assumptions underlying perfect markets are absent for a short while, checks and balances have to be built into the system, including an effectively structured board of directors, compensation for managers tied to shareholder interests and a fully functioning external market for corporate control to discipline managers and incumbent boards. This situation could occur when, for example, there is a temporary shortage of managerial talent or when there is a potential for serious market failure under monopoly conditions.

Newer versions of agency theory complicate the argument a little by positing a permanent hierarchy of control within the organization rather than the market metaphor. According to these new institutional economists, firms arise because of the nature of market imperfections and the need to keep down transaction costs among contractors. Nevertheless, attention still remains focused on the relationships between shareholders and managers, but this time shareholders are deemed to be facing a diffuse but significant risk of self-interested opportunism by managers because the assets of the firm are too numerous and too ill-defined to fully describe in contractual agreements (Roberts, 2004).

Whether in its neo-classical or institutional variants, however, agency theory relies on a mixture of converging economic incentives – pay tied to shareholder value – and power-sharing through bargaining and coalition-building to bring about cooperative behaviour between the two principal parties in governance – shareholders and managers. No other parties are really considered as having long-term and significant interests in the firm.

It is because of this last point that alternative theories of governance have been proposed. **Stewardship theory** and its progenitor, stakeholder theory, seek to explain how governance works in practice and how it should work in the future. As we have seen, agency theory proposes a self-interested model of management and in-built conflict with shareholders; stewardship theory proposes no such conflict of interests because good managers, by dint of both will and skill, are deemed to be naturally inclined to act in the interests of shareholders since their interests, and those of other stakeholders in the firm, are broadly similar and contingent on the long-term wealth creation of the organization. Essentially, this is a unitary ('we are all in it together with the same aims') and benign view of organizations which also posits a strong degree of managerial choice, based on their motivations to act as stewards on behalf of everyone in the business and its long-term survival. Although it recognizes that there are situations when managers may not always exercise good or well-meaning judgements, stewardship theories are not hung up on the downside risk of managerial misbehaviour that dominates agency theory; instead they focus on the importance of building trust relationships and social networks to coordinate actors in and across organizations; this, they argue, is more characteristic of institutional and funding arrangements more likely to be found in Europe and Asia, e.g. networks of banks, privately owned and family-owned firms, and the new forms of organizations we have discussed in the previous sections.

According to the **stakeholder theory** view, firms are not bundles of assets that belong to shareholders, nor can they be in a modern world when the key assets are largely intangible and under the control of employees. Instead, governance structures and the work of senior managers are aimed at maximizing the total wealth of the organization for the benefits of those *inside* it that contribute firm-specific assets, i.e. their knowledge and skills, as well as those outside it.

This theory fits in well with the assumptions of reputation management, which recognizes the importance of constituencies including customers, suppliers, employees, business partners, government, the press, investors and, increasingly, society at large. Like stewardship theory, this approach is closer to the models of governance found in continental Europe and Asia–Pacific countries than the Anglo-Saxon external focus on shareholder value model assumed by agency theory. It is also more consistent with insider control and newer forms of organizations discussed under stewardship theories that are a feature of continental Europe and Asia–Pacific.

Is there a possibility of **convergence**? The success of the USA and its new economy during the 1990s, coupled with problems in Asia and continental Europe during the same period, provided a great fillip for outsider, Anglo-Saxon market-based shareholder value models of governance, and the assumptions underpinning them. In countries such as Germany, Sweden and France, there were enthusiastic calls by certain sections of the business and financial community and supporting political parties to embrace shareholder value principles and to rid themselves of stakeholder constraints. However, as we are all aware, the problems of Enron and recent scandals in other firms have brought about a re-think in models of governance among American and British companies, resulting in the passing of US legislation such as Sarbanes–Oxley in 2002 and attempts by the OECD to set world standards on corporate disclosure and governance. They have also posed similar questions and problems to enthusiasts for change in continental Europe, with the most recent answer being a hung parliament in Germany in 2005 because the electorate could not make up its mind between the two views.

One solution proposed by financial economists and lawyers who remain wedded to the core principles and benefits of agency theory is an *enlightened shareholder value model*, balancing the interests of investors with those of other stakeholders to ensure that the long-term interests of shareholders are achieved. Such an Anglo-Saxon model is in line with global trends in the internationalization of finance, equity markets and various financial instruments, which is forcing organizations from all parts of the world that wish to borrow to conform to certain governance conditions, e.g. the OECD's principles of Organization and Governance. This convergence, inevitably, is on the Anglo-Saxon model, though critics argue there are limits to such convergence. A one-size-fits-all model of governance is insensitive to the institutions, cultures, history and business systems, particularly of Asian countries such as Japan and China (Kay, 1998).

However, as Clarke and others point out, the 'sharpest skirmish' has been over the idea of shareholder value in any form following the scandals of Enron and other examples of corporate malfeasance (Gordon, 2004). Though there are many Americans and British lawyers, financiers and business people who still stick to the dictums proposed by the neo-classical economist Milton Friedman in the 1970s, and adhered to by certain sections of the financial and economic media, critics are mounting a spirited and influential campaign. Friedman's moral as well as economic argument was 'that the social responsibility of business is to increase profits'; it was only by doing so that the interests of all were served in the long run.

Enron and other examples of the system breaking down – Tyco, Global Crossing, Worldcom, Qwest and Arthur Andersen – have caused economists and moralists to argue that even an enlightened shareholder value model is inappropriate in a modern world (Coffee, 2004; Kay, 2004). Critics believe the ability of directors to monitor executive behaviour and the temptations of making enormous gains by cashing in the huge stock options that form the basis of many executive pay packets have created an unworkable system (Gordon, 2004; Bebchuk and Fried, 2006). Enron was the classic example of how self-interested and financially motivated managers could not only poorly serve shareholders, but also its customers and employees in bringing companies down. Agency theory has been proven right by Enron in that such managers were all-powerful in governance and shareholders needed protection through governance mechanisms and the passing of legislation (such as Sarbanes–Oxley). However, according to critics, one of agency theory's most sacrosanct principles of tying pay to shareholder value was its undoing. Perhaps as important, the pursuit of shareholder value has disconnected corporations from their moral purposes, according to stakeholder theorists, which is to serve the wider interests represented within firms and changing values in society. Trustee theorists, such as John Kay, also argue that the job of governance is to 'sustain the corporation's assets', not merely its financial assets. 'The difference comes not only because the stock market may value these assets incorrectly. It also arises because the assets of the corporation … include the skills of its employees, the expectations of customers and suppliers, and the company's reputation in the community' (Kay, 1997, p. 135). It is in that sense in which the calls for a new, more socially responsible and sustainable theory of governance have been framed, which lead us into a more in-depth discussion of the CSR agenda, reputations and branding.

Corporate identity and corporate social responsibility

CSR has been touched on in most of the chapters of this book since it is one of the most rapid growth areas of interest for modern businesses and is the basis on which a corporate identity can be built. The case of GE is an excellent illustration but it is only one of many organizations claiming to follow a CSR agenda. But what exactly do we mean by CSR and why should it be of interest, especially given the dominance of the shareholder value model of governance among so many companies? To answer these questions, we will outline the case for CSR and then examine some of the criticisms of this contested concept from the right, the left and from within, the last of these positions probably being the closest to our own viewpoint.

The case for CSR

The case that is usually made for CSR is a business case for pursuing socially and environmentally friendly policies, rooted in a stakeholder theory of governance and Rawlsian theory of social justice. Rawlsian ethics are associated with a 'theory of good', which focuses on defining the characteristics of a just society. Imagine a society in which there were no laws, social conventions or political state. Then ask yourself the question: what principles might reasonable people agree on to guarantee order while placing few constraints on individual freedoms? When applied to organizations, a theory of good states that these principles and the outcomes that result from these principles must be distributed with full consultation and so that no organizational stakeholders are losers while others are clear winners. Responsible leaders should place organizational survival and the long-term interests of its stakeholders over any single interest (Legge, 1995).

Drawing on these ideas, CSR advocates contend there is a more or less fundamental tension between the pursuit of private profit and public good, usually because a pursuit of profit at the expense of society is unsustainable in the long run. The basic argument underlying the business case for CSR is two-fold. First, profit in its own right is not pursued by companies for the public good but for private gain, which has little or nothing to do with the public good. If the pursuit of profit is to advance social welfare, it cannot be left to the hidden hand of the market and powerful business leaders, a form of very rough justice. Instead, it often requires active regulation from outside bodies: in our case of the Financial Services Industry in the UK, this would be through the FSA and government legislation. Second, in the pursuit of private gain, companies are driven by their internal business logic of maximizing revenues and minimizing costs to place enormous burdens on society and on the environment. Economists call this placing *externalities* on society, defined as companies taking action that affects others' welfare without having the incentive to recognize this impact in their decision-making, nor fully accounting for it in their evaluation of the costs and benefits of particular decisions. The consequences are that these externalities lead to inefficiencies for society if businesses do not pay their fair share of costs (Roberts, 2004). For example, there is a concern over the true costs of encouraging people to fly on low cost airlines more than they need to because of the contribution of frequent flying to global warming. Thus for many governments, NGOs (non-government organizations) and critics of the Anglo-Saxon shareholder value model, the untrammelled pursuit of profit yields little or nothing for many ordinary citizens, but costs them plenty. Unless it is checked either by CSR or by government regulation, private enterprise is bound to make losers of everyone apart from private business and its owners.

The business case for CSR

As we have seen from the case of GE, CSR has become big business. Its agenda is supported by many governments, business organizations and professional bodies such as the CIPD in the UK. The British government has been prominent among them in making the business case for CSR through its relevant website:

> The UK government sees CSR as good for society and good for business. Better understanding of the potential benefits of CSR for the competitiveness of individual companies and for national economies can help encourage the spread of CSR practice. The Department for Trade and Industry (DTI) … has therefore supported work exploring the 'business case' for CSR. (http://www.societyandbusiness.gov.uk/businesscasecsr.shtm; accessed 28 February 2006)

The DTI has worked with 'Forum for the Future', a sustainable development charitable organization, and 'AccountAbility', an international organization concerned to promote business performance through social and ethical responsibility, on a range of projects. Its conclusion from these projects is that:

> sustainability makes a positive contribution to business success ... The key was to look at CSR as an investment in a strategic asset or distinctive capability, rather than an expense. The debate highlighted the importance of taking a balanced approach to assessing performance – and the risks of concentrating solely on one aspect, such as shareholder value. (ibid.)

There are several international networks promoting CSR and its more modern focus on sustainable development, including the World Business Council for Sustainable Development (http://www.wbcsd.ch/). Its membership is made up of 180 multinational enterprises including the European-based Shell, BP, Nokia, Michelin, SKF, Novartis, ABB, Volkswagen and Daimler-Chrysler, and major US-based Dow Chemicals, Ford, General Motors, Procter & Gamble, Time Warner, GE and HP. The Council invites 'companies committed to sustainable development and to promoting the role of Eco-Efficiency, Innovation and Corporate Social Responsibility'. One of the Council's publications acknowledges the legal requirement to promote 'acceptable returns for its shareholders and investors' but argues that 'business and business leaders have ... made significant contributions to the societies of which they form part' and that responsible leadership is necessary for business and societal progress.

The CIPD in the UK have also been vigorous in pursuing the CSR agenda and in promoting the need for HR specialists to champion CSR. Their position is informed by a stakeholder view of ethics in business, in which employees are one of the principal stakeholders, and a view that employees' beliefs and actions are also the main vehicle for putting CSR into action. Their policy document on this issue (CIPD, 2002) points out the traditional role of HR (or personnel) was and is to act as 'employee champion', one of the roles identified by Ulrich as core to the success of HR (see Chapter 10). So the profession 'has the unique privilege and challenge of reconciling employer and employee interests' (2002, p. 14). The document made the case for HR's involvement in CSR in helping organizations deliver on the rhetoric of CSR through systems of good practice in recruitment, development and communications, helping manage trust and risk, the management of psychological contracts and enforcing 'whistleblowing' policies when they observe managers breaching their CSR responsibilities. To do so, they argued, HR specialists need to broaden their own understanding and skills. Since publishing their policy document, the CIPD has commissioned a series of case studies that showed how a number of leading UK firms defined and implemented their CSR agenda, including diversity management at B&Q, environmental management at BAA, employee well-being at AstraZeneca and community involvement at British Gas (CIPD, 2005).

Measuring CSR

Inevitably, when making a business case for anything, this turns on measurement. Numbers are language that business people understand and need to use to convince the financial community that pursuing goals other than shareholder value is likely to pay off for all in the long run. Managers also need measurement for performance management reasons and to keep them focused. As a result, many of the companies mentioned in this section have adopted the 'triple bottom line' (3BL) as a performance measure. The idea was first offered in John Elkington's (1997) book, in which he described a framework for measuring and reporting corporate performance against economic, social and environmental parameters. However, he also made a more far-reaching claim:

> At its broadest, the term is used to capture the whole set of values, issues and processes that companies must address in order to minimize any harm resulting from their activities and to create economic, social and environmental value. This involves being clear about the company's purpose and taking into consideration the needs of all the company's stakeholders.

In effect, 3BL is a planning and reporting mechanism, and a decision-making framework used to achieve sustainable development. It has been adopted by organizations as diverse as local government in Australia, major corporations such as Monsanto, the BBC and British Petroleum, and a range of small firms (see for example the cases available online at the Business and Sustainable Development Global Website available online at http://www.bsdglobal.com/tools/principles_triple.asp). The financial community is also paying attention in the form of a new Dow Jones Sustainability Index tracking the economic, environmental and social performance of more than 300 global companies, such as Siemens, Nokia and Home Depot, whose business practices have received the green seal of approval from a Swiss-based organization, Sustainable Asset Management (http://www.sam-group.com/htmle/main.cfm). Not surprisingly, consultants have been at the forefront of CSR. Price-WaterhouseCoopers (2002) published a survey of 140 American corporations, arguing that companies that ignore the triple bottom line are 'courting disaster', concluding that it 'will increasingly be regarded as an important measure of value'.

Criticisms from the right

We have already discussed the credo of many businesses, 'the business of business is business', which was given moral support by neo-classical economists such as Friedman during the 1970s. Currently, there is a battle being waged by economists, corporate lawyers and business ethics writers who argue there are two reasons for sticking with the shareholder value/agency theory model. The first is the agency theory position that managers of public companies are not owners but are employed by the firms' owners to maximize the long-term value of the owners' assets, within a framework of law that sets out rights and wrongs, the responsibilities and accountabilities of managers and corporate leaders. Some business ethics advocates believe that putting those assets to any other use, such as CSR, is effectively robbing the owners of their just rewards, and that is unethical (Sternberg, 2000). The ethical decision for a manager who believes that the business s/he is working for is causing harm to society at large is either not to work for that business in the first place or to leave it.

Elaine Sternberg, a UK academic and former corporate executive, believes in two principles of business ethics that underlie a shareholder value model. These are *ordinary decency* and *distributive justice*, without which the conduct of business would not be possible. These principles are based on a theory of rights. Paramount among these rights are those of property owners, which must be respected; these, however, do not extend to 'lying, cheating, stealing, killing, coercion, physical violence and most forms of illegality'. Instead, managers should pursue 'honesty and fairness', reflecting the demands of 'ordinary decency'. Her second component of business ethics, distributive justice, refers to the alignment of organizational rewards and managers' contributions towards achieving shareholder value. Two canons of modern-day HR, performance-linked pay and merit-based promotion, are manifestations of distributive justice within the company. So, for Sternberg and others, promoting people on the basis of anything other than merit or to reward a manager for anything other than pursuing shareholder value is bad for business and bad ethics. No doubt she would applaud the findings of a survey of the attitudes and values of young financial analysts reported in August 2005, which concluded that despite all of the bad press following Enron and other scandals:

> many young analysts appeared unconvinced of the materiality of most [CSR] issues to business; unable to consider them because of inadequate information, training or tools; and unwilling to depart from business as usual because of conflicts with remuneration, career advancement or culture. (Available online at http://www.wbcsd.ch/plugins/DocSearch/details.asp?type=DocDet&ObjectId=MTYxNTc; 28 February 2006)

Criticisms from the left

As is often the case in social debate, the right and left of the political spectrum often agree on the analysis, but come to entirely different conclusions on the prescriptions. Such is the case over CSR. The left criticism, which has been acknowledged by some business leaders as a legitimate one, has been most recently put by Joel Bakan (2004), a North American law professor, who has written a very powerful book and made a film about the impact of modern corporations in society. We discussed this work earlier in Chapter 1, but it is worth repeating and extending some of his criticisms and those of others (e.g. Monbiot, 2000), who take a similar stance.

Bakan argues from an examination of legal documents that corporations are bound by mandate to pursue relentlessly and without exception self-interested shareholder value, regardless of the harmful consequences it might cause to others. This is an extreme version of agency theory, which few corporate leaders would openly subscribe to; nevertheless, he argues, they have very little choice because of the legal, political and economic logics and structures of capitalist societies. His view is that such mandated corporations have come to dominate our lives in the developed and developing world, determining our lifestyles, culture, employment, economic and political choices. Aside from the iconography and ideology of modern business, which is all around us, corporations go further in dictating the decisions of national governments and controlling societal decisions that were once part of the public domain and subject to genuine political decisions by ordinary people. So, according to Bakan, it is corporations that now govern society, not governments 'for the people and by the people'. Yet, in true Hegelian fashion, every thesis brings about its own antithesis: it is the very power of modern, global corporations that leaves them open to reputational risk in the form of public mistrust, fear and demands for social and environmental accountability from society. The response has been an acknowledgement by corporate leaders to understand and address the costs of poor reputations, and work hard to regain and maintain the trust of 'stakeholders', including an increasingly vociferous investor community and financial press. The vehicle for this identity and image change had been CSR, which is nothing but a means of persuading a sceptical public of the virtues of capitalism.

Like many critics from the left, Bakan's view of CSR is that it is largely fraudulent because corporations, in the final analysis, cannot do anything other than engage in the 'pathological pursuit of profit and power', his book's subtitle. He cites the case of Sir John Browne, an icon of the CSR movement, and

BP's pursuance of a green agenda as a mask behind which to 'maintain consumer demand for petrochemicals':

> The days when our business had a captive market for oil are probably ending ... So we have to compete to ensure that oil remains the fuel of choice (quote from Sir John Browne). (Bakan, 2004, p. 46)

On the potential for CSR, Bakan concludes:

> More generally, for Browne and all other business leaders, social and environmental goals are, and must be, strategies to advance the interests of their companies and shareholders; they can never legitimately be pursued as ends in themselves ... (p. 46)

Criticisms from within

Bakan's thesis is predicated on CSR being an important movement in society, yet even its adherents remain unconvinced of some of the arguments and evidence used to support it. First, the business case for CSR has often rested on the assumption that 'doing good leads to doing well'; that creating product or service differentiation through CSR is a way of satisfying the firm's needs for superior profits and serving societal goals. Daniel Diermeier (2006), a CSR supporter, has tempered this argument with a view that it is really long-run cost reduction that is the best justification for CSR, because it is concerned with managing the downside of reputation risk rather than the upside of differentiation. Note the similarity between this argument and Bakan's, but for very different reasons.

Diermeier began his thesis by making a values case for CSR, claiming that values matter and that the values of the newer generations in advanced industrial societies are more inclined to be post-materialist, with a concern for the environment, tolerance and social issues that are different from the materialist values of earlier generations that were influenced by hardship. Moreover, he argues that these values will remain relatively permanent throughout the lifetime of this new generation, precisely because their formative years were shaped by times of plenty rather than hardship. The consequences, according to Diermeier, are that the shift to CSR is real and permanent (though our example of young financial analysts earlier may be seen as evidence of influential 'Neanderthals', or as the exception that breaks this 'rule'). As a result, companies will be pressed into responding to these value-changes by outsiders and insiders, especially when competing in the global market for talent. However, CSR issues are likely to vary in the same way that cultural values vary; some emerging economies not only cannot afford CSR but do not value it so highly because the values of their nationals have been formed under conditions of relative hardship, exacerbated by the growing gaps between rich and poor and by the impact of modern communications in highlighting that gap to the poor. One only needs to see the good life invoiced by the skyline of San Diego in California from the run-down squalor of Tijuana in Mexico, literally within viewing distance, to have this gap rammed home forcibly.

The consequences of these value-changes for competitive positioning are that businesses must be able to adapt their strategies to different segments of product markets (and employment markets), as we have consistently argued throughout this book. As Diermeier argues, for a product differentiation strategy to work by creating and capturing value from customers for socially responsible brands (e.g. the Body Shop or Patagonia), three factors have to be present:

- Customers must be willing to pay more for socially responsible goods and services to cover the fixed and variable costs of providing them, implying that customers must be willing to pay sufficiently high marginal prices and the market segment must be large enough to cover the fixed costs.
- Socially responsible brands must be difficult to imitate to allow for both socially responsible and non-socially responsible brands to coexist.
- The claims for social responsibility must be credible and customers must be able to verify these claims in some way.

Thus, in sufficiently large markets, it is possible for firms to earn superior profits from socially responsible brands by charging a premium price for them if these three conditions hold. And there are examples of markets in which socially responsible brands do earn superior profits through charging more for their goods and services, such as the food market in which organic and 'fair play' producers are carving out a niche.

However, the case for CSR does not really rest on this 'doing business by doing good' argument, but in lowering long-run costs. This, Diermeier argues, is the main argument for CSR: it does not rest on offering higher consumption value to willing consumers, which is difficult for them to verify anyway, but in delivering goods and services at lower costs to the environment, which is simply a principle of good management and is independent of offering higher value. To prove his point he used the example of the contrast between BP and Shell in the 1990s. Clearly, there is only a small segment willing to pay higher prices for a commodity product such as petrol for their cars but BP's strategy is not driven by a differentiation strategy in small segment markets; it is driven by its reputation for CSR and in protecting it. Shell, on the other hand, has had a number of problems with its reputation, resulting from its confrontation with Greenpeace, its proposed disposal of rigs in deep water, and in its operations in Nigeria where human rights were an issue. As a result, Shell has had to invest heavily in CSR to lower its costs arising from reputational risk in the long run and has had to work very hard to catch up with BP in particular markets. However, this will only be worthwhile if the expected savings from avoiding reputational damage are greater than the costs of complying with CSR practices. So in essence these are cost-driven strategies, arising from the nature of the markets they operate in, not price differentiation, which is the usual justification.

This argument can also be extended to the market for talent. While there may be niche markets for talented people who are attracted by working for companies that offer socially responsible goods and services, more people are likely to be attracted to and remain with organizations with a history of avoiding damage to their reputations, since the individual reputations of talented individuals are likely to suffer from association with firms that have not invested in avoiding reputational damage.

Criticisms of measurement

While the idea of a triple bottom line has appeal to a number of firms and government departments that have used it in their public relations, including BT, AT&T, Shell and Dow Chemicals, the UK government and state governments in Australia, critics point out some fundamental problems with it, even as a metaphor. These are based on the contention that what is sound about 3BL isn't novel and what is novel isn't measurable (Norman and MacDonald, 2004). The claims of its proponents, in line with stakeholder theories of governance, are that firms should assess their overall long-term contribution to society as well as to shareholders, that the social and environmental impact of firms can be measured in much the same way as the financial impact and that these individual measures can be aggregated to provide something akin to a societal profit or loss. While those adhering to the strict shareholder value version of corporate governance, such as the editors of *The Economist*, may take issue with the first of these claims, in no way could they be regarded as novel, according to Norman and MacDonald, since they have been at the heart of the CSR agenda since the 1980s. The more important criticism, however, lies in the measurement aspects of 3BL.

First, there are no known, universally accepted standards for measuring an aggregated bottom line, and given different versions of ethics in business, it is probably not theoretically possible. The movement known as SEAAR, social and ethical accounting, auditing and reporting, which is probably the most rigorous body in this field, has influenced a number of standard-setting bodies in the past few years, including the Global Reporting Initiative, SA 8000 Workplace/employee relations, AccountAbility 1000 Stakeholders, ISO 9000 Organization and Governance standards (see Fombrun, 2005), but would not claim to have provided an aggregate measure of 3BL. Their job has been to identify performance indicators of the social and ethical behaviour of companies and to find ways of auditing it. However, this is some way short of providing valid and reliable aggregate measures of CSR, which is the novel claim of 3BL. Indeed, to be plausible, the concept has to remain vague, qualitative and generalized; the closer one gets to specifying a measure of 3BL, the less plausible it becomes.

Part of the reasoning for this is the 'apples and oranges' argument; there is simply no universal, common currency for equating financial performance with all aspects of social and environmental impact, or even one unit of social good with another, e.g. donating money to charity for food aid or donating money to education. So, is this a case of what is measurable isn't always meaningful, and what is meaningful isn't always measurable? Another part of the reasoning is a more fundamental one and relates to our debate over different versions of governance and their moral stance. CSR and stakeholder theory, according to Norman and MacDonald, are largely premised on a theory of good: how does a business add value to the world? However, this is sometimes at odds with a theory of rights, which underpins the case for shareholder value. This concerns itself, as we noted, with whether individual rights are respected and societal obligations exercised in relation to these individuals. Thus, fulfilling obligations to shareholders may not always have a net positive impact on society but it does respect their rights and discharge society's obligations to them. From a rights perspective, it is not possible to say that maximizing three lines of promises to shareholders, employees and the public at large, as required by 3BL, is better than fulfilling one obligation to shareholders.

Conclusions

In this chapter we have looked at the corporate-level drivers of the links between HR, reputations and brands. The importance of the RBV was stressed and the role of leadership in turning the clichéd rhetoric of the RBV – 'people are our most important assets' – into reality. Ultimately, this depends on leadership vision and on their interpretation of governance theories and models. Among commercial organizations, there is something of a contested terrain between shareholder value and stakeholder theory, both of which would lay claim to strong moral and ethical bases. Shareholder value has the support of many neo-classical economists and those advocating a theory of rights, while stakeholder theory stresses the business case for

CSR based on a theory of good. Currently in this battle of ideas, following the pall created by Enron, stakeholder theory is rapidly gaining ground as a philosophy for many large businesses, and CSR has become big business. Some of this activity is directed at making money from socially responsible brands, but most is directed at building up social capital to create and protect their corporate reputations. The arguments from the right (spending money on CSR is wasteful of shareholder assets) and those from the left (CSR is a sham that leaves corporations even more free to dominate the world) are powerful. Our view, however, is closer to those advocating CSR as a way of reconciling business with society, though we are mindful of the problems of measurement such as the 3BL and some of the more cynical attempts to hide behind CSR in some quarters while exploiting and polluting in others.

The core theme of the book is that reputations and brands are driven from the inside, which also applies to CSR, as both an outcome of business and as a new corporate identity for many businesses. Consequently, we are at one with the CIPD in arguing for greater understanding and skills among HR specialists in making CSR happen. However, it is really to the beliefs, policies, strategies and actions of leaders and line managers that we have to look for guidance and action in creating more socially responsible organizations, as our Financial Services and GE cases have shown. We conclude this chapter with a good example from the UK-based Diageo, a company that has been prominent in CSR activities through corporate citizenship programmes. Our thanks have to go to the authors of a very well researched case, Dave Bek, Ian Jones and Michael Pollitt, for allowing us to summarize their work in progress.

Box 9.3   Creating reputations by building social capital: Diageo's Corporate Citizenship Programme

Diageo is the global leader in sales of premium drinks, including high profile brands such as Smirnoff, Guinness, Johnnie Walker and Captain Morgan, formed in 1997 following a series of mergers. It sold some of its business, including Burger King and Pillsbury, to focus on beverages.

As a company it has attempted to establish a connection between its corporate brand and product brands since 1997, though, according to Bek *et al.*, it has had problems in doing so and in establishing a strong internal brand. In other words, it seems to have ambitions to become more of a branded house. An *Economist* article on the drinks industry noted an important contrast in this respect between Diageo and the number two in the industry, Pernod, which acquired Allied Domecq in July 2005. Pernod has a reputation for providing a great deal of local autonomy to its operations and brands (*Economist*, 2005c). The implication of the article was that Pernod will remain a house of brands and that this strategy would be an important point of contrast between the two market leaders. However, this may be oversimplifying the case, since Diageo 'can be conceptualized as a dynamic corporate entity, which is continually undergoing shifts with the substructures of its business through mergers, acquisitions, strategic alliances and sell-offs' (Bek *et al.*, 2005, p. 7).

Diageo's main markets are in North America, the British Isles and Spain (accounting for 75% of turnover), though it has other substantial 'key' markets in South America, Australasia, Africa, Europe and Japan, as well as smaller, 'venture' markets in other countries. Its Corporate Citizenship (CC) programme is at the heart of its marketing and branding strategy, along with involvement in local communities. Both sets of activities are core to 'creating long-term shareholder value'. Diageo aims to 'build and enhance its corporate reputation, help build a sustainable business environment, build team spirit and build trust and the licence to operate with shareholders' and is a leading company in community involvement. It was also one of the first to appoint a director of CSR.

A key aspect of the Diageo's approach to CC is that it is 'owned' by the main board and CEO. A CC strategy and policy committee has been established, which is chaired by the CEO and meets three times a year. Members of the committee are drawn from the company's executive level. Also of note in this respect is the company's intention to merge this committee and the Brand Committee, whose remit is to establish a strong corporate brand.

Whilst there is a strong degree of corporate activity in this field, Diageo's community programmes have arisen mainly from its acquisitions of businesses, which had a history of community involvement, such as Guinness in Ireland. Thus community involvement is embedded into the fabric of Diageo and in its day-to-day business operations. This history of community involvement, together with the corporate-level, senior leadership direction of the programme, and the merging of CC with corporate branding, indicate a serious attempt to integrate CSR into the strategic decision-making of the organization.

Diageo's CC activities are based on a policy of 'responsible drinking', to which a special fund has been allocated. In addition, community programmes have focused recently on three areas – Skills for Life, Local Citizens and Water of Life. The company also puts resources into disaster relief, leadership programmes and poverty relief. New markets require different projects and the company is presently examining the Chinese market for suitable CC programmes.

Projects can arise from different sources: through formal applications to a Diageo Foundation, a legally separate charitable body, for projects in the focus areas; informal requests; and key Diageo employees who wish to champion local or international initiatives. The work of the Foundation cannot support the commercial interests of the company but is designed to be complementary to its business, brands and people. A business case has to be made for funding. The Foundation aims to kick-start programmes, provide advice and push out responsibility for these to local markets. It contributed about 3 million pounds to the total CC spend of 17.5 million in 2003/4.

The company has also agreed a 1% of pre-tax profits allocation for community programmes, which is in line with best practice in other organizations. Diageo were ranked 24th among the FTSE top 100 for donations as a share of profits in 2003.

The CC programme is varied in its content ranging from on-going 20-year support for 'Tomorrow's People' totalling 20 million pounds, $200 000 disaster relief in Columbia, to providing senior executive time for voluntary organizations and employees painting a local classroom in a poor area of London. Following a strategic review, Diageo decided to concentrate on the themes of responsible drinking through alcohol education, Skills for Life, Local Citizens and Water of Life.

Alcohol education is aimed at curbing the social problems of 'binge drinking' in the UK, dealing with drinking by minors in the USA, drink-driving in Africa and Germany, and training bar staff worldwide. The company has also developed a code for responsible marketing and is a leading member of the Portman Group in the UK, a body established to deal with alcohol abuse. Water of Life focuses on projects that demonstrate a commitment to water and effective sanitation, mainly in

African countries. Since water is core to Diageo's production processes, this is entirely consistent with its business aims. Local Citizens focuses on ways in which the corporation as a whole can support Diageo's businesses in communities, such as providing matching funds to support young entrepreneurship programmes and relief operations following natural disasters. The Skills for Life programme aims to provide disadvantaged and unemployed people with help to find work or start new businesses.

Diageo evaluates its community involvement programmes using the London Benchmarking Group (LMG) model, which it helped found. The model differentiates between different types of donations provided by companies: charitable giving and philanthropy (no regard for returns to business); community investment, which is focused and is intended to provide long-term gains to the company; and commercial giving, which provides direct payback to the company. The model is used to evaluate inputs against outputs by the Corporate Citizenship Company, which manage the LMG, to audit individual programmes and companies if they so wish. The data on Diageo over the period 2001–2004 show a move away from philanthropy to commercially-led programmes and to social investment (see Table 9.1, adapted from Bek *et al.*, p. 15).

Table 9.1

Community-led investments, 2001–2004 (£m)

	2001	2002	2003	2004
Philanthropy	5.4	2.1	2.4	1.1
Social investment	8.2	12.1	11.3	11.8
Commercially led initiatives	1.6	2.7	5.3	4.7
Total	**15.2**	**16.9**	**19.0**	**17.5**

In addition to this financially independent evaluation, one of the authors of the case, Ian Jones, has established a quantifiable measure of how firms make themselves accountable to their communities. The criteria used in this comparative evaluation of companies are:

■ Use of a separate social report in the published report
■ Information easily linked to home webpage
■ The firm has explicit social values
■ The firm has a Foundation charity

- The firm has explicit funding application criteria
- Information is provided in the local language
- The firm subscribes to the Global Reporting Initiative, a multi-stakeholder process and independent institution that sets sustainability reporting guidelines.

Based on published information on the internet, Jones has rated Diageo as scoring the highest possible marks.

The conclusions of the authors are that Diageo's efforts at corporate citizenship have paid off in building 'social capital' inside and outside the firm. Social capital refers to the levels of trust, socially responsible norms of behaviour and social networks that are facilitated outside and inside an organization through investment in social programmes. CC activities have been especially positive in raising social capital with employees, allowing them to make positive contributions to society while working in an industry that presents some ethical concerns to people. The CC programmes have been very influential in recruiting talented graduates.

They also issue a word of warning, however, that:

---

subordinating corporate citizenship to commercial objectives reduces its values to the company ... There is an observable trend away from purely charitable projects motivated by community need to projects that directly serve the interests of Diageo's brands. While this is understandable it is a risky strategy as it undermines one of the major benefits of corporate citizenship projects which is the building up of goodwill towards the company based on altruistic involvement in the community. (p. 47)

Source: Based on Bek, Jones and Pollitt, 2005

References

Bakan, J. (2004) *The corporation: the pathological pursuit of profit.* New York: Free Press.

Bebchuk, L. A. and Fried, J. M. (2006) Pay without performance: overview of the issues. *Academy of Management Perspectives,* **20**, 5–24.

Bek, D., Jones, I. W. and Pollitt, M. G. (2005) How do multinationals build social capital? Diageo's corporate citizenship programme, *Working paper No. 302, ESRC Centre for Business Research*, March 2005. University of Cambridge.

CIPD (2002) *Corporate social responsibility and HR's role: a guide.* London: Chartered Institute of Personnel and Development.

CIPD (2005) *Making CSR happen: the role of people management.* London: Chartered Institute of Personnel and Development.

Clarke, T. (ed.) (2004) *Theories of corporate governance: the philosophical foundations of corporate governance.* London: Routledge.

Coffee, J. (2004) What caused Enron? A capsule of social and economic history in the 1990s, in T. Clarke (ed.), *Theories of corporate governance: the philosophical foundations of corporate governance.* London: Routledge, pp. 333–358.

Cox, A. (2004) *Win–win? The paradox of values and interests in business relationships.* Stratford-upon-Avon: Earlsgate Press.

Davenport, T. H. (2005) *Thinking for a living: how to get better performance and results from knowledge workers.* Boston, MA: Harvard Business School Press.

Diermeier, D. (2006) Leading in a world of competing values: a strategic perspective on corporate social responsibility, in T. Maak and N. M. Pless (eds), *Responsible leadership.* London: Routledge, pp. 155–169.

Economist (2005a) Another day, another probe, *Economist,* 17 December, p. 35.

Economist (2005b) The greening of General Electric: a lean, clean electric machine, *Economist,* 10 December, p. 79.

Economist (2005c) Local tastes: Pernod has ambitions for the global drinks industry. *Economist,* 12 November, p. 86.

Elkington, J. (1997) *Cannibals with forks: the triple bottom line of 21st century business.* Chichester: Capstone Publishing.

Florida, R. (2005) *The flight of the creative class.* New York: HarperCollins.

Fombrun, C. J. (2005) Building corporate reputation through CSR initiatives: evolving standards, *Corporate Reputation Review,* 8 (1), 7–11.

Galbraith, J. (2002) *Designing organizations: an executive guide to strategy, structure and process* (new and revised edn). San Francisco, CA: Jossey-Bass.

Goldsmith, P. (2005) Attracting weapons grade talent to the general insurance industry. Paper presented to the annual conference of the Reputation Institute Annual Conference, Madrid, Spain, 19–22 May.

Goold, M. and Campbell, A. (2002) *Designing effective organizations: how to create structured networks.* London: John Wiley.

Gordon, J. N. (2004) What Enron means in the management and control of the modern business corporation: some initial reflections, in T. Clarke (ed.), *Theories of corporate governance: the philosophical foundations of corporate governance.* London: Routledge, pp. 322–332.

Groysberg, B., Nanda, A. and Nohria, N. (2004) The risky business of hiring stars, *Harvard Business Review*, **82** (May–June), 93–100.

Hagel III, J. and Seely-Brown, J. (2005) *The only sustainable edge: why business strategy depends on productive friction and dynamic specialization*. Boston, MA: Harvard Business School Press.

Hamel, G. and Prahalad, C. K. (1996) *Competing for the future: breakthrough strategies for seizing control of your industry and creating the markets of tomorrow*. Boston, MA: Harvard Business School Press.

Joyce, W., Nohria, N. and Robertson, B. (2003) *What really works: the 4+2 formula for sustained business success*. Boston, MA: Harvard Business School Press.

Kay, J. (1998) The role of business in society. Inaugural lecture, Said School of Business, Oxford, 3 February. http://www.johnkay.com/society/133 (28 February 2006).

Kay, J. (2004) *The truth about markets: why some nations are rich but most remain poor*. London: Penguin.

Kochan, T. and Lipsky, D. (eds) (2002) *Negotiations and change: from the workplace to society*. Ithaca, NY: Cornell University Press.

Legge, K. (2004) *Human resource management: rhetoric and realities* (Anniversary edition). London: Palgrave.

Mintzberg, H. (1987) Crafting strategy, *Harvard Business Review*, **65** (Jul–Aug), 66–75.

Mintzberg, H., Ahlstrand, B. and Lampel, J. (1998) *Strategy safari*. Hemel Hempstead: Prentice Hall.

Monbiot, G. (2000) *Captive state: the corporate takeover of Britain*. Basingstoke: Macmillan.

Norman, W. and MacDonald, C. (2004) Getting to the bottom of the 'triple bottom line', *Business Ethics Quarterly*, **14** (2), 243–262.

Pettigrew, A. M. and Whipp, R. (1991) *Managing change for competitive success*. Oxford: Blackwell.

PriceWaterhouseCoopers (2002) *Global CEO survey*, January.

Roberts, J. (2004) *The modern firm: organizational design for performance and growth*. New York: Oxford University Press.

Sternberg, E. (2000) *Just business: business ethics in action* (2nd edition). Oxford: Oxford University Press.

Sung, J. and Ashton, D. (2005) *High performance work practices: linking strategy and skills to work performance*. London: Department of Trade and Industry in association with the Chartered Institute of Personnel and Development.

Wright, P., Dunford, B. B. and Snell, S. A. (2001) Contributions of the resource-based view of the firm to strategic HRM: convergence of two fields, *Journal of Management*, **27**, 701–721.

CHAPTER 10

The corporate agenda and the HR function: creating a fit-for-purpose future

Introduction

At the end of the first chapter we raised the question of the significance of the corporate agenda for the HR function. Given the central theme of this book has been about the key role of people management in creating difference through corporate reputations and brands and maintaining legitimacy through CSR and good governance, we have sought to provide our HR readers with a good grounding in these fields and some practical frameworks and tools to help them contribute to these key strategic drivers of organizational performance. However, the tensions between corporate and local agendas – what we might call the universal paradox in management – presents HR with difficult challenges but significant opportunities (see Box 10.1). These challenges and opportunities posed by reputation management and corporate branding, as well as the related issues of CSR and corporate governance are, we believe, among the most important the profession is likely to face, not least because they incorporate most of the issues identified by some of the leading academic thinkers on the future of HR who also have an impact on practice (Pfeffer, 1998; Sparrow *et al.*, 2004; Huselid *et al.*, 2005; Ulrich and Brockbank, 2005).

So, in this chapter, we examine research and the speculation about the changing role of HR, as well as current practice, to show how HR professionals can contribute to the corporate agenda more effectively. We also make some specific recommendations for HR leadership in this field, especially on improving HR's professional competence in this field and credibility with the other functions contributing to the corporate agenda, including marketing, branding, CSR and senior leadership (see Figure 1.1 in Chapter 1). These recommendations should be timely in an international context since there are a number of projects and investigations looking at the future of HR in various countries, including the CIPD, SHRM and the World Federation of Personnel Management Associations. Hopefully our contribution will help them with their reflections.

To begin with, let's look at a short case that deals directly with the relationship between HR and branding. We will use it to ground some of the ideas raised in the rest of this chapter.

The 'think global and act local' problem, HR and people management

Box 10.1 Scottish & Newcastle, branding and people management

Scottish & Newcastle (S&N) was the fourth largest European brewer in 2005 and in the top ten by sales volume in the world. It is a public company with a history dating back to 1749 and is listed on the London Stock Exchange. Its headquarters are in Edinburgh, Scotland. S&N has grown over the past decade or so through acquisitions and joint ventures to become an international brewer with strong positions in 14 countries in Europe and Asia and exports to more than 60 countries around the world. Its major markets are still the UK, but S&N also has a substantial presence in Russia, France, Belgium, Finland, Portugal and Greece. It also has emerging interests in China and India. The company has the market leading positions in the three core markets of the UK, Russia and France and three of the top ten beer brands in Europe – Baltika, Kronenbourg and Foster's. Its strategic objectives are brand growth through innovation and efficient operations. S&N's website puts some flesh on these objectives:

Successful international beer companies have strong market positions at home which provide the platform for their development overseas. Strong market positions allow cost efficiencies in production and distribution and are usually cash generative.

We consider Western Europe to be our homeland and there we have market-leading positions. Our markets in Western Europe are mature markets with significant value growth, where big brands tend to get bigger, medium-sized brands can be squeezed and certain niche brands prosper. The key challenge is to maximize value growth through brand strength and superior customer service. S&N's strategy is to create value by investing in a focused portfolio of premium and mainstream brands and by maximizing brand synergies from the integration of the new beer businesses.

As well as investment in marketing spend there will be continued investment in new product development, packaging and dispense. Investment to provide a better experience for the customer is as important as advertising.

Brand synergies will arise from launching international and speciality brands into new markets alongside strong national brands. Such products will benefit from the existing distribution network in those markets but will also add value by selling at a premium and by broadening the portfolio of products available.

In each market we look to ensure greater cost efficiency in production and distribution and by doing so ensure better customer service.

The emerging markets in which we will be operating are characterized by high volume growth, real price increases, emerging brands and current shortage of capacity. However, the key drivers of profitability are the same – market share, brand development, cost efficiency and route to market. We are entering all these markets with experienced partners holding strong market positions who understand the distinctive nature of their own

markets. (http://www.scottish-newcastle.com/sn/scottishnewcastle;
5 January, 2006)

Until the 1990s, S&N was largely a domestic company, exporting some of its products to overseas markets. Establishing an international presence in such markets through subsidiary companies and joint ventures is a more recent strategy, so it is undergoing a major re-think of its organization and management to support S&N's ambition to become a global company. Brewing is an industry in which there are a small number of global brands, such as S&N's Kronenbourg and Foster's, but is based on large numbers of domestic speciality brands that suit local tastes. This is particularly so in European countries such as Germany and Belgium, with their multiplicity of local beers. Consequently, S&N, probably more than most MNEs, has to act out the mantra of think global and act local, a fact well-recognized by their senior HR team.

Management and leadership development, talent management and performance management are seen as both a driver of these ambitions to become a geocentric company, and also a constraint. This is evidenced by the appointment of a senior HR director and team of HR specialists whose work is taken up with balancing national and local interests. The company is sometimes perceived internally, even by staff in England, as Scottish-centric; employees in the South of England have been known to complain that you have to be Scottish to 'get on'. However, to support global and internationally local brands, S&N recognizes it has to develop a cadre of geocentrically oriented senior managers and an HR team, process and systems to help them. So, for example, they have embarked on a major development across most of the business to attempt common HR process mapping on administration, performance management, development potential and talent management.

At the same time, they need to have the majority of managers aligned with the growth of domestic brands, aggressively promoting local interests. They also recognize that HR issues such as industrial relations, payroll and attendance are more likely to be issues best resolved locally, since they are constrained by domestic legal and institutional features.

A major question for HR is how to best achieve this balance through its management development, talent management and performance management policies and practices. It has begun to do this by growing its own cadre among an international graduate intake of 'high potentials' and putting them through a rigorous and systematic international leadership development programme. Following the process mapping, it is also in the throes of developing a common set of talent management and performance management policies for most of its European subsidiaries, although it has taken the decision not to involve subsidiaries which are joint ventures rather than majority owned. Most of these subsidiaries are in countries institutionally distant from the UK, including joint ventures in China and India.

To help the company develop a greater international identity, they have also considered locating the HR team responsible for management and leadership development in a location in subsidiaries in Brussels or Paris, though for reasons of cost they have sited it in the UK, at least for now. Also of interest are their ambitions to roll out an e-HR portal, which will help promote a corporate identity among subsidiaries. Again, this portal may be customized according to the advice received from national subsidiaries and partners.

Arguably, the HR team's contextually sensitive approach to internationalizing is likely to serve them well in the future, but they recognize that the challenges of aligning HR policies and practices to brand management in an ever-expanding international company will be something of a movable feast.

This case reveals the dynamic tensions between global and local branding, the emerging solutions of one company's attempts to deal with these tensions in its people management policies, and the role of the HR function in supporting these policies in conjunction with staff in corporate communications and brand management. As noted in earlier chapters, there is no single solution posed to the problem in the case of S&N, nor is there a feeling among HR staff that the accommodations reached at any one time will be other than temporary. To borrow from the insights of one influential commentator on management and change, we are always in a process of 'becoming' rather than in a state of 'being' (Chia, 1995). This view of change in the world is echoed by the insights of Zygmunt Baumann (2000), a well-known social philosopher, who has argued that we are increasingly moving towards a 'liquid modernity', in which the old 'heavy' and 'solid' modernity has given way to a 'light' and 'fluid' software-type modernity: life for many consumers and employees is increasingly lived in a process world in which mobility is the order of the day, especially for those privileged members of society, including highly qualified and increasingly footloose professionals and managers. In Chapter 8, we introduced that idea that sustainable change is not only preoccupied with laying down more permanent bases for new ways of working but is also concerned with laying down a foundation for further, continuous performance improvements (Buchanan *et al.*, 2005). In that sense we can talk about change as a dynamic process, punctuated with periods of (increasingly short) stability rather than change 'programmes' characterized by fixed beginnings and ends (Van de Ven and Poole, 1995). Such 'programmitis', arguably, is one of the most significant errors of perspective made by management teams in the past, and, no doubt, will be made again.

More specifically, the case also raises implicitly the issue of what kind of HR function might, to borrow the quality guru Deming's term, be 'fit-for-future purpose', bearing in mind our comments about the infrequent periods of 'punctuated equilibrium' in any dynamic change process and HR's needs for credibility with other functions responsible for the corporate agenda. So, what have writers proposed about the future developments in HR, how do they relate to the tensions experienced by S&N and similar companies, and what do they suggest for the links between HR and the corporate agenda?

The future of HR

Strategic partnerships or strategic drift: a very short history of the quest for credibility

As we argued in Chapter 7, in our discussion of culture, institutions and the lessons of history, often you have to look back to look forward; otherwise we may be 'destined to repeat the mistakes of the past'. From our reading of some of the practitioner-based literature, there is more than a whiff of that in recent times. For, as long as both of us have been practising and writing about HR, there has been an agonized debate over its role, relevance and credibility. In the UK this debate originated during the early decades of the 20th century when personnel management first emerged as a welfare function in manufacturing industry, championing the interests of employees in mainly Quaker-owned factories in the north and west of England. The personnel function's origins in America were slightly different, being more administrative in nature, but the welfare role and looking after employees' interests, often in a paternalistic and intrusive manner, were also prominent; witness the work of Ford's notorious 'sociology department' during the 1920s, which had little to do with the application of sophisticated sociological or human relations ideas to industry and more to do with 'socializing' mainly immigrant and agricultural labour into the rhythms and disciplines of factory work in Ford's motor vehicle plants located south of Detroit in Michigan.

Gradually, during the middle part of the last century, personnel evolved into the 'contracts manager' and policing roles, dealing with industrial relations problems, the negotiation of contracts and procedural agreements, payments systems, and discipline and grievance handling, in an ever more sophisticated fashion (Tyson and Fell, 1986). This more sophisticated approach to personnel has been portrayed as a response to increased militancy over pay and fragmented bargaining by trade unions in the UK and USA; it is equally likely, however, that the steps taken by personnel to professionalize itself by devising and encouraging individualized pay schemes and plant-level bargaining may have provoked more sophisticated responses from trade unions at local level (Batstone, 1982), a point worth noting for our later discussions on the future of the profession.

From the 1970s onwards, there were greater calls for personnel to become experts in organizational development and 'architects' of people management strategy (Tyson and Fell, 1986; Caldwell, 2001, 2003). Such early calls presaged the Cornell University architectural metaphor we described in Chapter 6. They also presaged the change in name and focus during the 1980s to HRM, associated with the decline in trade union membership and influence and the adoption of more sophisticated and strategically focused HR techniques (Caldwell, 2004). Finally, they were also a portent of the current focus on 'strategic partners' in HR, those people occupying the pinnacle of a new, hierarchical division of labour that has emerged in HR since the late 1990s (see Figure 10.1). In Box 10.2 we have summarized the findings of one report that exemplifies the clamour for strategic partnering (Ashton and Lambert, 2005), a report which has also

Figure 10.1
The new HR hierarchical division of labour.

influenced the CIPD in the UK. Note in addition how this report has argued for the division of labour in Figure 10.1.

There is a growing realization, however, that business partnering may not be appropriate in all organizations; some evidence points out that it may have negative and unexpected consequences even when it is successfully implemented (Hope-Hailey *et al.*, 2005). For example, in a recent discussion we had with one senior HR director who had attempted to implement business partnering in the UK university sector, he pointed out the problems of using such language and in gaining credibility with highly qualified academic staff who did not frame their problems in, nor relate to, the discourse of business and strategy. This is a point to which we shall return in this chapter.

Box 10.2   The future of HR

The Future of HR Report posed a series of questions to CEOs and HR leaders in 30 international organizations:

1   How does HR add value in your organization?
2   Where do you as an HR leader add value to the business?

3   What credentials do you have to justify a seat at the strategy-making table?
4   What returns on HR investment are generated in areas such as training and development, selection, rewards, etc.?
5   Do you have the right people in the right jobs to make a difference?
6   What advantages does your organization gain from the way it manages human capital stocks and flows?

The report argued that the future of HR depended on its ability to deliver three outcomes:

■   Excellent HR services at the least possible cost, consistent with service delivery.
■   Expertise in critical areas such as organizational design, development and change, and talent management.
■   Organizational capabilities and human capital, and making strong inputs to strategic issues by influencing and shaping the decisions of business leaders.

To achieve these outcomes, the report argued that HR had to transform itself by (1) shifting in gravity from mainly transactional activities towards those focused on an organization's performance, capability and effectiveness; (2) providing service excellence, value-adding work and an orientation to thinking about the future; and (3) HR people needed to advance their own technical and professional capability.

It is worth quoting a passage to reflect the contingency perspective they and other writers hold on HR business models:

Our proposition for the future of HR centres on the business context shaping what HR does. Clarity about business drivers and organizational capabilities is critical. This will define HR's core work and challenges – and what its purpose, position, structure, roles and capabilities should be. Yet such a scenario is far from stable. Business environments are constantly shifting. No one type or model of HR is automatically right. To be 'fit-for-purpose' an HR function must be adept at analysing and matching, through its work, the emerging success requirements and differentiators for the organization.

Source: Ashton and Lambert, 2005

HR, strategy and leadership

Perhaps more than any other figure, Dave Ulrich has helped shape thinking among HR professionals in their quest for relevance during the past decade, arguably because he has been one of the few HR academics who have been able to 'look both ways' – to the academy and practice – and claim credibility with both. He first put forward his ideas on the roles of HR in 1996 and has updated these by drawing on his more recent research (Ulrich and Brockbank, 2005). From our perspective this updating has been important because of the greater focus on HR's impact on stakeholders, including employees, customers and other managers dealing with branding and reputation management. In his earlier work, he defined HR's four roles as 'employee champion', 'administrative expert', 'change agent' and the 'strategic partner', shown in Table 10.1. In the more recent version with Wayne Brockbank, a fifth role of 'HR leadership' was added because it combined elements of the others but also signified an important change in direction for HR as thought leaders influencing board-level policies. Note how these roles mirror the historical development of personnel in the UK and USA and have captured the drift of management studies towards leadership during the past decade.

You might also want to reflect on how, like the findings of the Ashton and Lambert study, these roles mirror (and may have been the source of) the hierarchical division of labour in Figure 10.1.

This division of labour and new role nomenclature probably have been more widespread in Britain than America, perhaps reflecting the greater influence and exhortations of the CIPD than SHRM as a professional qualifying association, and the generally lower status of HR practitioners in the business hierarchy in the USA (Strauss, 2001). Moreover, the calls for HR to become strategic partners have also enjoyed greater intellectual support from four related ideas tied more closely to the career interests of British HR professionals (see Box 10.3). We cannot emphasize enough the importance of ideas in promoting the interests of those who become its champion, known in the 'trade' as 'elective affinity', especially in HR (Watson, 1977; Elwell, 1996).

Table 10.1

Developments in the 'Ulrich' model

Old roles (1996)	New roles (2005)	Description of new roles
Employee champion	Employee advocate	'Caring for, listening to, and responding to employees … while at the same time looking through [stakeholders'] eyes and communicating to employees what is required for value creation
Administrative expert	Functional expert	Developing specialist knowledge and skill in: *Foundational HR practices*, including recruitment, promotions, transfers, outplacement, measurement, rewards, training and development; and *Emerging HR practices*, usually not under the direct influence of most HR professionals, including work process design, internal communications, organizational structures, design of physical setting, dissemination of external information throughout the firm and executive leadership development
Change agent	Human capital developer and	Focus on the future of individuals and teams, developing plans that offer each employee opportunities to develop future abilities, match desires with opportunities and master new skills
Strategic partner	Strategic partner	Bring know-how about business, change, consulting and learning to their relationships with line managers. They partner with line managers to help them reach their goals through strategy formulation and execution by acting as devil's advocate, crafting strategies and developing the strategic IQ of the business
	HR Leader	The sum of the other, four roles of strategic partner, human capital developer, functional expert and employee advocate, plus Leading the HR function, collaborating with other functions by looking outwards and as network integrators, setting and enhancing the standards for strategic thinking, and ensuring corporate governance.

Source: Adapted from Ulrich, 1996; Ulrich and Brockbank, 2005

Box 10.3   Elective Affinity and HR in Britain

■ The growing influence of the RBV as a theory of strategic advantage

■ The promises of riches in achieving competitive success on the basis of knowledge and innovation like the USA

■ The negative, though receptive context of the 'British disease' – continuing low labour productivity associated with a low skills, low growth dynamic (Porter and Taylor, 2004), especially compared with competitor economies such as America, France, Germany and the Scandinavian economies (*Economist*, 21 January 2006)

■ Perennial shortages of knowledge-based talent to resource new, knowledge-based enterprises.

It is, perhaps, easy to see how such a combination of ideas and theories has benefited the interests of HR in the UK, since HR professionals have been able to point out how more effective HR/HRD, targeted on boosting the knowledge base of British organizations, may help Britain and British firms break out of the vicious cycle of low skills–low growth. As a consequence, many commentators in the UK in particular, but also in America and Asia–Pacific region, believe that the HR function appears to have transformed itself by appropriating a renewed sense of mission, or is at least on track towards such a transformation if it is able to address this agenda successfully. Measures of success for HR, as we discussed in Chapter 6, have moved away from internal, transaction costs, such as costs of recruitment and HR headcount, to externally focused ones that address the key strategic drivers of the business (Boxall and Purcell, 2003; Huselid *et al.*, 2005).

However, just how broad and deep such transformation has been in the majority of organizations, especially in the public sector, is very much open to question. De-bureaucratization has been very evident among large MNEs, in small to medium-sized organizations; while those in the public sector have remained remarkably stable structures in the UK and USA (Sennett, 2006). The probability that HR transformations have been noticeable and significant, outside of that small number of large firms discussed in the media and by academics, is relatively small (Sparrow *et al.*, 2004). However, the need for such transformation has been at the heart of this book and other investigations into the future of HR (Reddington *et al.*, 2005).

This progressive focus on strategic HR, performance and organizational capabilities has begun to re-designate the HR function and boundaries, and the processes it uses to demonstrate its worth. For example, much has been made recently of the impact of information and communications technologies (ICT) and outsourcing on the future of HR, with the prospects of a virtual future looming large among some organizations, especially given the impact on HR headcount and potential for improved service delivery (Snell *et al.*, 2001; Martin, 2005). One of the messages of this book is that HR needs to re-designate its boundaries and relationships with the marketing, corporate communications and public relations functions to serve the corporate agenda, in much the same way that ICT, supplier management and HR are coming together to cut costs and improve service delivery of HR. Nevertheless, at the same time as HR specialists are recognizing such opportunities, there are significant challenges, especially in convincing the ever-present sceptics of HR and reforming and re-educating the profession to understand broader agendas. We now turn to these challenges.

The limitations of HR

Low impact

Notwithstanding the positive claims for HR, there has always been a countervailing tendency. This has damned personnel and the re-labelled HR function for failing to live up to senior managers' expectations and its own rhetoric on delivering strategic results. Two such examples are drawn from surveys conducted by Accenture (2003) and Watson Wyatt (2003). Asked to state levels of satisfaction with the performance of their HR departments, almost half of 150 senior executives in Fortune 1000 companies in the Accenture survey said they were either dissatisfied or ambivalent about what HR had achieved. The main reason cited was business responsiveness. Only 34% of 1700 senior line managers in a Watson Wyatt study rated HR performance as good – yet 83% said HR was critical to business success.

According to observers, HR is often seen as too bureaucratic, mechanistic, expensive, schedule-driven, slow-moving, lacking focus on the needs of the business, especially in helping high performing talent, and too concerned with policing low performers (Michaels *et al.*, 2001), even allowing for the recent moves to strategic partnering. Quite simply, few firms have implemented the sophisticated HR policies discussed in the textbooks and at HR conferences (Burke and Cooper, 2005). This implies at least two possible 'culprits': senior managers who are not educated in the ways of HR, or HR people who are not educated in the ways of senior managers. Our natural inclination, based on previous experience of HR's frequent flirtations with the modish solutions proposed by consultants, is that the problem lies mainly with HR in trying to implement one-size-fits-all models to the reorganization of the function. More of this later.

Poorly trained and educated HR

Though reflexivity is generally considered to be a virtue, HR has suffered from what some consider self-indulgent navel-gazing as it deliberates on why it does not have board status, despite people management being recognized as a core function. The argument is often made that managing people is what is important, not what HR does. In that sense, HR or, more accurately, the people management function is perceived to be too important to be left to functional specialists with little grounding in the business of business, or in the case of other sectors, a grounding in education, social work, financial services, etc. This is especially the case when, even today, despite the work of professional organizations such as the CIPD and SHRM, the function is frequently populated by people with low levels of expertise and experience in management and low levels of education in what matters in management. For example, one recent evaluation of Masters degrees in HRM in the USA has suggested they are too technically focused and characterized by a lack of business management knowledge (Langbert, 2005), an issue that the CIPD at least is trying to address with its new leadership and management standards.

A more fundamental criticism of professionalization and professional education is a distinction made some years ago by one of our colleagues who argued that HR suffered from (a) too great a concern for a rather abstracted idea of scientific-technical excellence and (b) a 'thinking and planning' paradigm. Both of these were important characteristics of the British idea of professionalization (e.g. among accountants, lawyers, scientists). This British attraction to narrow professionalization has been accompanied by a downgrading of the view of man as 'homo faber', summed up by the Germanic idea of 'Technik'. This latter term promotes the notion that managers should be makers and doers, as 'true technocrats' and action wo/men, rather than British-style, disinterested professionals and scientists. Such technocrats are 'broadly educated technical or commercial and financial specialists whose experiences ... tend to be specific to particular sectors of employment' (Glover and Hallier, 1996, p. 234). Technical excellence and deep networks are the order of the day. According to this line of criticism, HR suffers from an 'officer-class and arm's-length mentality' by dint of professional training and because its occupants lack the well-roundedness to contribute directly to the main business of business, which is, when stripped to the basics, about making and selling goods and services (Paterson *et al.*, 1988). This criticism may seem slightly old-fashioned in the context of a knowledge economy, but certainly rings true for us in our concern to link HR with the key functions responsible for marketing and selling products, services and, even, knowledge.

Lack of 'well-roundedness'

Such internally focused reflexivity among HR, we believe, has been quite damaging to the reputation of the HR function. HR, in one sense, is a victim of a narrow, British-style mentality of professionalism and the new division of labour built on centres of excellence and shared services. Instead of building 'well-rounded' HR managers, professionalization has helped create a narrow, administrative or technically expert group of sub-specialisms in HR (increasingly in remote call centres or off-site centres of excellence) and a potentially disconnected band of strategic partners, whose justification is to be able to see the 'wood' instead of the 'trees'. This development is inimical to producing well-rounded HR generalists who can mix directly with stakeholders (employees, senior managers, customers, suppliers, network partners, etc.) and has disconnected them and the function from the top (Martin, 2006). It may also result in HR professionals becoming disconnected from the bottom as they lack the ability and inclination to form direct relationships with employees and to act as advocates for them. Finally, on the role of strategic partners, we might be well advised to remember the advice of a management classic, 'good managers don't make policy decisions' (Edward Wrapp, 1967). A number of subsequent studies have shown how good senior leaders are frequently observed to get involved in detail rather than 'feasting on a diet of abstractions, leaving the choice of what he eats in the hands of his subordinates'. Invoking another metaphor, Mintzberg (1991) has cautioned against seeing a wood or forest only from on high, the so-called helicopter view. This line of sight is likely to give you an impression of a rather uniform green rug and not much insight into detail; seeing from below, on the other hand, that is from the perspective of the trees, gives you a much more nuanced, variegated and grounded perspective on which to base strategic decisions.

Well-roundedness, an idea to which we shall return later in this chapter, is based on the ability of managers to heed such sound advice by striking a balance between managing at different levels – managing information flows to manage others, managing through people and managing by taking direct action and connecting with people first hand (Martin, 2006). It also requires HR to strike a balance in styles, reflecting three competing poles or pulls on managers – to see HR as a science and technical specialism (expertise), to see it as an art (vision and leadership) and to see it as a craft (experience) (Mintzberg, 2004). Finally, it is based on the capacity to manage outwards, across functions and, increasingly, organizations, and not just in them. This is especially important in the new networked economy and to meet the demands of stakeholders for positive reputations and brands, good governance and CSR.

Assessing the future challenges for HR: the implications of the corporate agenda

As far as we are aware, there are no reports that make the reputation management and branding agenda an explicit centre-piece of their recommendations. Yet, once the links between HR and the corporate agenda are pointed out, most senior HR staff and senior managers think these are obvious and agree that HR has missed a trick. We had a discussion with one of the leading European HR academics on this very issue, and his response was 'it's so obvious. It is one of these ideas that you want to say "why didn't I think of that myself?"'

However, as we have argued all along and as the S&N case illustrates, there is no single set of recommendations we can make because context is all important in shaping how leaders lead, what customers seek, what the financial community expects, how people work, what they want from work and who and what they identify with, to name but a few of these contingencies. Context is also important in shaping the nature and role of HR processes and their relevance, e.g. HR in certain knowledge-based organizations is likely to be a very different proposition from retailing or manufacturing. In trying to bring together some of these contextual factors, we have drawn on a number of sources, including material from earlier chapters, research into the future of work and from specialist HR reports. These are generalizations but raise a series of questions that leadership in HR should consider, especially in relation to our calls to address the corporate agenda – reputations, brands, CSR, governance and leadership.

Demographic and social change

There are significant demographic changes notably in developed economies of Europe and Japan (though not America) where the workforce is ageing, unlike the newly emerging economies in Asia. In addition, there have been significant social changes, as the UK Economic and Social Research Council project on the 'Future of Work' (Taylor, 2004) has shown. These include declining levels of job satisfaction and loyalty to employers combined with greater expectations from employment; increased demands for a better work–life balance resulting in more demands for flexible working; labour market turbulence and skills shortages; structural reforms in social welfare provisions combined with more emphasis on the employee to safeguard their future through personal pension provision; more remote working through virtual business-professional communities. In a beautifully crafted book, Richard Sennett (2006) has documented more fundamental changes in the 'new capitalism', reflecting Baumann's liquid modernity, with significant implications for organizational design, career management and skills:

1   The requirement of individuals to manage short-term relationships in 'careerless' organizations, while moving from task to task, job to job and place to place. This fragmentation of careers has a marked effect on the potential for organizations to achieve identification and for individuals to identify with one organization. For example, Baumann (2004) has pointed out that identity and identification is very much a local phenomenon and that attempts to engineer organizational and national identities go against human instinct. According to both of these writers, new careerless organizations lack the capacity to provide local identification, a basic human requirement.

2   The requirement for individuals to manage their talent, develop new skills and leverage their potential, given the increasingly ephemeral nature of technology, science and skills. Craftsmanship, in the sense of individuals being able to do something well and to be able to point to past achievements as a measure of one's status, has given way to the celebration of *potential* ability, the capacity to re-invent oneself in the future, to learn how to learn, and to be able to say, 'I get along with everyone'. Mastery and knowing something has given way

to transformative potential and knowing little in the
conventional sense of the term.

3   Ensuing from this ephemeral and fragmented nature
of modern working is the requirement for individuals
to learn how to let go of the past as organizations have
less need for their past skills. Such a characteristic is a
rare one among most people who value their achievements and prior investment in skills they thought they
had banked for future gain and is associated with the
spectre of 'uselessness'.

Questions for HR leadership

■   How is the HR strategy addressing the demands for flexible working and offering support for work–life balance?

■   How well do you measure employee identification, e.g. psychological
contracts, identity, commitment, internalization, psychological ownership and levels of employee engagement, and are these still meaningful ideas in the light of increasingly fragmented and 'careerless'
organizations?

■   How does your HR strategy address employees' career aspirations
and needs for craftsmanship, which are often associated with doing
a job well and being regarded for expertise? Or is it aimed purely at
buying in potential and the skills of learning how to learn, without
necessarily being expert in anything?

■   How well does your HR strategy and policy address more remote
and flexible working and the needs of such people to feel a sense of
belongingness and organizational identity?

■   To what extent do HR strategic business partners in your organization
fall into the category of over-celebrating potential in themselves
and under-valuing craftsmanship? (See the discussion on 'well-
roundedness' later in this chapter.)

Consumers

This focus on the outside has been one of the themes of this
book. Changing social structures in developed societies is associated with fragmentation and segmentation of product and

service markets. Most marketers are familiar with the basic tenets of geo-demographic neighbourhood classification systems. People with similar cultural backgrounds, means and perspectives naturally gravitate towards one another to form relatively homogeneous communities and identities. Once settled in, people tend to emulate neighbours, adopt similar social values, tastes and expectations and, most important of all, share similar patterns of consumer behaviour toward products, services, media and promotions. This behaviour is the basis for the development of computer-based classification systems, all of which classify neighbourhoods and their households into clusters or groups of neighbourhoods, based on their underlying socio-economic and demographic composition. We have argued that such variety in product markets is increasingly reflected in internal labour markets through workforce segmentation, based on the principle of requisite variety. This principle, drawn from organic sciences and systems theory, states that the degree of internal variation in a system must match the variation in its environment, and is one that is widely adopted when designing organizations.

We have also documented the increasing importance of brands in determining consumer purchasing decisions and organizational reputations for socially responsible behaviour among consumers, and their willingness to punish firms that do not match rhetoric and spin with action.

Questions for HR leadership

■ To what extent does your HR function understand and systematically use data on geo-demographics and changing consumer preferences and behaviour to inform its HR policies?

■ To what extent is the HR function teamed up with those responsible for marketing and branding to influence key decisions in these areas?

■ To what extent are staff in HR sufficiently knowledgeable and credible with colleagues in marketing and branding to be able to contribute to these key decisions on reputation management and brands?

■ Does your HR function have the requisite skills to segment the workforce to reflect/drive consumer segments, and to design different employee value propositions to align staff, existing and potential, with brand offerings?

■ How does your HR function measure up in its ability to communicate employee value propositions to different employee segments?

Internationalization and globalization

For the past three decades, the world economy has been growing at its fastest, with more countries sharing in that growth than ever before. For example, between 1980 and 1999, annual world exports more than trebled, but during the same period, foreign direct investment (a form of geographical integration) multiplied ten times (Whittington, 2000). Trade liberalization in Europe and Asia, the rise of the Asian economies, outsourcing and high levels of labour mobility, coupled with the use of the Internet to span across borders, have all contributed to the rapid rise in globalization. Peter Berger has helped lead a major international research project on the theme of globalization, which does indeed point in the direction of an emerging global culture heavily American in origin and content, though this is increasingly challenged by eastern centres such as Tokyo, Hong Kong, Singapore, Shanghai and Mumbai (Berger and Huntington, 2002). This emerging culture, according to Berger, has four faces, based on a 'world made in English' as the cultural, as well as business, *lingua franca*:

■ the Davos culture, centred on the discussion held by big business and the World Economic Forum at Davos in Switzerland, which has led to a form of economic globalization through the spread of MNEs' influence

■ the Faculty Club culture, which reflects the impact of Western intelligentsia and its liberal ideas of environmentalism, feminism, universal ethics, human rights and multiculturalism; this culture sometimes merges with the Davos culture but also sits in tension with it

■ the McWorld culture, which reflects the impact of mainly popular Western youth culture, propagated by the celebrity firms such as McDonald's, Nike, Disney, Apple, Google and MTV, and by the universal access to American-based media such as television and the Internet, and

■ evangelical Protestantism, which is the re-emergence of the Protestant ethic in new parts of the world (e.g. in parts of Latin America, East and South-East Asia, sub-Saharan Africa), providing a morality highly appropriate for developing economies seeking to become part of modern capitalism – disciplined, frugal and science-based, rationally ordered societies.

These trends look set to continue and hold significant challenges for HR practitioners and for HR strategies. However, Berger and his colleagues recognize significant localization and modifications, which shade into a form of hybrid culture. We also used this term in describing the dominant mode of HR systems in Sino-foreign joint ventures (Zhang and Martin, 2003). 'Hybridization', which involves synthesizing foreign and native cultural traits, is likely to be the most common form of adaptation of management practices in the new economies of China, India and the Arab world.

Questions for HR leadership

■ How aware are HR leaders of these trends in globalization, localization and hybridization?

■ To what extent are these trends relevant to your organization's future and what are you doing to prepare your HR team and the organization's leadership to take advantage of these trends? For example, how are these trends likely to influence branding strategy and reputation management?

■ What kinds of HR strategies and policies are necessary to reflect/ drive international branding strategy and reputation management?

■ What proportion of current and future leaders will need developing in international management and leadership development to support global branding and what are the best ways of developing them?

- What are you doing to identify talent and labour pools to support your organization's international ambitions over the next 3–5 years?
- What implications does internationalization have for segmentation of the workforce and for performance management?

Shareholder interest, governance and social responsibility

Through the book we have discussed the debates between shareholder value and stakeholder models of governance and their implications for the CSR agenda. The risk to organizations' reputations through actions/inactions in the field of CSR are increasingly being realized by senior executives, and HR leaders have an important role to play in helping shape the agenda in these areas. They also have an important role to play in corporate governance, as the case study on Paragon/Enron illustrated well. At one level at least, Enron was a failure of talent management, which should carry warning signs for other organizations adopting talent management philosophies. Again, our discussion of the Financial Services Industry in Chapter 8 illustrates this point.

The findings of a report by McKinsey, one of the world's largest and most influential management consultancies, is worth highlighting in this regard (McKinsey, 2006). The report dealt with the survey of senior executives on their worries over the societal expectations placed on their companies. The overarching conclusion was that they can and must do better in meeting them. In this report, the overwhelming response of 84% of executives was that they had a responsibility to balance public good with meeting shareholder obligations; this is a rather different proposition from the one advanced by Milton Friedman, that generating high returns for shareholders should be a corporation's sole focus (see Chapter 8). However, they were less certain about which concerns would affect them and what responses were most appropriate. Among the most cited issues that would impact positively or negatively on their companies' shareholder value in the near future were job loss and off-shoring, political influence and involvement of companies, environmental issues, including climate change, pensions and retirement benefits, healthcare and other employee benefits, opposition to foreign investment, demand for safer products and pay inequalities between senior executives and other employees.

Interestingly, they perceived a mismatch between the tactics used by companies to manage such socio-political issues in their organizations – media and public relations, lobbying, CEO statements, CSR reports and philanthropy – and the most effective methods of doing so. These they deemed to be increased transparency about risks of products and processes, developing and implementing policies on ethics and CSR, engaging stakeholders and improving compliance.

Unsurprisingly, HR were not seen to be key players in taking the lead in these issues, deemed to be a CEO responsibility, and too important to be left to public relations, line managers or HR. Yet, given that so many of the issues have significant HR implications or fall directly within the sphere of competence of HR, our belief is that with a better understanding of these issues it is incumbent on them to take the lead as a form of corporate conscience.

Questions for HR leadership

- To what extent does HR leadership in your organizations understand the key debates over corporate governance and leadership, and CSR?
- Are these issues part of the internal agenda of HR at senior levels?
- To what extent is HR represented in the senior management team in discussions of governance and CSR? Do they contribute to policy making in these areas, particularly in discussions over shareholder value and stakeholder issues, including pay policies and performance management?
- Have HR in your organization taken a lead in the issues raised by the McKinsey report, including job loss and off-shoring, political influence and involvement of companies, environmental issues, including climate change, pensions and retirement benefits, healthcare and other employee benefits, opposition to foreign investment, demand

for safer products and pay inequalities between senior executives and other employees?

■ To what extent has HR implemented the recommendations of reports such as the CIPD's policy document on CSR, and contributed to the measurement of CSR?

■ To what extent is HR taking a lead in developing CSR initiatives such as those implemented by the Diageo case in Chapter 9? To what extent is HR developing policies on ethics and transparency and ensuring those responsible for making and selling products and services are compliant with good practice?

■ How do you partner with your suppliers to sustain service excellence?

■ What are you doing to plan for the succession of your top talent?

Change through communications and communications technologies

In Chapter 8 we discussed the importance of change through communications and in telling sustainable corporate stories. We also highlighted the role of employer of choice policies, employer branding and linking specific employee value propositions to different employee segments. Our change model also emphasized the importance of measuring employer brand equity and its links with psychological contracting and engagement behaviours. Advances in ICT have also resulted in the potential to improve and engage employees through online surveys and provide them with new ways of working. Finally, employee portals can provide an important method of communicating a sense of corporateness, as well as allow for significant localization. However, much of the current advice from consultants and practice among firms in the global roll-out of e-HR is to follow a technology-driven solution and only allow for limited customization to reflect local differences, a solution that may suit short-term administrative and cost targets to the detriment of longer-term service delivery and strategic aims (Martin *et al.*, 2006).

Questions for HR leadership

■ Do HR understand the potential of sustainable corporate stories and how they differ from many mission statements?

■ To what extent have we made use of internal marketing techniques to develop employee value propositions; do we know what different groups of employees and potential employees most value, what they would choose and advocate particular employer brands?

■ What are the best means of engaging and communicating brand values, and how can we best use employee surveys and employee HR portals in this process?

■ To what extent do we measure employer brand equity?

■ Do we have a convincing change model that can be used to address the issue of sustainable change?

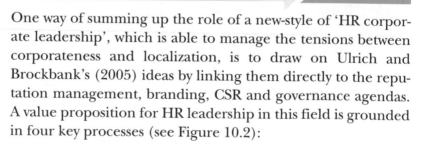

Delivering the corporate HR value proposition

One way of summing up the role of a new-style of 'HR corporate leadership', which is able to manage the tensions between corporateness and localization, is to draw on Ulrich and Brockbank's (2005) ideas by linking them directly to the reputation management, branding, CSR and governance agendas. A value proposition for HR leadership in this field is grounded in four key processes (see Figure 10.2):

1   Understanding the external environment of the organization and how it shapes its 'corporate' agenda, especially the relationship between HR, customer/client satisfaction, customer/client loyalty and building awareness of the corporate brand, and strengthening and maintaining corporate reputation, leadership and governance.

2   Addressing the individual career, motivation, identification and engagement issues to help manage the tensions between corporate and local identities, and corporate and locally relevant talent management policies.

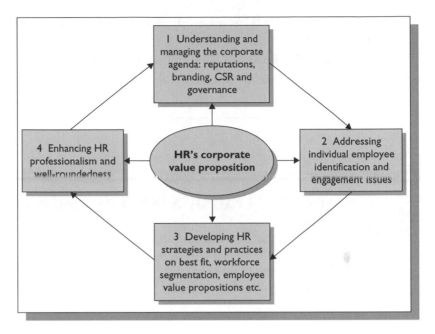

Figure 10.2
HR's value proposition for the corporate agenda.

3   Developing HR strategies and practices to address the corporate agenda, which are also locally sensitive, including high performance HR policies, workforce segmentation and employee value propositions.

4   Enhancing the credibility of HR group by improving its reputation for well-roundedness, a business orientation, true rather than narrow professionalism, and up-to-date thought leadership and innovative action by addressing the corporate agenda in an innovative way.

That said, however, we caution against the idea of leadership disconnected from followership, a point made throughout this book. We would be well advised to heed a warning by Caldwell o*et al.* (2005) that the new HR leadership models more often than not repeat the mistakes of visionary or transformational paradigms, which are based on an unhelpful model of top-down, inspirational leadership, passive followership and lists of competencies or emotional intelligences that are not joined up or linked to context. As we have discussed in previous chapters, leadership and followership are different sides of the same coin;

moreover it is increasingly inappropriate to discuss leadership purely in terms of organizational boundaries, which are ever more irrelevant in modern networked forms. Leadership, like strategy, has to leverage value from people in organizations over which it has no direct authority.

The well-rounded HR leader

The need for craftsmanship as well as potential

So what does a well-rounded HR leader look like? The first point to reflect on is the dangers pointed out by Sennett (2006) in over-valuing potential and the 'learning how to learn' model, and in under-valuing craftsmanship, expertise and experience. This warning is especially relevant in the context of the new hierarchy of HR professionalism and the emerging division of labour between strategic partners and centres of excellence, both of which reflect trends in the 'cutting-edge' firms of Sennett's new capitalism and help embed these trends in society. As he points out in the book, the basis on which esteem in society is accorded to individuals has been based on merit and expertise; ask most people in developed economies who they would hold in high esteem, as many international surveys have done, and you are likely to get the answer doctors, nurses, teachers, engineers, social workers, and even lawyers, academics and entrepreneurs in certain country rankings of occupational prestige. Such surveys will also include skilled manual crafts, but, interestingly, rarely include managers in the top echelons of the rankings. The reasons for this are that people are valued for abilities developed within themselves, for their craftsmanship. This notion of craftsmanship evokes a world where a job well done in its own right, a concern for standards and expertise, and knowing something well is valued above all else.

In 'liquid modern' societies, however, there is little that is stable about work, talent and consumption; transactions have replaced relationships in people's dealings with one another. The new institutional architecture, according to Sennett, more closely resembles the infinitely flexible architecture of the MP3 player than the classic bureaucratic pyramid; thus it is potential that counts. So 'cutting-edge firms and flexible organizations need people who can learn new skills rather than cling to old competencies ... human "potential" consists in how capable he or she is in moving from problem to problem, subject to subject' (Sennett, 2006, p. 115). Perhaps the classic metaphor for such potential is the management consultant who flits from job to job, organization to organization and industry to industry without having a deep understanding of any single location, problem or body of expertise. In fact, the idea of skill and expertise is often an anathema to consultants who are frequently taken on to 're-engineer' organizations that embody craftsmanship and creativity. He cites UK research on the use of young MBA-trained, McKinsey consultants at the British Broadcasting Corporation (BBC), who tended to devalue creative work because they did not understand it, were paid to re-engineer the organization by reducing the number of creative people, and then left it in turmoil after a quick departure.

One of the main lessons from Sennett for this book is that potential is a damaging measure of talent, and we are inclined to agree; witness the emphasis placed on such young talent at Enron. The decline of craftsmanship in cutting edge organizations, he contends, leaves three 'social deficits'. The first is low organizational loyalty or potential for organizational identification. As Baumann (2000) argues, identification is a naturally occurring and local phenomenon born out of being valued and in valuing the 'local', not something which is planned or forced on people by (corporate) identity engineers. And loyalty for most organizations is essential during business cycles when the going gets tough, or when labour markets encourage frequent moves among talented people. The second social deficit is trust, which we discussed in an earlier chapter. Ever more frequent change in business cycles and re-engineering through change programmes diminishes informal trust among employees, but at the same time, makes trust more essential to cope with such circumstances. The third deficit, and perhaps the most important point for our discussion of the future of HR professionals, is the requirement for institutional or organizational knowledge. What is required in many large, bureaucratic organizations is knowledge of how to make the system work, which, according to Sennett, has developed into an art form in learning 'how to oil the bureaucratic wheels' (2006, p. 69). Yet such people are often low in the pyramid, frequently let go or outsourced, or subject to replacement from a talent management system that privileges the outsider over the insider. But organizational knowledge – both inside and among the increasing external relationships on which organizations depend for survival – is also a feature of craftsmanship. Skilled accomplishment is as much a function of internal and close external networks as it is of inherent skill. Karl Weick (2001) describes how effective managers need to be good 'bricoleurs' – to be able to fashion innovative solutions from an intimate knowledge of the materials they have to hand – which is highly dependent on in-depth organizational knowledge and their internal and external networks.

All three social deficits are being accelerated by the new version of talent and the premium placed on potential, and the narrow idea of professionalization. We fear that the Ulrich HR architecture may be a product of such thinking, at least as it has been interpreted by many organizations, and perhaps part of the problem rather than the solution. Instead, we propose a more balanced view of HR professionalism and leadership, based on the work of people such as Mintzberg, Weick and others. In a recent book by one of us, there was an attempt to construct a model of a well-rounded manager, which is particularly apposite to the present discussion of HR leadership and the corporate agenda (Martin, 2006).

The need to manage at different levels

To be effective, we believe that HR leaders have to translate their personal qualities or competencies into the kinds of effective behaviours needed inside, across and outside of their organizations. According to Mintzberg (1994), well-rounded managers demonstrate these behavioural competences at three levels, moving outwards from the conceptual level to the doing or action level. So, good HR leaders need not only to conceptualize, plan and manage on the outside and from on high, as the Ulrich model is often taken to imply, but also to:

- manage **action**, by doing things directly themselves
- manage **people**, to get things done through others, and
- manage **information**, to influence people to take action.

As Mintzberg pointed out, leaders and managers can choose to focus on any of these levels but action taken at one of them has 'knock-on' consequences for action taken at other levels.

HR leaders will also be stylized by the level at which they prefer to work and, most importantly, by how other, often sceptical, managers and employees see them working. Thus, some leaders who favour a more 'hands-off' style prefer to work at the informational level; 'people-oriented' HR leaders will prefer to work through others, namely line managers and HR staff; whilst 'doers', often in more front line roles or who wish to take a direct lead by 'rolling up their sleeves', will take direct action. The main point of this discussion is that though the Ulrich model suggests a balance among such levels, current interpretations of the model by many organizations and the new hierarchy in HR implies no such balance.

Furthermore, the idea of a balance itself is a rather problematic concept. In his most recent work on management, Mintzberg (2004) has reworked these issues of preferences in managerial styles and levels into a model of three poles of managing that touch on our earlier discussions of narrow HR professionalism and the need for craftsmanship as well as potential. This model is highly relevant to our desire to link HR leadership to the corporate agenda and tackles the notion of balance head-on. Mintzberg depicts management (note that he has a problem with the idea of leadership as somehow distinct from management, and so do we) as a science, as vision and as a craft (see Figure 10.3).

Translating his ideas into an HR context, there will be those HR leaders who prefer to work at the informational level, typically framing their roles in terms of **management as a science**, which involves applying rational techniques and thinking about leadership and strategy best achieved through systematic assessment and planning. There will also be HR leaders and

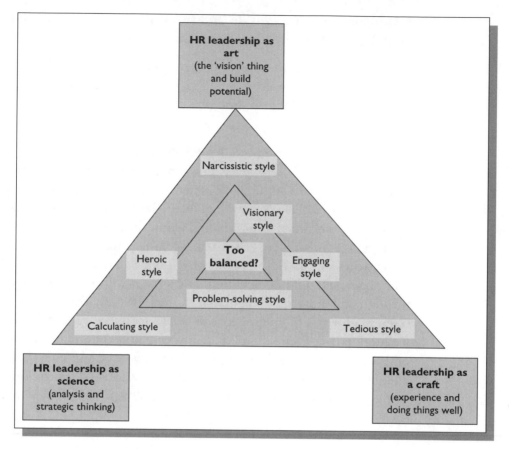

Figure 10.3
HR leadership styles (based on Mintzberg, 2004 and Sennett, 2006).

managers who prefer to work through people, who are more likely to be influenced by the idea of **management as an art**, which relies on creative insights and holding out a novel and compelling vision that others can buy into. Finally, there will be those HR leaders and managers who prefer to work by taking direct action, typically influenced by the notion that **management as a craft**, learned and practised through direct experience, experimentation and doing.

The critical point, according to Mintzberg, is that the well-rounded manager (for our purposes, read HR leader) needs to function effectively at all three levels and achieve balance among all three poles in Figure 10.3, a message also mirrored by the ideas of Sennett discussed earlier. Balance, however, comes in the form of three choices of style:

- A **problem solving style**, which combines the strengths of rational analysis with practical experience (and just enough people-management intuition and contact thrown in). Such a style is reminiscent of the broader professionalism invoked by the German notion of Technik as a well-rounded maker and doer.

- An **engaging style**, which is people-oriented and experienced-based, but with just enough science to take it out of the 'gifted amateur' category. Such a style may be associated with those HR leaders and managers who prefer to coach and facilitate others, and to interpret their role as an employee advocate in situations in which employees have no other source of 'voice'.

- A **visionary style**, which is strong on art and vision, but is also rooted in experience, again with just enough science thrown in to give the ideas credibility. This style is reminiscent of Ulrich's HR leader and strategic partner, and is close to the view of strategists as creating the sustainable corporate stories we discussed in Chapter 8.

Mintzberg, however, suggests that balance lies in reconciling two out of the three of these styles, with just enough of a third style to keep things in check. His view is that if we try to achieve a balance among all three simultaneously, we run the risk of either having no style at all or of not making a choice over how to manage. Furthermore, given our over-riding concern in the book to highlight the importance of context, balance will not only be a matter of choice but also of the nature of the organization, industry and kinds of employees HR leaders hope to lead. Returning to our example of the problems of the HR director in the university sector, it is likely that his ideal balance and those of his 'business partners' will be rather different from that of HR leaders in manufacturing environments or voluntary organizations.

In his own iconoclastic fashion, Mintzberg also highlights the dangers of too little balance among styles, an issue which we have already taken onboard in our discussions of bad leadership in Chapter 9. Thus he warns against *calculating* leaders and managers who manage purely at the informational level, thus running the risk of dehumanizing organizations and being criticized for lacking sufficient grounding in experience and organizational knowledge. This style is one of the dangers that Sennett has alluded to in his discussion of the over-valuing of potential. It is also a reasonable analysis of the Paragon/Enron case in Chapter 5, since a charge has often been made against the recruitment strategies of firms that target inexperienced MBA graduates and provide them with high degrees of responsibility early on in their careers. It also provides a warning to those inclined to take on consulting firms who employ such people to carry out their business.

Though Mintzberg and Sennett have a fondness for leadership as a craft, both would recognize there is a danger in focusing too much on this interpretation of the role of HR leaders. **Tedious** leaders and managers, according to Mintzberg, are frequently guilty of not being able to see the 'big picture' since they rarely move out of their own comfort zone of experience or professional mindset. Often this charge is made against engineers or HR managers who are promoted into leadership roles because they have been good at their professional 'craft', but who fail to provide the organization with a compelling vision or well-worked-out strategy. This point provides the necessary balance between seeing the wood from the trees and from a helicopter, which we introduced earlier.

Narcissistic HR leaders, as we discussed briefly in Chapter 4 run the danger of being strong on vision, but with little else other than a concern for their own celebrity. Finally, **heroic** HR leaders, at least according to Mintzberg, are perhaps the most dangerous of all. Their style is likely to be influenced above all else by the need to promote shareholder value, involving a shift away from hard analysis but not from calculation. This time, however, the calculation is about how best to promote their careers. The heroic style is largely about providing drama, rather than true art, and is focused on selling stories without substance to corporate leadership whose interests lie principally in satisfying the investment community. His 'tongue-in-cheek' recipe for heroic leaders involves looking out rather than in and ignoring existing business since anything established takes time to fix; then do anything to help get the stock price up, for example, recommending swingeing cuts in numbers, and cash in before you are found out. Many readers, we are sure, will have experienced this phenomenon and its HR equivalent: for 'looking out', read 'the big change programme'. Few leaders ever got on in their careers by maintenance work!

Conclusions: rounding out the HR leader for the corporate agenda

In this chapter we have tried to bring some of our ideas together to help a modern and ambitious HR function and leadership achieve its goals of being relevant to business by being relevant to the corporate agenda. We began by looking at a case of how branding and reputation management directly impinges on the HR function and how that function has to meet the universal paradox of managing globally whilst acting locally. Our plea to them, and indeed all HR managers, is that in order to do so, they have to develop a well-rounded style of HR leadership that understands and is able to contribute to the corporate agenda – those agenda items that make organizations different (corporate reputations and corporate brands) and those items that make them legitimate (corporate social responsibility and corporate governance).

Though the present models and advice for reorganizing HR may have been circumspect in selling the idea of a one best way – Ulrich's model and the Ashton and Lambert study are two cases in point – our feeling and experience is that they have been read as such. Thus we have a new and rigid hierarchy emerging in which HR leadership, centres of excellence and shared services are in danger of repeating the mistakes of previous hierarchical solutions in management, not the least of which is divorcing thinkers from doers, and in creating a disconnected group of strategists and narrow professionals.

HR's contribution to corporate reputation, brands, CSR and governance, issues that permeate every aspect of organizations, can and should occur at every level inside an institution, across its functional and divisional boundaries and, especially outside of it, among key stakeholders and partner organizations. Thus we have adapted the work of Mintzberg, and other writers that have something new and potentially controversial to say, to re-introduce an element of generalism into HR leadership, to round out HR leaders and to resurrect the notion of craftsmanship as an antidote to the current preoccupations with the 'visionary' leadership, the veneration of potential and the narrowly 'scientific' professional. It is also a call for adapting HR leadership to the context. The danger of one-size-fits-all models applied to re-organizing the HR function, or anything else for that matter, especially when existing staff are forced kicking and screaming onto a Procrustean bed, is that they rarely fit anything well – other, that is, than those organizations and people that fall within the ambit of normal. To paraphrase Michael Porter, where is the reputational and brand advantage in that?

Allied to the need to be able to tailor solutions to context, is the requirement of HR leaders to be able to read situations through multiple lenses and to act on these more complex readings to organize and manage effectively (Morgan, 1997). As the eminent American writer F. Scott Fitzgerald once said, the sign of intelligent people is the ability to hold two or more contrasting ideas at the same time and work with them. This is a key competence for HR leaders who seek to reconcile the ambiguities and uncertainties embedded in the universal paradox of thinking global and acting local. Acting local, if it means anything, is the ability to lead by looking from the bottom up or the perimeter in to see the wood as a nuanced collection of trees, branches, plants, spaces in between trees and so on. Thinking global is often a metaphor for looking down on a wood from on high and seeing nothing other than a blanket of green cover. As Weick (2001) points out, 'acting your way into thinking' (from the perspective of the local) is often preferable to 'thinking your way into acting' (from the perspective of the global), which is a recipe for learning, experience, craftsmanship and well-roundedness.

References

Accenture Consulting (2003) *Provision of human resources services survey*. New York.

Ashton, C. and Lambert, A. (2005) *The future of HR: creating a fit-for-purpose function*. London: CRF Publishing.

Batstone, E. (1982) The reform of industrial relations in a changing society. The Seventh Countess Markievicz Memorial Lecture, Irish Association of Industrial Relations, University of Limerick. http://www.ul.ie/iair/publications.htm (28 February 2006).

Baumann, Z. (2000) *Liquid modernity.* Cambridge: Polity Press.

Baumann, Z. (2004) *Identity.* Cambridge: Polity Press.

Berger, P. L and Huntington, S. P. (2002) *Many globalizations: cultural diversity in the contemporary world.* Oxford: Oxford University Press.

Boxall, P. and Purcell, J. (2003) *Strategy and human resource management.* London: Palgrave Macmillan.

Buchanan, D., Fitzgerald, L., Ketley, D., Gollop, R., Louise Jones, J., Saint Lamont, S., Neath, A. and Whitby, E. (2005) No going back: a review of the literature on sustaining organizational change. *International Journal of Management Reviews,* **7** (3), 189–204.

Burke, R. J. and Cooper, C. L. (2005) *Reinventing HRM: challenges and new directions.* Oxford: Routledge.

Caldwell, R. (2001) Champions, adapters, consultants and synergists: the new change agents in HRM, *Human Resource Management Journal,* **11** (3), 39–52.

Caldwell, R. (2003) The changing roles of personnel managers: old ambiguities, new uncertainties, *Journal of Management Studies,* **40** (4), 983–1004.

Caldwell, R. (2004) 'In search of strategic partners', in *Business partnering: a new direction for HR.* London: CIPD, pp. 6–13.

Caldwell, R. (2005) *Agency and change: rethinking change agency in organizations.* London: Routledge.

Chia, R. (1995) *Managing complexity or complex managing?* Paper presented to the British Academy of Management Annual Conference, Sheffield.

Elwell, F. (1996) *The Sociology of Max Weber,* retrieved 9 February 2006 from http://www.faculty.rsu.edu/~felwell/Theorists/Weber/Whome.htm.

Glover, I. A. and Hallier, J. (1996) Can there be a valid future for human resource management?, in I. A. Glover and M. Hughes (eds), *The professional–managerial class: contemporary British management in the pursuer mode.* Aldershot: Avebury, pp. 217–244.

Hope-Hailey, V., Farndale, E. and Truss, C. (2005) The HR department's role in organizational performance, *Human Resource Management Journal,* **15** (3), 49–66.

Huselid, M. A., Becker, B. E. and Beatty, R. W. (2005) *The workforce scorecard: managing human capital to execute strategy.* Boston, MA: Harvard Business School Press.

Lado, A.A., Boyd, N. G., Wright, P. and Kroll, M. (2006) Paradox and theorizing within the resource-based view, *Academy of Management Review*, **31**, 115–131.

Langbert, M. (2005) The Master's degree in HRM: midwife to a new profession, *Academy of Management Learning and Education*, **4**, 434–450.

McKinsey (2006) *The McKinsey global survey of business executives: business and society*. http://www.mckinseyquarterly.com/article_print. aspx?L2=39&L3=29&ar=1741 (26 January 2006).

Martin, G., Alexander, H., Reddington, M., & Pate, J. M. (forthcoming)

Martin, G. (2005) *Technology and people management: challenges and opportunities*. Wimbledon: CIPD.

Martin, G. (2006) *Managing People and Organizations in Changing Contexts*. Oxford: Butterworth–Heinemann.

Michaels, E., Handfield-Jones, H. and Axelrod, B. (2001) *The war for talent*. Boston, MA: Harvard Business School Press.

Mintzberg, H. (1991) Strategic thinking as seeing, in J. Nasi (ed.), *Arenas of strategic thinking*. Helsinki: Foundations for Economic Education.

Mintzberg, H. (1994) Rounding out the manager's job, *Sloan Management Review*, **36** (1), 11–26.

Mintzberg, H. (2004) *Managers not MBAs: a hard look at the soft practice of managing and management development*. Harlow: Pearson Education/Financial Times.

Morgan, G. (1997) *Images of organization*. London: Sage.

Paterson, B., Martin, G. and Glover, I. A. (1988) *Who incorporates whom? Managerialism versus professionalism among a sample of personnel specialists in Scotland*. Paper presented at the Sixth Labour Process Conference, Aston University Birmingham.

Pfeffer, J. (1998) *The human equation: building profits by putting people first*. Boston, MA: Harvard Business School Press.

Reddington, M., Williamson, M. and Withers, M. (2005) *Transforming HR: creating value through people*. Oxford: Elsevier Butterworth–Heinemann.

Sennett, R. (2006) *The culture of the new capitalism*. New Haven, CT: Yale University Press.

Snell, S. A., Steuber, D. and Lepak, D. P. (2001) Virtual HR departments: getting out of the middle, in R. L. Henan and D. B. Greenberger (eds), *Human resource management in virtual organizations*, Information Age Publishing, pp. 81–102.

Sparrow, P. R., Brewster, C. and Harris, H. (2004) *Globalizing human resource management*. London: Routledge.

Strauss, G. (2001) HRM in the US: correcting some British impressions, *International Journal of Human Resource Management*, **12**, 873.

Taylor, R. (2004) *Skills and innovation in modern Britain*. ESRC Future of Work Programme Seminar Series. http://www.leeds.ac.uk/ esrcfutureof work/downloads/fow_publication_6.pdf. (23 December 2005).

Tyson, S. and Fell, A. (1986) *Evaluating the personnel function*. London: Hutchinson.

Ulrich, D. (1996) *Human resource champions*. Boston, MA: Harvard Business School Press.

Ulrich, D. and Brockbank, W. (2005) *The HR value proposition*. Boston, MA: Harvard Business School Press.

Van de Ven, A. H. and Poole, M. S. (1995) Explaining development and change in organizations, *Academy of Management Review*, **20** (3), 510–540.

Watson, T. (1977) *The personnel managers: a study in the sociology of work*. London: Routledge and Kegan Paul.

Watson Wyatt (2003) *The HR scorecard alliance*. Watson Wyatt Worldwide, Washington, DC.

Weick, K. E. (2001) *Making sense of the organization*. Oxford: Blackwell.

Whittington, R. (2000) *What is strategy and does it matter* (2nd edition). London: Thomson.

Wrapp, H. Edward (1967) Good managers don't make policy decisions, *Harvard Business Review*, Sept–Oct, 91–100.

Zhang, H. and Martin, G. (2003) *Human resource management practices in Sino-foreign joint ventures*. Nanhchang: Jiangxi Science and Technology Press.

Index